Graphic Opinions

Graphic Opinions:
Editorial Cartoonists and Their Art

edited by

Jack Colldeweih
and
Kalman Goldstein

Bowling Green State University Popular Press
Bowling Green, OH 43403

Library of Congress Cataloging-in-Publication Data
Graphic opinions : editorial cartoonists and their art / edited by Jack
    Colldeweih and Kalman Goldstein.
          p.   cm.
    Includes bibliographical references and index.
    ISBN 978-0-8797-2758-1
    1. Editorial cartoonists--United States--History--20th century.
  2. American wit and humor, Pictorial.   I. Colldeweih, Jack.
  II. Goldstein, Kalman.
NC1426.G73   1998
741.5'092'--dc21
                                                                97-52131
                                                                    CIP

Cover design by Dumm Art

THIS BOOK IS DEDICATED

*To Kay, who points up the glories of life
and to Corrina, who makes me laugh.*

To the memory of my beloved Susanne.

Contents

Acknowledgments

The editors would like to thank University College of Fairleigh Dickinson University for a grant-in-aid and research release time for the editors, as well as technical assistance in its support of this project. They would also like to acknowledge the encouragement and aid of the faculty and staff of the Schools of Communication Arts and History and Political Science. Finally, we would like to express our appreciation for the cooperation and assistance of the cartoonists included herein and their respective distribution syndicates.

Acknowledgments

Introduction

Kalman Goldstein

In his preface to an anthology of cartoons about the O. J. Simpson trial, former cartoonist and now president of Cartoonists and Writers Syndicate, Jerry Robinson illustrated his contention that "just as Watergate was the catalyst for a renaissance of the political cartoon in the 1970s, the O. J. story has similarly inspired the world's great satirists" (Robinson 5). Beyond its comparing a political and constitutional crisis to a celebrity murder trial, Robinson's hyperbole might seem strange to aficionados of political cartooning who are convinced that since the so-called Oliphant Revolution of the late 1960s and early 1970s, editorial graphics have steadily enjoyed a Silver Age of inventiveness, influence, and serious notice second only to the era of Thomas Nast and Joseph Keppler. After all, since Richard Nixon's debacle the cartoonists have continued to draw inspiration and ammunition from twenty years of political controversies, peccadillos, and fiascos. And over this past generation, editorial cartoonists have paid more critical attention to the political implications of a greater variety of social and cultural issues than did their predecessors. What need of the profession for a *new* renaissance?

But for current political cartoonists themselves, the O. J. case may have represented less an inspiration for satire than a tiresome topic which, however, might boost their newspapers' circulation figures or their own syndicate marketability. If the *Seattle Post-Intelligencer*'s David Horsey is any barometer, an increasing number of editorial cartoonists, especially those who entered newspaper work after Watergate and the Oliphant Revolution, seem transfixed by the attenuating state of their medium and their constricted room for expression within it. During the last months of 1995, Horsey drew several cartoons berating the current computer hoopla. One compiled "Three Reasons computers can't replace newspapers" (pilfered newspapers cost less, swatting flies with a computer is costly, and sand in your paper is less destructive). Another empathized with a print reader annoyed by the noisy advertising for "Windows 95" (*Best Cartoons of the Month* Sept. 1995, 71; Oct. 1995, 43). Charles Brooks's annual collections, *Best Cartoons of the Year,* and the anthologies of individual cartoonists' work offer similar examples of this attitude. Horsey is representative of a generation of political car-

1

toonists, too young to anticipate retirement but too established in their profession comfortably to contemplate radical new methods of composing and distributing their work, bedeviled by pressures to be technologically as well as aesthetically innovative while creating culturally important statements on a daily basis. How they see themselves and their profession is what this book is about.

Kalman Goldstein has written an introductory chapter about the generally edgy feelings among newspaper editorial cartoonists today, and Jack Colldeweih one that surveys how cartoonists' newspapers and syndicates are being buffeted by the unprecedented legal and cultural challenges of global computer information networks. But at the heart of *Graphic Opinions* are two dozen essays about the current work and opinions of selected editorial cartoonists whom the authors believe have much in common besides their similar ages. They were chosen to represent the larger group of their generation's cartoonists in an admittedly subjective manner. The authors were fortunate to recruit half a dozen colleagues, identified in the Contents and in the Contributors section, interested enough in our project to take time from their own researches, and we thank them profusely. We and they were drawn to certain cartoonists' eye-catching styles, particularly pungent satire, or a shared sense of humor, and sometimes the mundane consideration of interviewing cartoonists who worked within reasonable travel distances.

We made every effort to be geographically inclusive, though unfortunately we were unable to find colleagues willing to visit certain corners of the nation or get there ourselves. So we apologize to those cartoonists who do intriguing work but were not profiled in our book. But a glance at the Table of Contents reveals that we have included representative cartoonists from both coasts and many sections of the Heartland.

Roughly between their mid-30s and their mid-40s in age, all of the cartoonists studied got interested in cartooning during the upheavals of the late 1960s, and obtained newspaper editorial positions about 1980. Almost all of them were inspired by or early copied Pat Oliphant, Paul Conrad, Jeff MacNelly, or Mike Peters, and consider themselves inheritors of the "revolution"; but all of them have moved on self-consciously to create more personal styles. Almost all are recognized, even distinguished, among their peers, garnering awards for their work; four of the most recent Pulitzer Prize winners are represented in this volume. Almost all seem aware or convinced that their profession is in serious flux, but almost none seems anxious yet to confront that challenge.

Beyond these shared characteristics, all two dozen maintain individuality in many ways. When we began our research and interviews, we thought vaguely about presenting our subjects geographically—then ideologically—and finally along both sides of the Great Divide: graphic satirists versus political gag cartoonists. In the end, we have retreated to alphabetical order. However, in a concluding chapter, Colldeweih and Goldstein offer what we hope are useful summaries about the extent and ways in which these cartoonists have "agreed to disagree." We have distinguished between liberals, moderates, conservatives, and libertarians; partisans and nonpartisans; and single- versus multi-panel preferences. Further, despite the perils of pigeonholing, we've designed and assigned suggestive categories by which to comprehend these cartoonists' choices and treatment of subjects: headline- versus issue-driven commentary; techniques used (emphasis on text or on image); and styles of humor (from graphic satire through bland gags). Finally, we illustrate and summarize their attitudes about computerization as syndicates point artists toward sophisticated delivery systems, and even on-screen composition.

Graphic Opinions opens new ground in writing about editorial cartoons. A number of scholarly studies of editorial cartooning in the United States exist, but either they are broad historical surveys or, except for Roger Fischer's recent *Them Damned Pictures,* were published in an earlier period (see Sources). In any case, they do not approach editorial cartooning the way we do, through interview-based and analytical essays about current young leaders. From autumn 1981 through summer 1987, Richard Samuel West edited and published *Target,* a quarterly trade journal whose every issue contained interviews with leading cartoonists and illustrators such as Don Wright, Tony Auth, Ralph Steadman, Ben Sargent, and Jim Borgman. These are invaluable, but except for Mike Keefe, in his final issue, West's subjects were older or are not profiled in our book. Similarly, the quarterly *Cartoonist Profiles* contains useful interviews with contemporary cartoonists, but in separate issues, so that a sense of the profession or attitudes of its younger leaders can be gained only segmentally. Both Richard S. West's "Selected Bibliography" in *Inks* and John A. Lent's superb book of references reaffirm current scholarly interest in American political cartooning: academic and trade articles, and collections of cartoons. But these bibliographies also reveal that none collect essays about contemporary cartoonists in one volume, and neither books nor journals profile many of those included here. There are monographs that analyze political cartooning during a single generation, but they generally focus on earlier periods like the Gilded Age (West, *Satire on Stone*), or the Progressive Era (Fitzgerald, Sheppard, Zurier). We hope that this book encourages other scholars to create similar studies, as this one is hardly definitive. In fact, Jack Colldeweih and I have already begun a companion study of graphic artists, some still in their 20s, who don't have regular newspaper pulpits.

We deeply appreciate the graciousness of those cartoonists who readily agreed to be interviewed, allowed us to tape our conversations, and provided open and frank responses to our questions (some by necessity off the record!). We also hope that including four representative cartoons for each artist does their work justice, and proves useful to the reader's understanding and appreciation of how cartoonists interpret issues, and also how they express themselves as graphic artists. For despite their nagging disquiet about failing newspapers, harried or dismissed colleagues, tussles with editors and syndicates over theme and content, and whatever may be lurking in cyberspace, the cartoonists profiled in this book maintain their joy in artistic experiment, their sense of satisfaction in daily creativity, and the comedy of those visceral responses to their pungent commentary, which reassure them that their readership is still "out there" and paying attention.

Sources

Brooks, Charles A., ed. *Best Editorial Cartoons of the Year.* Gretna, LA: Pelican. 1982–.

Fischer, Roger A. *Them Damned Pictures.* North Haven, CT: Archon, 1996.

Fitzgerald, Richard. *Art and Politics.* Westport: Greenwood, 1973.

Hess, Stephen, and Milton Kaplan. *The Ungentlemanly Art.* New York: Macmillan, 1968.

Hoff, Syd. *Editorial and Political Cartooning.* New York: Stavron Educational, 1976.

Lent, John A. *Animation, Caricature, and Gag and Political Cartoons in the U. S. and Canada.* Westport: Greenwood, 1994.

Murrell, William. *History of American Graphic Humor.* 2 vols. New York: Cooper Square, 1933.

Press, Charles. *The Political Cartoon.* Madison: Fairleigh Dickinson UP, 1981.

Robinson, Jerry, and Jens Robinson. *OD'd on O. J.* New York: Universe, 1995.

Sheppard, Alice. *Cartooning for Suffrage.* Albuquerque: U of New Mexico, 1994.

Szabo, Joseph, ed. *The Finest International Political Cartoons of Our Time.* North Wales, PA: Witty World Books. Since 1992.

Target. Ed. Richard S. West. Washington, D.C., 1981-1987.

West, Richard S. *Satire on Stone: The Political Cartoons of Joseph Keppler.* Urbana: U of Illinois, 1988.

——. "Selected Bibliography of Political Cartoon Collections." *Inks* 1.3 (1994); 2.1 (1995).

Zurier, Rebecca. *Art for the Masses.* Philadelphia: Temple U, 1988.

1

Recent Editorial Cartooning—
Wither or Whither?

Kalman Goldstein

Pat Oliphant's arrival at the *Denver Post* in 1964 has taken on by now almost the same mystique for political cartoonists as jazz's trip "up the River" from New Orleans in 1917 has for musicians. Until Oliphant revitalized the profession, American political graphics was judged to have degenerated from an earlier stance of high moral outrage and visually dramatic artwork, to what Bob Taylor of the *Dallas Times* once derided as the "poster period." Cartooning had once been driven by causes and characterized by angry reformers such as Art Young, Boardman Robinson, and Robert Minor; by feminists Lou Rogers and Nina Evans Allender; and by those two greasepen giants, sardonic Rollin Kirby of the *New York World* and populist Daniel Fitzpatrick of the *St. Louis Post-Dispatch.*

By midcentury it was stale: ideologically predictable, and visually boring. In a now-classic 1954 essay for the *Saturday Review,* Henry Ladd Smith eulogized "The Rise and Fall of the Political Cartoon," deploring contemporary artists' lack of energy and creativity, their overreliance on hackneyed allegorical figures, and kneejerk posturing as a substitute for critical commentary. In fairness, Smith did take into consideration the Cold War atmosphere as well as the artists' alleged mediocrity: "a cartoonist thrives on the hot issues of the crusader, not on apathy and desperation" (Smith 11). Audrey Handelman, writing 30 years afterward, also conceded that a period of simmering low-level anxiety had discouraged creative thinking. Even so, she reminded readers, cartoonists prided themselves on being a special breed who "make no claims to objectivity," and whose "products almost certainly reflect their own views" (Handelman 137). So she concluded that they should have been more courageous or inventive despite the smothering atmosphere.

It is therefore tempting to over-dramatize both the changing times, the political and social upheavals of the 1960s, and the sudden appearance of a "new wave," as Everette Dennis called those artists who took

5

inspiration from Pat Oliphant's biting, satiric iconoclasm. For after all, Herbert Block was already creating new images and standards of pugnacious caricature. Bill Mauldin was drawing ordinary folk commenting on issues, reducing our leaders' pomposities to childish posturing, and turning the era's stock phrases into visual metaphors. Jules Feiffer had taken a radical departure from the single-panel cartoon with his borderless narrative "talking heads," and integrated political with complex social commentary in order to contextualize as well as expose the authorities' doubletalk and obfuscation. As Julius Novick put it, "his political strips are essentially not about statesmen and nations but about the moral problems imposed on us by political events" (Novick 58).

But in the end, the new group of artists who appeared during the late 1960s and 1970s did reinvigorate their profession, developing significant innovations and setting new standards for artistic as well as critical expression. Bill Mauldin had for a decade insisted to his colleagues: "If it's big, hit it;" he now found a younger, more responsive audience. Oliphant went straight after the Presidents, depicting them as liars or buffoons. His ribald humor, an ability to mix naturalism and "bigfoot" grotesquerie in the same drawing, or to combine subtle caricature with surreal symbolism—Uncle Sam as W. C. Fields—all were an inspiration, as was his footlight bystander Punk the Penguin, who provided even more ironic commentary. Paul Conrad joined Oliphant in insisting that cartoonists should not just illustrate the news, but should take their own editorial stances. He jettisoned many old abstract images, drew characters so meticulously that fewer now needed name tags, and similarly shortened or entirely abandoned wordy captions and dialogue balloons.

Everette Dennis reminds us that during the 1960s, offset printing was beginning to increase the market for cartoon art. Other developments in graphics and the mass media similarly helped expand artistic repertoire and broaden social attitudes, among those younger cartoonists who would gain editorial jobs and rise quickly in the profession during the 1970s. Bill Sanders and Bob Taylor remember that early in the 1960s, while in their late 20s, they were very conspicuously the youngest members of the Association of American Editorial Cartoonists (AAEC), most of whose members were in their late 50s. As the veterans retired, they were quickly succeeded by cartoonists who had grown up with very different historical experiences and diverse visual models. For example, younger artists would credit the comic books of their childhood, satiric magazines like *Mad,* and those inexpensively reproduced political graphics so abundant in 1960s popular culture: posters, buttons, T-shirts, bumper stickers, van graffiti; what Gary Yanker called "prop art." The era's alternative press also contributed to cartooning's reorientation. Not only did the "counterculture" artists violate all the older canons of permissible subject matter, artistic style, and choice of images; but some among them—particularly Gilbert Shelton, Ron Cobb, Bill Griffith, and Skip Williamson, were political as well as social satirists. Finally, television itself was beginning to increase the recognizability of references and subjects among many readers who used to look at cartoon humor but "didn't get it" (Carl 533). TV's cornucopia of mass culture provided a new, shared vocabulary of popular images that favored both the use of visual metaphors and a less word-cluttered, comparatively minimalist cartoon panel.

Following in the inkprints of Oliphant's cohorts, those who entered the profession during the Nixon era and the later 1970s have opened up the genre in so many ways that a very few examples must suffice. Jack Ohman has demonstrated that multipanel cartoons, resembling one-shot comic strips, make extended commentary possible on an issue within a single visual editorial. Besides following Oliphant in creating a footlight character for ironic emphasis, Tom Toles showed how much mileage a cartoonist could get from recurrent images and commentary on an issue as well; Ronald Reagan flying an open-top rocket ship while daydreaming about Star Wars (SDI), was priceless. And no one, except perhaps the Progressive Era's Frederick Burr Opper, had used cartoony distortion of visage and posture in order to reduce political leaders to goofiness the way Mike Peters now would.

During the "decadent" midcentury period, editorial cartoonists, especially those working for partisan newspapers, were expected to hew closely not only to a party line but to the lead editorial. Now they would feel freer to produce the equivalent of an Op-Ed feature rather than simply to reinforce their editor's views or illustrate the daily headline. A zealous environmentalist, over the years Tom Toles has compiled a portfolio of urgent advocacy for environmental issues regardless of their changing daily notoriety. Signe Wilkinson similarly has done this for various women's issues. As Chip Bok of the *Akron Beacon Journal* puts it, describing his own behavior at editorial board meetings: "I'm always glad to weigh in on any issue under discussion and from time to time I can actually have an influence on an editorial position of the paper. My cartoon on the other hand is strictly my own production, tolerated but not necessarily endorsed by the paper, which is the way I like it" ("Chip Bok" 34).

By the 1980s, American political cartoonists had evolved tremendously in style, critical boldness, in their range and treatment of both political and social subjects, their involvement with distribution syndicates, and their use of humor: from sarcasm to satire, slapstick, or one-liners. Some among them even ignored the traditional outer limits of the genre as well. For the first time since Walt Kelly's heavily politicized "Pogo," cartoonists such as Garry Trudeau, Mark Stamaty, Bill Griffith, and Berke Breathed wrote continuity strips whose ensemble characters frequently commented on politics and even interacted with actual political leaders. Both Trudeau and Breathed won Pulitzer Prizes for their strips, though editors were unsure whether their work was editorial or belonged on the comics pages. Some scholars cautioned that perhaps only an elite leadership could decode their "stylized message system" (De Sousa and Medhurst, "The Editorial Cartoonist" 58), but cartoonists were convinced that they could now make substantial demands on their readers' awareness of current events.

While scholars also argued that it seemed impossible to prove whether any particular cartoon or cartoonist had swayed public opinion, except occasionally on a local issue, to an increasing extent political cartoonists were perceived as inventive and influential graphic communicators rather than simply as pictorial adjuncts to the editorial page. Many cartoonists certainly shared this perception. Mike Ramirez of the *Memphis Commercial Appeal* considered himself a "pit bull of journalism . . . paid to be obnoxious" (qtd. in Hernandez 14). Rick Bragg called editorial cartoons "winks on the gray face of the editorial page" (12). And those same scholars who warned cartoonists against overestimating their impact, still judged their art "a subtle framework within which to view the American political process and its players [whose] ability to tap the collective consciousness of viewers . . . help to maintain the ties which identify us as a people" (De Sousa and Medhurst, "Political Cartoons" 84). Mass journals like *Time* and *Newsweek* periodically surveyed the state of political cartooning, more distribution syndicates were created to market political cartoons nationally, many newspapers ran additional cartoons to supplement the work of their staff artists, and publishers more frequently issued collections of individual cartoonists' works. William F. Buckley, Jr., who certainly disagreed with Trudeau's views, nonetheless credited "Doonesbury" with being a keynote of contemporary humane letters; in a 1987 *Esquire* article he admitted that "in many ways, political cartoons have presented the truest history of our times" (qtd. in Neave 29).

One would expect, then, that full-time editorial cartoonists, some of whom are profiled in this book, would be generally satisfied with the state of their profession. Some are, of course, and feel well appreciated as well as purposeful. 1995 AAEC President Kevin Kallaugher (KAL) of the *Baltimore Sun* and *The Economist* offered an upbeat assessment of his calling: "Political cartoons touch on so many aspects of contemporary life. I love the feeling that I'm doing something vital. I feel that I'm contributing to the democratic process because I'm getting a political discourse moving, getting people to talk about issues" (qtd. in Wepman 11).

Yet why have recent AAEC conventions generated so many downbeat comments, some of which echo those lamentations written just before the Oliphant Revolution? When Ralph Steadman retired in 1991, he sneered that the political cartoon had become outdated, outmoded, a tired equivalent of Muzak. David Wiley Miller said roughly the same thing when he left the *San Francisco Examiner* the next year in order to do a comic strip. A national survey of editorial cartoonists conducted for *Editor & Publisher* in October 1995 found that over half felt the state of their profession "bad" and only 11% found it "good"; fewer than 15% saw as much opportunity in it as ten years previously. Respondents blamed crises in the newspaper industry, conflicts with editors, artistic constraints, the vogue of gag cartooning, and the baneful effects of both "political correctness" and syndicate caution. Signe Wilkinson long has been concerned about the paucity of women and non-whites entering her profession. "Aspiring satirists of color or breasts wisely skip this dying medium and go directly to film or the Fox Channel, but it leaves a rather pale, breast-challenged contingent at the drawing board" ("Mightier" 47). Steve Kelley of the *San Diego Union-Tribune* has quipped that current editorial pages had all the spice and variety of shopping malls. (Their editors were far less pessimistic.)

Certainly any careful reading of monthly or annual anthologies of political humor reveals much repetitiveness or imitativeness in the images cartoonists use while dealing with certain issues. From late 1994 through early 1995, House Speaker Newt Gingrich was pictured either as a figure out of Charles Dickens or as Dr. Seuss's Grinch; the Whitewater investigations produced myriad *Jaws*-like sharks or takes on the Clintons reprising Richard Nixon's stance, gesture, and "We are not a crook" disclaimer. The crisis in Haiti inspired a pincushion full of voodoo references, and the Joe Camel cigarette logo was fodder for endless burlesques. Some cartoonists have tried to explain, if not justify, this occupational hazard. Rob Rogers of the *Pittsburgh Press* and other cartoonists feel forced into using faddish or lowest common denominator symbols in order to make their work accessible to a mixed audience. Don Wright of the *Palm Beach Post* is more apologetic: "You're on a deadline, and you have three ideas, and you throw out the first one, and you throw out the second, and you're running out of time, and before you know it, the cliché is looking better" (qtd. in *New York Times* Apr. 3, 1994, 4, 12). Garry Trudeau has savaged colleagues who even take refuge in labeling symbols; from January 25 through 29, 1994, his TV reporter Rollie Headley navigated the ludicrously mis-tagged shoals of "Whitewatergate." And for the past few years an AAEC "committee on clichés," headed by Steve Benson, Jack Ohman, and Joel Pett, has chided colleagues for becoming so predictable, even boring, trying good-humoredly to shame them into rethinking their craft.

Many of the cartoonists we interviewed are self-conscious about this. They have recently changed their styles of lettering, inking, shading, or blocking out figures in an effort to distinguish their work from that of their colleagues, as well as to maintain their zest for daily creativity. Rex Babin loosened his lines, dropped balloon captions, employed more idiosyncratic metaphors or popular culture references, and impressionistically explored odd lines of perspective or camera angles. David Hitch concentrated increasingly on replicating Gilded Age crosshatching; David Horsey moved toward more complex draftsmanship so that many of his cartoons resembled easel paintings. Jack Ohman mixed his styles and panel arrangements, and stressed words more than he used to. Mike Shelton moved back and forth from anger- to humor-driven representations. Steve Sack felt that his work was in constant flux. Many essays in this book further underline cartoonists' continuous search for an individual statement within a constraining medium. They seem worried that after thirty years of innovations in their profession, once again cartoonists are being challenged to avoid rigidification or trivialization.

In the past, editorial and strip cartoonists inhabited separate niches, with the occasional and notable exceptions of giants like Frederick Burr Opper and Rube Goldberg. Or they moved from one field to the other, like H. T. Webster and Winsor McCay. But today an increased number of editorial cartoonists also create successful comic strips. A partial list would include Doug Marlette ("Kudzu"), Jeff MacNelly ("Shoe"), Mike Peters ("Mother Goose and Grimm"), Mark Cullum ("Walnut Grove"), Larry Wright ("Wright Angles"), Dana Summers ("Bound and Gagged"), Wayne Stayskal ("Ralph"), and Jack Ohman ("Mixed Media"). From 1993 to 1995 Tom Toles drew "Curious Avenue," until he took on an editorial position with the New York *Daily News* as well as with the *Buffalo News*. Dave Horsey, Jeff Danziger, Sam Rawls, Bob Gorrell and Garry Brookins, among others, simultaneously drew strips and cartoons during the 1980s.

Not only do editorial cartoonists' comic strips often present political and social analyses, but both weekly and daily comic strips have generally become more hospitable toward references to contemporary issues: Nicole Hollander's "Sylvia" and Barbara Brandon's "Where I'm Coming From," "Jump Street" by Robb Armstrong and "Curtis" by Ray

Billingsley, "Herb and Jamal" by Stephen Bentley, and "Sally Forth" by Guy Howard and Craig Mackintosh are some recent examples. And like Trudeau's "Doonesbury," or Berke Breathed's "Bloom County" (1980-1989) and "Outland" (1989-1994), the politically conservative strips "Mallard Fillmore" by Bruce Tinsley and Carl Moore's "Culture Shock" have re-opened the question of whether some comic strips belong on the Op-Ed pages rather than with the "funnies."

Branching out into comic strips probably reflects a hedge against unemployment. The number of newspapers has been steadily declining; any perusal of *Editor & Publisher*'s monitory articles or editorials about bankrupt papers pounds that fact home. And by 1995 only 120 of the nation's 1,500 daily newspapers employed editorial artists full-time. Some, like the *San Francisco Examiner, Providence Journal,* and *St. Paul Pioneer Press Dispatch,* decided not to replace retirees. Others, most notably the *St. Petersburg Times* and *Seattle Times,* have fired their resident cartoonists (Clay Bennett and Brian Basset, both in October 1994).

Moving to strip cartooning may also reflect a search for more creative outlets and less pressure to respond to daily events or provide serious commentary without pause; Signe Wilkinson once noted wryly that editorial cartoonists "have to care about something every day, whether we do or not" ("Signe Wilkinson" 17).

Despite assertions to interviewers about how well they get along with their editors, political cartoonists increasingly are wary of disputes either with them or with their readers over irreconcilably emotional subjects. A mid-1980s survey by Reffe, Sneed, and Van Ommeren ("Uneasy Alliance") concluded that cartoonists were often locked in conflict with editors who believed themselves better able to predict public reactions to sensitive issues; a 1992 international survey by Joe Szabo and John Lent, *Cartoonometer,* elicited the same feelings. And at the 1995 convention of the AAEC, artists and editors were unusually blunt about matters of creativity and censorship. During 1994 and 1995, *Editor & Publisher* disclosed a number of serious controversies over cartoons involving Signe Wilkinson, Pat Oliphant, Mike Ramirez, Rex Babin, Mike Luckovich, and Doug Marlette. Were it not for cartoonists' self-censorship, there would probably be more. Except for pro-choice crusaders, few editorial cartoonists will now comment on the abortion issue; one admitted that he had been expressly prohibited by his publisher from drawing any. Some we interviewed explained that past references to racial issues had resulted either in their being picketed or being accused of racism, and they now shunned that subject also. When the *Atlanta Constitution* published one by Mike Luckovich that seemed to carry a racial overtone, local radio stations exploded. The paper received thousands of phone calls, and subsequently ran pages of readers' letters, along with an explanation of the cartoon by both the artist and his African American editor. Doug Marlette has insisted that "good cartoonists are the point men for the First Amendment, testing the boundaries of free speech. If they are doing their job, their hate mail runneth over" (ix). Yet even he had two angry, open debates with his editor in 1994 over cartoons that had been pulled from *Newsday*. (The AAEC annually exhibits such suppressed works, and awards a Golden Spike to the best.) No one was fired in 1995 as a result of a cartoon, but in at least one case, that of Dennis Renault of the *Sacramento Bee* who drew Klansmen lauding statements by Nation of Islam leader Louis Farrakhan and using the word "nigger," visceral reader reaction led to a significant rash of cancelled subscriptions. And in a particularly messy contretemps, the *Miami Herald* had to destroy over 500,000 copies of a Sunday magazine because of a cartoon inadvertently run showing a young Martin Luther King Jr. having wet his bed, intoning "I had a dream!" The syndicated feature was cancelled.

After many years with the *Dayton Journal Herald* and the *Hartford Courant,* Bob Englehart reminisced in 1983 that he had "worked with a gaggle of editors and [had] learned how to cope with just about every situation an editor can invent. I've had my cartoons approved by a committee, a liberal Socialist, two conservative Reaganauts, a closet psychotic, a Victorian patriarch, a nit-picker, and the role model for TV's Lou Grant" (qtd. in Engelhart 32). But since some editors or publishers are tempted to consider staff cartoonists a luxury compared to cheaper syndicate products, or are anxious to be inoffensive or to "dumb down" coverage in the interests of circulation, fewer younger cartoonists may believe that they will ever achieve Engelhart's longevity or equanimity.

In addition, historian Roger A. Fischer recently concluded that the latest generation of cartoonists have moved "even further away from the art of moral indignation to that of irreverent humor" (22). This certainly seems a back-handed compliment. For in one way or another, most of the artists we interviewed have admitted to ambivalence or dissatisfaction with what one privately damned as an editor- or syndicate-driven demand that they be "funny" rather than trenchant, if they couldn't be both. There is at present a deep, noisy, and sometimes quite nasty schism among political cartoonists about the gag cartoon, and many agree with the complaint of the *Miami Herald*'s Jim Morin that while "humor used as a means toward enlightening your audience and getting them to care about the world around them is a potent weapon, when the editorial cartoon is used merely to entertain and distract, then the vast potential inherent in this great and unique art form is wasted" (53).

Some of those who vehemently oppose gag cartoons generally also regret having to use faddish popular culture images in order to get reader attention. Some scholars like De Sousa and Medhurst blame the cartoonists themselves for promoting a "cultural gap," continuing to use formulaic metaphors more suitable to an earlier mass readership than to today's faster-paced political and cultural environment. Some artists, in turn, disparage reader impatience with decoding cartoons due to an ever-shortened attention span: Garry Trudeau has even offered tongue-in-cheek a "tech support hotline" where cartoon staffers explain news stories and symbolic references to readers of "Doonesbury" (Dec. 24, 1995). Signe Wilkinson dislikes using topical references. She considers them trifling compared to those ideas drawn from history and literature which in earlier generations were familiar to a broadly educated public, but currently sees no alternative. Pat Bagley of the *Salt Lake Tribune* would prefer to use Biblical allusions rather than popular metaphors, "because this stuff is going to dry up and blow away. Five years from now, nobody's going to care much about Madonna" (qtd. in Harvey 55).

Cartoonists who have entered the profession in order to teach or preach may also resent pressures placed on them to be entertainingly faddish if they feel that more "serious" work could make a difference to public policies or political careers. None of them realistically expects to become a Nast, Keppler, or Gillam, turning elections with a floodlit image, or even a Herblock hounding politicians with caricature. The targets of their jibes are more likely to request the original cartoon than to take offense. But they do occasionally touch a nerve. House Speaker Newt Gingrich became so incensed at a Luckovich cartoon that he refused to grant press conferences to the *Atlanta Constitution;* former President George Bush has revealed how much Garry Trudeau's jabs wounded him. And most of the cartoonists we interviewed do believe that pointed commentary on local government and politics may prove effective as well as *ad hominem* neighborhood fun. Mike Shelton of the *Orange County Register* syndicates local-issue cartoons throughout Southern California in hopes of scaring county solons; Steve Greenberg of the *Seattle Post-Intelligencer* has done the same thing both in California and in Washington State. Signe Wilkinson claims that Philadelphia officials "get their pictures in the papers, sober stories written about them, and ponderously critical editorials wagging fingers at them, but when they feel the unexpected sharp point of a cartoonist's pen, they squirm and they hate it" (qtd. in Judge and West 42). Rex Babin believes the same is true in Albany, New York, as does Dave Coverley of the *Bloomington (Ind.) Herald-Times*. On the other hand, if they have shared Walt Handelsman's earlier experience of having had to explain the local issues to rural Maryland readers *as well as* to draw cartoons commenting on them, they might conclude that being "funny" is less disillusioning if less rewarding.

As much as they insistently deplore gag cartoons and claim that they draw them only when humor may slyly serve to educate their readers, for some cartoonists developing humorous, even goofy perspectives on the news may also be comforting in the face of fundamental professional challenges and changes in the offing. In 1995 the Board of Directors of Washington's National Gallery of Caricature and Cartoon Art (NGCCA) expressed concern that the decline of newspapers threatened cartoonists with the loss of traditional apprenticeship training grounds. The board also lamented a decline in "the sort of liberal education which informs editorial cartoonists": knowledge of Greek mythology and Shakespearean allusions were to them as vital as popular culture references to ensure creative outlooks and historical perspective. Ranan Lurie has become concerned enough to establish youth interships in editorial cartoon political analysis; and the NGCCA plans both video documentaries interviewing older cartoonists, and a multimedia clipping reference and resource matrix for the aspirant editorialist (Rodman 17). Such projects may be more a boon to the historian than to the working artist, however. For if Signe Wilkinson is prophetic, the next crop of influential cartoonists will come neither from the AAEC nor museum schools but from the alternative presses.

Graphics theorist Scott McCloud is convinced that cartoons as well as comics are on the brink of a dramatic reinvention. If so, the cartoonists featured in this book are not only engaged in differentiating themselves from their predecessors and from one another, but have to look to their laurels while being hotly pursued by an even younger, hungry cohort. Some cartoonists unable to obtain newspaper staff positions are being packaged by syndicates; the best known are probably Ann C. Telnaes (North American Syndicate) and William A. Costello (Newspaper Enterprise Association). In exchange for abandoning cartoons about local politics or issues, they have been given broad exposure and emancipated from worries about the health of "their" paper. Some have syndicated themselves, distributing their work either by fax or, now more likely, through Internet; examples include Paul Fell (since late 1995 once again with the *Lincoln [Nebr.] Journal-Star*), T. Brian Kelly, Geoff Yorke, and Harley Schwedron. They lack guaranteed wages or steady venues, but their work benefits from more direct feedback from their readers. At least, this is the claim of Dan Perkins ("Tom Tomorrow"), who was by 1995 being carried in 80 weekly papers, and occasionally featured on the *New York Times* Op-Ed page. Lesbian cartoonist Alison

Bechdel has been able since 1990 to earn a living wholly from "Dykes to Watch Out For," without a staff position or mainstream newspaper exposure, through an alternative press network, seven published collections (Firebrand Press) and successful product marketing.

At a session on alternative cartooning at the AAEC in June 1995, three of the "new breed" who have won some recognition and publication (Nina Paley by T. H. C. Press, Dan Perkins by St. Martin's, Ted Rall by Rip-Off Press) shared their belief that they have an artistic and ideological advantage over current mainstream newspaper cartoonists. Their outlets grant them more space in which to draw, so they can create multi-panels, cartoons heavy with verbiage, even graphic political novelettes. Further, according to Paley:

What I try to do is get below the issues of what I consider superficial politics. Most mainstream political cartoons are about mainstream politics. I try to do issues that are more universal. The way I analyze society now is to look at class differences or race or gender discrimination. I do a lot about capitalism itself, which you don't see in the mainstream press. . . . I'm highly politicized and reflect my own political concerns rather than the concerns of the paper or the editor. ("Alternative" 18)

Perkins agreed: "There are too many cartoons about Judge Lance Ito and too few cartoons about the societal analysis such as you are describing" ("Alternative" 18). And Ted Rall touched on a generational nerve that former Young Turks like Trudeau have come ruefully to recognize: "There is a gulf currently between people who are under 35 and people who are over 35. . . . There are no political figures out there doing anything to address the needs of younger Americans" ("Alternative" 18).

Behind these young firebrands strides an even younger group of aspirant political cartoonists. Each year since 1989, *News Currents* has held cartooning contests for middle and high school students. In 1994 and 1995, the hundred best of ten thousand entries each year were published as *Editorial Cartoons by Kids*. The most promising of these reveal influences from cartooning history: from Winsor McCay to 1930s Social Realism, to 1960s Agitprop; the inspiration of current artists like Jack Ohman, Tom Toles, and Dave Horsey is obvious. But also included are tributes to "Tom Tomorrow" and to Japanese *manga*—and examples of wholly original syntheses and viewpoints. So there are even younger and probably hungrier cartoonists on the horizon.

Sources Consulted

"Alternative Cartooning." *Funny Times* Sept. 1995: 18-19.

Astor, David. "Cartoonists' Group Decries Job Losses." *Editor & Publisher* 22 July 1995: 34.

——. "Cartoonists Launch a Media Committee." *Editor & Publisher* 11 June 1994: 30.

——. "Doonesbury Man Discusses His Strip." *Editor & Publisher* 30 Sept. 1995: 30-31.

——. "Editors Editorialize at Cartoon Session." *Editor & Publisher* 19 Aug. 1995: 34.

——. "Future of Comics Is Discussed by Panel." *Editor & Publisher* 7 Oct. 1995: 35.

——. "Meeting Speakers Display Even More Clichéd Editorial Cartoons." *Editor & Publisher* 16 July 1994: 50.

——. "Paul Conrad Wants Angrier Cartoonists." *Editor & Publisher* 18 June 1994: 42.

——. "This Young Creator Is a Big Yuk Hater." *Editor & Publisher* 18 Dec. 1993: 42.

——. "Trio of Cartoonists Offer Fresh Content." *Editor & Publisher* 12 Aug. 1995: 34-35.

Beckerman, Jim. "Even in the Funny Papers, No Comic Relief." *Bergen Record* 2 July 1995: A: 1.

Beniger, James. "Does Television Enhance the Shared Symbolic Environment?" *American Sociological Review* 48 (Feb. 1983): 103-11.

"Bill Sanders." *Cartoonist Profiles* 78 (June 1988): 48-55.

"Bob Engelhart." *Cartoonist Profiles* 60 (Dec. 1983): 32-36.

Bragg, Rick. "Some Cartoons Are Original: Alas, the Also-rans Also Run." *New York Times* 3 Apr. 1994: 4, 12.

Brinkman, Del. "Do Editorial Cartoons and Editorials Change Opinions?" *Journalism Quarterly* 45 (Winter 1968): 724-26.

Campbell, Sandy. "Bob Taylor." *Cartoonist Profiles* 73 (Mar. 1987): 64-69.

Carl, Le Roy M. "Editorial Cartoons Fail to Reach Many Readers." *Journalism Quarterly* 45 (Summer 1968): 533-35.

"Chip Bok." *Cartoonist Profiles* 103 (Sept. 1994): 30-37.

Dennis, Everette E. "The Regeneration of Political Cartooning." *Journalism Quarterly* 51 (Winter 1974): 664-69.

De Sousa, Michael A., and Martin J. Medhurst. "The Editorial Cartoon as Visual Rhetoric." *Journal of Visual Verbal Languaging* Fall 1982: 52-61.

——. "Political Cartoons and American Culture . . . Campaign 1980." *Studies in Visual Communication* (Winter 1982): 84-97.

Editorial Cartoons by Kids. Compiled by *News Currents.* Madison, WI: Zino, 1989.

Edwards, Janis. "Wee George and the Seven Dwarfs: Caricature and Metaphor in Campaign '88 Cartoons." *Inks* 2.2 (Spring 1995) 26-34.

Fischer, Roger A. "The Lucifer Legacy." *Journal of American Culture* 13.2 (1990): 1-19.

——. "The Monumental Lincoln as American Cartoon Convention." *Inks* 2.2 (Spring 1995): 12-25.

Groth, Gary. "Art Spiegelman." *Comics Journal* 180 (Sept. 1995): 52-114.

Handelman, Audrey. "Political Cartoonists as They Saw Themselves During the 1950s." *Journalism Quarterly* 61 (Spring 1984): 137-41.

Harvey, Robert C. "Chip Bok." *Cartoonist Profiles* 103 (Sept. 1991): 30-37.

——. "Pat Bagley: Cartooning in Salt Lake City." *Cartoonist Profiles* 93 (Mar. 1992): 50-56.

Hernandez, Debra. "Cartoonists Confront Political Correctness." *Editor & Publisher* 6 Aug. 1994: 14.

"Jim Morin." *Cartoonist Profiles* 83 (Sept. 1989): 46-53.

Judge, Lee, and Richard S. West. "Why Political Cartoonists Sell Out." *Washington Monthly* Sept. 1988: 38-42.

Lamb, Chris. "Editorial Cartoonists Pessimistic about Their Profession." *Editor & Publisher* 14 Oct. 1995: 48.

Marlette, Doug. *In Your Face.* Boston: Houghton Mifflin, 1991.

Mauldin, Bill. *What's Got Your Back Up?* New York: Harper, 1961.

"Mightier Than the Sorehead." *The Nation* 11 Jan. 1994: 45-54.

Moore, Carl. "Culture Shock." *Cartoonist Profiles* 108 (Dec. 1995): 59-67.

Moxley, Cynthia. "This Is a Fair Cartoonist." *Cartoonist Profiles* 60 (Dec. 1983): 66-70.

Muncie, Howard. "Lurie." *Cartoonist Profiles* 108 (Dec. 1995): 27-31.

Neave, Charles. "Drawn to Politics." *Esquire* Mar. 1987: 29-30.

"Newspapers Serve as Pulpits for this Editorial Cartoonist." *Christianity Today* 17 Feb. 1984: 42-43.

Novick, Julius. "Jules Feiffer and the Almost-In Group." *Harper's* Sept. 1961: 58-62.

Oliphant, Pat. *Four More Years.* New York: Simon & Schuster, 1973.

"Open Season on Editorial Cartoonists?" *American Journalism Review* Dec. 1994: 15.

Phifer, Greg, and Thomas R. King. "Censoring (Editing) the Comics." *Journalism Quarterly* 63 (Spring 1986): 174-77.

Rodman, Larry. "Full of Spice." *Comics Journal* 181 (Oct. 1995): 17-20.

"Signe Wilkinson." *Bull's Eye* 2 (Dec. 1988): 16-21.

Smith, Henry Ladd. "Rise and Fall of the Political Cartoon." *Saturday Review* 29 May 1954: 9-11.

"Steadman Quits Cartoons." *Comics Journal* 140 (Feb. 1991): 21.

"Steven Greenberg." *Cartoonist Profiles* 71 (Sept. 1986): 30-36.

Stevens, John. "Comics and Editorial Cartoons: An Essay on Five Books." *Journalism Quarterly* 56 (Spring 1979): 180-82.

Szabo, Michael, and John Lent. *Cartoonometer.* North Wales, PA: Witty World, 1993.

——. "An Uneasy Alliance." *Target* 12 (Summer 1984): 13-15.

"Walt Handelsman." *Cartoonist Profiles* 84 (Dec. 1989): 62-68.

Wepman, Dennis. "KAL: Cartoonist for the World." *Witty World* 19 (1995): 8-12.

"William Costello." *Cartoonist Profiles* 84 (Dec. 1992): 74-79.

Wines, Michael. "Cartoonists See a Future That's No Joking Matter." *New York Times* 3 July 1995: 41.

Wood, Art. "Origins: Mauldin and Oliphant." *Cartoonist Profiles* 54 (June 1982): 12-21.

2

Editorial Cartooning in a Digital Age: Problems and Prospects

Jack Colldeweih

The art of creating graphic political images and messages has advanced in virtually every respect since humanity first scratched or painted images upon stone—save one: durability. Each advance in the medium seems to give more control over the image but a shorter lifespan for it. Newspaper editorial cartoons today are printed by marvelous high-speed presses on paper that is comparatively inexpensive, but also acid-based; that means that the time it takes to turn brownish-yellow and crumble away is fairly short. The current electronic versions of these same cartoons can in some senses be said to barely exist at all; without the proper imaging device they are incorporeal. While there may be those who feel that such evanescence is their proper status, there are many who are concerned with the future of editorial cartooning as both a profession and as a useful commentary on the political health and direction of society, its institutions and its leaders. This chapter is an attempt to examine some of the likely effects of current electronic developments in the field.

When we began interviewing the cartoonists included in this book, in the summer of 1994, we asked a number of questions dealing specifically with the use of computers in cartooning for drawing or image manipulation, storage and transmission, and of problems of copyright, libel, contractual relations with publishers and syndicates in relation to the Internet and service providers such as America Online, Compuserve and Prodigy. Despite an earlier 1991 American Association of Editorial Cartoonists (AAEC) convention panel, we found few that had any experience at all, or much concern, with these issues. And even though at the 1995 annual convention of the AAEC, a special session was held to deal exactly with these kinds of issues, many cartoonists still preferred not to discuss the issues with us at length, or considered it a nuisance. But editorial cartoonists clearly were retreating from denial to confused ambivalence. One believed, for example, that the hype about the decline of newspapers and his profession was overblown; another, when asked about potential Internet copyright/plagiarism problems, replied that he was unconcerned because "nobody cares enough." What had happened?

As is frequently the case with new communications technology, growth of applications of the Internet, the digital World Wide Web of interconnections for computers, suddenly exploded. This was due in large part to the convergence of a number of factors:

- Widespread availability of computers to a sufficiently large group of potential users
- Development of modems fast enough to make using the Internet for data transmission and retrieval economical in terms of time and expense
- Development of useful databases accessible through the Internet
- Development of computer software that made finding and searching these databases sufficiently easy
- Economic pressure on newspapers by expanding cable television, satellite services and telephone companies as information providers and advertising vehicles
- Increasing interest by advertisers in utilizing the Internet to reach potential consumers;
- Consequent establishment of Web sites, i.e., Internet addresses for electronic databases, by newspapers and syndication services

It is this last development that is of most interest to us here because it most directly affects the political cartoonist. Although some newspapers had forged ties with Internet service providers early on, such as the *San Jose Mercury News* and the *New York Times* with America On Line, the current trend is for individual papers to establish their own Web sites, independent of such service providers (ISPs). Each weekly issue of *Editor & Publisher*, for example, reports additions to the list of these papers. In either case, the paper is presenting access to its news and features without cost to the user, at least for now, although some charge may be made for access to a database of previous information, the morgue files. This may well include graphics such as political cartoons, if the paper carries them. Material that appears on the Internet is considered "published," whether or not it has any other corporeal existence.

A number of thorny questions arise here. A cartoonist is hired to draw for a newspaper, which publishes his or her work. Contracts normally allow for him to sell his art through syndication for profit. If the newspaper makes that same work available for free at a Web site, i.e., republishes it, should the paper pay extra for that? Does such republication detract from the salability of that cartoon either for the syndicator or for the artist personally? We found that none of our interviewees had considered the issue, nor, having been made aware of it, was disposed at this point to challenge it, perhaps in light of the precariousness of cartoonists' position on their newspapers.

A related point is that newspapers, like other businesses that go to the trouble of establishing a Web site, do so with the intent of attracting "surfers" or browsers to view their content. Most businesses on the Web are unclear as to how money will be made from it, but they don't want to be left behind when that puzzle is solved. Journalism business organs such as *Editor & Publisher* and *Presstime* frequently run stories on discussions and developments in this area as the print media try to compete with newer electronic media. The debates usually focus upon the possibilities of immediate value of current news, features and advertising or upon the long-term value of archived information.

To attract surfers, to be known as a "cool site," attractive and interesting content is needed. Comics, like some television series, often have a long shelf life and can usefully be archived and still be attractive. For editorial cartoonists, however, this requirement means creating cartoons that strangers, nonlocals, can easily understand; cartoon content therefore must be on national or international issues and figures, or be drawn from popular culture. It is even better, perhaps, if it is a gag cartoon that makes the reader laugh and feel good. If that is the case, then the need for a local newspaper-employed cartoonist is diminished, for a syndicated cartoon by a famous artist can be used at much cheaper cost (Astor "Cartoonists," "Downbeat"; Lamb). The original purpose of having an editorial cartoonist may be lost for the local reader, but the publisher may now balance that loss against fewer potential problems with angry local targets of the cartoonist, a larger readership and the enhanced advertising potential that goes with it, and corporate benefits of a reduced payroll. While it is unlikely that any one newspaper feature, news column, cartoon or comic, is going to determine the success or failure of a Web site, an enhanced mosaic of features cannot hurt (Rykken).

Companies that syndicate features have also created Web sites to promote their offerings of comics, columns, crossword puzzles, editorial cartoons and the like (Astor, "Electronic," "United," "Syndicates"). For example, as a promotional feature, the United Media Syndicate has established The Inkwell, a Web site that displays editorial cartoons by the ten artists they represent, along with personal data and commentary. The AAEC also created a site to display art, news and information related to its members and their interests.

Some cartoonists, especially those without a regular newspaper contract, have established Web sites themselves to promote their art. For example, despite a new and interesting style, Ted Rall has been unable to catch on with a newspaper on a permanent basis, although he is widely printed. He has his own site on the Web now which contains his cartoons and a weekly opinion column that he self-syndicates. The *Denver Post's* Mike Keefe, who has long been involved with computers and other high-tech media, also has his own address on America On Line, an ISP. A number of cartoonists have begun including their e-mail address in the signature line within their cartoons so that readers may address them directly. While some cartoonists, such as Mike Luckovich, feel that the fuss over computers and the Internet and consequent danger to the health of newspapers is overdrawn, others are self-protectively dipping their mice into the digital stream. Bruce Plante, for example, does not draw on the computer, but he uses it for transmittal to customers and is establishing a Web site to enhance availability to individual computer users. Although perhaps not as viable a concept for more time-bound editorial cartoonists, The Cartoon Bank was established on the Web by gag cartoonist Robert Mankoff to make use of his unpublished cartoons. It now serves as an alternate distribution source for other cartoonists who want to sign on. Cartoons are scanned in, filed, organized and retrieved by computer (Miller).

This very useful set of computer processes has its own hazards as well for the cartoonist as artist and copyright holder. Although some cartoonists are not much concerned about the problem of plagiarism, others have been beset from time to time. Joel Pett, for example, feels that the cartoonist community is sufficiently small and tight-knit to handle any abuse that occurs, and that therefore it is not much of a problem. The 1990 AAEC convention, however, felt the issue was important enough to have a panel session on it (Astor, "They"). Jeff MacNelly felt that "similar" cartoons more likely reflected "influence" than plagiarism, and that those who drew exact duplicates were people who were looking to get caught. Panelist Richard West felt that there was little "legal recourse" for those who have been copied, but those who were discovered plagiarizing usually became quickly unemployed.

Domestically, then, plagiarism has not seemed much of a problem economically or artistically for editorial cartoonists. Other aspects of copyright law may prove to be more troublesome and costly, however. A number of observers have noted that there is a need to "reconcile 21st-century computer technology with 19th-century laws protecting intellectual property" (Markoff). The problem currently most vexing relates to those selling access to copyrighted work through "indexes," without compensating the creator or owner of the work (Carmody; Baker; Muchnick). The artist's material is incorporated within an index, and then access to that index is sold to the customer without compensation to the copyright holder. At a 1995 conference on Intellectual Property Rights and the Arts: The Impact of New Technologies, lyricist Hal David bemoaned that "creative people these days are feeling like road kill on the information superhighway," unable to protect their work from end-less reduplication (qtd. in Frankel).

Two approaches have been proposed to deal with the problem. The first is a technological solution; MOR Ltd., a company based in Notting-ham, England, has announced the development of "a digital image copy-right identification technique that leaves an invisible ID that survives even vigorous electronic retouching." This would "defeat image piracy by threading a combination of header, 'fingerprints' and alphanumeric ID sentences throughout an image" (Fitzgerald, "Invisible"). Another suggested technique is to provide each information product with its own "unique digital coding," a 128-bit name. "Combined with available tech-niques, such as public-key encryption, information providers [would] have the privacy to create information, protect against counterfeit—and yet make the information available to the public" (Fitzgerald, "Solu-tion"). Joel de Rosnay, a French scientist, suggests that "original materi-al could be locked by codes until the user sent payment by E-mail" (Blumenthal). And a small group of companies have joined together to develop "information by the slice" technology, Information Marketplace, wherein providers "can safely put information on Internet and have it copyright protected, and have metering and billing in place" (*Editor & Publisher* May 27, 1995, 29). Brian Kahin, the general counsel of the Interactive Multimedia Association, feels that "contract is taking prece-dence over copyright as a means for managing the flow of information on this environment" (Blumenthal).

The second approach to the problem is to update the concept of copyright by modernizing it for a digital world. Cartoonist Bob Thaves called attention to the copyright problems posed "when comics are used electronically." "Technology is ahead of the rest of the world, and the legal profession hasn't caught up yet" (Astor, "Thaves"). Knight-Ridder/ Tribune Information Services felt compelled to withdraw two of its fea-ture columnists from an Internet-distributed newspaper, *ClariNet,* because of unauthorized and extensive copying, which it believed jeop-ardized the copyright (Carmody, "Barry"; Muchnick, "Crackdown"). Efforts to revise the Copyright Act have taken place under the Clinton Administration, although not without controversy. Some feel that the whole concept of copyright is out of date, focusing on the work itself, and should be perhaps replaced with a term such as "mediaright" (Wincor). Still others believe that information should be readily and freely available in "cyberspace," so as not to impede the free flow of information (Veliotes). Nevertheless, the Copyright Reform Act of 1993 was introduced but failed to pass. In 1994, the Working Group on Intellectual Property Rights, under the direction of Bruce A. Lehman, as part of the Information Infrastructure Task Force, issued a "Green Paper," *Intellectual Property and the National Information Infrastructure,* which examined existing copyright law in the context of NII (Lehman, "Greenpaper" 39). Following a period for comment, the final report was released the next year suggesting revisions in the present law (Lehman, *Intellectual*). The issue was promptly taken up by Congress in the NII Copyright Protection Act of 1995 (S. 1284 and H.R. 2441). Despite the apparent interest, however, the bill's ultimate passage into law remained uncertain during the election year of 1996 (Truitt; Hernandez). Aside from the obvious distractions of the presidential race, scientific, educational and commercial interests weighed in with conflicting opinions reflecting their concerns. The Association of American Publishers, for example, was prompt in sending in its comments on Lehman's "Green Paper," including previous statements on scanning and document availability. The Association for Computing (ACM) responded to the House and Senate bills on the Information Infrastructure Copyright Act of 1995 by suggesting that the legislation "fails to recognize legitimate needs and interests of academic, professional, scientific, and ordinary users of telecommunications technology . . . [by impeding the] needs of the scientific and academic communities to disseminate and study information in a free and speedy fashion" (Association for Computing).

Protection for copyright holders may be a bigger problem in the foreign markets than it is domestically. Syndicates and news services are finding that business is growing at a much more rapid pace abroad than it is in the United States. In 1991, United Media reported that its overseas business had "more than tripled" in the previous five years, and Cartoonists & Writers Syndicate also reported that foreign sales had been "very important" for it (Astor, "Sales"). The delivery of the various features, including comics and cartoons, is increasingly by fax, computer and satellite—i.e., digitally. Because of the growing importance of the overseas markets, the syndicates are simultaneously becoming more concerned with the overseas sales potential of the features they sign on and carry. "We definitely discuss its overseas potential," said United Media Vice President Sid Goldberg. "Every syndicate with both strong comics and text features will say they sell more comics abroad. Comics are the crux of the syndication industry in the U.S., so it's not necessarily surprising that it holds true overseas as well" (Astor, "Sales" 40). Internationally, then, the material, the attraction and the means are all available to copy and plagiarize or steal.

And steal they do. For computer software, it is reported that piracy in Japan cost American companies more than $1.1 billion. In China the rate of piracy is 98%, exceeded by Indonesia at 99% (Holleyman). *WittyWorld,* the international cartoon magazine, recently published an illustrated accusation by an Australian editorial cartoonist of plagiarism by a German cartoonist, Peter Kaste, detailing the thefts. The magazine also published a reply by Kaste admitting to the plagiarism, and apologizing for it, but not promising that it wouldn't recur. Kaste had merely modified the cartoon slightly for his own purposes. Digitally, this is very easy to do, although any decent craftsman could do so manually as well.

The emerging problem lies in both the ready availability, through computers, and the various degrees of support for the rights of copyright holders throughout the world. Stanford University expert Paul Goldstein believes that "countries that were net copyright importers often had little incentive to meet American demands for expanded copyright protection." Bruce Lehman adds that, "There are a lot of very serious political problems. The European copyright system is vastly different from our own, and there is a great reluctance on their part to adopt our system" (qtd. in Markoff, "Unraveling" D18). "At the February 1995 G-7 Ministerial Meeting on the Global Information Infrastructure (GII), the ministers noted that unless rules for the effective protection of the intellectual property are taken into account from the outset, the development of the international information superhighway will be severely hindered" (Lehman, *Intellectual* 130). It is further pointed out:

When the globe is blanketed with digital information dissemination systems, a user in one country will be able to manipulate information resources in another country in ways that may violate that country's copyright laws. Indeed, it may be difficult to determine where and when possible infringements may take place because, under the present level of development, a user in France can access a database in the United States and have a copy downloaded to a computer in Sweden. Whose copyright law would apply to such a transaction? Because copyright laws are territorial, and the standards of protection embodied in the international conventions leave room for national legislative determinations, acts that may constitute infringement in one country may not be an infringement in another country. (Lehman, *Intellectual* 130)

Cartoonists, then, are squeezed into a strange position; syndicates want work that is more salable internationally, which means less locally meaningful material. Their newspapers also want cartoons that are attractive beyond the local circulation for the newspapers' Internet database Website. But if the cartoons are all readily comprehensible nationally and internationally, why need the newspaper have its own staff cartoonist? In addition, the material that is made available internationally by digital means is increasingly subject to plagiarism and consequent loss of potential income.

Libel is an area from which political cartoonists have little to fear in the United States, especially since the extensions of the First Amendment into libel law consequent to *New York Times v. Sullivan* in 1964. Many cartoonists take some pride, glee even, in being sued for libel because they know they have virtually nothing at risk and feel that they have been effective in their work. Their identifiable subjects are all public figures of one sort or another who are by that fact subject to harsh opinion *which need not be fair*. I know of no successful libel suit against a political cartoonist since 1964. Rep. Newt Gingrich was nearly angry enough to want to try in 1994, when Mike Luckovich drew him asking his bedridden wife for a divorce (Astor, "Gingrich"). Instead, he contented himself with banning the *Atlanta Constitution* from his appearances until he received an apology and retraction.

Internationally, the situation may be quite different. Few other nations have anything approaching the protections provided freedom of speech and press in the United States. Most are much more restrictive, especially in regard to government personnel and their policies; those are precisely the areas that have been the typical target of editorial cartoonists. Although conceivably cartoonists could be personally subject to some form of penalty in a foreign country for a cartoon drawn in the United States, such as in Iraq for cartoons about Saddam Hussein, it is unlikely unless the cartoonist appeared there. Iran did not promulgate death penalties for cartoons about Ayatollah Ruhollah Khomeini as it did for for the author Salman Rushdie. But that may have only been for lack of access to a foreigner. Manouchehr Karimzadeh, an Iranian cartoonist, was thought to have blasphemously drawn the image of Khomeini on the face of a soccer player and was heavily punished, along with his editor (Trudeau 19). A Palestinian cartoonist, Naji Salim al-Ali, was assassinated in London for his work, supposedly by the Palestinian Liberation Organization. Johnny Hart escaped punishment by being absent from Saudi Arabia when one of his "B.C." strips was charged as blasphemous, but the newspaper editor there did not. Similar events have taken place in the former Soviet Union, Israel, Turkey, Eastern Europe, Latin America, and elsewhere.

Whether or not syndicates try to sell cartoons and other features abroad, they are often available there through the Internet, and can be forwarded to still other destinations. Therefore, a cartoonist can be technically in violation of a foreign libel law without any intention of distributing his art there. Or, on the other hand, the ISP may be held responsible for content that violates some other nation's laws. In December 1995, for example, Compuserve was informed by a Bavarian prosecutor that some material appearing in Usenet group sites carried by the company might be in violation of German law; furthermore, if access to these sites by German subscribers was not eliminated, the company might be penalized in some way, such as being unable to do business in Germany. Compuserve, claiming that it had no immediate means to close access by subscribers of any particular country, responded by eliminating some 200 Usenet groups from its service *everywhere*. In February 1996, it was able to provide software controls to subscribers to permit customer control of access, and restore access to the Usenet groups it had closed off. In this case the issue was pornography, particularly that involving minors; but that need not be the case, as Prodigy, another ISP, discovered when it was named co-defendant in a $200 million lawsuit over statements made by a subscriber charging a brokerage house with illegal activities (Lewis, "New Twist," "Libel"). Margaret Chon, a Syracuse University law professor, believes, "Libel seems to be emerging as a locus of dispute on the Internet" (Lewis, "Libel" D2).

The potential for a myriad of other nations to confront ISPs with demands similar to those of the German government presents significant problems (Helle). As noted above, countries vary greatly in what they will tolerate in public communications. If even a modest number of them exercise their sovereignty in this manner, ISPs that want to do business there will have to conform by screening their offerings, reducing content to that which offends as few as possible. That screening may well eliminate much of what editorial cartoonists see themselves as doing.

The Communications Decency Act, signed into law by President Clinton in February 1996, only compounds the problems faced by those publishing opinions. Initially, what the Act forbids, relating to pornography and indecency related to children, is unlikely to affect editorial cartoonists. But the concept of "decency" is vague and subject to differing interpretations over place and time. For example, America On Line eliminated groups dealing with certain body parts, such as breasts. That action included groups focusing on problems of breast cancer, and following protests, was rescinded. If such reactions occur in the United States, one can imagine the blizzard of interpretations and responses abroad, especially in the more religiously fundamentalist parts of the world.

In sum, it appears that recent trends in digital communications and commerce do not favor editorial cartoonists at this time. They are being pushed from several directions either to reduce the bite of their opinions or to become gagsters. Their bewilderment is evident in their repeated but so far futile attempts at conventions and business meetings to address satisfactorily, or even agree on, the pressures facing them. Their employers, the newspapers, and their distributors, the syndicates, all want to enhance the salability of the material by reducing local and irritating content. If the cartoonists do so, however, they tend to make themselves less needed as part of an editorial staff. The future for the cartoonists then may be to become independent agents doing funny cartoons through the Internet that offend as few as possible. This is not an amusing prospect.

Sources

Association for Computing. "Letter on the Information Infrastructure Copyright Act." Dec. 1, 1995.

Association of American Publishers. "Comments by the Association of American Publishers on the Preliminary Draft of the Report of the Working Group on Intellectual Property Rights entitled 'Intellectual Property and the National Information Infrastructure.'" Sept. 7, 1994.

Astor, David. "Cartoonists' Group Decries Job Losses." *Editor & Publisher* 22 July 1995: 36-37.

——. "Consortium Formed for Feature Delivery." *Editor & Publisher* 21 Oct. 1995.

——. "Cyberspace Draws AAEC's Attention." *Editor & Publisher* 29 July 1995: 32-33.

——. "Downbeat Look at a Profession's Future." *Editor & Publisher* 25 June 1994: 110-11.

——. "Electronic Delivery of Comic Coming." *Editor & Publisher* 16 Oct. 1993: 36-37.

——. "Gingrich Bans the Constitution after Seeing Luckovich Cartoon." *Editor & Publisher* 19 Nov. 1994: 41.

——. "'High-Tech Update' on Editorial Cartoons." *Editor & Publisher* 11 May 1991: 36-39.

——. "Sales Are Booming in Overseas Markets." *Editor & Publisher* 26 Jan. 1991: 38, 40-42.

——. "Syndicates Race into Cyberspace." *Editor & Publisher* 6 May 1995: 36-38.

——. "Thaves Talks 'Tech' at Cartoon Meeting." *Editor & Publisher* 4 June 1994: 54-55.

——. "They Discuss Originality and Plagiarism." *Editor & Publisher* 30 June 1990: 30, 41.

——. "United Starts Web Site on the Internet." *Editor & Publisher* 8 Apr. 1995: 28.

Baker, Nicholson. "Infohighwaymen." *New York Times* 18 Oct. 1994: A25.

Blumenthal, Ralph. "Thieves in the Idea Marketplace." *New York Times* 11 Feb. 1995: 13, 14.

Carmody, Deirdre. "Barry Feature Pulled." *Editor & Publisher* 8 Oct. 1994: 46.

——. "Newspapers Surge into New Media." *Editor & Publisher* 4 Feb. 1995: 33.

——. "Writers Fight for Electronic Rights." *New York Times* 7 Nov. 1994: B20.

Fitzgerald, Mark. "Invisible Digital Copyright ID." *Editor & Publisher* 25 June 1994: 62.

——. "One Solution to Copyright Problems in Cyberspace: Unique Digital Names." *Editor & Publisher* 17 Dec. 1994: 16.

Frankel, Max. "Cyberights." *New York Times Magazine* 12 Feb. 1995: 26.

Garneau, George. "Big-time, Online Alliance formed." *Editor & Publisher* 22 Apr. 1995: 15-16.

——. "A Calling in Cyberspace." *Editor & Publisher* 13 May 1995: 35, 44.

Gipson, Melinda. "Bill's OnLine AdVenture." *Presstime* Oct. 1995: 28-33.

Glaberson, William. "Press Notes." *New York Times* 14 Mar. 1994: D7.

——. "Press Notes." *New York Times* 10 Oct. 1994: D5.

Helle, Steven. "Libel in Cyberspace." *Editor & Publisher* 24 Dec. 1994: 16, 30.

Hernandez, Debra Gersh. "Congress Considers Updating Copyright Law to Cover Online Information." *Editor & Publisher* 25 Nov. 1995: 31, 39.

Holleyman, Robert. *Bergen Record* 7 Mar. 1995: B4.

Lamb, Chris. "Editorial Cartoonists Pessimistic about Their Profession." *Editor & Publisher* 14 Oct. 1995: 48, 36.

Lehman, Bruce A. "Greenpaper." *Intellectual Property and the National Information Infrastructure* Information Infrastructure Task Force, July 1994.

——. *Intellectual Property and the National Information Infrastructure*, Information Infrastructure Task Force. Sept. 1995.

Lewis, Peter H. "Libel Suit Against Prodigy Tests On-Line Speech Limits." *New York Times* 16 Nov. 1994: D1, 2.

——. "A New Twist in an On-Line Libel Case." *New York Times* 19 Dec. 1995: D10.

"Making Archives Pay." *Presstime* Oct. 1995: 57.

Markoff, John. "In a World of Instant Copies, Who Pays for Original Work?" *New York Times* 9 Aug. 1992: E-18.

——. "Unraveling Copyright Rules for Cyberspace." *New York Times* 9 Mar. 1995: D18.

McKenna, Kate. "The Future Is Now." *American Journalism Review* Oct. 1993: 17-22.

Miller, Bryan. "What High-Tech Cartoonists Do with the Leftovers." *New York Times* 11 Sept. 1994: F4.

Moeller, Philip. "The Age of Convergence." *American Journalism Review* Jan./Feb. 1994: 22-28.

——. "The High-Tech Trib." *American Journalism Review* Apr. 1994: 14-21.

Muchnick, Irvin. "Electronic Copyright" (Letter to the Editor). *New York Times* 18 Feb. 1995: 20.

——. *Presstime.* "Crackdown on Copying." Nov. 1994: 22.

Rykken, Rolf. "Funny Business." *Presstime Planner* Apr. 1995: S1-10.

"Technology Guards Other Copyrights." *Editor & Publisher* 27 May 1995: 29.

Toner, Marl. "Getting on Boards." *Presstime* May 1995: 47-50.

Trudeau, Garry. "Drawing, Dangerously." *New York Times* 10 July 1994, Sec. 4: 19.

Truitt, Rosalind C. "Protecting Digital Property." *Presstime* Oct. 1995: 24.

Veliotes, Nicholas A. "Don't Lose Creators' Rights in Cyberspace." *USA Today* 16 Aug. 1994: 11A.

Webb, William. "Intelligent Agents on the Internet." *Editor & Publisher* 25 Mar. 1995: 50, 56.

Wincor, Richard. "Unrest on the Frontiers of Copyright." *Communications and the Law* 16.3 (Sept. 1994): 83-89.

Wines, Michael. "Cartoonists See a Future That's No Joking Matter." *New York Times* 3 July 1995: 40.

WittyWorld 18 (Summer/Autumn 1995): 28-29.

3

Rex Babin, *Albany Times-Union*

Kalman Goldstein

On August 23, 1994, the day I interviewed Rex Babin, the *Albany (N.Y.) Times-Union* ran his captionless cartoon on President Clinton's Health Care bill. Laboriously carrying a giant, cross-like caduceus on his back, the President struggled toward a political Calvary (see illustration). Having already read some of the letters to the editor his work inspires, I predicted that some reader reaction might be visceral. Babin agreed: "I'm anti-Establishment, God dammit. I'm going to cause trouble. I found my voice. I was on shaky ground for a while. Sometimes I'm still on shaky ground. The paper gets letters. The paper should like that. It should like to have talk in the local media, discussions about these crazy cartoons" (Babin, interview). His comment earlier that month about the murder of an abortion doctor in Florida, simply drawing a car with a bumper sticker that read "Guns Don't Kill People—Pro-Lifers Kill People," had already generated a lot of mail (*Albany Times-Union* Aug. 2, 10, 13, 1994). So had a cartoon in May, a parody of Michelangelo's "Creation of Adam," likening controversial euthanasia doctor Jack Kevorkian to God while connecting Adam to tubes of lethal drugs (*National Forum* May 22, 1994, 20). Clearly Babin enjoys being provocative, describing himself as a young blond surfer dude come East, where it's more acceptable to be outrageous rather than mellow.

Babin was born in 1962 in Los Angeles and raised in a one-parent family (his father died when he was four). He showed an interest and ability in drawing at an early age, and came from a politically aware family. While he had no formal art training, he was in California's first "Newspapers in Education" program and drew for his high school paper. Earning a B.A. in English (minor in journalism) from San Diego State University in 1985, he became involved in newspaper cartooning upon graduation. From 1985 to 1988 he was senior artist and cartoonist for the *Orange Coast Daily Pilot* in Costa Mesa, California, where he did graphics, illustrations, editorial page layouts, and four cartoons a week. For nine months, September 1988 to July 1989, he filled in for Mike Keefe at the *Denver Post,* then began his present position that

31

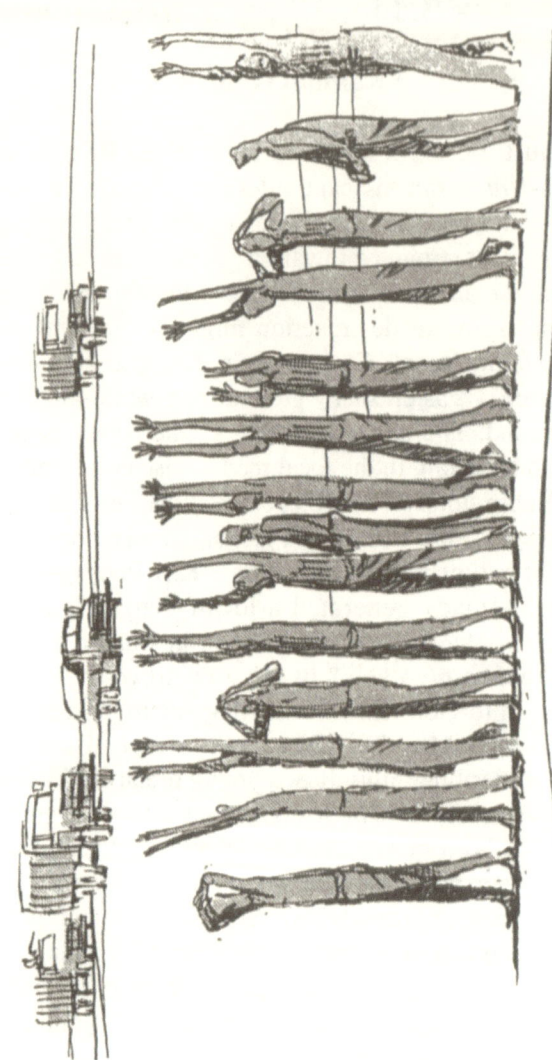

IRAQI TROOP MANEUVERS

Rex Babin (1994) *Albany Times-Union*. Reprinted with special permission of North American Syndicate.

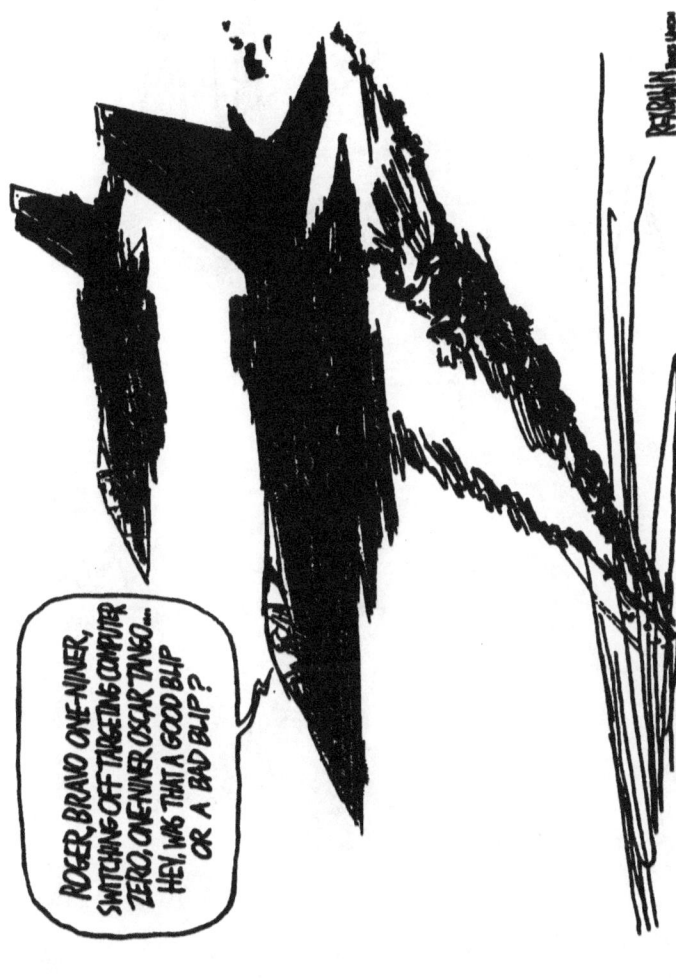

Rex Babin (1994) *Albany Times-Union*. Reprinted with special permission of North American Syndicate.

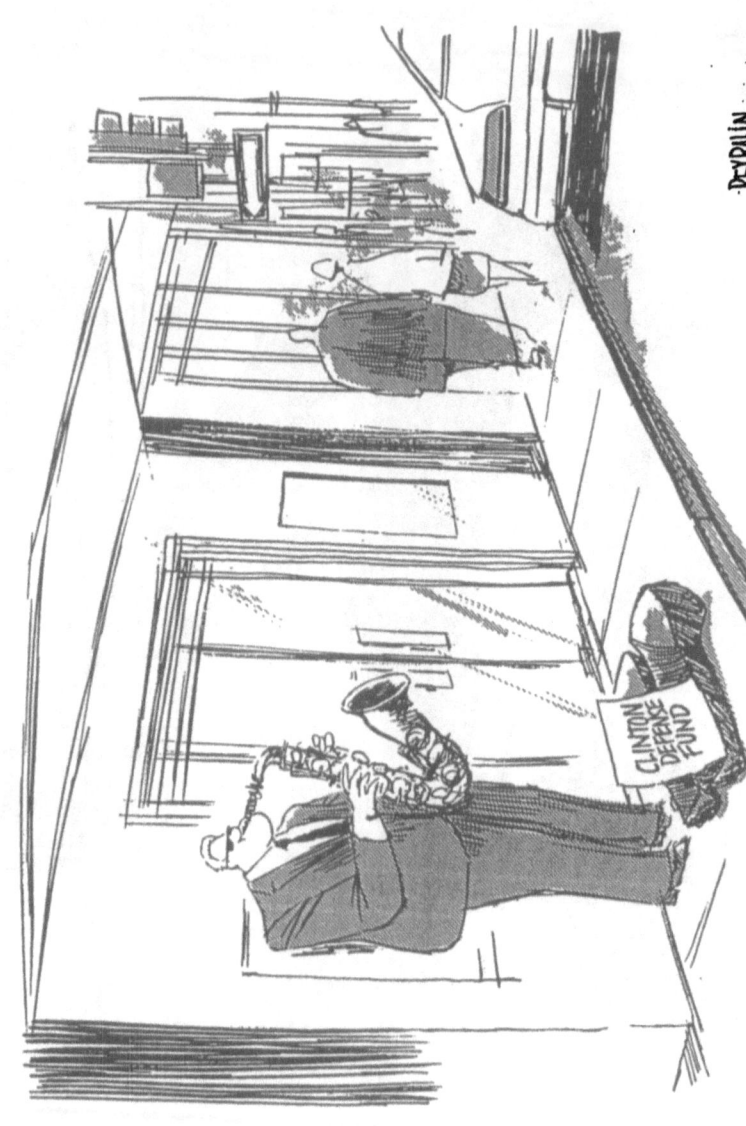

Rex Babin (1994) *Albany Times-Union*. Reprinted with special permission of North American Syndicate.

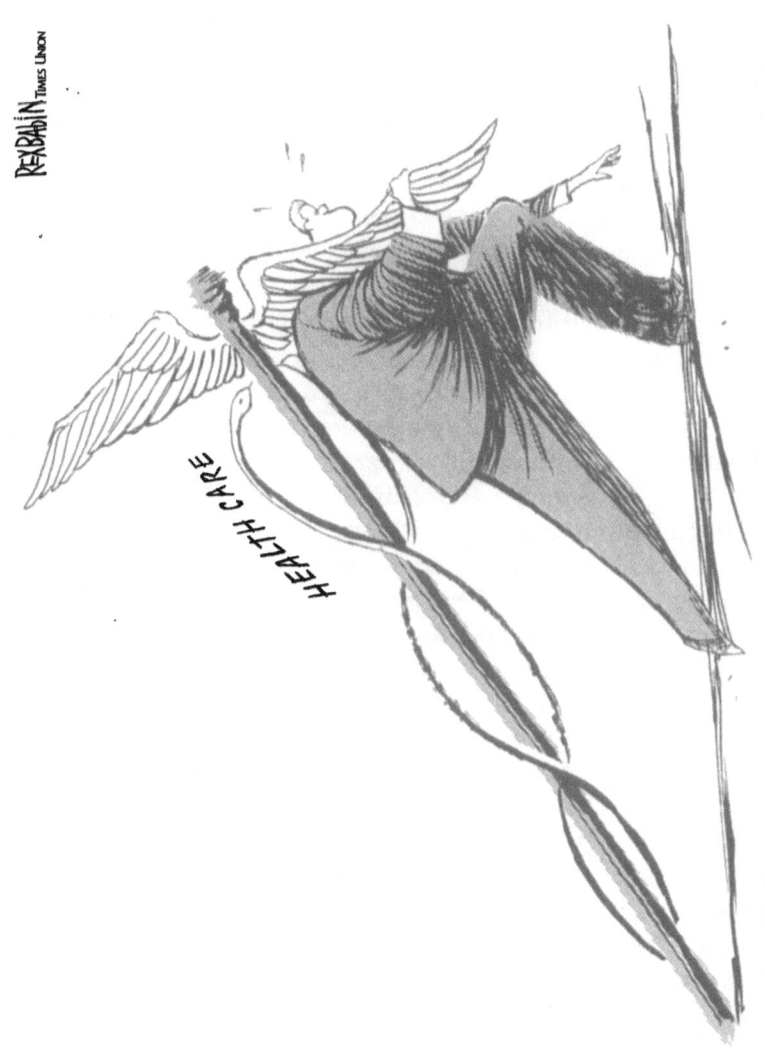

Rex Babin (1994) *Albany Times-Union*. Reprinted with special permission of North American Syndicate.

September. He has won awards in California and New York for his work, the Fischetti Editorial Cartoon Competition in 1991, and the Hearst Newspapers Eagle Award in 1994. Since September 1993 he has been affiliated with North American Syndicate.

Much of his art, both in concept and execution, shows how much he revels in belonging to a new, younger artistic generation. His drawing has changed dramatically since he first joined the Albany paper, becoming looser, less exact, and more impressionistic; he no longer tries to copy the styles of more established political cartoonists. In fact, he cites as his leading influences right now the work of Charles Addams, current *New Yorker* staff artists, and New York City's Museum of Modern Art exhibitions. Hokusai, Matisse, Giacometti, and Frank Lloyd Wright have particularly inspired his interest in sketching line and movement rather than in thinking about filled in backgrounds, detailed caricatures, or gag situations—the approach of "traditional" editorial cartoons. Fascinated by the power of simplicity and restraint, he has also stopped using balloon captions. "There's no law that says editorial cartoons have to have balloons just because MacNelly did them really well back in the '70s. . . . Editorial cartoonists are still struggling with what they want to be— Do they want to be editorial cartoonists or do they want to imitate what a few cartoonists were doing during Watergate?" (Babin, Interview).

On June 30, 1994, Babin drew President Clinton as a street musician trying to raise money for the Whitewater Defense fund. While drawing the President playing a saxophone has been done by any number of cartoonists, Babin's version illustrates a uniquely New York City–inspired aesthetic: architectural and cultural lines of dynamic perspective through which to enrich his captionless cartoons. "Look at the buildings, my backgrounds, they're all linear—fast lines—New York City backgrounds." Clinton's figure and posture alone makes the political point, "but to give it the dynamics and the energy that I want, it has these lines running through it" converging toward the traffic light and parking arrows. "The drawing stroke I use is neurotic—like I've had five cups of coffee. Wired. The New York architecture encourages that" (Babin, Interview; see illustration).

His Clinton Health Care cartoon provides a further opportunity to examine Babin's distinctive compositional techniques. Selecting a caduceus came to him as he thought of the simile of two snakes and two houses of Congress, and while doodling the similarity of caduceus and cross. Visual ideas connected with and reinforced literal ones. He left much white space in order to allow concentration on the sole, dynamic figure. Diagonal lines abounded, reinforcing a sense of strained movement. Babin is unconcerned with exact perspective or proportion, and in a spoof of Clinton's involvement in the restaging of D-Day showed him gingerly entering the surf with outrageously rubbery legs, exaggeratedly elongated thighs, and foreshortened shins (*National Forum* June 12, 1994: 7). While including a verbose dialogue balloon, his portrayal of jet fighter plans and a burning target provide another stark example of his impressionistic technique (*National Forum* May 1, 1994, 3; see illustration).

Babin credits his assignment to cover the August 1994 Woodstock festival with continuing his artistic development. From the 13th to 21st, the *Times-Union* pubished his on-site drawings. Doing sketches in acrylic amid the rain and mud forced him further away from tightly outlined drawing and suggested an experiment of allowing water to drip on his sketch book, affecting lines and hues. It also tickled him that he was one of the few artists from a nonalternative journal young enough to rock and roll with the crowd.

Being young and experimental affects Babin's choice of subjects as well as his compositional approach. As well as local, state and national political issues, many cartoonists tackle items of popular culture and its transient icons. When Babin presents them, however, frequently his references reflect the interests and concerns of young adults. One of his most effective was a multipaneled soliloquy by a member of Generation X about alienation and drug use, which rings true in viewpoint and jargon (*National Forum* June 12, 1994, 21). Frequently Babin sets his satires within the world of computer hackers and virtual reality enthusiasts. Or he cites unusual popular culture references such as the Genevieve Bujold movie *Coma* or the children's book *Where's Waldo?* in order to make a political point (*Albany Times-Union* Sept. 21 and 28, 1994, Oct. 29, 1994).

As do many other political cartoonists, Babin enjoys being sarcastic, but often manages to make his point using unusual juxtapositions or angles of view. As he remarked: "I'm basically lucky because my mind doesn't think in the same way that a lot of cartoonists' do" (Babin, Interview). One cartoon that he particularly enjoyed doing was a comment on March 9, 1994, in which Hillary Rodham Clinton, rather than Whitewater documents, was shredded. Here he was inspired by the double entendre of the word, the visual image, and the sufficiency of the image to make captions superfluous. In fact the metaphor built up: shredder machine, Hillary as shredded paper, political credibility shredded, media shredding of the First Lady's financial probity.

Babin believes cartoons like this are in sharp contrast to trends of the past 20 years, where cartoonists searched for "humorous-switch" captions. He used to do them himself, but felt uncomfortable at it, and has never been good at the classic gag-editorial cartoon. However, he does concede that as he gets better at doing gags, he might run some. One example reveals a sign-painter amending the door of former Congressman Dan Rostenkowski's office to read "Chairman—Ways and Misdemeanors," while the politician puts his hand to his head. On the wall is a plaque referring to "U.S. Commemorative Stamps," a reminder of one of the scandals associated with him. This is not typical of Babin's work, but even here there is much use of white space. Lines of molding and desk lead the eye from the hunched painter, to the gag, then to the wall plaque, then to a window framing a sketchily suggested Washington Monument, and finally to the politician, cowering in a far corner of the cartoon (*National Forum* June 5, 1994, 6).

Another cartoon that he especially enjoyed doing was his January 14, 1994, take on the Tonya Harding affair, in which a competitive figure skater allowed her husband and bodyguard to attempt to injure the competition. Babin has her routine being "judged," with one judge awarding her "5 to 10." His delight with it was increased when other cartoonists, doing similar variations on the situation, had judges fearful of physical reprisal giving her "9.5." They did not realize that, in this sport, "6" is a perfect score, which makes the "5 to 10" gag funny.

A third cartoon, which took an old metaphor and did something visually unique with it, was a March 17, 1994, attack both on New York Senator Alphonse D'Amato and President Clinton, a visualization of the metaphor of the pot calling the kettle black. Drawn from a child's perspective, looking upward toward a stove top, the cartoon shows D'Amato emerging from a large pot to point dramatically and accusingly at Clinton, cowering under a teakettle lid. To Babin, the cliché is now no longer shopworn because people have to recognize the metaphor themselves, because it is presented in unusual perspective, it alludes to a stove without drawing it completely, and it portrays an unusual dynamic relation between the two caricatured politicians. Babin partly credits a college education in literature for his ease at visualizing metaphors afresh, but adds that "it helps to have a lot of stuff in your head already: historical, pop culture, literary references, Bugs Bunny cartoons, classic humorists, New York icons" (Babin, Interview).

A final example of unusual perspective or juxtaposition can be seen in his October 16, 1994, piece, "Iraqi Troop Maneuvers." Here he transforms a column of surrendering soldiers into a monumental Giacometti-like frieze (see illustration). A line of figures only sketchily drawn as human, their hands and postures suggestive of complete despair, the prisoners file off as if into the wings of a stage, with some troop trucks in background as if on a scrim. The ample white space contributes a hush; the entire political cartoon partakes of sculpture and tableau.

Babin thinks that his youthfulness might make a difference in the kind of response, both positive and negative, that he gets from readers. In Albany, a "small political town," he finds himself a big fish in a small but culturally interesting pond, though even during his nine months in Denver people responded to his work. In both cities he found numbers of interesting, bright, intelligent readers looking for an iconoclast. Babin is convinced that the "in your face" arrogance that his work exudes is sorely needed, after 20 years of gag-oriented humorous cartoons. He does, however, note a growing problem in the profession for cartoonists of his generation. During the 1970s, a transition time when older cartoonists were retiring and newspapers were hiring young energetic artists, many could quickly gain peer and professional acclaim. In Albany, Babin succeeded a veteran of 44 years with the paper, but now some newspapers whose older cartoonists retire choose for reasons of economy to carry syndicate-packaged artists rather than pay a staff cartoonist. So he is concerned not only with his own growth and recognition but with the future of editorial cartooning as an art form. While the apparently shrinking size of the field does allow cartoonists to be well aware of one another's work, job opportunities are very tight. This might frighten aspirants into copying the work of accepted leaders rather than take risks on their own. "If I had a family and a mortgage, I don't know if I would have the nerve to say things that would get me in trouble, where the paper might think I was a liability and get rid of me. I think a lot of editorial cartoonists are getting less aggressive and trying to hold onto their jobs. They are good at being funny and not really saying anything" (Babin, Interview).

Babin is equally convinced that both cartoonists and their papers should be more thoughtful about content. People want information, and no cartoonists should try to compete with television by providing simplistic "bits" and "bites." "I'm still aiming to do sophisticated humor in a traditional medium that goes all the way back to the days of woodcuts. . . . People want art to transcend their lives. It's content, not how you do it that counts" (Babin, Interview).

Sources

Albany Times-Union July-Oct. 1994.

Babin, Rex. Interview. By Kalman Goldstein. 23 Aug. 1994.

Brooks, Charles, ed. *Best Editorial Cartoons of the Year*. Gretna, LA: Pelican, 1992-1997.

National Forum Gallery of Cartoons. Washington, D.C., weekly.

4

Linda Boileau, *Frankfort State Journal*

Jack Colldeweih .

"Draw what you're familiar with and get published." With that advice from one of her mentors, and a lot of determination, Boileau has become one of but a handful of female editorial cartoonists employed at daily newspapers. She draws for the *Frankfort State Journal*, an afternoon paper in the Kentucky state capital, a location that provides her with a lot of local targets with statewide implications, and when she comments on them she hits hard and often. Governor John Y. Brown, and his wife, the former Miss America Phyllis George, were among the early favorite victims of her cartoons—"worth a cartoon a day," she claims (Boileau, Interview). She scores no low blows, though. While groaning and feebly protesting to the editors, the subjects often surreptiliously request copies of the original cartoons.

Very shy in her youth, Boileau found that cartooning "changed my life—it gave me a voice, a personality, a tiny bit of grit; it turned on a light" (Boileau, Interview). Although she took some classes at a community college and received advice from other artists, such as Kate Sally Palmer, then cartoonist for the *Greenville News* in South Carolina, Boileau is essentially self-taught as an artist. A Frankfort native (born May 17, 1960), she initially wanted to do a strip, and in October 1980 proposed that to the editors of the *Frankfort State Journal*. She was told, "We don't want any damned comic strip, but we do want an editorial cartoon—can you do that?" (Boileau, Interview). Accepting without really knowing what she was doing, she soon found out that she could "do that." Her editors, who were "like fathers" to her, made suggestions for the subjects of cartoons for the first few years, but she has been on her own in that regard since then.

Boileau takes her local paper responsibilities seriously and draws half her cartoons on local and state topics. She feels that "you have to hook [the readers] first, and then you can do the national or international material. I think the reader wants to see something local or state—that kind of gets the readership going. . . . So you do the local first, and then you embellish yourself when you do the national and international"

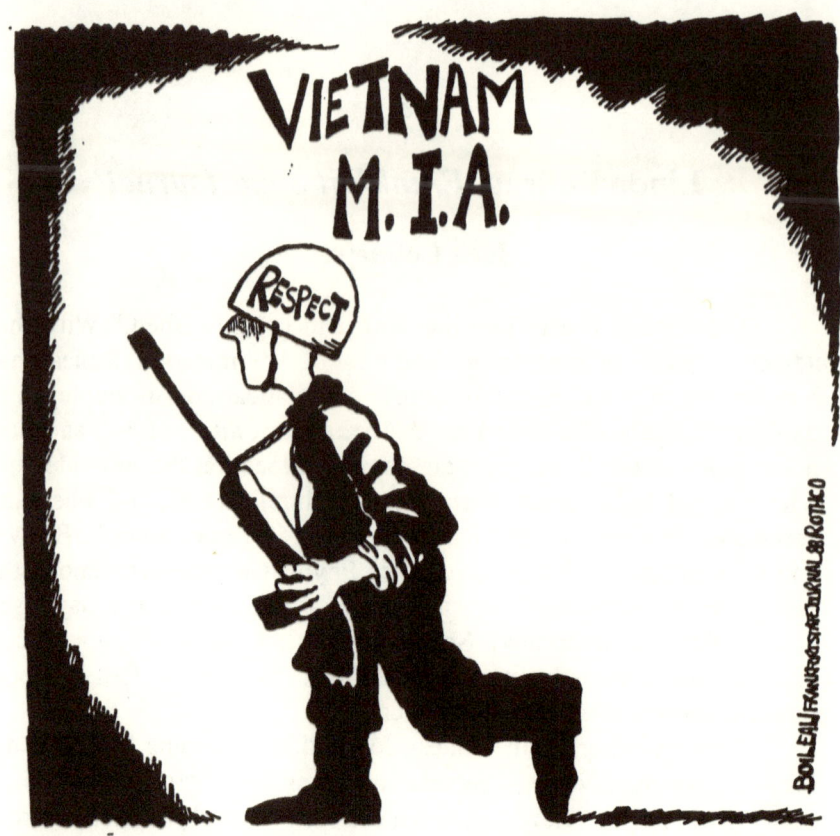

Linda Boileau (1988) *Frankfort State Journal* and Rothco. Reprinted with permission.

(Boileau, Interview). She does believe, however, that if one is going to be in the cartoon business, national and international topics have to be covered.

Boileau's working schedule is somewhat different from that of most other artists because the *State Journal* is an afternoon paper, one of the few extant. She draws her cartoons is bunches, over the weekend and then through the week, working primarily at home. If a breaking story hits after Friday's submission for the Sunday edition, she will draw a new one for it. With such a schedule, she arises very early in the morning to get through all the newspapers for cartooning ideas. She prefers to read for the news, rather than pick it up on radio or television, feeling that one gets "a different interpretation of the news when you read it rather than have it read to you" (Boileau, Interview).

Despite her habit of keeping very current with the news, her preference for a broad humanistic approach to that news, to its longer-term

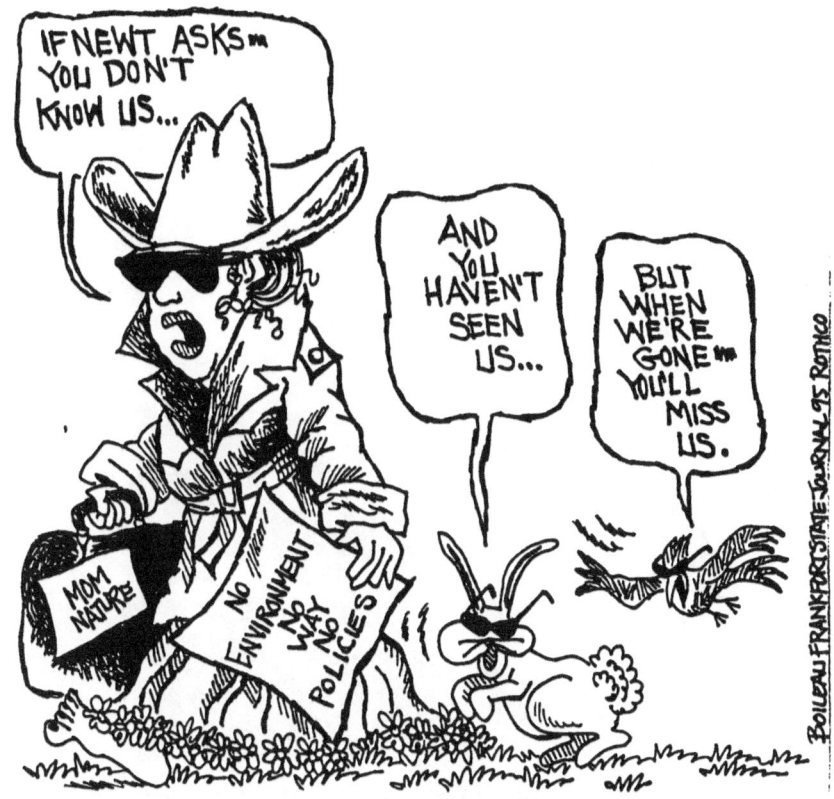

Linda Boileau (1995) *Frankfort State Journal* and Rothco. Reprinted with permission.

implications for the ordinary person, keeps her work from falling rapidly out of date. This permits her to go on vacation while having left an ample stock of suitable cartoons to cover her absence. As her editor once told another potential contributor, Boileau "sucks up all the cartoon ink on that page."

Boileau's drawing style is stark and straightforward, with the emphasis on the foreground; there is little background detail or filler. She sometimes uses crosshatching for shadow or to highlight text balloons, but even that is kept to a minimum. Early in her career she tended to use up every bit of space, but as her style matured, she has moved to the less-is-more viewpoint. "Now I think that a really good cartoon does not have a lot in it, does not have a lot of art, does not have a lot of words that you have to wade through" (Boileau, Interview). Before she begins to draw, she writes down the idea as clearly as possible. Then, after drawing it, she edits the drawing to see what can be eliminated so

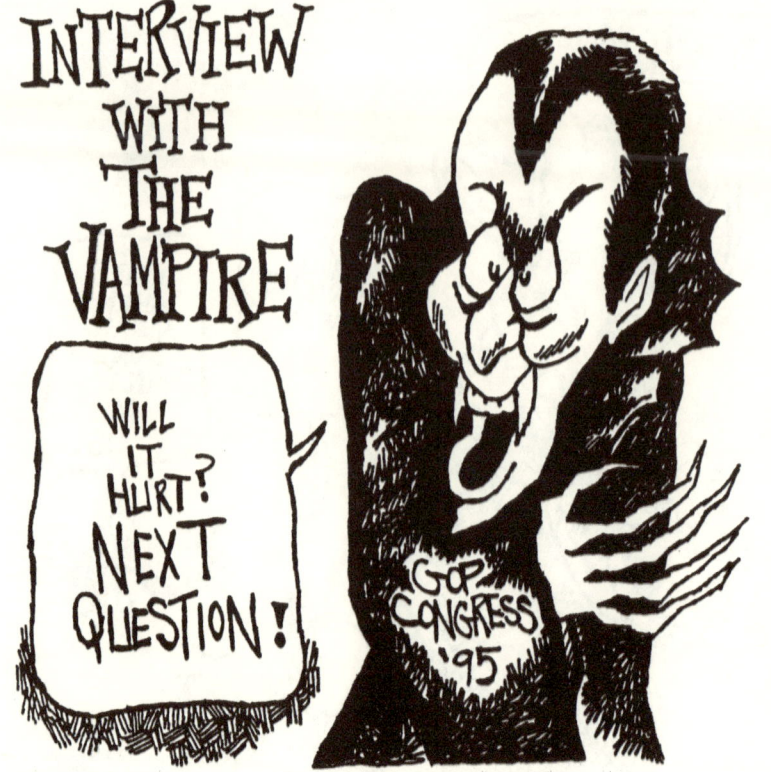

Linda Boileau (1995) *Frankfort State Journal* and Rothco. Reprinted with permission.

as to highlight the message. She wants the reader to "zoom right in on the part of the page that I want him to see. One of the best things about a cartoon is that it's quick; you've got one shot and it's sort of like shooting an arrow: it's quick and clean and you get right to the target. The stuff in the background just gets in the way." She does not use graphic paper or a brush but generally sticks with a fine point pen. Her figures and crosshatching are consequently clean and distinct.

In other ways, her cartoons are more traditional. She rarely uses the multipanel cartoon style favored by many contemporary artists because she thinks in single-panel formats when conceiving her images. Occasionally, she does draw before-and-after, then-and-now, yesterday-and-today divided formats, but two panels is about the limit. She also does not favor color cartoons for the editorial page, believing that color belongs with the comics. Black and white go along with the message, she feels, while color tends weaken it. Whereas many cartoons today are very wordy, especially in the multipanel style, Boileau's usually don't

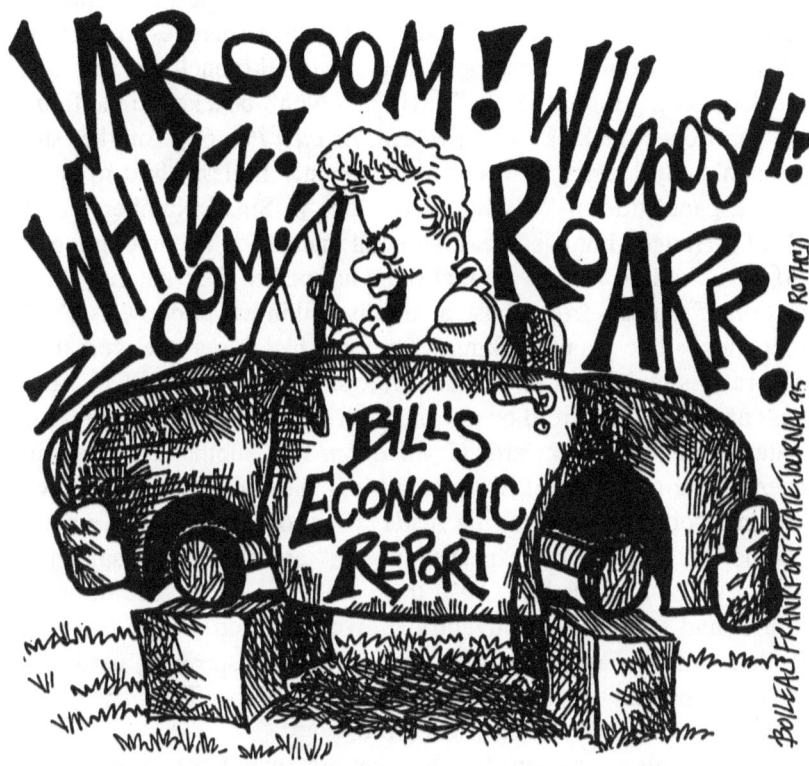

Linda Boileau (1995) *Frankfort State Journal* and Rothco. Reprinted with permission.

contain a lot of dialog or labels. They all have dialog, but it's at a minimum. She thinks dialog when conceiving the cartoon because she thinks of what someone is going to say, whether she actually lets them say it that way or not.

Although from a Democratic Party background, she aims to be "equally unfair to both democrats and republicans. . . . I try to be as mean to one as the other" (Boileau, Interview). She claims to be able to find fault with just about anyone. Her real goal, however, is to assist the underdog against the forces of government, business, society or individuals that may be oppressing him. Boileau has great difficulty understanding those who would be hostile or indifferent to the difficulties of the downtrodden. Therefore, she wants to be a voice for those who perhaps could not have another voice, "whose plight could not be known if [I] didn't do something about it. I try to do cartoons about people who are always being pushed back, held down, by whatever circumstances . . . I don't really try to speak for either political party" (Boileau, Interview).

Two of her most frequent "clients" in this regard are children and animals, both often victims of cold and violent societies in many countries. One cartoon, for example, depicts a child, enclosed in a padlock labeled "Rising Poverty Rate," saying, "I won't be a key to the future . . . if I can't open the lock . . ." (Boileau, *Loaded Pen* 67). Another shows a woman sadly looking down at an apparently lifeless child in her arms, with a panel title of "Civilian Casualties in Small Numbers" (*Loaded Pen* 6). Hunger, homelessness, parental inattention are among the conditions of children worldwide that draw her pen to their defense. The protection of animals from abuse also falls within her purview. A 1994 cartoon shows two people talking, with a leashed dog at the woman's feet. The man is saying. "If all animals were supposed to be treated with kindness and respect, there'd be a sign . . . ." A thought-balloon from the dog states, "Spell dog backward" (*Loaded Pen* 12). Another cartoon depicts a deer, a bear and a rabbit, with sunglasses, hats and a camera, arriving at a man's door; the cartoon title reads "If national park wildlife respected people the way people respect them . . ." and the deer is saying to the man, "We're on vacation! We'll trash your house, doo-doo on your furniture, and sell human souvenirs! Move your butt!" (*Loaded Pen* 59). Boileau also occasionally uses a rat as either a speaking participant in the cartoon or as a commentator on the main action. Thus, she gives animals a voice in both senses of the word.

She is also very sensitive to what are sometimes called "women's issues," but which she sees as human issues. These prominently include wife- or women-battering by abusive husbands or boyfriends. A 1994 cartoon, for example, dramatically depicts only the right half of a woman's face that has a large and ugly black eye; the text states, "Domestic violence abusers need a cool-down time before release. All in favor . . . say eye" (*Loaded Pen* 27). On another front, birth control, she is a strong supporter of women's control over their own bodies. On the occasion of the 1994 United Nations Conference on Population, she drew a cartoon depicting an obviously pregnant woman labeled as "Third World," with one infant in her arms and two at her feet. She is being told by a priest that "Certainly women have rights. . . . Women have the right to always be wrong" (*Loaded Pen* 41). Artificial barriers to women's advancement in business, i.e., the glass-ceiling effect, and the strain of double-duty work as co-provider and homemaker are other topics that she has dealt with in her cartoons.

Boileau usually sticks with the straight political material because she feels that she would weaken herself if she didn't. She is very conscious of being one of just a few women in the field and has to be careful of her topics and approach. "I feel that I have to be just a little bit stronger than a man would have to be; a guy could maybe zigzag a little bit and do topics that weren't political, but if I did that, they would say 'It's just a woman thing.' I watch myself" (Boileau, Interview).

She does take up causes that some might not consider political, however, such as the illiteracy project that many cartoonists participated in; some might call that a social issue instead. The Vietnam War MIA issue is one that Boileau is involved with and is generally accepted as a political one. Other aspects of the war that she deals with, such as the treatment of its veterans, are now more marginal politically. Usually Vietnam appears in contemporary cartoons only as a cautionary note compared to other actual or contemplated actions, or related to the qualifications of political candidates.

Violence in general, and war in particular, is one of her primary targets. She returns to this topic frequently not only because of its overall importance to her but also because of its plentiful and continuing examples. Bosnia, Somalia, Haiti, Rwanda have all been visited in her cartoons. She also thunders against those that contribute to the violence, even though not actually participating in it. One example has a smiling, trench-coated Russian in dark glasses offering the reader a rather large "Terrorist Coupon good for Free Armageddon with purchase of nuclear materials," and saying, "Thanks for shopping and have a nice doomsday" (*Loaded Pen* 40). Another shows a couple of labcoated scientists watching an nuclear explosion in the distance; he is carrying a clipboard reading "Nuclear Testing" and saying, "We must keep testing until nuclear weapons are safely dangerous!" She holds a clipboard reading "Ban the nuke test ban" and responds "or dangerously safe . . ." (*Loaded Pen* 30).

Boileau also deals with violence in its many guises on the domestic scene. Anti-abortion violence was remarked on, for example, in a cartoon showing a rat sitting upon a pile of garbage that has a sign reading "History's trash heap." The rat is holding a newspaper with a story about "clinic shootings" and is commenting, "If violence is the answer—justice is never the question" (*Loaded Pen* 80). Other aspects include children versus children in schools, youth-gang violence in the streets, the National Rifle Association, and violence in the media. Her work reflects an angry bewilderment at the callousness and stupidity of much of what she sees people doing to each other; in this she seems quite representative of her "middle-America" readership.

She feels that an editorial cartoonist must always make a statement, and therefore resists any urge to do "gag" cartoons for their own sake. On the other hand, she thinks that "most of the time the funny cartoon will get people's attention more than something that is dark and dramatic, even though I have done some things that are very dramatic and sad." She believes that people will remember what is funny more than what is sad. Political cartoons must have a "bite" to them, she feels, "you've got to burn some ego, get the knife out now and then, because if you don't, you're just not worth your stuff" (Boileau, Interview).

Images from popular culture appear frequently in her cartoons because she feels that it gets the reader's attention. As an admitted movie buff, she likes to use film titles when they work with the message of the cartoon. It gets another side of the audience that is missed when using classical references like great literature. She believes that if you employ classical references too frequently, you may lose some of your audience because currently many people don't have the educational background to grasp the allusions, and your syndicate would have trouble placing the work. On the other hand, "there are times when you just have to go ahead and do it, because no matter what you do there is always going to be a certain percentage of your readers who aren't going to understand. You just have to go ahead and trust what you think is going to be a good idea" (Boileau, Interview).

Boileau has continued her initial interest in doing a comic strip, like many other editorial cartoonists. She has been working with a newspaper columnist and book author who developed a strip a few years ago in conjunction with two others, but never got beyond character concepts and dialogue. She has drawn the strips using that material and is awaiting a response from a distributor. In addition, she has been practicing her talent as an illustrator for the *State Journal*, which doesn't have a separate position for that role, for community fundraisers for the Humane Society and the Arts Foundation, and for children's books.

Although she takes great delight in what she is doing, Boileau has a very sober view of the role of the editorial cartoonist for both the newspaper and the community. She feels that the cartoonist is "kind of the heart of the paper," prominently featured on the editorial page where the newspaper displays its conscience. If the cartoonist is regularly dealing with local issues, a bond is created between the paper and the community it serves. And by giving voice to those whose viewpoints might not otherwise be able to be expressed, the cartoonist is facilitating a community dialogue much needed in modern stressful times.

Sources

Boileau, Linda. Interview. By Jack Colldeweih. 23 Aug. 1994.
———. *Loaded Pen*. Gretna, LA: Pelican, 1995.
———. *Stink Ink*. Self-published, 1990.

5

Mark Cullum, *Birmingham (Ala.) News*

Robin Weitzen

"When you draw three hundred cartoons a year, it's hard to say which is your favorite," Mark Cullum claims. When pressed, however, he points to one of former Surgeon General Jocelyn Elders as Joe Camel. The difference between the two, according to Cullum, is that Joe pushes cigarettes, Jocelyn pushes condoms. Both are panderers; both are trying to make the unacceptable acceptable. While he is teaching kids how to smoke, she is teaching them what to do in the back seat of a car. Hesitant to further explain his cartoons to readers, Cullum says, "If they don't get it, they don't get it." For the cartoon to work, the viewer has to understand its message without elaboration.

A sharp example of the social conscience and the biting satire that Cullum combines as one of America's leading young and "nast-y" cartoonists, the Elders cartoon works according to the formula: the viewer "gets" it. How did Mark Edward Cullum, born in Philadelphia, Pennsylvania, on July 25, 1962, brought up in Nashville, Tennessee, and now living in Birmingham, Alabama, develop such a hard moral edge? And where does he get ideas for editorial cartoons like these?

Rush Limbaugh, right-wing America's notorious media star, is one source of inspiration. Another is former Education Secretary, present public moralist, and bestselling author, William Bennett. Bow-tied Princeton Ph.D., George Will, whose name often appears on late night talk-show guest lists, also provides Cullum with material. In addition to the moral and political concepts of others that Cullum integrates into his work, the cartoonist relies heavily on home and family for ideas. He calls himself a "conservative Christian" and attempts to express these values in the cartoons he writes and draws. He says that "home base is important," and that his parents were influential in shaping him (Cullum, Interview).

Cullum thinks of himself as a southerner. He moved with his family to Nashville when he was young, where his parents still live in the same house in which he was brought up. His father, Alan, works for the State Department of Education; his mother, Beverly, works at home. After

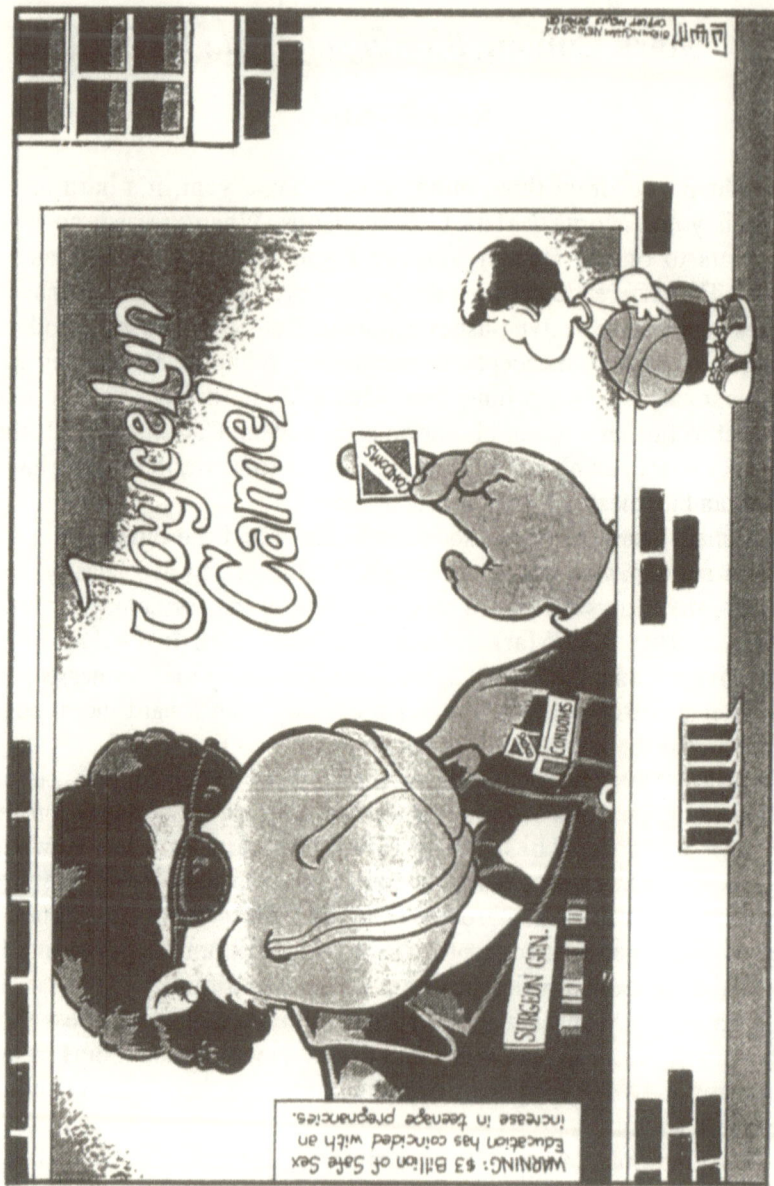

Mark Cullum (1994) *Birmingham (Ala.) News.* Reprinted with permission of Copley News Service.

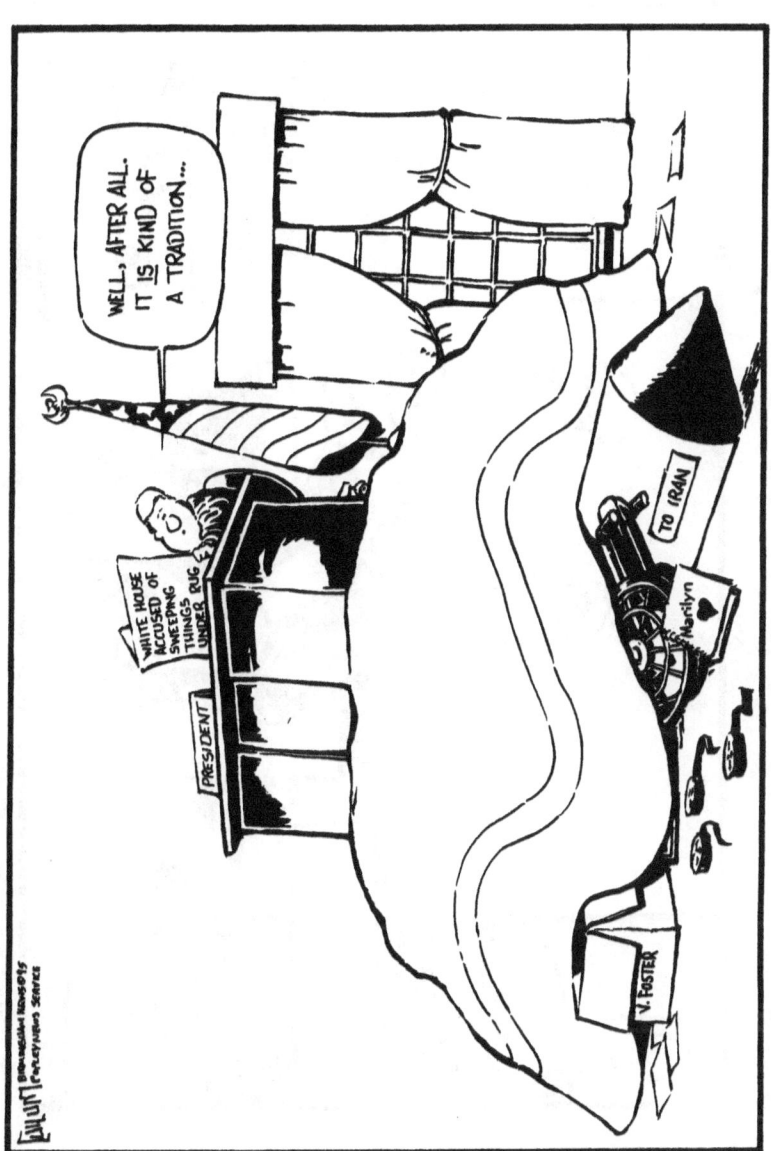

Mark Cullum (1995) *Birmingham (Ala.) News*. Reprinted with permission of Copley News Service.

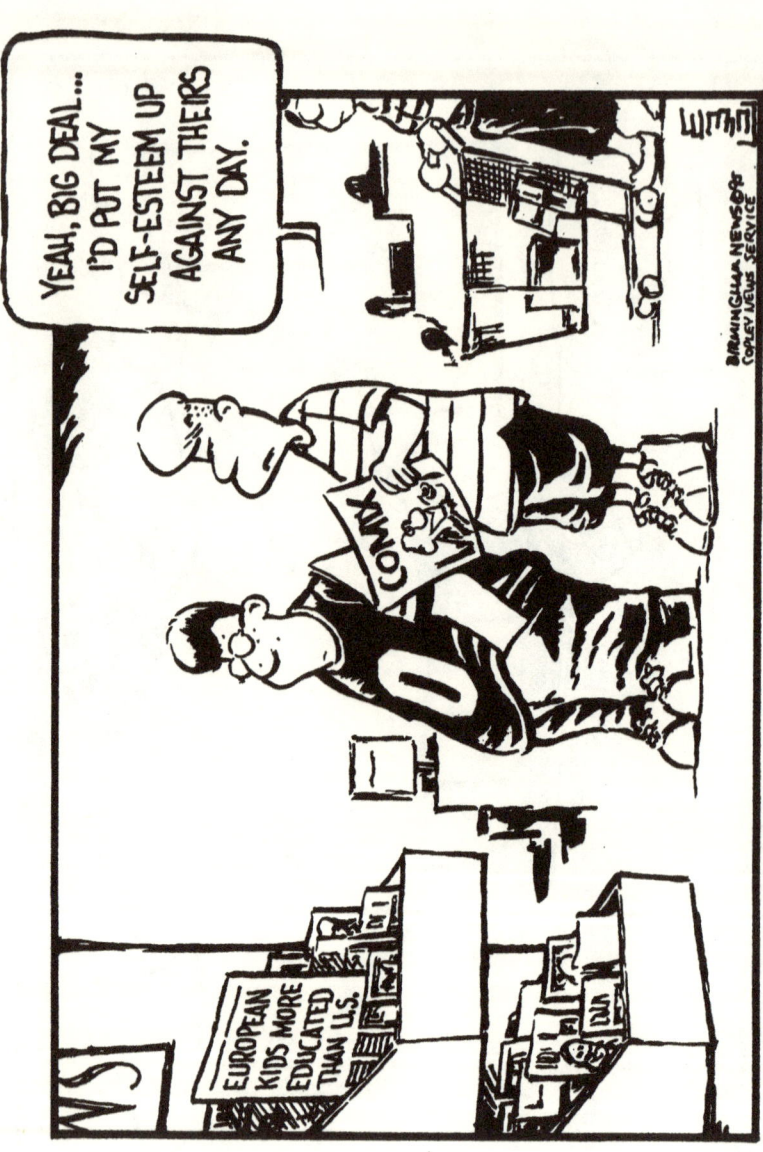

Mark Cullum (1995) *Birmingham (Ala.) News*. Reprinted with permission of Copley News Service.

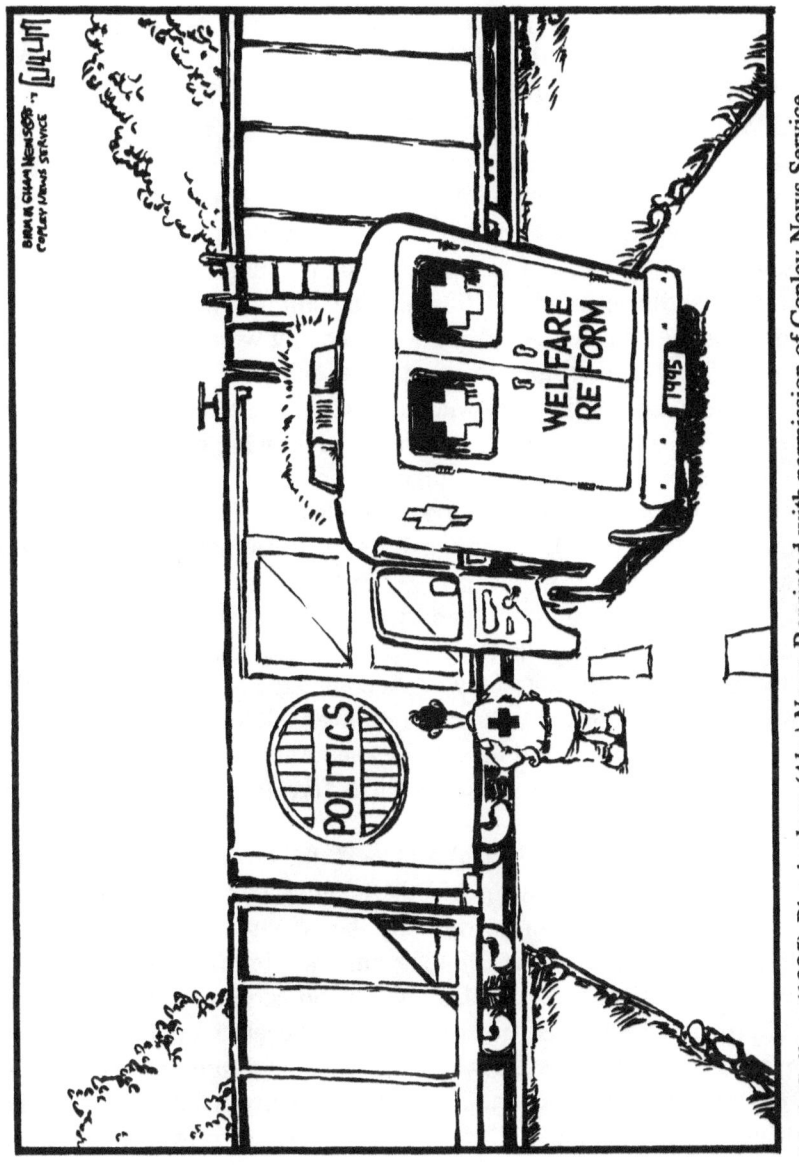

Mark Cullum (1995) *Birmingham (Ala.) News.* Reprinted with permission of Copley News Service.

high school Cullum moved from Tennessee to Texas to attend college. He spent four years at Abilene Christian University earning not only his Bachelor's degree in Mass Communications but also wide recognition for his cartooning talent. Once the young satirist's rage captured an audience, awards began to accrue. He was recognized as one of ten young cartoonists by the Chicago Tribune's Campus Cartoonist Contest in 1983. In 1984 he was awarded first place in the College Media Advisors National Cartoon Strip Competition. That same year he captured first place in the Editorial Cartoonists Southwestern Journalism Congress Awards competition and the Alabama Family Alliance Award. The next year he walked away with top prize in both the regional and national Public Policy Editorial Cartoon Contest. Winning the Sigma Delta Chi Green Eye Shade Award in 1988 placed Cullum squarely in the editorial cartoonist big leagues. Although he has not yet won a Pulitzer, he clearly has the talent and discipline to garner that laurel.

Unlike cartoonist Doug Marlette, who, according to Kalman Goldstein, wears a tie when he sits down at the drawing board to indicate the serious nature of his project, Cullum maintains a casual demeanor. "My habit is to avoid work," he says. "That's why I became a cartoonist" (Cullum, Interview). Although he may not consider what he does "work," he certainly works at it. He follows a disciplined routine. Five days a week he is up early and in his office at the *Birmingham News* before 9 a.m. writing the text for the editorial cartoons which he will later draw. Once his editorial work is completed he turns to his syndicated comic strip, "Walnut Cove." By eleven o'clock he is ready to don headphones. When asked the significance of the hour, he replies, "Rush comes on. I draw and listen to Rush five times a week" (Cullum, Interview).

Lest he be considered a "ditto-head" (the term for blind devotees of the current Rush Limbaugh cult), he is quick to qualify his devotion to Limbaugh. "He sometimes rubs me the wrong way. He will criticize Clinton just because he is Clinton." Insisting on his natural suspiciousness, his independence, and his own "vivid sense of right and wrong," Cullum says he listens to Rush primarily because Limbaugh is funny. Perhaps he appreciates the way Rush Limbaugh presents ridicule neat. Ridicule, according to cartoonist Jeff MacNelly whose work has been influential in shaping Cullum's, is "the basis of effective humor in a political cartoon" (*Gang of Eight* 75).

Other influences, in addition to MacNelly, include the artistry and wit of cartoonists Don Martin and Charles Schultz. Even as a child, Cullum enjoyed writing and drawing. His subject matter is a compilation of his own ideology and religious beliefs, and the synthesis of readings as diverse as the religiophilosophical work of C. S. Lewis and, of course, the daily diatribe of Rush Limbaugh. Although, according to Cullum, the ideas churn constantly, the brush, the ink, and the headset are set aside on the weekends.

Birmingham is a town where Mark Cullum has found not only professional success at the *Birmingham News* but also a lifetime companion. Married on September 9, 1995, he spends most of his time with his wife, Melissa, and—her gift to him—his pet cat, Eliot ("as in T. S." Cullum explains) (Cullum, Interview). He also jogs, runs, plays basketball, and reads. Just as predictably as he can be found every weekday morning sitting at the drawing board while listening to the radio, on every Sunday morning he and Melissa can be found in church. They attend the Church of Christ, the same church Cullum has attended since childhood. He not only is committed to his church, but he also reads and quotes the Bible. Mark Cullum takes his religion seriously.

"I guess you could say I take a traditional approach to social values," Cullum explains. In a typical Sunday editorial, he attacks what he calls "the silly emphasis on stopping school prayer" (Cullum, Interview). In the cartoon there is a schoolroom. Facing the corner a bulky schoolboy sits on the dunce stool. He wears a vest with a skull and crossbones on its back. On the floor, next to the globe another chubby schoolboy is stretched out, a dagger protruding from his back. Standing over the body, arms on her hips, a heavy-bosomed schoolteacher wearing the label ACLU turns to chide the corner-keeper. Her mouth wide open, she says, "OUGHT TO BE ASHAMED OF YOURSELF! DON'T YOU REALIZE THAT TYPE OF BEHAVIOR CAN LEAD TO SCHOOL PRAYER?" For Cullum, the American Civil Liberties Union, in focusing on prayer as more significant a threat to school children than crime, is morally irresponsible. To be opposed to school prayer in the classroom is, in Cullum's cartoon world, to be fat, female, and over forty. His schema is logically fallacious, but that is the point: he does not have to be fair. He can create a false dilemma, an "America: Love it or leave it" universe in which the only alternative to violence is prayer, and he can make his point over the dead body of a schoolboy.

Not only the American classroom but local educational reform is a continuing theme in Cullum's work. In Alabama, before the recent gubernatorial election, there was a strong push to reform education. The previous democratic governor's big, new educational bureaucracy failed. The incumbent Republican governor, Fob James, is now concentrating on a return to traditional values in the schools. Cullum illustrates this aspect of James's policy with a cartoon once again located in the classroom, this time an Alabama classroom.

The door to Room 404 is ajar. A puzzled student, clutching a pillow, stands staring at the new teacher who is surrounded by a nimbus of white light. The teacher, identified as James by the ribbon across his chest, is dressed in the uniform of a highly decorated military hero. He stands at attention in front of the blackboard, holding a riding crop in his hands. On the board is written the name of the class: EDUCATION REFORM. The student, sensing he is in the wrong place, says, "OH . . . SORRY, DUDE. I THOUGHT THIS WAS THE ROOM FOR REMEDIAL SELF-ESTEEM."

The student is an example of what Cullum calls the "touchy-feely" school of education. What James is doing, in cracking the whip on educational reform, is returning the power to the state, the place where Cullum, an ardent advocate of states' rights, believes it should rest. The cartoon is praise for James's leaner and meaner educational policies. It is not that Cullum does not believe in experimenting and seeing what works, but he finds it ludicrous that officials in Washington, D.C., are managing the schools in Alabama, or any other state for that matter. While Cullum's opinions on education and social values are consistently Republican, he prefers to think he does not "blindly defend Republicans." "Sure," he says, "you're always looking for ways to defend the guy you like" (Cullum, Interview). Instead, he believes in concerning himself with issues. His opinions are certain to rub some the wrong way.

Tom Brokaw points out that "sooner or later cartoonists offend just about everyone" (*Gang of Eight* v.) As offensive as he can be, however, Cullum has few revisions he would make in his political cartoons. He does acknowledge that if he had it to do over again, there are a few he would not publish. An example of what Cullum has in mind is what he admits as too hasty a leap to make humor out of a national tragedy.

In 1986, the day the Challenger disaster occurred, Cullum memorialized the event with a sensitive rendering that met the public's need for national mourning. A week later, though, he moved into what he calls his "fun mode." He probed the political fallout that the disaster precipitated. In retrospect, he thinks he would either not have acted so quickly after the event, or perhaps not submitted the cartoon at all.

Whether or not Mark Cullum is a natural born cynic or a born again one is uncertain. He says that once he recognized the mentality of public officials and the sleaziness of politics he became naturally suspicious. When asked whether or not editorial cartoonists aren't just as much to blame for undermining authority as the rest of us, Cullum replies, "One part of me says, 'I hope so,' while the other part wrestles with the notion that somewhere in the Bible it says that mockers are not necessarily good" (Cullum, Interview). As young as he is, Mark Cullum has developed the skills and instincts of the great editorial cartoonists. His dilemma, a personal struggle between his conscience and his sense of the absurd, results in three hundred statements a year, some of them pretty nasty.

In early autumn, 1996, Cullum received a Rotary International Fellowship to the University of Bristol, England, to read Classical Literature. He was succeeded at *The Birmingham News* by Scott Stantis.

Sources

Brokow, Tom. Introduction. *The Gang of Eight.* By Tony Auth. Boston: Faber, 1985. v-vi.

Cullum, Mark. Interview. By Robin Weitzen. 16 Nov. 1994.

MacNelly, Jeff. "Jeff MacNelly." *The Gang of Eight.* By Tony Auth. Boston: Faber and Faber, 1985. 74-96.

6

Brian Duffy, *Des Moines Register*

Roy E. Blackwood

It's not difficult to believe Brian Duffy when he says that he rides a bike 6,000 to 7,000 miles a year, or that he enters four or five races in Minnesota, Iowa, and Wisconsin each year. He's tall and fit looking, and gives the impression that he could take the physical punishment of bike racing. He says he likes biking, but that he's not "crazy" about it. He holds up for comparison a friend who each year enters a transcontinental race, in which the riders traverse the United State both ways. "Now that's crazy," Duffy says. What Duffy *is* crazy about is cartooning—and has been for as long as he can remember.

Brian Thomas Duffy was born on May 9, 1955, in Chicago. He says he remembers drawing a lot in kindergarten, but doesn't everybody? On the other hand, not everybody spends as much time as he did in first grade copying "Pogo" and "Li'l Abner" cartoons. By the time he was in junior high school in New York and Connecticut, where his father had taken a sales manager job with J. C. Penney, Duffy had succumbed to the influence of *Mad* magazine—a seemingly obligatory step for future cartoonists. By the time he graduated from a Milwaukee high school in 1973, he was an average student, but a better-than-average artist.

In addition to "drawing more on papers than writing notes," Duffy contributed cartoons on school issues to *West Winds*, the monthly newspaper of his high school. He says that although his parents, Thomas and Rene, as retail salespeople, weren't exactly inspirations for his art career, "They encouraged me to do what I wanted to. They knew I had a talent for art, and encouraged me to follow it." His older sister Joanne, he says, was properly "noncommittal," as befits siblings (Duffy, Interview).

Duffy says that when he first called Bill Sanders, editorial cartoonist for the *Milwaukee Journal*, to tell him he wanted to be a cartoonist, Sanders wasn't much more supportive than his sister. Sanders agreed to look at a few of Duffy's cartoons. The "few" became a flow. "I brought some more cartoons back to him after a couple of months," says Duffy. "He tried to discourage me, but I persisted." They began to meet regularly in a sort of informal apprenticeship that Duffy says is "the best way

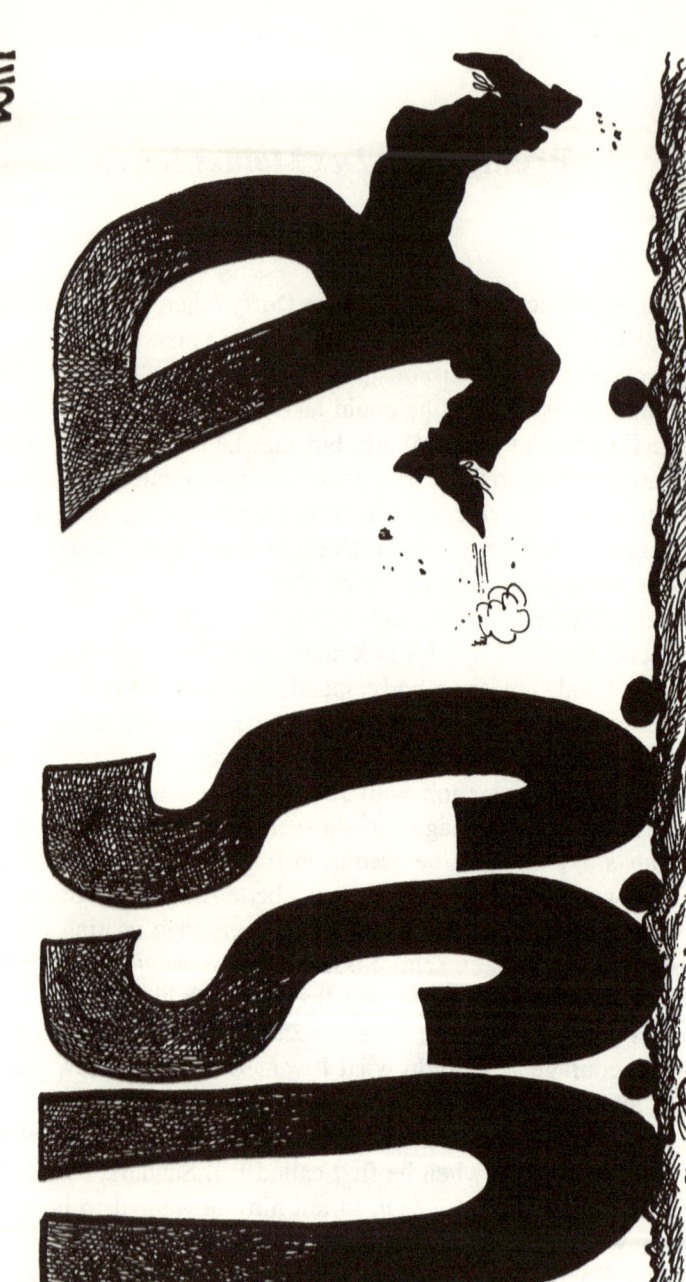

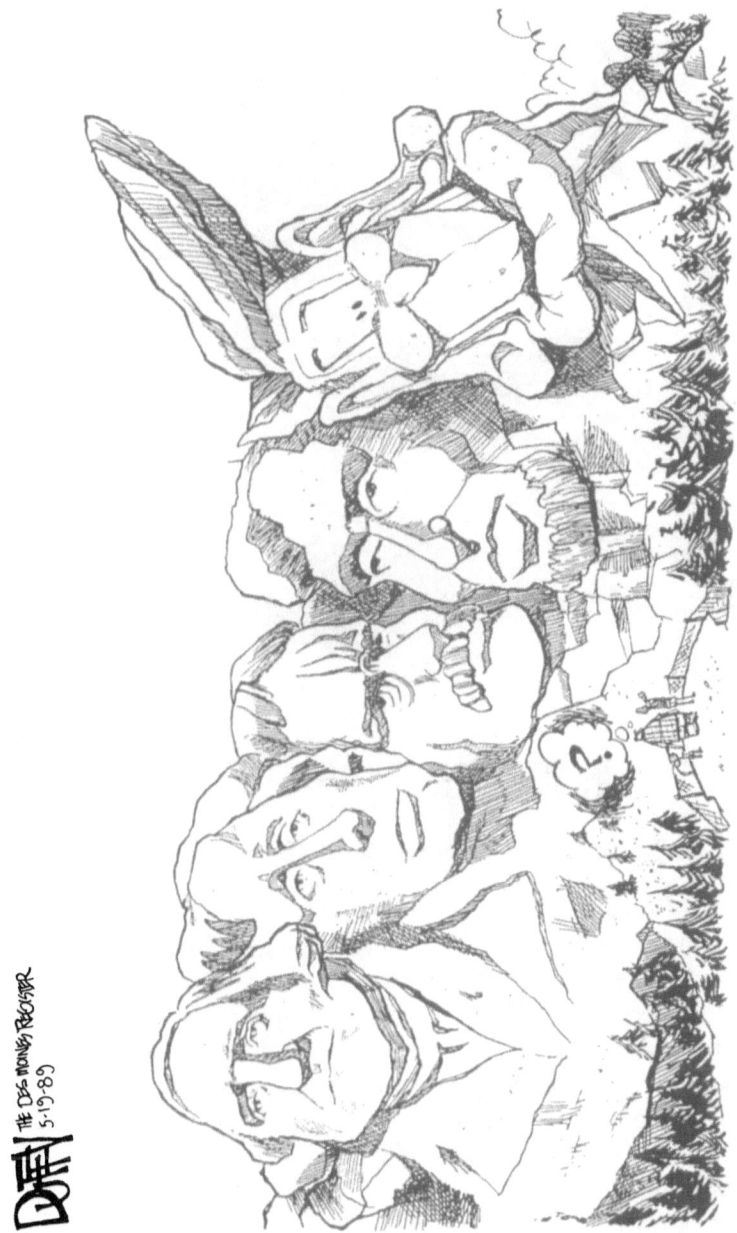

Brian Duffy (1989) *Des Moines Register.*

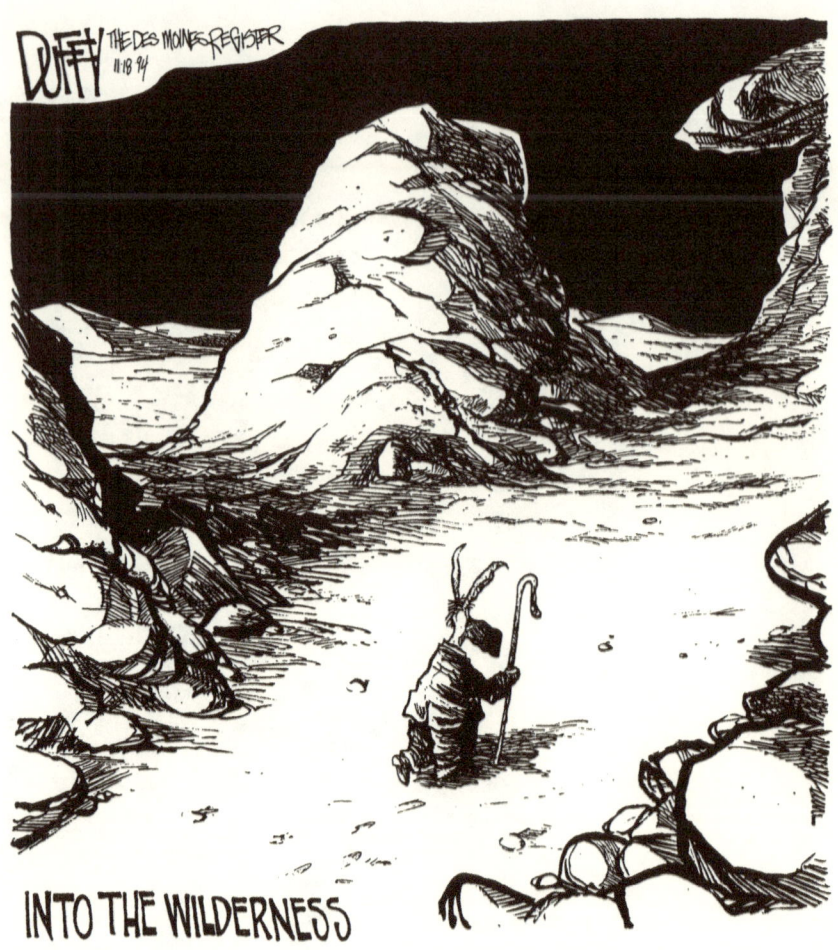

INTO THE WILDERNESS

Brian Duffy (1994) *Des Moines Register*.

to learn the profession." Duffy puts a lot of stock in persistence for advancing in a career with so few openings: "I get a lot of calls from young people now" (Duffy, Interview).

Sanders provided Duffy with the proper tools, and taught him how to effectively express his ideas. "He taught me that you have two or three seconds to get the idea across before you start to bore the reader" (Duffy, Interview). According to Duffy, his style has developed from so many sources that he finds it difficult to pinpoint one as more influential than the others. He does see Sanders as the biggest early influence on his work, however, and admits that "when you're talking about influence, early usually means ever." He is of the strong opinion that cartoonists should work with a person whom they admire, not just copy that person's work. "One of the things that has hurt cartooning is the number

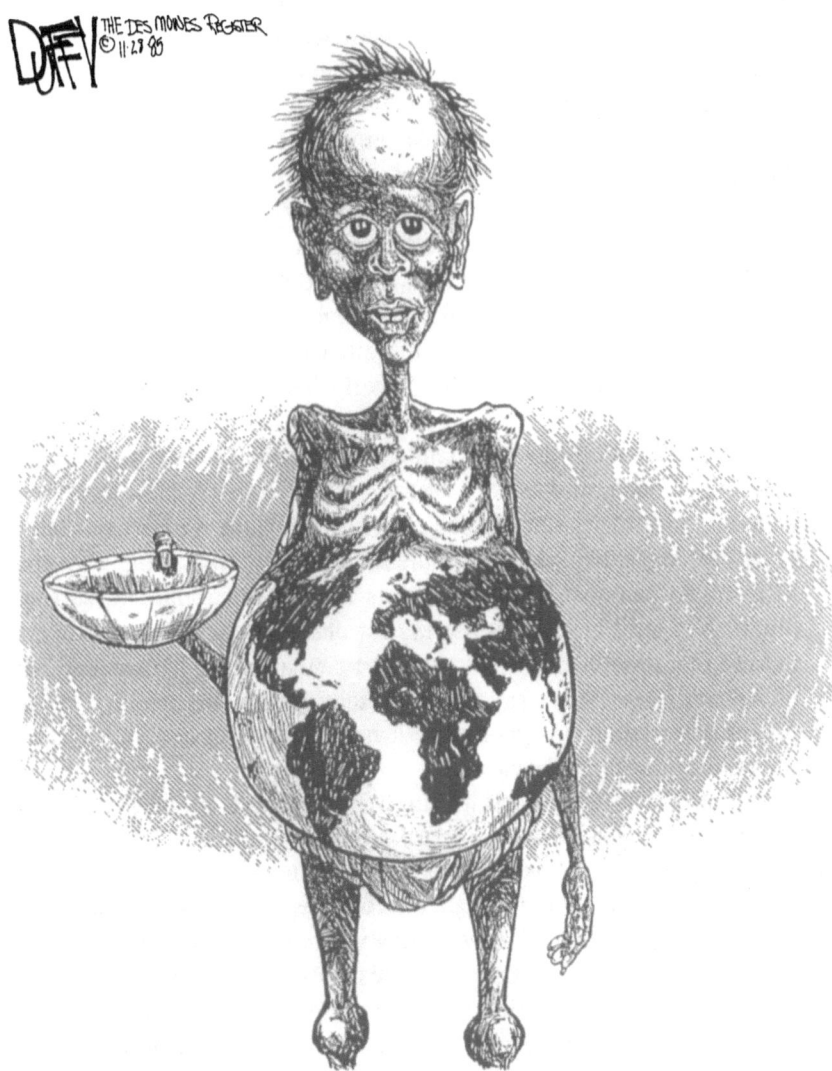

Brian Duffy (1985) *Des Moines Register.* All rights reserved.

of people who have imitated somebody's style and have never grown past that" (Duffy, Interview).

Worse than similarity of style, according to Duffy, is dependence on cheap humor. "Cartooning has gotten too gag-oriented," he says. "The drawing is just the dessert; the main course is your position. You may get a laugh out of a gag cartoon, but what does it say? People have to be able to get your position." He also sees a problem with some of the new styles that rely on funny-looking caricatures. "They work real well when you want to be funny, but when you want to draw on something like

Bosnia, it just doesn't work." On the other hand, he doesn't think overly harsh caricatures work, either. "Sometimes the image is so hard, maybe so offensive, that people don't get past the image. Then they get stuck on the image at the expense of the message" (Duffy, Interview). He's not advocating pulling punches, just tempering the vehicle so it doesn't detract from the point the cartoonist wants to make.

Duffy's June 1987 portrayal of Oliver North is evidence that he means what he says about not pulling punches. He has North in the classic Patton pose: helmeted, bemedaled, in riding boots and britches; saluting, in front of a wall-sized American flag; but with dollar bills sprouting from every opening in his uniform, rather like the straw from the scarecrow in *The Wizard of Oz*. Not "overly harsh," perhaps, but certainly pointed.

His apprenticeship with Sanders continued as Duffy took sociology, political science, and history courses while drawing cartoons on state, national, and international issues, first for the daily *Cardinal* at the University of Wisconsin, Madison, then the weekly *Post* at the University's Milwaukee campus. While there, his ratio of academics to cartooning diminished until he was registering for classes only to stay on the paper. During that time, he also took some art courses at the Milwaukee School of Art and Design. He says, though, that those courses didn't do much for his cartooning: "Anybody can learn to draw, not everybody can be a cartoonist" (Duffy, Interview).

Not that he was yet, if making a living at it is a criterion. He began free-lance work in 1976, while still drawing for the *Post*, but wasn't able to give up his day job at the J. C. Penney catalog store warehouse. As he persisted, however, his free-lance efforts began to pay off. Sanders provided him with a list of newspapers with more than 60,000 circulation that had no cartoonist, and he sent résumés to all of them. By 1981 the *Waukesha Freeman*, which was owned by the same group as the *Des Moines Register*, was using a cartoon or two a week on their editorial pages. *Milwaukee* magazine began using some of his work, and by 1982 he was supplying them a monthly cartoon, as well as illustrations for some of their feature stories. When Frank Miller, the *Register*'s cartoonist, died in 1983, some of the *Freeman* editors who had worked at both papers suggested Duffy submit some cartoons to the *Register*.

"I knew everybody else who wanted the job would be sending what the *Register* had been carrying," Duffy says; "I knew I had to look different, so I sent a group of cartoons I had drawn based on what I'd read in the news and editorial pages of the paper" (Duffy, Interview). Told that publisher Jim Gannon was "considering," Duffy got an opportunity to go to Des Moines and show them some more of his "tailor-made" cartoons. Duffy credits the fact that he had provided cartoons drawn especially for use in the *Register* with his getting the position. That it was his first full-time cartooning job was impressive, especially since the paper is the only daily in the country that carries its editorial cartoons on the front page and had attracted more than 100 applications. The *Register,* according to Duffy, is a traditional statewide paper, and people throughout Iowa have traditional expectations of it. Miller had been only the paper's second cartoonist, and "If I'd known how much the people had taken the previous cartoonists to heart I may have thought twice about applying for the job" (Duffy, Interview).

When he began his career in Des Moines, Duffy says, the editor of the paper thought it would be a good idea to introduce him to Iowans at the State Fair. "So I set up my drawing board amidst the horses, hogs, and the corn dogs. Feeling very much like one of the animals being judged, I sat there as a line of people came by and informed me that I had big shoes to fill" (Duffy, *Decade* ix). His editor at the time, Geneva Overholser, remembered that "when Brian Duffy took the job he stood in the shadow of two giants of cartooning—Ding Darling and Frank Miller. Now, ten years later, Duffy has made the *Register* cartoon very much his own. [Iowans] know to expect every Sunday the snapshots of state life that he renders with special warmth, poking fun at all of us (often in the guise of his own family) as we make our way through the seasons, through the holidays, through economic ups and downs, through harvest and planting season and harvest again . . ." (Duffy, *A Decade* vii-viii).

For Duffy, the cartooning process generally begins when he arrives at his office between 6:00 and 7:00 a.m. to read the morning papers. He spends about an hour on the *Register,* then usually moves on to the *New York Times,* the *Chicago Tribune,* the *Wall Street Journal,* and *USA Today.* He says that by the time he finishes the *Register,* often even after only the front page, he probably has at least one idea, "in the form of a smoke cloud." "I read the other papers to see if I find words or phrases that hadn't caught my eye in [my] paper." He gets his ideas often from the details of a story, "maybe some ridiculous quote." Two important elements must be present for an idea to become a Duffy cartoon. "The number one thing," he says, "is to find something people have already read about. They must have the background." According to Duffy, for a cartoon to work the topic must be at the right place in people's minds. "Cartooning is like driving a little car under a semi—too far up, you get squished by the front wheels; too far back, you get squished by the back wheels." Second, it has to be an idea he can express with very few words. Both these criteria arise from his belief, inherited from Sanders, that readers must understand quickly; if they have to spend a lot of time reading, or trying to figure out the context, the cartoon won't work (Duffy, Interview).

Duffy is syndicated with King Features, and says he tries to get at least a couple of cartoons a week to them. Syndicates are not interested in local issues, and to be useful to them, cartoons must have a long "shelf life"—they must still be of interest to readers by the time they are distributed and printed in subscribing papers. Duffy claims, however, that what the syndicate needs is only one of many criteria he keeps in mind while working. He says he naturally draws on a broad mix of local, state, national, and international topics because of his wide-ranging interests. He insists that "it's important to give every topic an equal chance of coverage in cartooning. A cartoonist is a person who is interested in everything" (Duffy, Interview).

He says the drawing is the easy part. First he has to "push the cloud to see what develops out of it." He tries to visualize the idea, and may go immediately to rough sketches—"sometimes one, sometimes eight or ten" (Duffy, Interview). He may wander around talking with people, working the idea about in his mind, trying to push pieces together. He tries to force himself to consider alternative presentations of the idea, making sure the one he has selected will be the fastest to read and comprehend. In the interest of having readers grasp the point of his cartoons quickly, he almost always draws only one panel. He says some cartoonists do well with multiple-panel cartoons, but only if each panel makes its own quick point. Just as frequently, he says, the words and images in a multi-panel cartoon may clash, to the detriment of both, and cause readers to lose track of the message.

After "pushing the cloud" for anywhere from ten minutes to six hours, Duffy spends a couple of hours drawing. "Most of the time I get really excited about drawing the cartoon that day. At the time, the cartoon is of ultimate importance, but the next day it's gone. After I've finished it, I sort of put it out of my mind" (Duffy, Interview).

Reader response usually averages a couple of letters and calls a week. These are more likely to contain complaints rather than compliments; when people like a cartoon, Duffy says, they tell a friend, but when they don't they tell the cartoonist. Duffy insists he is neither Republican nor Democrat; neither liberal nor conservative. "I'm iconoclastic, and look at each issue on the merits of that issue," so may offend all sides equally (Duffy, Interview).

Representative Duffy cartoons are quickly grasped and incorporate very few words. For example, following the huge Republican victory in the national elections of 1994, he drew a little donkey wandering off through a rock-strewn, barren landscape off toward darkness. He titled this "Into the Wilderness." Duffy, who considers himself a craftsman, notes that he particularly liked the way his rocks turned out.

Others seem to like the way much of his work turns out. In both 1985 and 1986, he won the cartooning section of the World Hunger Media Awards for coverage of sustainable agriculture and world hunger issues. In keeping with his "quick read" style, one of those award winners pictured a small emaciated child, empty bowl held forward in supplication, a map of the world imprinted on its distended stomach. Also in 1986, Duffy was a finalist for the Fischetti Award, a national honor for general excellence in cartooning. He has also won "several seconds and thirds," as he puts it, in the annual Best of Gannett Awards. His lack of specificity here results from the fact that he does not get very excited about awards. "I have no favorite cartoons. We have somebody else who picks them and sends them out. I like to just do my cartoons, and if somebody likes them, that's great."

Somebody must. Duffy says three or four of his cartoons have appeared annually in the past eight issues of *Best Editorial Cartoons of the Year,* a national collection published by Pelican Press. Also, his second published collection of individual cartoons, *More of Duffy,* includes some cartoons from the 1994 elections, as well as some omitted from his first, which "somebody" liked well enough to have reprinted.

Sources

Duffy, Brian. *A Decade of Duffys*. Ames: Iowa State UP, 1994.
——. Interview. By Roy Blackwood. 21 Nov. 1994.

7

Linda Godfrey, *The Week*

Diana Beeson

Linda Roberts Godfrey, the 1959 president of Milton Junction, Wisconsin's Three Stooges Fan Club, can still do a dead-on imitation of Curly's trademark, "Nyuk, nyuk, nyuk," but the intervening decades have honed her humor from appreciation of slapstick to the writing and drawing of pointed political and social satire. Her editorial cartoons have appeared periodically in the *Janesville (Wis.) Gazette* and *The Walworth County (Wis.) Week* since 1990. Godfrey's work was selected for three consecutive editions of *Best Editorial Cartoons* (Brooks, 1991, 1992, 1993).

Godfrey, a life-long resident of Wisconsin, was born in Madison on March 20, 1951, grew up some 30 miles away in Milton Junction and now lives in Elkhorn. Except for a summer when she studied drawing in Spain and Italy, her college education was a virtual tour of the Wisconsin State University system. She attended its branches at Whitewater and Platteville, and finished her bachelor's degree in art education in 1976 at Oshkosh.

In college Godfrey's focus was fine arts. Her drawings and fiber art pieces were accepted at juried art shows throughout Wisconsin even before she graduated. Her desire to work as an artist was tempered by her need for a regular paycheck, so she opted for a teaching certificate along with her degree in fine arts. This is emblematic of two of her dimensions that seem to be at odds with one another. On one hand, she is wildly creative and leans toward the whimsical; on the other, she is practical and firmly grounded in the Midwestern work ethic and conservative political points of view.

Godfrey describes herself as a Republican and tends to align philosophically with political stances taken by Wayne Stayskal and Mike Ramirez in their editorial cartoons. But she is by no means doctrinaire. She agrees with Northrop Frye that for a society to exist there must be a delegation of prestige and influence accorded to organized groups: the church, the army, the medical and teaching professions and the government. All consist of individuals given more than individual power by the

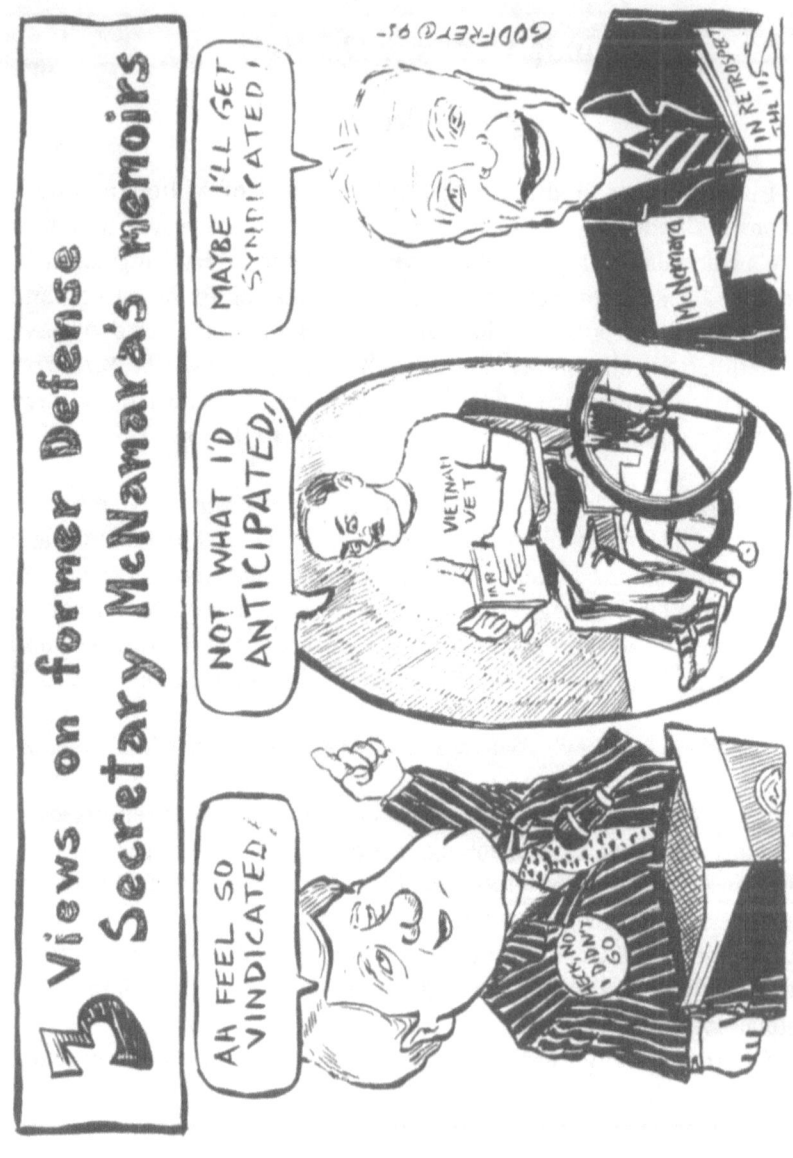

Linda Godfrey (1995) All rights reserved.

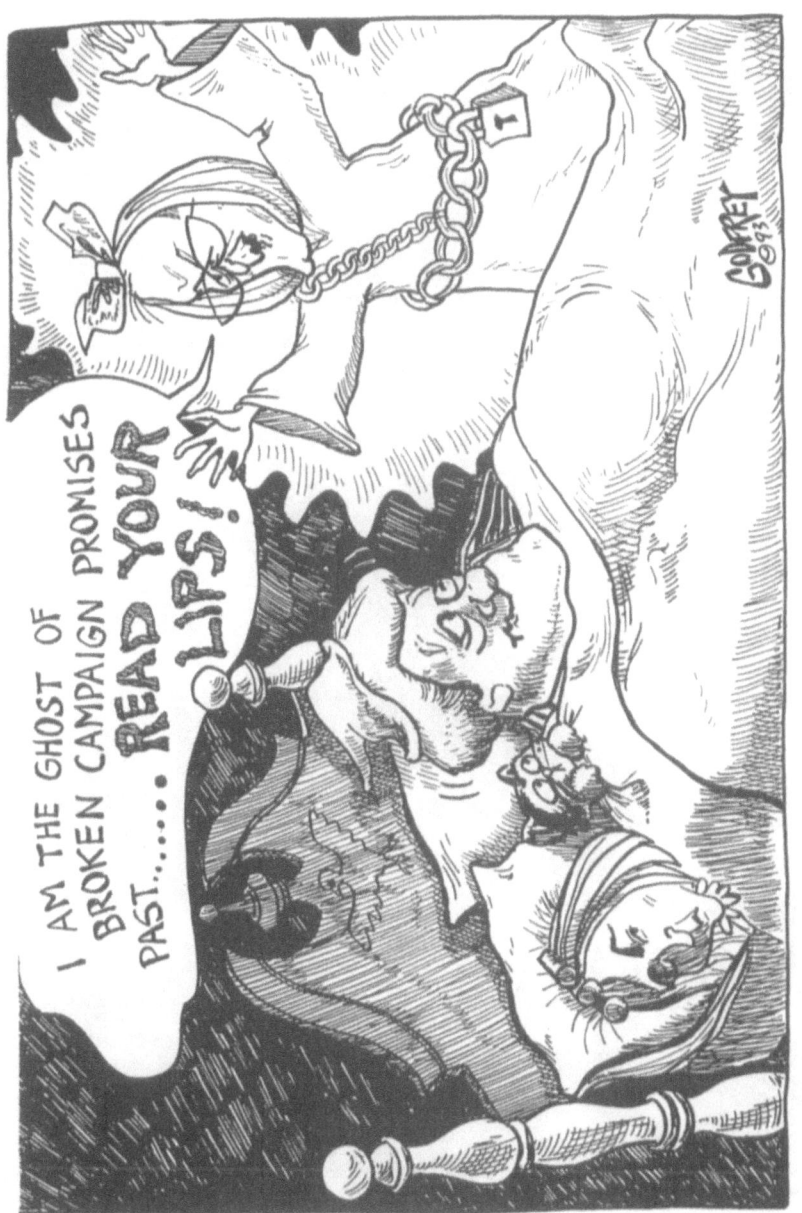

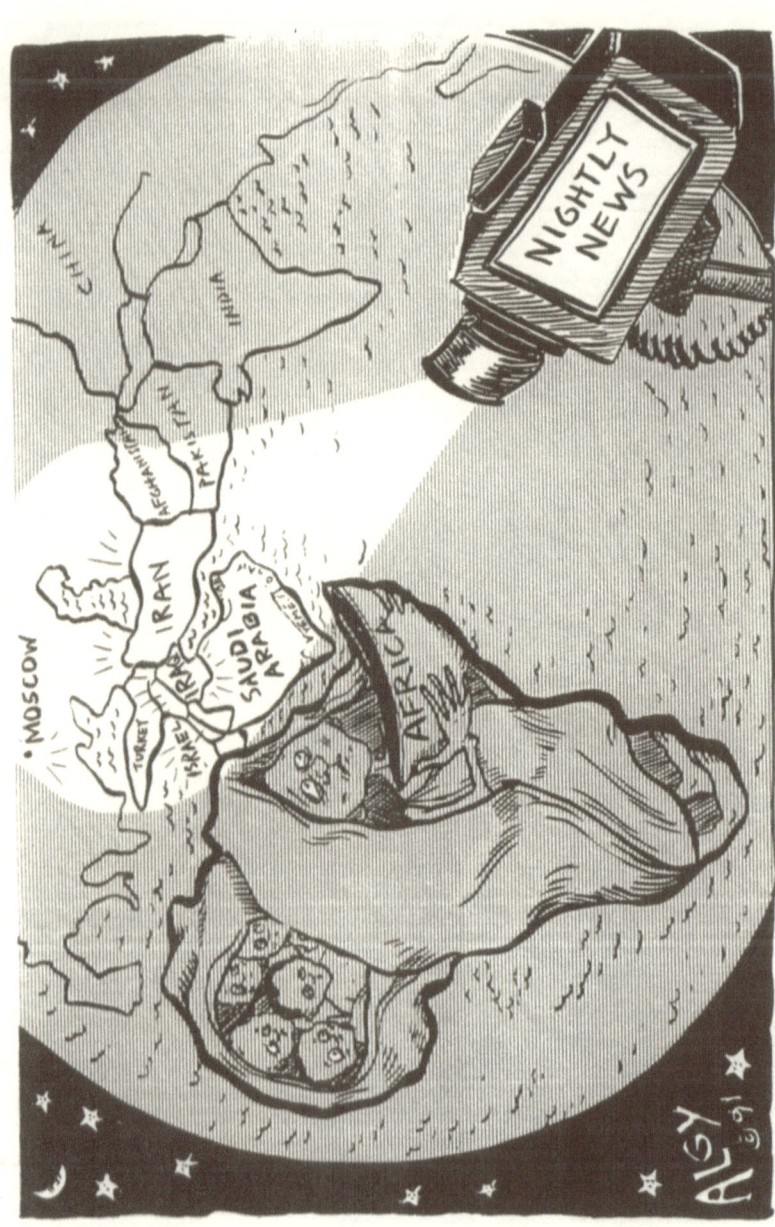

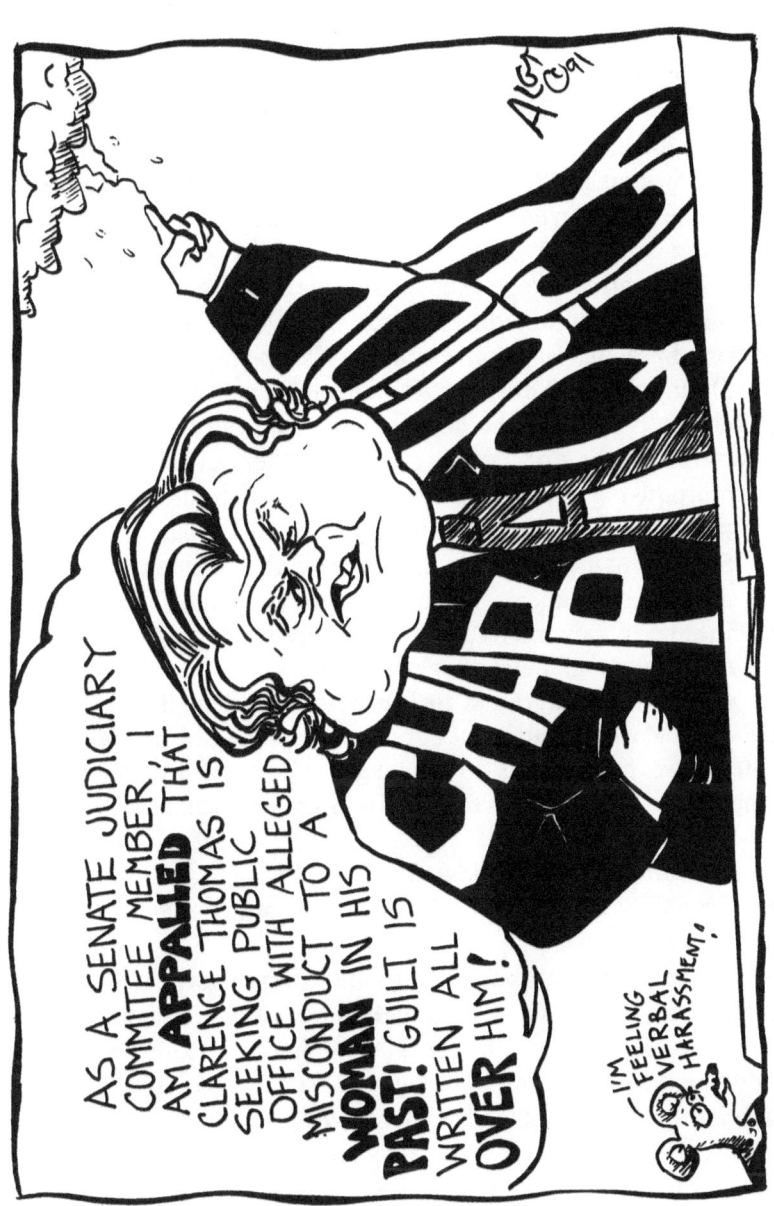

institution to which they belong. "Whether they are given this power for good or evil depends largely on them. If a satirist presents a clergyman, for instance, as a fool or a hypocrite, he is primarily attacking neither the man nor his church. The former is too petty and the latter carries him outside the range of satire. He is attacking an evil man protected by the prestige of an institution. As such, he represents one of the stumbling blocks in society which is the satirist's business to clear out" (Allen and Stephens 20).

Her work is not designed to skewer liberals or liberal points of view. Rather, she targets hypocrisy, irony and institutional foibles. For example, one of her works points out the hypocrisy of Senator Edward Kennedy's moral indignation over sexual harassment charges against Clarence Thomas during confirmation hearings in 1991, in view of the Senator's checkered past and involvement in the Chappaquiddick scandal.

During the 1992 presidential campaign, she was struck by the irony of both George Bush, who had been labeled a wimp, and Bill Clinton, known for waffling on issues, comparing themselves to the eminently uncompromising Harry Truman. Each candidate drawn in miniature, stands in an enormous pair of wing-tips labeled Truman's shoes.

She nips at the superficialities of network television news in a panel that shows their tendency to focus on international flash points while ignoring the world's more complex and far-reaching problems, such as hunger, poverty and imbalances of power.

Godfrey's background in fine arts is evident in her cartooning, although she is quick to point out that cartoonists are largely self-taught. Nonetheless, her years as an art student are revealed in her attention to composition. Her cartoons rarely have a single visual focus; she tends to draw highly detailed panels, characterized by balanced elements of form and space or light and shadow. She judges herself and other cartoonists by their ability to execute not only a concept and message, but by the quality of their artwork.

Growing up in a small town as the oldest of seven children, her life revolved around family, school and church. Materially, the family was comfortable, but as Godfrey says, "With that many kids, we didn't have a lot of extras" (Godfrey, Interview). One extra the family had was an abundant supply of large format drawing paper. Her father, Roland Roberts, worked for a glass company and designed storefronts. The plate glass her father delivered to construction sites was protected from breakage by yards of blank newsprint. He brought the paper home in bundles for his children's after school art projects. Godfrey describes her mother, Elaine, as "a frustrated artist." One of her earliest memories is of standing at the kitchen table, watching her mother draw Rosie the Riveterstyle cartoon figures of women, and trying to imitate the caricatures in her own hand.

Always small for her age and not good at athletics, Godfrey spent her childhood drawing and reading. In grade school, she earned the nickname "Brain." She remembers being bored in class and spending time doodling and drawing caricatures of her teachers. While most teachers were unappreciative, at least one allowed Godfrey to paint murals on the classroom's window shades. Other teachers encouraged her by letting her illustrate class newspapers. She drew her first comic strip in fifth grade for mimeographed distribution to her classmates, and first considered cartooning as a possible future career.

In high school and college, Godfrey tried to become a more serious artist. In 1975, she placed third in a juried competition at the Wisconsin Women in Arts Spring Show and she won a Best of Show at the University of Wisconsin Priebe Gallery in Oshkosh. Her work has been displayed in at least six galleries throughout Wisconsin. "I was always really, really drawn to humor, though," Godfrey said. "Even when I was preparing drawings for galleries, I think you can see a kind of humor in them. I was doing kind of surrealistic drawings of real things that were juxtaposed in humorous ways" (Godfrey, Interview).

The incongruity that adds humor to Godfrey's gallery pieces also characterizes her career path toward cartooning. Over the years she has worked as an elementary and high school art teacher and an inventory control clerk for a firm that customized vans. She wrote a successful grant proposal that initiated a statewide juried college art show and she was an Amway distributor. She served for nine years on the board of directors of the Walworth County Arts Council, developing children's art workshops, giving demonstrations and lecturing, and tried to be home every afternoon when her two sons, Benjamin and Nathan, returned from school. Godfrey juggled multiple careers and art projects to help put food on the table without interfering with the time she wanted to spend with her children, especially when they were younger. She never lost sight of her goal to become a cartoonist, but as a wife and mother, priorities in her life, she could not pursue her goal with the same single-mindedness as do many men in the field.

The chance discovery that she lived only a few miles from a successful, nationally syndicated cartoonist and the fact that her children were in school and required less of her time combined to help Godfrey focus more fully on a cartooning career. While browsing through a copy of *Artists' Market*, she noticed that Joe Martin, author of "Mr. Boffo" and two other nationally syndicated comic strips, was from neighboring Fontana, Wisconsin. Godfrey had been developing an idea for a comic strip and thought he might offer her some advice before she submitted her drawings to syndicates.

When she located Martin, Godfrey was president of the Walworth County Arts Council. She approached him in that capacity and asked him to speak at an arts council function. Afterwards, she asked for advice. Martin told her he couldn't offer any substantive advice after seeing only a few samples, but if she provided him with six weeks worth of cartoons, 42 comic strips, he might be able to help her. A few weeks later, Godfrey returned with her portfolio case and 42 strips of a series about a farm family called "Fly Corners."

"Joe was shocked. He was really surprised," Godfrey said. "He told me lots of people had asked him to look at their cartoons and he always told them the same thing he had told me. I was the only person who ever went back and did the work" (Godfrey, Interview).

Martin became Godfrey's mentor, offering advice that might make her strips more appealing to syndicates. She submitted "Fly Corners" to several syndicates and shortly thereafter received her first rejection letters. Most included encouraging words, but none offered her a contract. Her second attempt was a panel called "Pretty Real Home Town News," based on actual news items she culled from small town newspapers, such as stories on chicken parts festivals and make-it-with-lard cooking contests. She submitted it and received her second round of rejection letters, again with words of encouragement but no commitments. Her third attempt brought her both her greatest encouragement and her most devastating rejection.

Her previous submissions were done in a drawing style she describes as loose but detailed. "It was really a lot of work to draw them, so I decided to go with something really graphic, black and white, almost art deco-looking, just to be different." The result was "Razzberries," a distinctively drawn panel featuring commentary on national and international events. For example, in 1989 when Raisa Gorbachev visited Beverly Hills, looking distinctly un-Soviet while shopping on Rodeo Drive, Godfrey drew a send up of a popular television commercial, labeling the sable attired, rounded woman and her entourage as the "California Raisas." Godfrey said writing "Razzberries" was more difficult than drawing it (Godfrey, Interview). She submitted samples to King Features. Some time later, she received a personal letter from Jay Kennedy, the syndicate's comics editor. Kennedy's letter spoke highly of the artwork and concept and suggested the cartoon be reformatted as a strip instead of a panel since strips were easier to market to newspapers. He even included a sketch, showing Godfrey how she could change it from a vertical to a horizontal format.

She called Joe Martin for advice. Martin was thrilled and told her the letter indicated that King Features was close to signing her. "He told me it was a test. They wanted to see if I could produce. He told me that no matter what I had planned, even if my kids were graduating from high school that weekend or if my grandmother died, I had to stay home and redraw the entire strip and get it in the mail Monday morning." For two-and-a-half days, living on sandwiches, coffee and very little sleep, Godfrey stayed in her studio, redrawing, reinking and pasting up the 42 strips. She met her deadline and sent them back by express mail. She waited for a response. Nothing came. Weeks went by without a word from Kennedy or King Features. Finally, she wrote to Kennedy. Still, she heard nothing. "I was so dejected," Godfrey said, "but I decided I had to get published somewhere, somehow" (Godfrey, Interview).

Godfrey submitted some editorial cartoons to the *Milwaukee (Wis.) Journal.* "They'd say they were going to print them and then they wouldn't. It was just killing me to put forth all this effort and never get anything published." Finally, she called Herb Moering, former editor of the *Walworth County Week* which then was a supplement to the *Janesville Gazette,* and offered to do editorial cartoons for free. He took her up on her offer, but reneged on his agreement not to pay her. "I might have done one or two cartoons for free," Godfrey said, "but very early on, Herb started paying me. I think he paid me eight bucks a cartoon at first" (Godfrey, Interview).

Her stint as an $8-a-week editorial cartoonist was short-lived. Moering hired Godfrey full time in 1990 and her workload expanded to include a weekly editorial cartoon, a comic strip called "This Week's Special," a column, one or two feature stories per week, and spot art for the newspaper's calendar of events. After joining *The Week,* some of her editorial cartoons received wider exposure. One was reprinted in a college textbook, *U.S. Government: Fundamentals and Alternative Viewpoints* (Holmes et al.). Another became part of a traveling exhibit entitled "America's Cartoonists Celebrate the First," and is now in the permanent collection at the Cartoon, Graphic, and Photographic Arts Research Library at the Ohio State University in Columbus.

Godfrey's work also is archived at the University of Wisconsin at Oshkosh, more by accident than by design. One evening in 1976, Godfrey noticed three men drawing cartoons on large pieces of paper in the student union. She joined the student audience until one of them drew an indelicate image of a young woman and labeled her "Little Annie Fannie." Discomfited, she asked for a marker, and drew "Annie's" male counterpart, a scantily clad caricature of a macho sheriff with a large star pinned to his bare chest, blood spurting from behind his badge.

She labeled him "Big Tannie Mannie." The cartoon amused and delighted the crowd. At this point, Godfrey found out that she had just satirized the work of Denis Kitchen, an underground cartoonist; R. Crumb, the creator of *Zap Comix;* and Harvey Kurtzman, whose "Little Annie Fannie" appeared regularly in *Playboy* magazine. The three cartoonists had been invited to lecture at the university and create a work for the university's archives. Godfrey's work inadvertently became part of it. In addition, she had won a small victory for her gender by showing that cartoon art was an equal opportunity petard.

Cartooning may offer equal opportunities to the artist for targets to satire, but the profession hardly provides equal opportunity employment. In 1990 Godfrey was accepted for membership in the Association of American Editorial Cartoonists (AAEC). The following year she attended the AAEC national convention in Memphis, Tennessee. Godfrey, Etta Hulme of the *Fort Worth Star-Telegraph,* and Signe Wilkinson of the *Philadelphia Daily News* were the only women there. Godfrey described the experience in a column she wrote for *The Week* after returning: "We were a tiny island of femininity awash in a sea of mustaches and bass voices. We got indignant together when one of the workshop topics for discussion was 'How to draw women and blacks' (The two black men didn't seem to care much for it either)" (Godfrey, *Walworth* 13).

The cartoonists who conducted the workshop had good intentions, hoping thus to prevent sexist and racist portrayals. "It just sounded funny to us," Godfrey said, "to think that there had to be a different way to draw women and minorities than there would be to draw white males." Aside from exchanging exasperated glances at the workshop, the three women went their own ways at the convention.

Godfrey was not interested in scoring points for women's rights. She had come to the convention to learn the secret of editorial cartooning success, and to learn why Jay Kennedy had never responded to her letter. Godfrey spotted Kennedy in the hotel bar and prevailed upon a bystander to make an introduction. To her surprise, Kennedy, who reviews thousands of submissions each year, remembered her comic strip series and apologized for not getting back to her. He told Godfrey that he had been impressed by the art and humor in "Razzberries," but decided to reject the strip because it did not have a recurring character. "It wasn't my art. It wasn't my humor. It was a marketing decision more than anything else," Godfrey said. "Jay told me comics with some kind of cute little animal that people can become attached to are less likely to be dropped by newspapers; 'Razzberries' didn't have that." Godfrey had solved one mystery, and the last days of the convention would help her answer her other question: What is the secret to success in editorial cartooning?

For years, Godfrey had studied work by artists such as Pat Oliphant, Maurice Sendak, Walt Kelly, Al Capp, and Bill Sanders. She examined the line quality in Oliphant's work and noted how it had the ability to evoke emotions. She admired the thick brush strokes in Sanders's work and looked for ways to incorporate that. She was inspired by the humor and conservative political stances of Wayne Stayskal and Mike Ramirez. "Nobody can teach you how to cartoon," Godfrey said, "and it's very different from what you're taught in art school about drawing. It's a good background and I'm glad I have it, but developing a cartoon style of any kind is something that takes a lot of work." At the convention she was surrounded by some of her heroes, but if they knew the secret of success they weren't sharing it. Finally it came to her as she was dropping off to sleep on the last night of the convention. "The big secret is that there is no secret," Godfrey said. "There's just me, and my paper, and my pen" (Godfrey, Interview).

Sources

Allen, Charles A., and George D. Stephens. *Satire: Theory and Practice.* Belmont, CA: Wadsworth, 1962.

Brooks, Charles, ed. *The Best Editorial Cartoons of Year.* Gretna: Pelican, 1991-1993.

Godfrey, Linda R. Interview. By Linda Beeson. 21 Jan. 1995.

——. "That's All She Wrote." *Walworth (Wis.) County Week* 6 May 1991: 13.

Holmes, Jack, Robert E. Elder, and Michael J. Englehardt. *U.S. Government: Fundamentals and Alternative Viewpoints.* New York: McGraw Hill, 1993.

8

David Hitch, *Worcester Telegram & Gazette*

Kalman Goldstein

During October 1994, David Hitch of the *Worcester Telegram and Gazette* published two cartoons about that year's elections which suggest his thoughtful, pedagogical approach to many issues and his refusal to be typecast. One derides those "liberals" who "turn conservative" while campaigning, and temporarily or expediently espouse pro-business, the death penalty and family values. The other, less predictably, scolds ideological excessiveness by having his John Q. Public figure demand that a candidate for dog control officer reveal his stance on the death penalty (*National Forum* Oct. 2, 1994, 10; Oct. 23, 1994, 7). David Hitch describes himself as a "conservative Republican," but while a G.O.P. partisan, and often of strong opinions, his is seldom doctrinaire. On a number of issues: environmentalism, gun control, health care and welfare and gay rights, he recognizes ambiguities, ironies and contradictions in public issues and would rather educate than propagandize his readers.

David Hitch is a Midwesterner working in a blue-collar New England town. Born in Omaha in 1958, he began drawing and cartooning at a very early age, dabbling in politics during high school but equally interested in abstract art and painting. He attended the University of Nebraska from 1979 to 1982, drawing for its newspaper *The Gateway* and winning national awards. By then he had become so interested in political commentary that he dropped out of college with only 20 credit hours left in order to better develop his cartooning skills. Despite advice from professional cartoonists to simplify his imagery and presentation, he gravitated toward a style in the tradition of Thomas Nast, using Rapidograph mechanical pens with ink cartridge, ideal for detailed cross-hatching techniques; he was willing to take six hours to do a cartoon (Hitch, Interview). For the next six years, he did freelance commercial work and occasional cartoons for the *Omaha Herald* while delivering parcels for UPS and worked briefly for the *Papillion Times* and *Millard Times*. In 1987, he won the National Newspaper Association award for the best original cartoon. The next year, he became the *Telegram and*

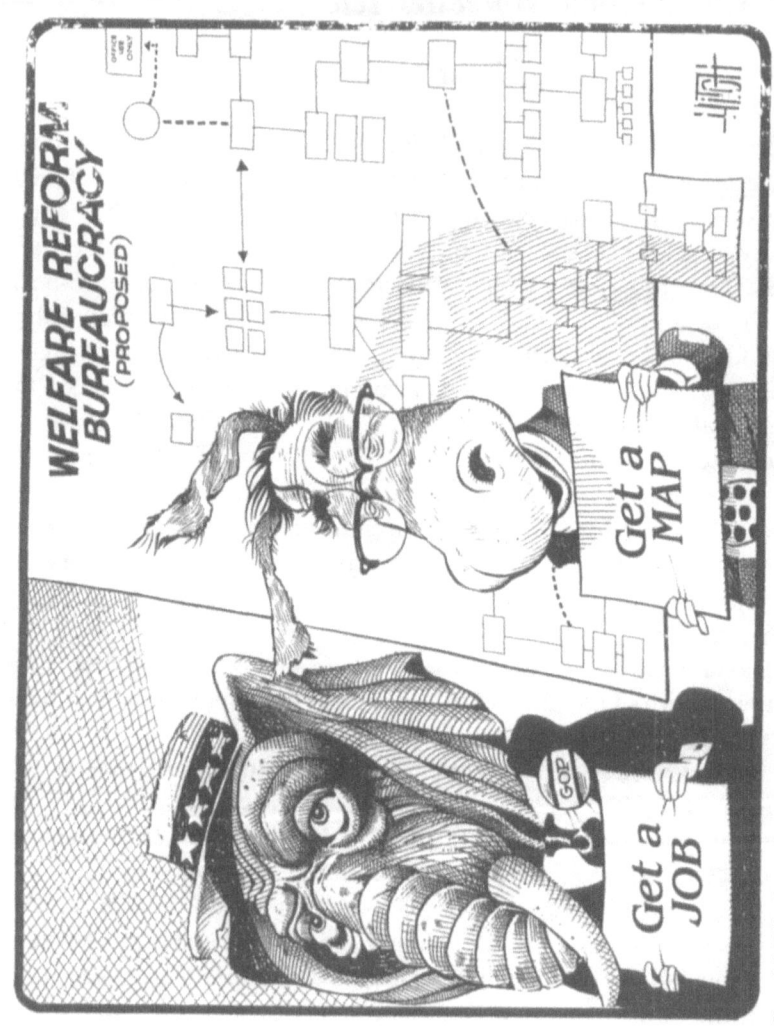

David Hitch (1994) *Worcester Telegram & Gazette.* Reprinted with special permission of North American Syndicate.

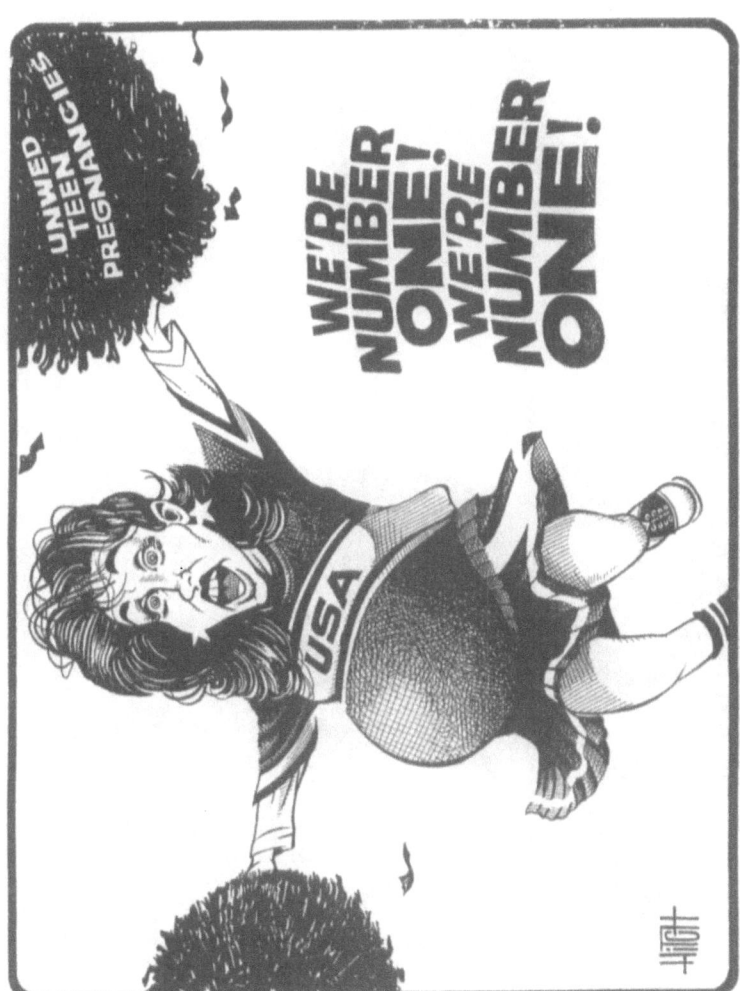

David Hitch (1994) *Worcester Telegram & Gazette*. Reprinted with special permission of North American Syndicate.

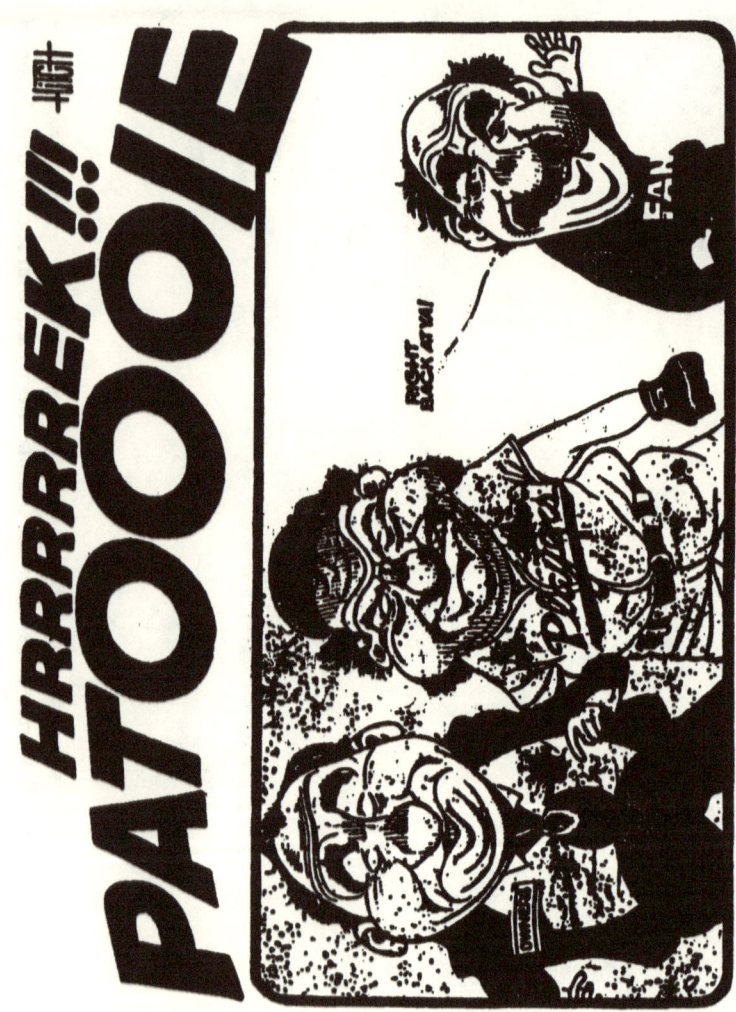

David Hitch (1994) *Worcester Telegram & Gazette.* Reprinted with special permission of North American Syndicate.

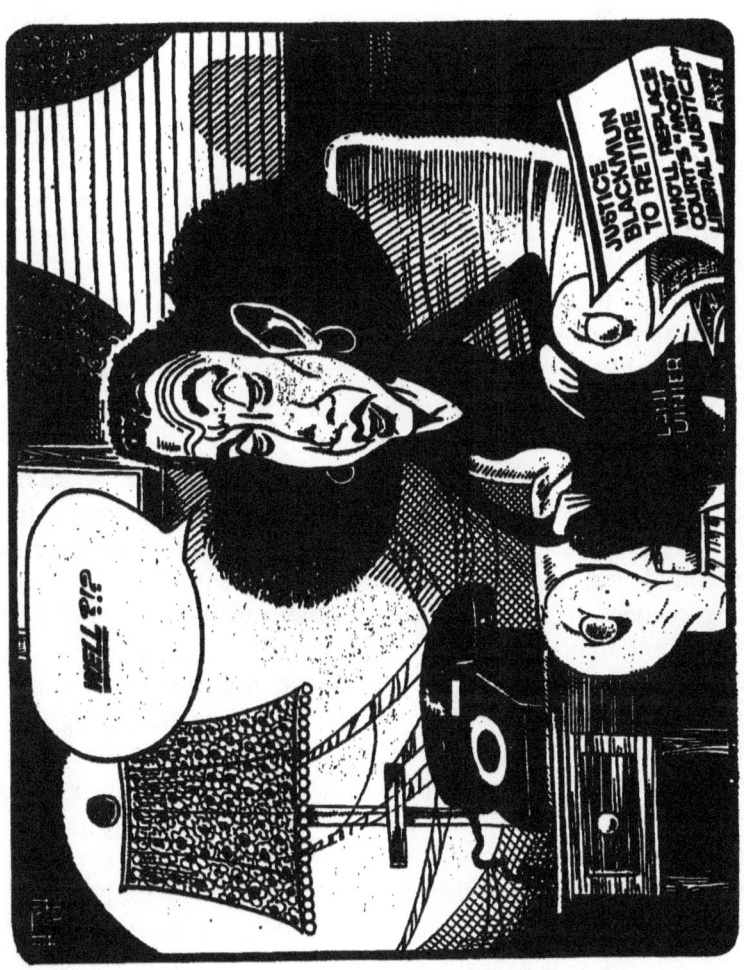

David Hitch (1994) *Worcester Telegram & Gazette.* Reprinted with special permission of North American Syndicate.

Gazette's editorial artist, and currently both his cartoons (since 1990) and caricatures (1992) are distributed by the North American Syndicate.

Hitch credits Ed Fisher of the *Omaha World Herald*, Tony Auth of the *Philadelphia Inquirer*, and Canadian artist Roy Peterson (whose elegant crosshatching designs his own often resemble) as among his most important mentors and influences, but his draftsmanship most closely honors Thomas Nast. So his cartoons sometimes remind one of Victorian era magazine illustrations (Hitch, Interview). Like Nast, he is a meticulous craftsman who may spend several hours on the execution of a cartoon full of monumental figures enhanced by cross-hatching, and carefully rendered textures, shadows and shading. (His renditions of antique locomotives are particularly precise.) Also, like Nast, he is a vigorous GOP partisan, as any of his sarcastic comments on Bill Clinton's character and administration make clear.

Above all, like Nast, Hitch is a moral traditionalist; he can become especially outraged and sarcastic when confronted by societal hypocrisy about basic values. During one recent controversy over the exclusion of gays from St. Patrick's Day parades, he drew a window placard at "South Boston Parade Committee Headquarters" which read "Gay Irish Need Not Apply," a reminder that at one time the excluders were themselves excluded. While he generally considers environmental activists largely intrusive pests, he will twit McDonald's for banishing smokers but serving "artery clogging" food, and chide consumer advocates for decrying coconut-oil saturated movie popcorn while ignoring the ultra-violent content of many movies.

A moral traditionalist, he has produced a number of cartoons reflecting how disturbed he is by irresponsible behavior among today's young people. During the summer of 1992, Hitch drew bored youth wondering how to entertain themselves, while sitting with their backs to the local library. Another cartoon on the theme of morally misguided youth is "We're Number One" (see illustration), a curdled comment on youthful pregnancy, which also decries our misuse of statistics and of sports analogies. He has similarly offered some pungent remarks on youth violence and the availability of weapons; he is an advocate of gun control (*National Forum* Apr. 10, 1994, 22). So while essentially a conservative, he has broken with the "party line" over the National Rifle Association, the death penalty, and sex education in schools. David Hitch is a traditionalist conservative rather than a reactive one.

In his close-up, naturalistic facial caricatures, Hitch's approach is similar to that of Ranan Lurie and Paul Szep. He has done treatments of political and entertainment figures, presenting them in frontal poses, larger than life, and with only a genial exaggeration of their features. But he has also incorporated extraordinarily detailed, expressionistically rendered caricatures into his editorial cartoons, which give them a distinctive dimension. These require not only attention from the readers, but presuppose that they, too, closely follow politics almost daily. For example, in June of 1994, during our imbroglio with Haiti, Hitch drew President Clinton in conference with media aide and Republican David Gergen. Much in the cartoon is not startling: the President has "voodoo" pins stuck in his face after the Haitian military leaders had threatened that an invasion by U.S. forces would meet occult opposition. And there is a bag of McDonald fries to comment on Clinton's junk food binges. But David Gergen's expression of lanky, dour exasperation not only at the Haitians, but at the President's policies, creates not only a fine caricature, but an extra-dimensional commentary. Similarly, Hitch has done a wicked caricature of controversial liberal legal theorist Lani Guinier waiting impatiently among cobwebs to be nominated to the Supreme Court (see illustration). He has also created a slapstick of former Surgeon General Joycelyn Elders, who favors drug legalization, with a comically outstretched tongue on which is a sticker: "Warning: Excessive Use May Create Credibility Loss."

Unlike Thomas Nast, Hitch is not averse to poking fun at the foibles of his preferred political party. An excellent example of both his attention to artistic detail and wry thoughtfulness as a faultfinder, is a captionless cartoon comparing Republican and Democratic nostrums about welfare reform proposals. Hitch suspects all "big-government" solutions to social problems: his conviction that bureaucracy is pork-barrel profligacy colors his reactions to welfare and health care proposals. He is adamant that "for every right, there is a responsibility. When I see people abusing their rights, then too I have to comment on that" (Hitch, Interview). But he will also agree that reforms of pressing social problems are sorely needed, and while he is not amenable to government enlargement or entitlement without accountability, he recognizes that solutions cannot be found in a simplistic appeal to "rugged individualism." So while in this cartoon his stylized Democratic donkey refers to a government flow chart, his naturalistically rendered Republican elephant glibly advises people to "Get a Job" (see illustration).

As a graphic educator, Hitch prefers his cartoons to clarify complex issues for his readers rather than simply to reflect his own convictions, so he will not comment glibly on them until he has given them careful study and is prepared to stake out a reasoned position. "I spend a lot of time drawing, but more time than that is spend researching and reading and ideating and daydreaming. Deciding how you feel about a certain issue. Sometimes that's the hardest part of the job, forcing yourself to have an opinion." He is sometimes diffident about his soapbox opportunities. "Sometimes I wonder what gives me the right to say something I've said in a cartoon. Am I somebody who has an agenda, who's trying to tell people how to run their lives?" And only recently has he concluded that after careful examination of how he feels about issues he can label himself a conservative: "It is only recently that I have come to terms with how I feel about issues and politics. It's not something that was in my genes. My parents are Democrats. My wife is a liberal Democrat." Because of this scrupulousness, he will not do cartoons on the abortion issues. As an adamant right-to-lifer (though characteristically he is not an activist demonstrator), he would have to take issue with his own paper's editorial position. But that is relatively a minor concern, for while some past cartoons on very volatile social issues have resulted in his being picketed, they at least got reactions from the readers which opened a dialogue. Rather, he is concerned that his comments on this emotional issue might make him a preacher rather than a teacher. He would simply be comforting the converted and outraging the opposition, and thus would forfeit that educative role which he believes to be the purpose of his editorial art: "Not only to say what is on my mind, but make something in their minds click on a given topic as well" (Hitch, Interview).

Hitch's cartoons are not unrelievedly didactic. While part of a growing reaction among younger cartoonists against the "gag" editorial cartoon, he acknowledges that he must be humorous in order not to drive his audience away by seeming preachy. And he does enjoy being funny as well as sarcastic. Further, there are slow times when a cartoonist may be reduced to making jokes about the weather. Above all, some political and social events may best be handled by a non-tendentious pun or sight gag. While he is sparing in the use of references to popular culture symbols or products, he could employ the *Batman* movie fad to portray H. Ross Perot as "Bratman Returns," surrounded by mock movie blurbs. Or use the ubiquitous Christmastime television showings of Frank Capra's *It's a Wonderful Life* as a springboard for a reference to "suicide doctor" Jack Kevorkian. He has had his fun with the non-sequitur soundbite juxtapositions produced by "channel surfing" and with the Michael Jackson/Lisa Marie Presley wedding (*Funny Times* Sept. 1994, 13; Oct. 1994, 14).

As a traditionalist conservative, Hitch is bemused by the fatuity of much of popular culture. But as a sports buff, he has been particularly angry about those departures from professional tradition demonstrated in the 1994 baseball and hockey strikes, and a tendency toward melees in basketball, a sport (unlike hockey) where violence is not "traditional."

He is certainly not unique among editorial cartoonists to comment, but the exasperated vitriol of showing baseball players and owners splattering one another, and most of the cartoon background, in tobacco juice, is an unusually graphic expression of his disgust (see illustration).

Hitch loves to be sarcastic, but is not driven daily to testify against the perceived devils of this world. Some issues call for a sledge hammer; others for a tweak. "I don't think I'm arrogant enough to think that I can solve the world's problems with a cartoon. I think maybe I can influence some people, but not maybe the right ones. . . . I'm a public servant, a watchdog for the public. I try to alert them as to what is going on behind the scenes. I try to be a reference point too. I like to see my stuff on the refrigerator, because I like people to be able to relate to what I have to say. . . . Maybe a cartoonist can express something in a unique way, and people can say, that's what I feel, that's what I was trying to say" (Hitch, Interview).

Sources

Brooks, Charles, ed. *Best Editorial Cartoons of the Year.* Gretna, LA: Pelican, 1988-1997.
Funny Times. Cleveland Heights, OH, monthly.
Hitch, David. Interview. By Kalman Goldstein. 26 July 1994.
National Forum Gallery of Cartoons. Washington, D.C., weekly.

9

David Horsey, *Seattle Post-Intelligencer*

Kalman Goldstein

When Jacqueline Kennedy Onassis died in mid-1994, David Horsey of the *Seattle Post-Intelligencer* drew her as a monumental, iconic figure, "the embodiment of grace under pressure" (*National Forum* June 5, 1994, 1). In the introduction to *The Fall of Man,* he described the former First Lady's life as a metaphor, invoking comparison with a coarsened contemporary American culture.[1] Horsey composes his cartoons meticulously, with a careful eye for design and representation; he could easily have become a commercial illustrator. Often his cartoons are given a computerized shading finish. Their varied hues, textures, and lines would not be out of place in a graphic animation shop. He excels at creating beautiful women with well-toned figures; he could easily have done what cartoonists call "good-girl" pin-up art. Instead, his cartoons consist of narrative tableaux or instructive conversations, designed to teach lessons in civic responsibility or policy-making. His lovely women either festoon moral (even Biblical) parables or comment satirically on social issues. He will render a naturalistic tiger, but make it into Exxon's logo in order to excoriate the company over the Valdez oil spill (Horsey, *Greatest Hits* 78). Editorial cartoonists can be divided into gag artists, political partisans, ideological preachers, and graphic pedagogues; and David Horsey's work belongs in this final category.

Horsey very seriously prepared to become a humorous teacher. Born in Evansville, Indiana, in 1951, he grew up in Seattle and for years drew cartoons for the University of Washington student paper. *Politics and Other Perversions,* an early collection of his collegiate work, was published in 1974. Before gaining his present position as staff cartoonist in 1979, for four years he had been government reporter and political columnist for a consortium of regional newspapers when just out of college. Now the North American Syndicate (he affiliated in 1988) distributes his work nationally. Horsey had edited the University of Washington's paper as well as drawing for it while an undergraduate communications major there, and despite his artistic skills, he still believes that what he writes has as much importance as how he illustrates his ideas. He

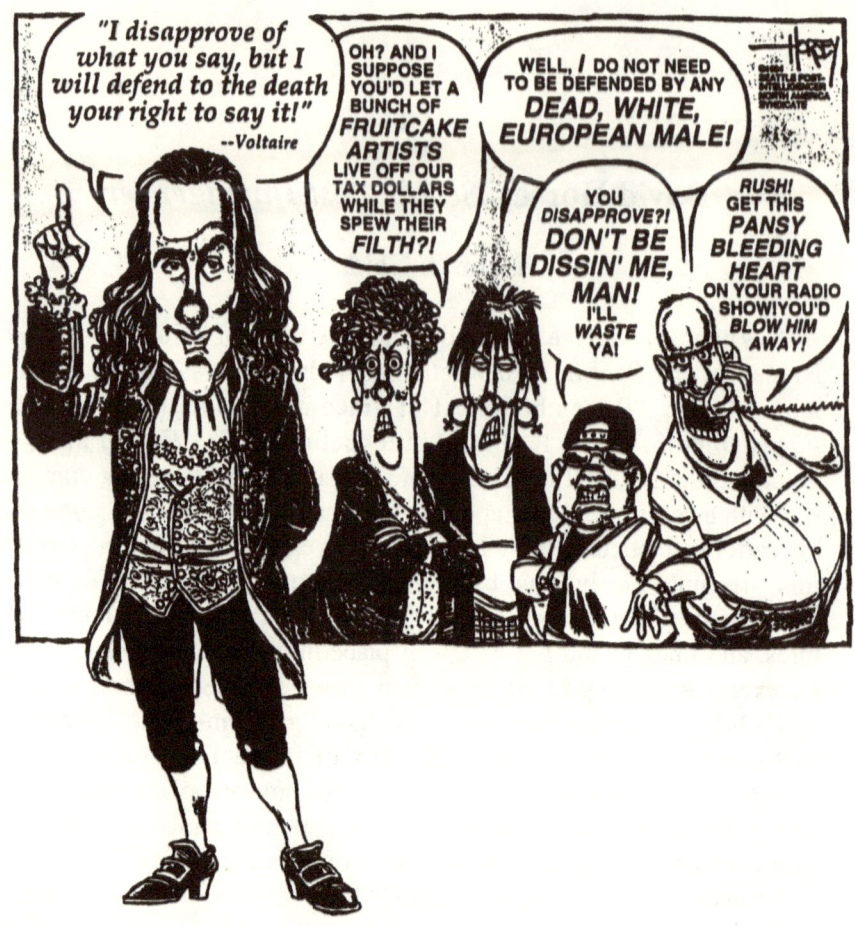

David Horsey (1994) *Seattle Post-Intelligencer.* Reprinted with special permission of North American Syndicate.

accepts many speaking engagements, and not only about cartooning. Horsey is one of the few American political cartoonists with a master's degree in political science, having been Rotary Scholar in International Relations at Great Britain's University of Kent during 1986.[2] In 1993 he spent a period in Brussels as a European Economic Union Visitor.[3] Though born in Indiana, Horsey is a fourth-generation Washingtonian. He has a deep sense of community rootedness, and here too Horsey finds time to teach—as a coach of youth soccer and Little League baseball.

Even though most of his cartoons focus on issues rather than personalities, they employ cinematic rather than symbolic techniques. Horsey prefers to create a story line or show people conversing about issues and ideas rather than glibly parody popular culture references or

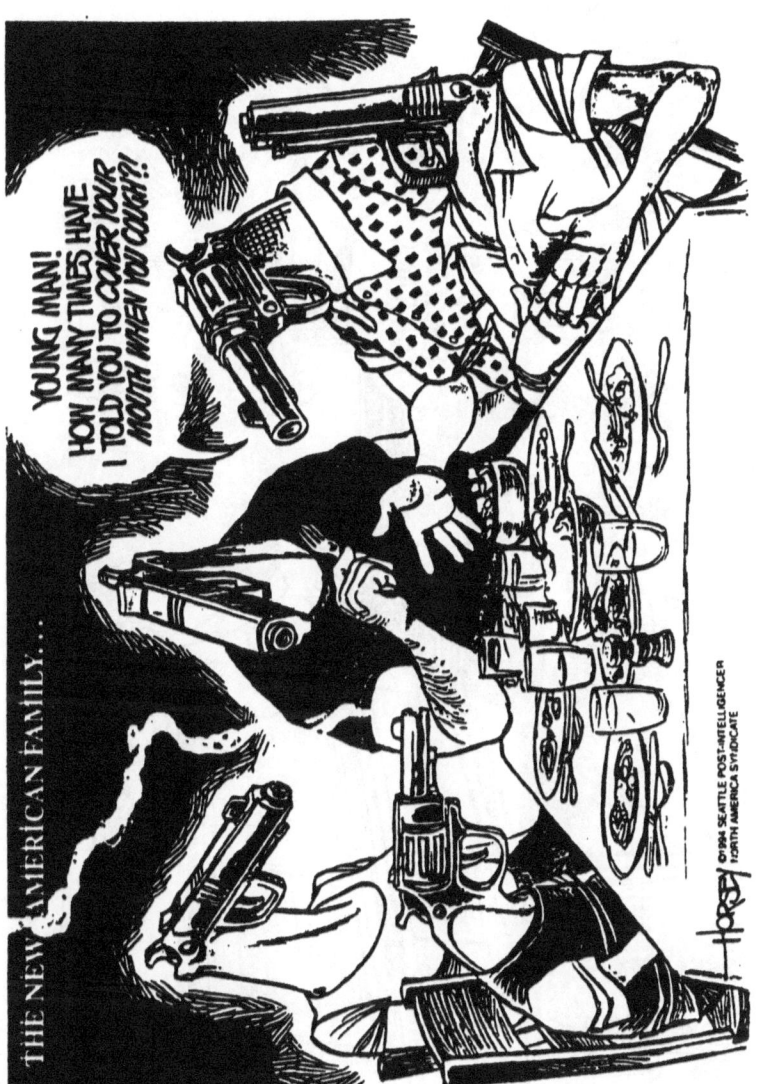

David Horsey (1994) *Seattle Post-Intelligencer.* Reprinted with special permission of North American Syndicate.

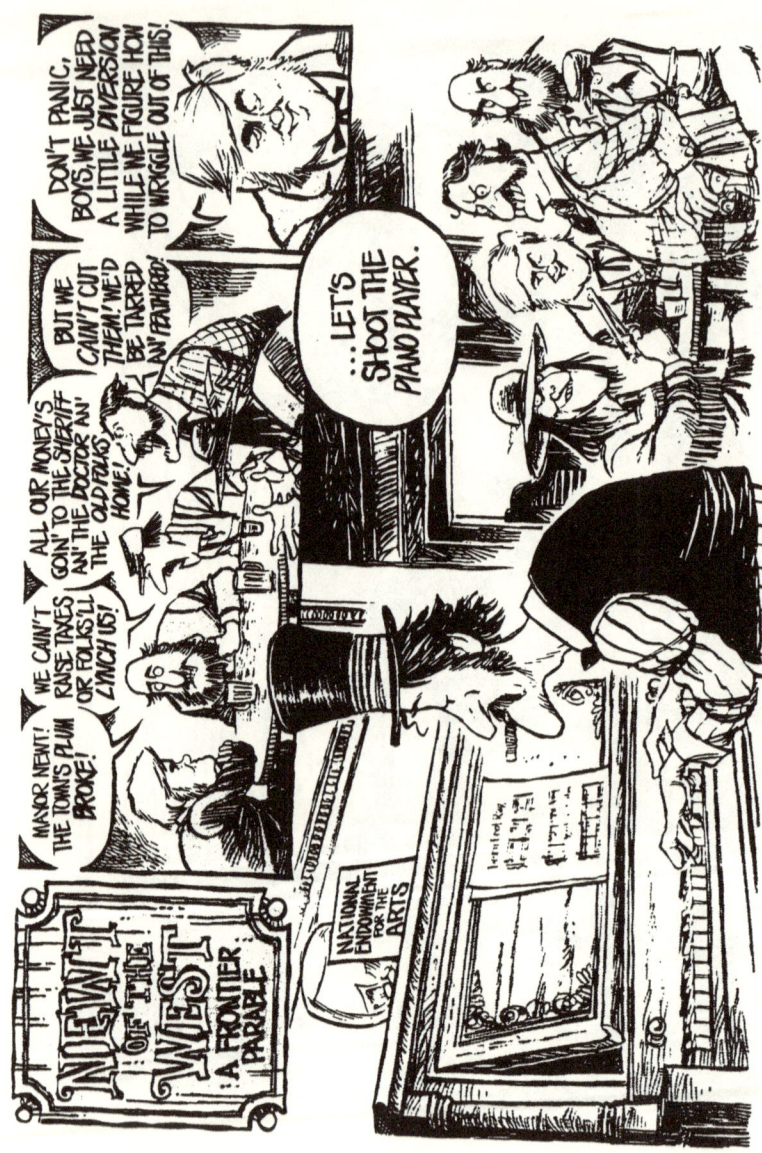

David Horsey (1994) *Seattle Post-Intelligencer.* Reprinted with special permission of North American Syndicate.

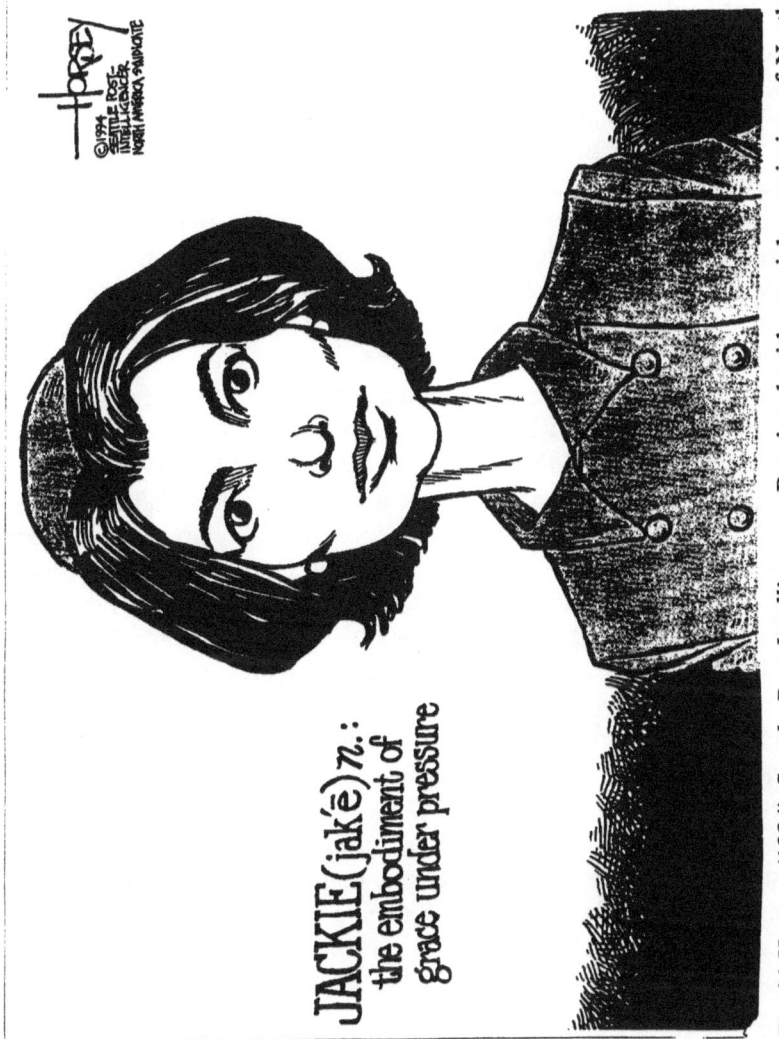

David Horsey (1994) *Seattle Post-Intelligencer.* Reprinted with special permission of North American Syndicate.

attach labels to caricatures of state, national and world leaders. Some of his work, for example "Newt of the West," could almost pass for a series of dialogue-ballooned motion picture stills (*New York Times* Feb. 5, 1995). Nor is he comfortable with gag cartooning, while he would not condemn it outright. For Horsey, political cartooning is one part art, one part journalism, one part humor and one part serious commentary. "It's all right to be funny, as long as you're making a point about it. I find humor extremely difficult. Political cartoons are there to make a point, only incidentally funny. When I do [gags], I betray all my impulses to be a serious commentator and I try to entertain (Horsey, Interview). Therefore it is fortunate that his paper allows him an unusually large space on the editorial page. Whittling down a complex presentation to one panel may result in wordiness, but that may be the only way for him to convey an important point. In fact, he admits that visual metaphors which really deliver a message are extraordinarily difficult for him to compose, because his ideas come to him through words. They would be trivialized and simplistic if reduced to a shorthand picture. "I try to say more than I can with a simple image. It's not very often that one image really captures the depth of an issue" (Horsey, Interview). In order to include a number of related political or social positions within one panel, he will on occasion compare the writings of a political philosopher like Voltaire or Jefferson with paradoxically hostile reactions by narrowly ideological listeners (*Funny Times* Dec. 1994, 15; *Greatest Hits* 3, 19).

On the other hand, sometimes he is able to use symbols or cultural references effectively and economically, with or without dialogue. He has frequently caricatured the Statue of Liberty, largely to criticize administration policies in Central America (Horsey, *Greatest Hits* 56, 66, 70). Since his interest in foreign policy is so strong, and his cartoons on world affairs so frequent, he has found it necessary and useful to use shorthand symbols such as Uncle Sam, Japanese geishas, atavistic Europeans in gold-braided uniforms, and current national leaders. One of his most striking devices on behalf of gun control has been showing people with pistols instead of heads. In "The New American Family," for example, a bit of ironic humor (visual, oral and narrative) underlines the deadly situation presented (*Funny Times* Nov. 1994; "Saturday Night in America" July 1993). And Horsey used a scene from the motion picture *Casablanca* to poke fun at both Presidents Reagan and Bush, as a tongue-in-cheek reference to Reagan's repeated use of movie scenarios when explaining his policies.

More frequently, however, one should look at several of his cartoons on any subject rather than any one example, in order to follow Horsey's exploration of issues. On some weeks he has done variations on the same topic, but normally Horsey explores sensitive questions incrementally over some time. These questions include foreign as well as domestic policies. Horsey's depth of interest in international relations, and the inherently complex nature of global trade or regional diplomacy, require that he develop his views carefully and clearly. These cartoons reveal his impatience with parochialism, whether American, European or Asian; and a desire that his readers be fairly conversant with the issues.

Race relations present the most ticklish subject for editorial cartoonists to handle, and after a scarifying experience or two, most have decided to avoid it entirely. Over the last several years, however, Dave Horsey's readers have been able to react to a large number of cartoons in which he explores race relations in a number of different contexts. *The Fall of Man* collection shows African Americans as victims of urban social problems as well as contributing to them. One of his most telling cartoons including inner-city blacks compared an African American store looter with white men in business suits busily stealing fortunes through banking or corporate-takeover manipulations (*New York Times* May 10, 1992). Many cartoons show black and white families equally affected by such problems as school violence, rampant drug use and unimaginative education bureaucrats. Nowhere here will the reader find a facile stereotype; it would take determined myopia for any reader to confuse Horsey's photographic portraits and specific comments about a leader like Jesse Jackson with any implied judgments about "all" African Americans.

Horsey has felt uncomfortable cartooning about abortion, because "there are so many loaded symbols, so many people on all sides." He would rather engage the issue than avoid it, "but as carefully and as clearly as possible." The problem is that "most political cartoons are ambiguous, almost by nature. I am amazed at what people can read into a cartoon, things that have nothing to do with what I was saying" (Horsey, Interview). Horsey also has to worry about his marketability. But during the last several years, he has felt an increased responsibility to do fewer cartoons on straight politics and comment on a variety of issues, especially social mores and sexuality. He has protested media pandering to "bimbo" exposés that distract voters from serious questions and link politics to celebrity voyeurism. He tries to portray current anxieties over gender orientation in an unpatronizing and instructive manner. He urges parents to deal with their children's urges by remembering their own adolescent behavior and offering them role model guidance, rather than simply bemoaning current media salaciousness or the newly discovered bogey of "Internet smut" (*National Forum* July 21, 1995, 17). The same is true of drug usage. Horsey has former marijuana smoker and current House Speaker Newt Gingrich with a joint in his hand, contemplating a lava lamp symbolic of the "flower power" era, while rationalizing his own smoking "as a means of supporting free trade in an agricultural commodity unfettered by the intrusive hand of the federal government" (*National Forum* Jan. 1, 1995: 4). Horsey tries hard to pose clear and intelligent moral choices and accountability over such issues, without becoming ensnared in the shackles of "political correctness."

On the surface, Dave Horsey might be someone who could be quite comfortable with "political correctness." He is pro-choice, feminist and liberationist, and vigorously opposed to all sorts of offenses against women, including such recent developments as the "wonderbra," "miracleboost jeans" and the return of stiletto heels (his fashionable woman discovers that she can neither breathe or walk, and may be wetting her pants! (*Funny Times* Aug. 1995, 10). He is also multicultural, anti-xenophobe, antitobacco, antidrugs, and a green-hot environmentalist. Horsey is even a labor union activist, and currently a shop steward in the Pacific Northwest Newspaper Guild.

But he is as unsparing of the "politically correct" as he is of our nation's Yahoos, and exposes their excesses to *reductio ad absurdum*. Among his barbs are endlessly differentiated and separatist school drinking fountains, small-print dating consent sexual-behavior forms, and hypocritical PC bowdlerization of Shakespeare. Horsey considers himself an iconoclast rather than an ideologue, and worries that the current wave of sensitivity is undercutting and restraining vulnerable editorial comment. So many late night television comics and even news readers have become the "court jesters" of political commentary that perhaps only editorial cartoonists remain capable of trenchant humor. And even they are under increasing pressures to take refuge in "pack cartooning," following evanescent media-dictated issues and repeating the day's gossip.

To Dave Horsey, this amounts to betrayal of a high calling. While editorial cartoonists are not necessarily smarter or more insightful than other folk, "we do what we do precisely because we take citizenship seriously" (Horsey, *Greatest Hits* 2). Horsey is even more serious than others; during his early years with the *Post-Intelligencer*, he added the Christian fish symbol to his name on his cartoons. As an educated, committed moralist with a well-honed pen and intellect, Horsey believes that he must be pedagogic, though not dogmatic: "To an extent it's my job to call attention to important issues that I think people should be thinking about" (Horsey, Interview). Censoring his syllabus would only impair his ability to teach.

Notes

1. "In the three decades between her days in the White House and the day of her death, the grace of Jackie has been replaced by the boorishness of Roseanne. The style of Jackie has been eclipsed by the trashiness of Madonna. The manners of Jackie have been replaced by the comportment of Beavis and Butt-head. The refined taste of Jackie has disappeared in the glare of Las Vegas aesthetics. And as for the personal privacy that Jackie saw rightly as an indispensable part of any individual's personal integrity, that has been submerged in the effluent of tabloid journalism and television talk shows (Horsey, *The Fall of Man,* Introduction).

2. His thesis topic was "Visions of the Bear: Western Perceptions of the U.S.S.R. 1947-1980 through British and North American Political Cartoons."

3. In August 1995, he transferred for a year to the Washington bureau of the Hearst Newspapers, the *Post-Intelligencer*'s parent company.

Sources

Funny Times. Cleveland Heights, OH (monthly).

Horsey, David. *The Fall of Man.* Seattle: *Post-Intelligencer,* 1994.

——. *Horsey's Greatest Hits of the 80s.* Seattle: *Post-Intelligencer,* 1989.

——. *Horsey's Rude Awakenings.* Seattle: Madrona, 1981.

——. Interview. By Kalman Goldstein. 6 Jan. 1995.

——. *Politics and Other Perversions.* Seattle: Shambala, 1974.

National Forum Gallery of Cartoons. Washington, D.C., weekly.

10

Mike Keefe, *Denver Post*

Jack Colldeweih

"Here, look at this," Mike Keefe said, "another demonstration that four-color theory really works," pointing to the screen of his laptop computer (Keefe, Interview). He had just finished colorizing a map of the world he had scanned into his computer so that each nation was a color different from all its neighbors. As one of the most technologically oriented of contemporary cartoonists, working with computers and graphic programs comes naturally to Keefe. Technology does not, however, dominate the content of his work, which ranges widely over the social and political scene. Not as finely detailed as some other cartoonists' work, Keefe's cartoons focus on the concept and keep the frame spare so as not to detract from it. On the other hand, he frequently favors multi-panel cartoons in which the dialogue presents an argument, somewhat in the manner of Jules Feiffer. In the spectrum between gagsters and ideologues, Keefe falls somewhere near the middle: his cartoons are nearly always at least amusing, sometimes uproarious, but never without a point—the pure gag is not part of his political repertoire.

Although he frequently sketched as a child and was encouraged by his father to explore art as a career, Keefe was more interested in science. Born in Santa Rosa on November 6, 1946, he grew up in St. Louis, Missouri, where his family had moved in the early 1950s. In an academic career interrupted by a two-year hitch in the Marines during the Vietnam War, in the totally-out-of-character role of an MP, he studied mathematics at the University of Missouri, completing coursework through the doctoral level. While still in school, he became interested in the work of the *Kansas City Star*'s new cartoonist Bill Schorr, and with some guidance by Schorr soon began to draw for his college paper. With his GI Bill expiring and no response to his applications for a teaching position while he finished his thesis, Keefe "decided [he] better learn how to draw" (Black 45). At Schorr's suggestion, he sent samples to Bill Sanders at the *Milwaukee Journal*, who told him of an opening at the *Denver Post*. Remarkably enough, the *Post* took him on, over the applications of many other more experienced artists. He speculates that this was because the

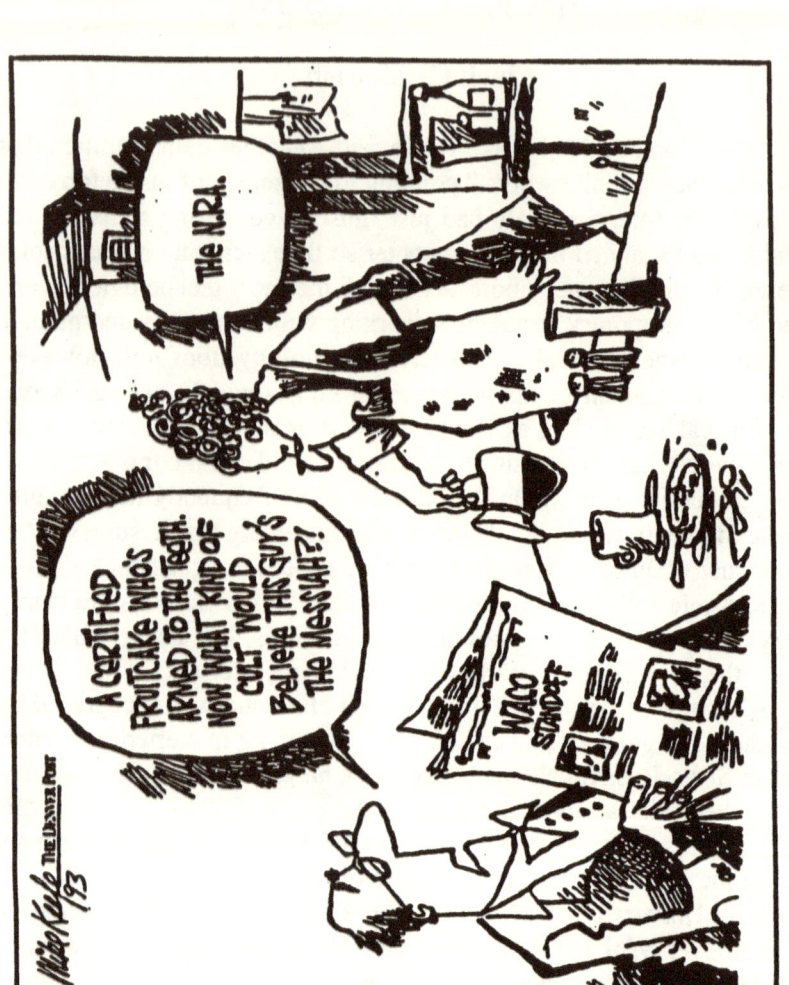

Mike Keefe (1993) *Denver Post* and dePIXIon Features. Reprinted with permission.

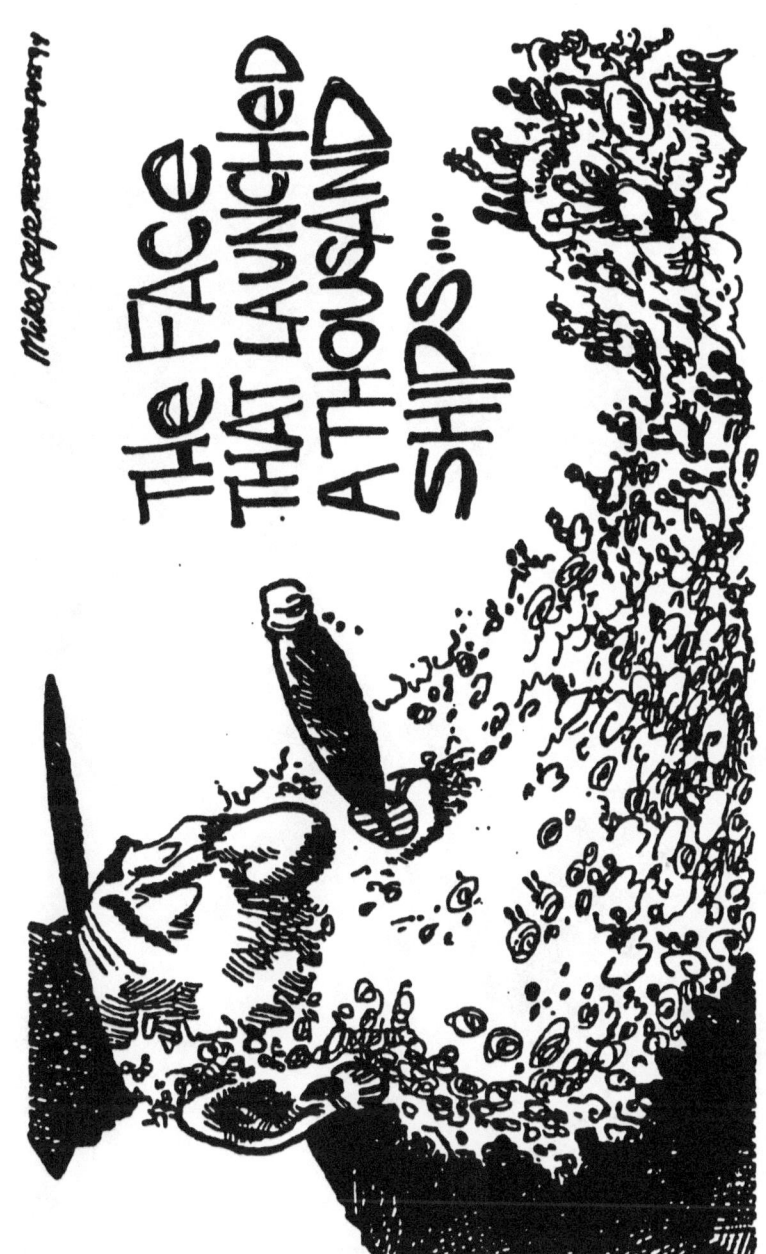

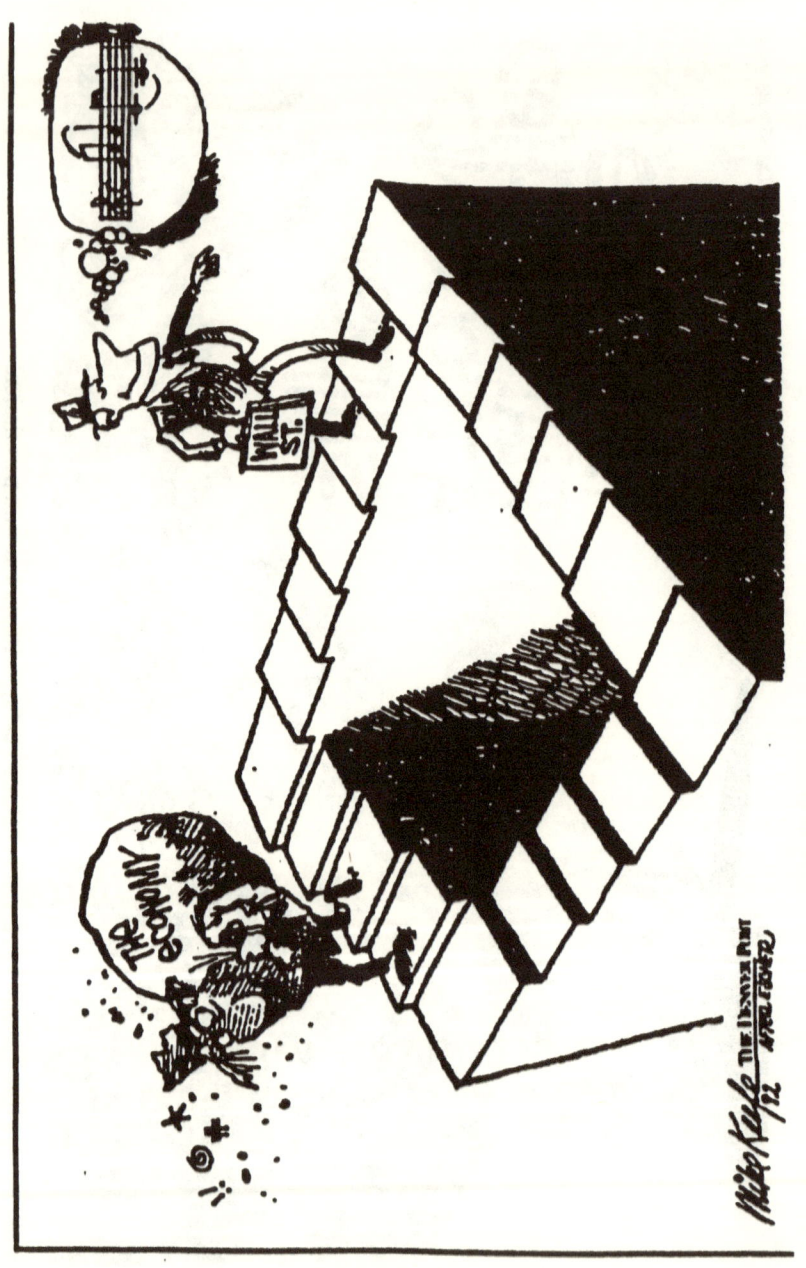

Mike Keefe (1992) *Denver Post* and dePIXlon Features. Reprinted with permission.

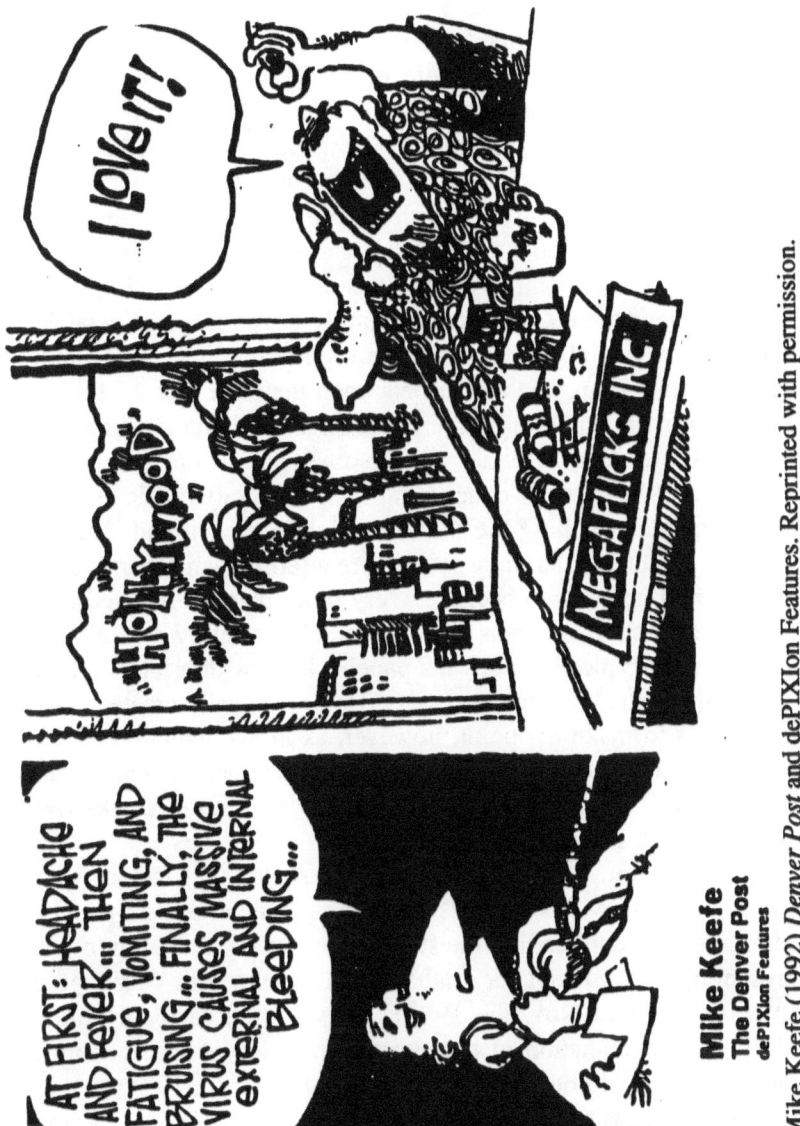

Mike Keefe (1992) *Denver Post* and dePIXIon Features. Reprinted with permission.

management may have felt that the others would have been much more difficult to work with and, besides, he certainly came a lot cheaper.

Keefe was totally unaware of whom he was replacing, Pulitzer winner Pat Oliphant, or that the *Post* had employed Paul Conrad, another Pulitzer winner, before that. When he found out, he was so depressed that he could hardly work for six months. Consequently, unlike many young artists starting out, Keefe pointedly did not further model his work on Oliphant, but tried to distance himself by creating his own style. Although it was a long process, he is now satisfied that he has done so.

Keefe used a lot of shading and crosshatching details in his drawings in the 1970s and 1980s, with careful attention to architectural and structural detail in both foreground and background. For example, a 1980 cartoon depicts three generations of a family in a king-sized brass bed, the grandparents and parents snugly covered by a Social Security blanket, the two children awake and shivering. The walls and floorboards of the room, and the carpets upon the floor and the furniture are all carefully drawn, with both crosshatch and splatter shading filling the frame (Keefe, *Keefe-Kebab* 48). A somewhat different technique was used in a 1981 cartoon concerning heavy aircraft traffic. Here he has drawn the planes filling the frame, so tightly packed and interwoven in different directions that they seem more a fabric than separate machines; the effect is heightened because every other plane is hatched in exactly the same direction, much as a cloth would be (Keefe, *Keefe-Kebab* 86).

Now he typically keeps his panels clean, with a lot of white space and no more shading than necessary. He occasionally creates some striking effects to make his point, however, as in his depiction of a woman seated on a raft with a *Roe v. Wade* flag on the mast, floating in a stormy sea labeled "Supreme Court" and filled with circling sharks (*National Forum* Feb. 2, 1992).

In addition, he frequently uses the multipanel format within the frame, although with variations. For example, he uses a six-panel format, semi-bordered and reading the standard left to right and top to bottom in presenting an argument for establishing democracy in Washington, D.C. (*National Forum* Nov. 13, 1994). A five-panel cartoon, unbordered, offering an explanation of the current operation of the economy, reads clockwise and without end (*National Forum* Feb. 12, 1995).

Keefe tends to see images not as stills but as continuous action; his cartoons therefore are reflective of the skewed perspective and animated action of film cartoons. In fact, he describes his drawn characters as "cartoony" (Keefe, Interview). He makes little attempt to draw real people as more than reminiscent of their actual appearance; on the other hand, he does not engage in grand exaggeration or distortion of facial features that is the usual style of cartoonists. His Bill Clinton, Jimmy Carter, Newt Gingrich, Ronald Reagan and George Bush, for example, are only slightly distorted, generally focusing on one major feature. For Clinton, it's the jawline; Carter, the lips; Gingrich, the overall shape of the head and face. He generally avoids caricature, perhaps because he believes he does not do it very well.

Early influences on his work include, of course, Pat Oliphant and Jeff MacNelly, but also Ronald Searle and the Czechoslovakian artist Adolf Born. He got interested in European artistic style, especially that of a group of animation specialists from Zagreb, while doing some animation work of his own. His later influences included Gerald Scarfe and some of the Zagrebian animators who subsequently came to work at the National Film Board of Canada.

There is a definite consistency to Keefe's views on a wide variety of subjects, although there have been some changes over time. On social and political topics he remains fairly liberal, but his views on economics have gradually become more conservative as he has gotten older and acquired a wife and two children. Growing up in a nonpolitical family, his liberal political views were formed during the turmoil surrounding the Vietnam War. The shooting of students at Kent State influenced him very deeply. Neither a bleeding heart nor a cynic, he could more accurately be described as a reasoned skeptic.

On the issue of abortion, he comes down on the pro-choice side, as in the *Roe v. Wade* cartoon described above. His harshest views of the pro-life side, however, are restricted to those who use violence to influence the public. For example, he has drawn a rather ape-like fellow grinning as he aims his rifle directly at the reader, the scope-sight and crosshairs forming the "o" in the word "pro-life" over his head (*National Forum* Jan. 22, 1995).

Violence, and the threat of it, in fact form the thread that runs through Keefe's cartoons on a variety of seemingly disparate topics. He persistently takes on the National Rifle Association (NRA) in an area in the Rocky Mountains where they might seem to be the strongest and most influential. For example, one, involving the relationship of the NRA to congressmen during Brady Bill discussions, has a cowboy loading his six-gun with congressmen shaped like bullets as he thinks, "Best Dum-Dums money can buy!" (*National Forum* Mar. 14, 1995). He continues in this vein, depicting unofficial militias as an armed cuckoo-clock bird shouting about Janet Reno fluoridating drinking water (*National Forum* May 21, 1995).

This thread extends into another of his major interests, education, wherein he has the students so well armed that the Secret Service cites as one of the reasons Clinton moved his daughter Chelsea to a private school: the eighth grade had her protection outgunned (*National Forum* Jan. 24, 1993). Due in part to his long involvement with education as both student and teacher, Keefe weaves across that thread other educational concerns such as prayer in school, and the poor career prospects of graduates; he has graduates being told "Go forth and serve mankind," and given spatulas instead of diplomas (*National Forum* May 29, 1995).

Keefe's antagonism toward violence is not limited to its organized form in militia groups or the promotion of gun use by the NRA but extends to the social attitudes that have permeated American society. In one drawing, for example, he has a family cowering behind their window drapes and heavily armed because everyone else is heavily armed (*National Forum* Jan. 15, 1995). Contrary to current popular opinion, he does not lay all the responsibility for these attitudes on the mass media. In one drawing depicting a liquor store clerk using a television controller to zap a robber, the caption says: "Want to get serious about violence in America? Forget television. . . . Install a 'V-chip' in every felon's buttocks" (*Denver Post* Aug. 9, 1995).

Many of his foreign policy cartoons also deal with violence and his frustration at the inability of international organizations to prevent or stop it. He has done an extremely pointed series on the wars in the Balkans. Other areas of conflict he has dealt with include Haiti, Cuba, Grenada, Somalia, Palestine and Rwanda.

Keefe is not, of course, a single theme thinker; other favorite subjects include ecology, health, and military leaders, bureaucrats and politicians whose inflated posturings and policies seem to have been designed for puncturing. Nor does business escape his brush, especially the tobacco companies and their approach to youthful smokers. He is also critical of the problems presented to employees by mergers, plant shifts, outplacement of work to foreign workers and other corporate practices.

He tries to avoid both illustrating the news and covering popular culture events and personalities. When he does deal with them it is usually in terms of some broader theme that he feels they illustrate. Keefe feels that "cartoons last long enough to line the birdcage, so pop culture is fine; if you want to have anything that lasts longer, then references to myth and literature are great." He feels that cartooning is a great tool of education, "but you have to get the reader on the page first; and once there you like to think that they have some sense of history and culture. . . . I'm fairly happy with the balance of my cartoons in that way" (Keefe, Interview).

Keefe's restless mind is constantly exploring new avenues of interest and new ways expressing himself. He has one book of collected cartoons from the *Post, Keefe-Kebab* and he is currently drawing his third comic strip, *Cold Facts Avenue,* now 12 years old.[1] He shared creative duties with Tim Menees, of the *Pittsburgh Post-Gazette,* on his first successful strip; *Cooper,* about a high school teacher, after their proposed first co-production, *Earl,* was a nonstarter. They later coauthored a second one called *Iota,* somewhat more political, which Keefe left in order to take a journalism fellowship at Stanford University that led to short story work with the Stegner Fellows.

Cold Facts Avenue is published every Friday and deals with aspects of life in Denver. Keefe thought of taking it national, but Jim Borgman beat him to it with *Wonk City,* so he kept it local. Sometimes his daily cartoon is very similar in style to his strip and could even pass for it with a title change. He does not feel that doing both detracts from either; rather, he claims to feel energized by the strip because it gives him an alternate outlet for some of his ideas that don't seem to work well in the daily cartoon. He also draws an editorial cartoon that appears every Tuesday in *USA Today* and a weekly sports cartoon for the *Post.*

His Sunday cartoon is done in color, which he enjoys; the others are black and white. Keefe acknowledges that "it's real easy to have color get in the way of the cartoon, to detract from the message," but feels that he is learning to use it advantageously. He does not color the cartoons directly, but scans them onto his computer and then colors them there where he feels he has a much greater palette to choose from and the control to use it. On the other hand, he does not generally draw directly on the computer, although he has done so in the past occasionally, because he has much more control with brush and pen.

Keefe indulged his interest in animation in 1990 by doing animated editorial cartoons for a local news station once a week and then decided to try them nationally. Fearing that his name would not sell nationally by itself, he recruited a group of eight cartoonists, including Tom Toles, Jim Borgman, Jeff MacNelly and Signe Wilkinson, with the idea of animating their cartoons. That meant that he had to learn to draw in each of their styles. He would scan in their frames, and when there was movement he drew in the missing frames by positioning the characters in relation to the background and each other. Since there were no morphing programs at that time, an animation program was used. His wife Anita, "a former aerospace engineer and computer whiz" and partner in their production company, dePixion, Inc., helped with the programming and editing. Sound, in the form of voice, effects and music, was added in the editing process.

Although more and more cartoonists are putting their e-mail addresses in their cartoons for reader feedback, and some are now appearing at various locations on the Internet, Keefe believes that he was the first to go on line with his cartoons, starting in 1992.[2]

Virtually all public commentators, graphic or textual, want to have some effect on society, and Keefe is no exception. Aside from the recognition of his artistic talent reflected in the award of First Place in the John Fischetti Competition in 1991 and the National Headliners Award in 1986, Keefe has also been honored for his service to his profession, receiving the Sigma Delta Chi Distinguished Service Award in 1986, and was elected president of the American Association of Editorial Cartoonists in 1991. While direct effects of one's cartoons are usually problematic at best, Keefe can point to at least one instance where his art affected national policy on the highest level. In the conflict of views between Secretary of Defense Caspar Weinberger and Secretary of State Alexander Haig over different MX missile proposals, a cartoon by Keefe relating to the whole concept of MX missiles was shown to President Ronald Reagan by Weinberger. "Reagan chuckled and approved the Weinberger plan" (*Keefe-Kebab* 8).

Notes

1. Keefe has also written two humorous-but-useful books on his hobbies of running and cycling, which he also illustrated, and he provided illustrations for a book about water conservation in the Southwest.

2. Keefe can be reached at dePixion@aol.com, where one can view several years of both editorial cartoons and the strip *Cold Facts Avenue*. Generally, other cartoonists have appeared only under the sponsorship of their distributor. Keefe is now self-syndicated so perhaps the same could be said of him.

Sources

Black, Ed. "Mike Keefe—The Cartoon Bug Bites Even Ph.D's." *Cartoonist Profiles* 55 (Sept. 1982): 44-50.

Keefe, Michael. Interview. By Jack Colldeweih. 2 Aug. 1995.

——. *Keefe-Kebab*. Denver: *Denver Post*, 1984.

——. *Running Awry*. New York: McGraw Hill, 1979.

——. *The Ten Speed Commandments*. New York: Dolphin Doubleday, 1987.

Keefe, Michael, and Tim Menees. "Cooper." *Cartoonist Profiles* 69 (Mar. 1986): 44-47.

Obmascik, Mark. *Consumer's Guide to Water Conservation*. Denver: American Waterworks Association, 1993.

11

Steve Kelley, *San Diego Union Tribune*

Kalman Goldstein

Steve Kelley of the *San Diego Union Tribune* is an unabashed champion of the humorous editorial cartoon. Growing up in Richmond, Virginia during the 1960s and 1970s (he was born Jan. 2, 1959), he admired clown-comic Red Skelton as well as Jeff MacNelly. Doing drawings about politics through his high school years as well as at Dartmouth, where he received a degree in English in 1981, he discovered that his freelanced "funny" pieces were the best received, and began cartooning for the San Diego paper immediately upon graduation. Four years later, he learned that Frank King, a stand-up comic at a local club, was using his cartoon punch lines as part of an act. Kelley struck up a professional relationship with King, and himself developed a nightclub standup routine in 1986. Steve Kelley has contributed to pilot episodes for comic shows, appeared on others, and been an opening act for various peole, including Dolly Parton, Lou Rawls and Peter Allen. By 1990 had been booked three times on NBC's *Tonight* show. Frequently he will arrange a comedy club performance during conventions of the Association of American Editorial Cartoonists in order to entertain colleagues. So in the profession-wide dispute over cartoon gags, it is clear where he stands; referring to a noted senior cartoonist's disparagement of editorial humor, Kelley responded that "he has his prizes, but *I'm* getting published" (Kelley, Interview).

Despite what might seem a crass, opportunistic attitude toward his job ("In a sense, my motto is give people candy, because people want candy"), Kelley disputes charges that he and younger artists turn to gags simply because syndicates such as Copley News Service, which carries his work, encourage humorous cartoons for increased sales. In fact, he is convinced that gag cartoons can deliver serious messages more effectively than those that are angry, didactic, somber or tendentious: what he calls the "self-important, self-possessed" and ultimately condescending approach. "I find nothing more insulting than a cartoon that assumes the cartoonist knows so much more than the readers do. I think that readers prefer that the cartoonist assumes that they have done their homework.

111

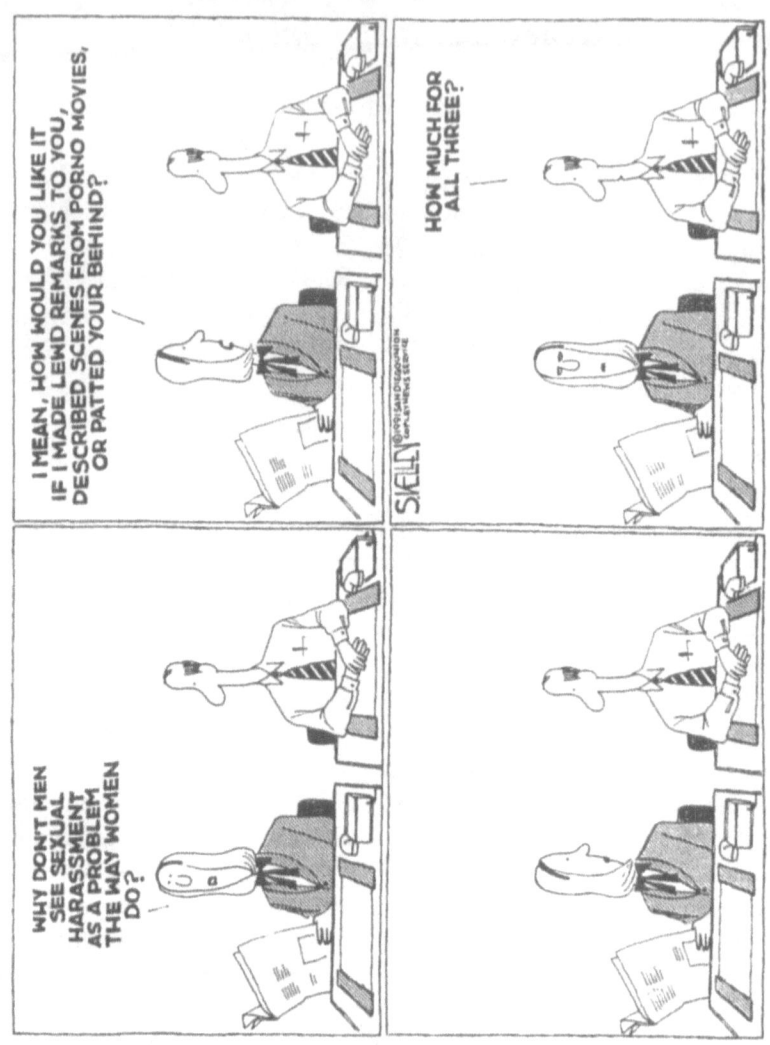

Steve Kelley (1991) *San Diego Union Tribune.* Reprinted with special permission of Copley News Service.

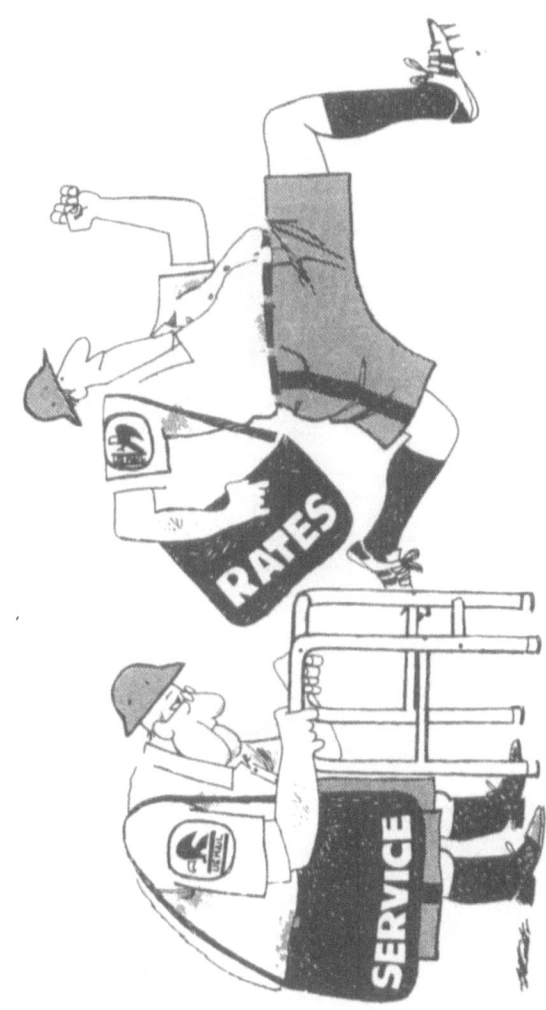

Steve Kelley (1994) *San Diego Union Tribune.* Reprinted with special permission of Copley News Service.

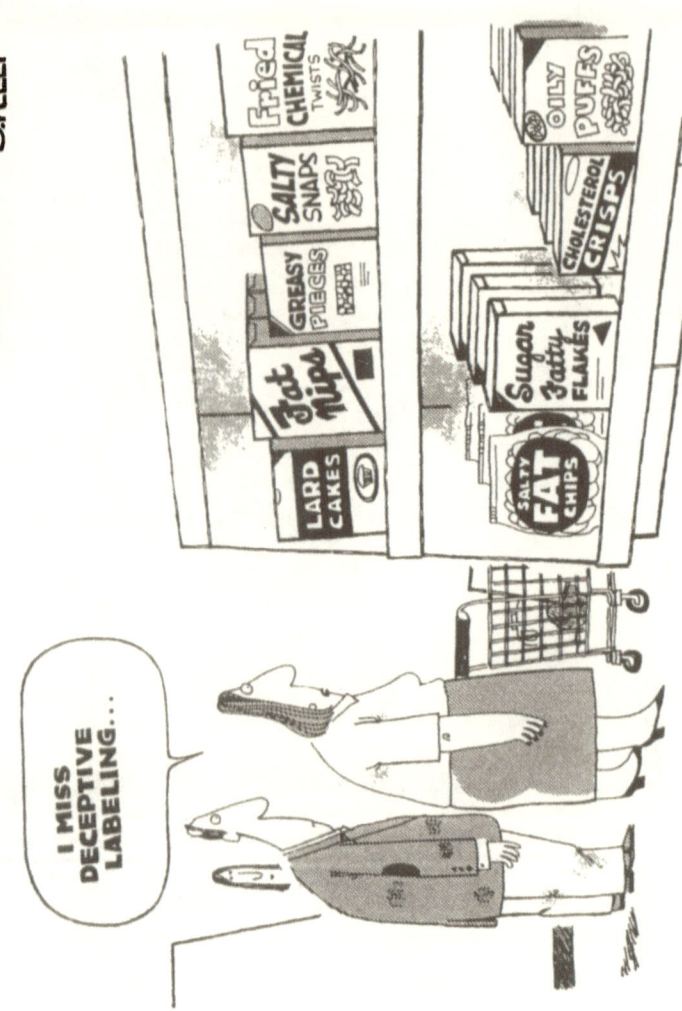

Steve Kelley (1994) *San Diego Union Tribune*. Reprinted with special permission of Copley News Service.

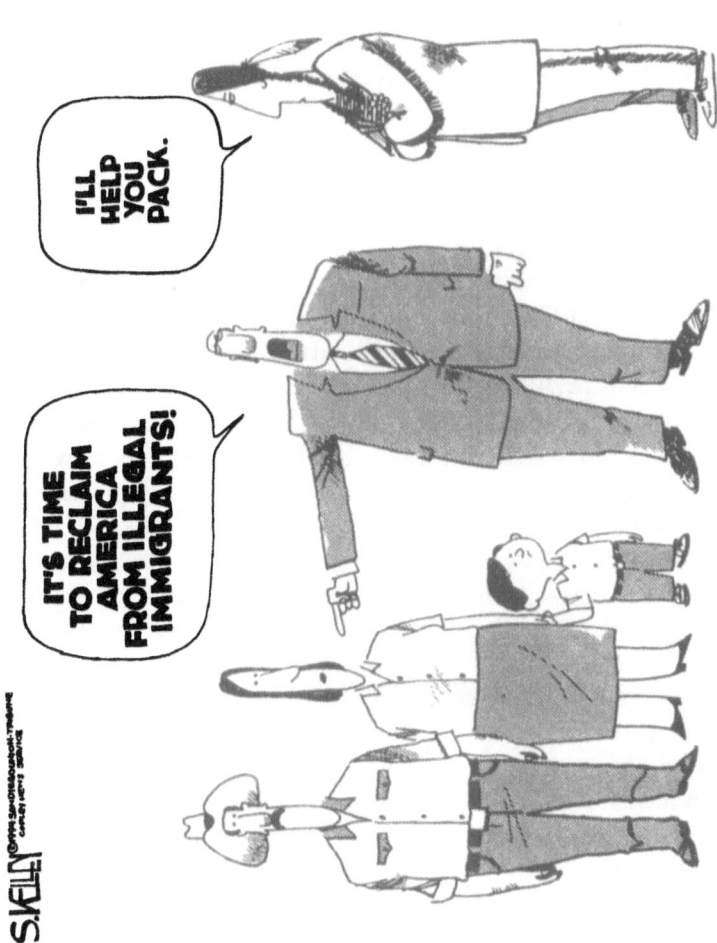

Steve Kelley (1994) *San Diego Union Tribune.* Reprinted with special permission of Copley News Service.

One of the measures of a humorous cartoon is that it does give the reader credit for that" (Kelley, Interview). Making light of a situation is not the same as dismissing its seriousness; rather, humor can be a catalyst for deeper reflection and discussion. Being portentous every day will not hold an audience, and might desensitize them.

A humorous approach rather than a preachy one encourages both cartoonist and reader to think further about complex or many-sided issues, to see that they don't have simplistic solutions, even to change their minds without being accused of ideological backsliding. For example, Kelley finds it impossible to express his feelings on the health care controversy within one cartoon or one consistent viewpoint. He believes that the nation needs a health care program, and that no one should be excluded; but no policy can provide indefinitely for all citizens, and a comprehensive national program would be ruinously expensive. So his cartoons on the subject illustrate his shifting perspectives (*National Forum* Aug. 7, 1994, 5; Dec. 4, 1994, 11; May 28, 1995, 6). He may ridicule groups that clamor for "undeserved" entitlements as lazy or self-righteous, and portray affirmative action literally as a crutch (*National Forum* Mar. 12, 1995, 17), but he also scorns those xenophobes who blame undocumented aliens exclusively for rising public expenditures (see illustration). Similarly, to Kelley the death penalty presents an issue that "I have very strong convictions about on both sides" (Harvey 48). Since he considers himself neither a political nor an ideological partisan, but rather an absurdity-sensitive opponent of stupidity, opinions offered through visual metaphor or dialogue punch line serve him better than do furious denunciations.

Using humorous cartoons for an offbeat approach has enabled him at times to outflank publisher, editor or syndicate-driven taboos about issues related to sexual or moral shibboleths such as gay lifestyles or gays in the military. At one point he was told point-blank not to do cartoons about abortion. However, he has gained approval for those that don't comment directly on legal questions, but instead remind readers about our very earthy and often hypocritically expressed drives, and their social consequences. Usually these are presented in multipanel stories, with a skipped beat or "take panel" just before the punch line (see illustration). By creating a ribald context, Kelley tries to play even such an otherwise horrific event as the 1994 bombings of abortion clinics for an instructive laugh. In this case, he had motorcycle daredevil Evel Knievel asking an abortion clinic nurse for *her* autograph (*National Forum* Jan. 22, 1995, 19).

Kelley will, in fact, avoid no issue, if it reflects current popular concerns and interests; he reads *USA Today* to confirm "what people are talking about." Even admittedly trivial, day-wonder faddish issues, precisely because they are so evanescent, provide cartoonists an unhackneyed context from which to work. Among the younger cartoonists with regular urban newspaper positions, he epitomizes clearly their willingness to broaden editorial coverage beyond the traditional parameters of government, diplomacy, public policy and partisan follies. For example, no prior cartoonist had, to Kelley's extent, discoursed so on editorial pages about health issues such as "wellness maintenance," nutrition and food content, and smoking in public places. Over the past two years, Kelley has also commented repeatedly on the greediness of sports figures and the tunnel vision of their fans, on celebrity vulgarities, dysfunctional families, the travails of commuter airlines, and the public's impatience with banalities of television programming. Sometimes, as in his juxtaposition of Rwandan starvation with a man incensed at forty grams of fat in a burrito (*National Forum* 7 Aug. 1994, 8), he intends ironic moral commentary; at other times, he is simply responding to our current obsession with quality of life issues. As a humorist, Kelley will not only address American foibles but usually try to present them in an unusual or arresting context. One example, captioned "As the Strike drags on, frustrated baseball fans roam the city," has a small crowd heckling a house painter using disparaging insults normally heard in a ballpark (*National Forum* Sept. 26, 1994, 20).

Using humor in editorial cartoons allows Kelley not only breadth of subject coverage but enables him to combine two or more topics in a single, versatile cartoon. Charles Brooks's 1994 edition of *Best Editorial Cartoons of the Year* included four by Kelley. One quoted a comment by President Clinton on his Iraq policy to raise the larger question of fudged 1992 campaign promises; a second deftly juxtaposed references to Medicare, Social Security and "suicide doctor" Jack Kevorkian within a single panel; a third reminded readers of two titillating and risible sex scandals of 1993 (Joey Buttafuoco's priapic misadventures and Lorena Bobbitt's "penisectomy" on an abusive husband) purely for comic effect; a fourth one used a toppled school bus as a visual metaphor for the possible effect of private school vouchers on public school education (Brooks, 32, 37, 130, 157).

Kelley's career as a stand-up comic shapes his newspaper art as well as his nightclub performances, not only in his always going for a laugh but in how he composes a cartoon. Until about 1990, his figures were drawn with thin lines, and he commonly caricatured national and world leaders, using a substantial amount of dialogue and an unremarkable lettering style. He has not since foresworn caricature and labeling of relatively unfamiliar figures; there are still donkeys and elephants rampant, and Speaker Newt Gingrich has been portrayed in a host of postures and situations. But in other respects, even compositionally, his cartoons are fundamentally different. He draws in pencil on Bristol board, and then traces the drawing in ink onto transparent vellum (wearing a photographer's dust glove), then photocopies it onto duoshade vellum, spray mounts the vellum onto bristolboard, and finally applies tone developer. Typically his single-panel cartoons will feature two or three figures representing common folk, often a husband and wife; they are posed either in profile or facing the reader in order to deliver their lines. Their conversations may either be reproduced or implied; that is, the punch line will be in response to a probable but unseen earlier remark. The figures are drawn in bold, thick outline and are anatomically indifferent, simply and even crudely executed; background details are spare. Captions or dialogue are lettered in thick, very heavily inked capitals. Kelley calls this "fast drawing," driven more by the idea than the art; it is also effectively eye-catching.

Similarly eye-catching is his offbeat use of visual metaphors. Sometimes, as he will admit, they do not quite click. Early in April 1994, in reaction to the announcement that "shock-jock" radio personality Howard Stern was considering running for governor of New York, Kelley drew the Statue of Liberty with a paper bag over her head, to communicate her shame. He told me that "I didn't know if it was going to work or not. To this day, I don't know if it did. In a sense it was dumb. You could never fit a bag over the head of the Statue of Liberty. She has a hat with all those points on it. A statue doesn't think or feel. It's one of those cartoons where either you get it and laugh at it or you don't" (Kelley, Interview). And one wonders how many readers, even now, will recognize the earlier-cited reference to Evel Knievel.

But usually Kelley is on safer ground drawing Disney characters, Charles Schulz's "Snoopy," or Superman, and using bad puns or relatively familiar metaphors such as crystal balls, glass ceilings and lame ducks—even quotations from classic comic routines such as Abbott and Costello's "Who's on First?" He reasons that the basis of a cartoon is to "take something that is known and distort it a little bit," and that this is as valid for popular culture icons as it historically has been for caricature or literary references. As he puts it, "Mr. Magoo is today's Hamlet!" When he feels particularly comfortable with an appropriated icon that is neither too sophisticated nor too simpleminded, he will use it or variations upon it a number of times. The Wizard of Oz is one of his favorites, and over the past year or so he had referred to it over a dozen times. From October 1994 through May 1995, I found three such quotations, from the Democrats' health reform proposals melting the Wicked

Witch of the West through a questionably effective association with the
Oklahoma City bombing (*National Forum* Oct. 29, 1994, 17; Feb. 19,
1995, 9; May 19, 1995, 3). And during the Christmas season, Santa
Claus was trotted out a half dozen times to comment cynically on illegal
immigrants, pay raises, tax cuts and (inevitably) the O. J. Simpson murder trial.

Another favorite technique, directly taken from standup comedy, is
the tag line, a repeated phrase associated with the performer and used in
a variety of situations. "Most jokes," he explains, "and many cartoons,
when broken down, conform to one of a dozen or so basic structures. We
just change the variables" (Harvey 41). Kelley has found the phrase "I
miss . . ." dependable, and over a six-month period he either "missed"
voter apathy (incumbents imperiled), the Middle East (assassins firing at
the White House) or (see illustration) "deceptive labeling."

Whether using single or multipanel cartoons, tag lines or punch
lines, whole or completed exchanges, and even in dialogueless cartoons
such as "Service Rates" (see illustration), as you read them from left to
right, there is a skipped beat, visual and/or verbal, between the "set-up"
character or situation, and the punch-line character. Therein lies the tim-
ing of the standup comic, and when it works, Kelley believes that one
can even hear a drummer's rimshot punctuating the joke.

Steven Kelley is obviously a realist about the economics of his profession; the decline in positions due to daily papers folding or merging
makes cartooning seem like a game of "musical chairs" (Harvey 49). So
the wise cartoonist sells papers and become indispensable both to the
organization which employs him and the syndicate which distributes his
work. He draws and writes to communicate with a mass audience, not to
impress his peers, and likens himself to other cartoonists whose work is
criticized by students but loved by consumers. At the same time, he is
convinced that what he does is "brain work," and whimsically likens his
art to physics. "I believe there's a certain theory of relativity about political cartooning; force equals mass times acceleration. The mass would be
how many people turn to see what you've done that day" (Harvey 42).
So Kelley's humor is the result, not the abrogation, of serious knowledge
and intent: "If you force enough information in one end, something
funny will come out the other end" (Kelley, Interview).

Sources

Brooks, Charles, ed. *Best Editorial Cartoons of the Year 1994.* Gretna, LA:
Pelican, 1995.

Harvey, Robert C. "Cartooning and Comedy with Steve Kelley." *Cartoonist Profiles* 108 (Dec. 1995): 40-49.

Kelley, Steve. Interview. By Kalman Goldstein. 10 Jan. 1995.

——. *Steve Kelley's Greatest Hits*. San Diego: Union Tribune, 1996.

National Forum Gallery of Cartoons. Washington, D.C., weekly.

12

Chan Lowe, *Fort Lauderdale Sun-Sentinel*

S. L. Harrison

Chan Lowe, one of the nation's most promising cartoonists, is feature editorial artist for the *Sun-Sentinel*. Lowe's career began in 1975, in Oklahoma with the *Shawnee News-Star*, where he drew Sunday supplement covers and editorial graphs, maps and charts and contributed his after-work-hours editorial cartoons. These are the kinds of graphic work chores associated with the apprenticeship of past generations of newspaper artists, but it was sound experience and he remained in Shawnee through 1978. His next newspaper job was with the *Oklahoman and Times* that year. Writing ability more than artistic talent provided the ticket to this position. Lowe began as a feature writer although he also drew three editorial cartoons a week. His main task was writing, however; in addition to his feature stories, Lowe occasionally wrote music criticism and regularly contributed a television column. After three months, he began to concentrate more on drawing cartoons, even while continuing his television column. However, the *Times* folded in 1984. He then decided to reverse Horace Greeley's famous advice and went back East. For the prior decade Florida had been the fastest-growing state in the union and prospects looked more inviting. So Lowe quickly found a niche with the *Fort Lauderdale News and Sun-Sentinel*. He and the paper, now simply the *Sun-Sentinel*, are both prospering.

He considers his editorial cartoons much the way an independent columnist views his work: they contain his personal statements about things political and social, in art rather than words. The cartoons bear his signature, and reflect views which are not necessarily those of his newspaper. He draws what he wants to draw and when he wants to draw it. Lowe is a member of the newspaper's editorial board, helping to set policy, but they do not dictate subject matter for the editorial cartoon. In fact, shortly after joining the Fort Lauderdale paper Lowe was quoted as convinced that, while most editors consider cartoonists prima donnas, they have insufficient appreciation for the effort "and frequent panic" involved in editorial cartoonists' "pulling a usable idea out of the ether" (Lowe, Interview). So, at least in the past, he had fumed while an editor

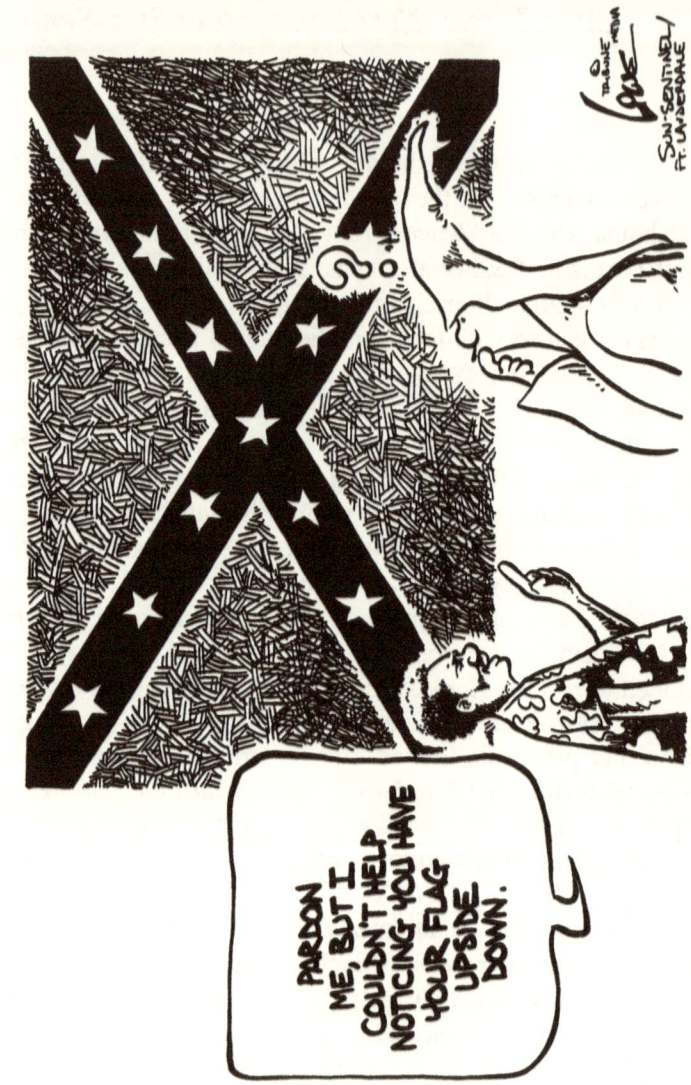

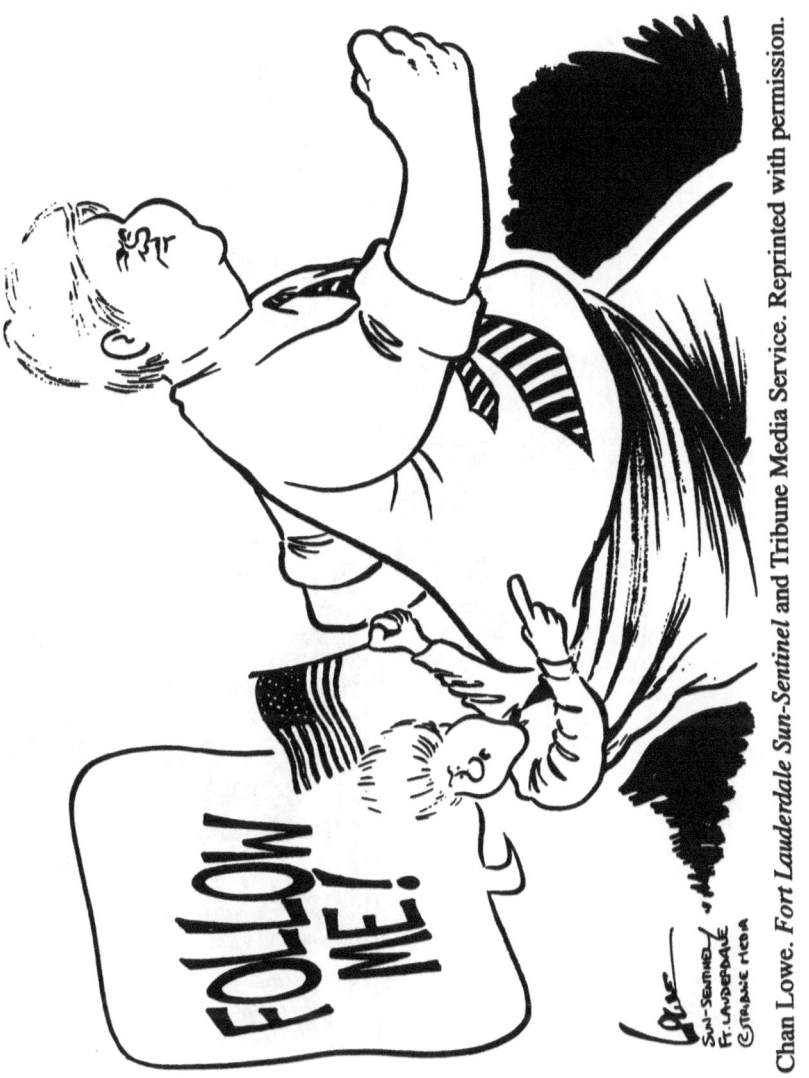

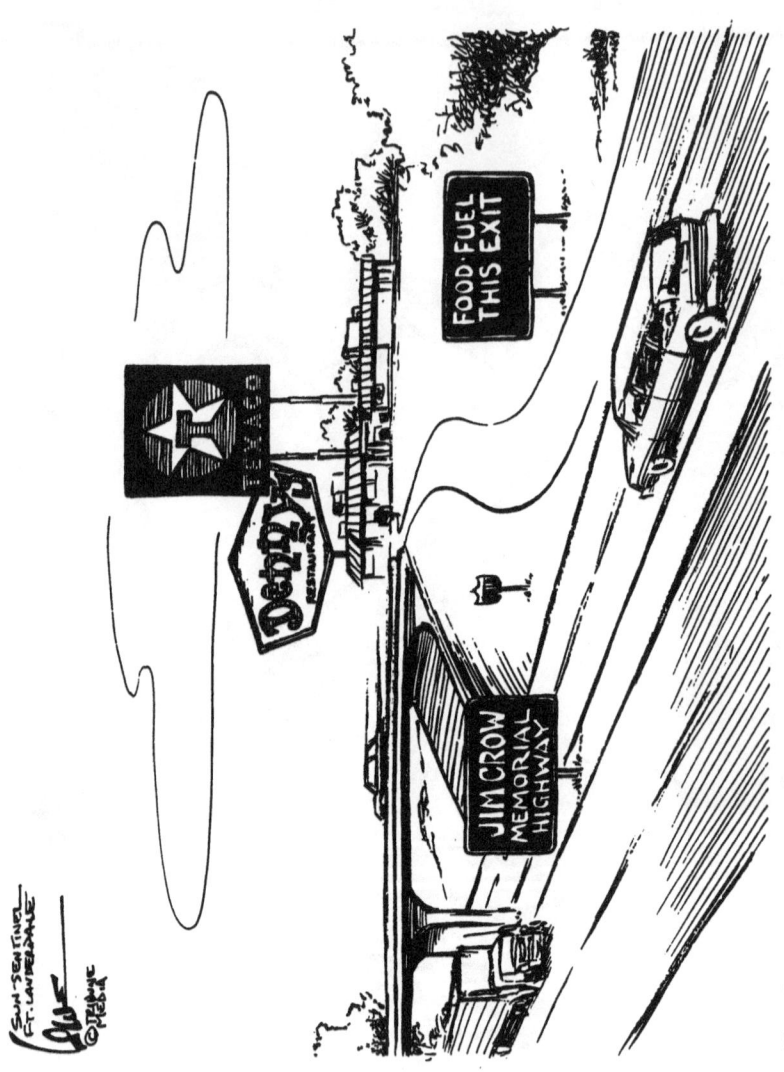

Chan Lowe. *Fort Lauderdale Sun-Sentinel* and Tribune Media Service. Reprinted with permission.

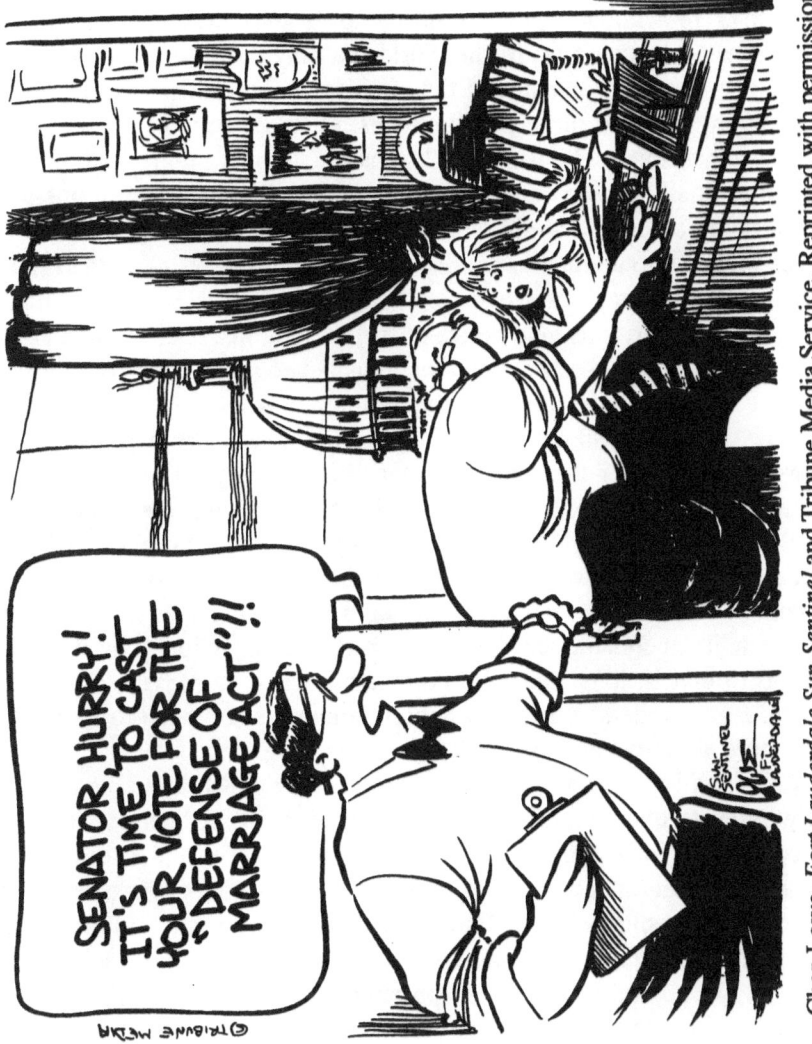

mucked about with one of his roughs, "wanting to change a little word here, soften something there, and sort of get their thumb in the pie" (Lowe 75). Apparently, Lowe no longer suffers from such intrusive supervision of his work, or is now associated with an editor whose reasoned opinions help rather than hinder artistic creativity.

Lowe, a self-confessed "news junkie," describes his working day as lengthy. He acknowledges that he spends a good deal of time catching up on what is going on in the world; he may spend almost half a day doing so. He reads as many of the morning newspapers as he can lay his hands on and from these compiles a list of topics suitable for a cartoon. He watches some television and listens to National Public Radio. When he does finally decide on a subject, Lowe sketches a number of possibilities, being careful to avoid what he calls "Cartoonist's Night-mare" (an idea identical to another cartoonist's, but run a day later), and then shows these to his editor (Lowe, Interview).

Lowe's cartoons take notice of the international scene, when appropriate, but he focuses attention on national events and points of view that affect the average reader directly. While any selection of his cartoons likely will deal with a variety of topics, he intends and hopes that none are too arcane for the typical reader. For as every editor knows, subscribers have opinions, and don't relish either having their intelligence belittled or topics of interest to them ignored. And he has in the past observed that his area of the country boasts a large concentration of senior citizens who tend to remain avid newspaper readers. They may provide a dependable and large audience, but may equally be depended upon to call in long and loud complaints when so moved. Obviously, then, Lowe understands that a lighter, humorous approach to issues will be more attractive and effective than a hectoring one.

When Lowe comments on a complex or ticklish issue, he does not try either to oversimplify or to preach. For example: busing, which has been around for a generation, has still not solved the troublesome dilemma of integration and has even added to the difficulties of education. His take on this topic makes that fact crystal clear. The cartoon in this article, presented as *reductio ad absurdum,* has the schoolroom—teacher, desk, globe, blackboard and all—transported onto the bus for a mobile schoolday. This is not the commentary of a bleeding-heart liberal but a mind that looks with ironic comment on a cause gone wrong.

Lowe's editorial views on another "lost cause" are perhaps more in line with what a liberal view might produce. His sly portrayal of a black man confounding a low-IQ Klansman while deflating the Confederate Battle Flag's image provides a focal point for a visceral issue, but one posed more palatably by containing deliciously barbed humor. And that kind of humor pervades many of Lowe's cartoons. He may picture a self-righteous Navy admiral, congratulating himself for uprightness during the Tailhook scandal, but trailing a brassiere on his coattails. Or show a Senatorial paladin of "family values" interrupted by an aide while in mid-assault on his secretary.

However, there are also times when more serious condemnations are called for. And so Lowe shows the logos of Denny's restaurant chain and Texaco, both recently accused of corporate racism, as roadside services on the "Jim Crow Highway," thus compiling and associating references to social archaism.

Lowe's cartoon simultaneously deriding President Clinton's inability to lead and House Speaker Newt Gingrich's huffing and puffing, manages with a few penstrokes to identify the subjects and portray their character and relationship, without those conveniently attached labels which seem so necessary to many other editorial cartoons. The tag line: "Follow me!" could as easily have been its caption, rather than a talk balloon. But this is Lowe's style, along with an economy of approach that makes his art so effective.

Such subjects provide only part of his range, for Lowe never forgets that an editorial cartoonist has an obligation to comment on local events as well. Every newspaper, no matter its national reputation, is a community enterprise that reports on local and state issues as well as the more "profound" national or international events. Accordingly, Lowe has satirized the proclivity of Florida as well as other states to issue special-issue auto license plates that celebrate local schools, places, mottoes, or historic events (and also make additional revenue for state coffers). His solution, typically, contains more burlesque than outrage, showing people yelling "Enough Already!" at the ludicrous vanity plates.

Once he has decided on content and context for his cartoon, its actual drawing time takes about two to three hours. Lowe works with brush and pen and ink on a thin Bristol board 9" x 11" and takes his drawings right to the border. Typically, his cartoons contain a lot of pen-and-ink cross-hatches with an eye focus of black, and dialogue enclosed in balloons, as in a comic strip panel. Lowe does not expend a lot of energy discussing the execution of his art—the cartoon speaks for itself; it's the planning and preparation that he believes makes an effective statement. Once he's completed his cartoon, his evenings are spent in more television watching and more listening to National Public Radio; his pursuits are cerebral (Lowe, Interview).

Lowe's intellectual capacity was recognized when he was one of the recipients of the John S. Knight Fellowship in 1993 and took a sabbatical to pursue academic interests at Stanford University in Palo Alto,

California. The *Sun-Sentinel* allowed him time off and temporarily filled its editorial page with syndicated material. Lowe's talents have been recognized with a number of other awards: in 1992, he won the Sigma Delta Chi Green Eyeshade and in 1990 he was a finalist for the Pulitzer Prize. He won second place in the 1996 Fischetti Awards.

Chan Lowe was born in New York City in 1953 but grew up in Los Angeles. He knew at an early age that he wanted to be an editorial cartoonist; then and now, he especially admired the work of Paul Conrad and Pat Oliphant. During high school, Lowe began his cartoon work for his school newspaper, and did the same at Williams College (B.A. 1975), while majoring in art history. So he's shared the earlier experiences of many other cartoonists, including striking out on his own to pursue a career in a enterprise that has witnessed its share of business failures.

Lowe returned to Williams early in 1997 to teach a brief course in editorial cartooning, an experience that left him with high hopes for the future of the profession. The newspaper in modern America has to compete with a variety of media, and the habit of reading is eroding among a population on the run, with a short attention span. But Lowe's cartoons, with their prominent place on the editorial page, and wide distribution through the Tribune syndicate, are compelling and vital. Chan Lowe has a promising future in a competitive industry.

Sources

Harrison, S. L. *Florida's Editorial Cartoonists.* Sarasota: Pineapple, 1996.
Lowe, Chan. "Get the Lowe Down." *Cartoonist Profiles* 70 (June 1986): 74-78.
——. Interview. By S. L. Harrison. Jan.-Feb. 1997.

13

Michael Edward Luckovich,
Atlanta Journal/Constitution

Kerry Soper

Mike Luckovich is a person of striking contrasts. His personal appearance is impeccable—he's thin, athletic, and dresses in vintage suits, ties, and flashy two-toned shoes. His working environment, however, is messy and chaotic—there are scraps of paper and cartoons spread on every available surface and littered across the floor. Luckovich also presents a dichotomous personality. On the one hand, he is very polite and kind in personal conversation, is given to self-deprecation, and walks and gestures in a youthful, energetic manner; on the other hand, when you get him talking on subjects about which he is passionate, he can exhibit an intensity and mischievousness that resemble the sardonic, biting persona he projects in his hard-hitting cartoons.

This combination of good-natured civility, and subversive, world-wise confidence is perhaps an ideal character composition for an editorial cartoonist. In Luckovich's case, it allows him to create cartoons that are sharp, funny and biting, but that are also grounded by a compassionate, consistent political vision. Having come from a privileged, middle-class background, Luckovich has felt an obligation in his work to champion the causes of the poor and underprivileged. He takes pleasure in creating cartoons that make people laugh, but feels that a satirist's most effective work is that which mounts a humorous attack in the name of those who don't have a voice in society. He has the following to say about this combination of humor and pointed commentary: "I really try to use my humor not gratuitously but to actually get a point across. Humor makes cartoons more fun and easier to read. You can make it very hard-hitting, but humor sweetens it. Even those who disagree may pay more attention to it" (Bookman B8).

Luckovich's sense of responsibility toward people with little power or voice has garnered him the respect of his colleagues, who awarded him the Robert F. Kennedy cartooning prize for championing the causes of the poor and underprivileged in 1994, and nominated him as a runner-

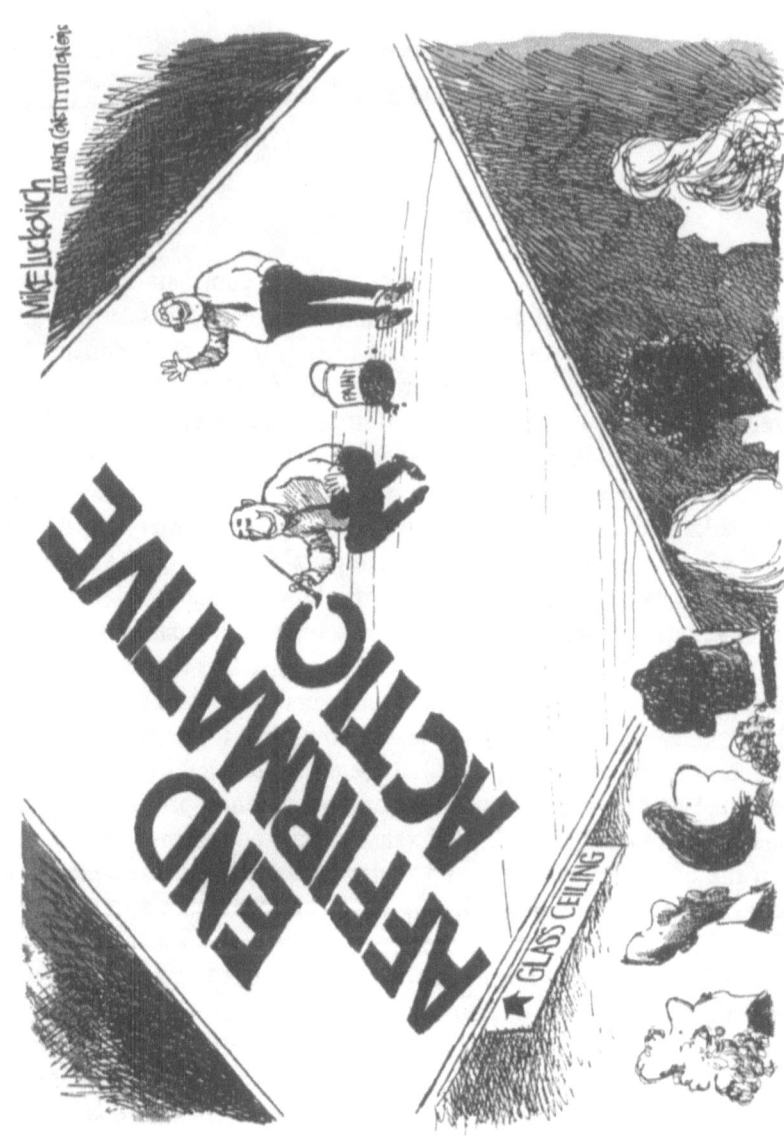

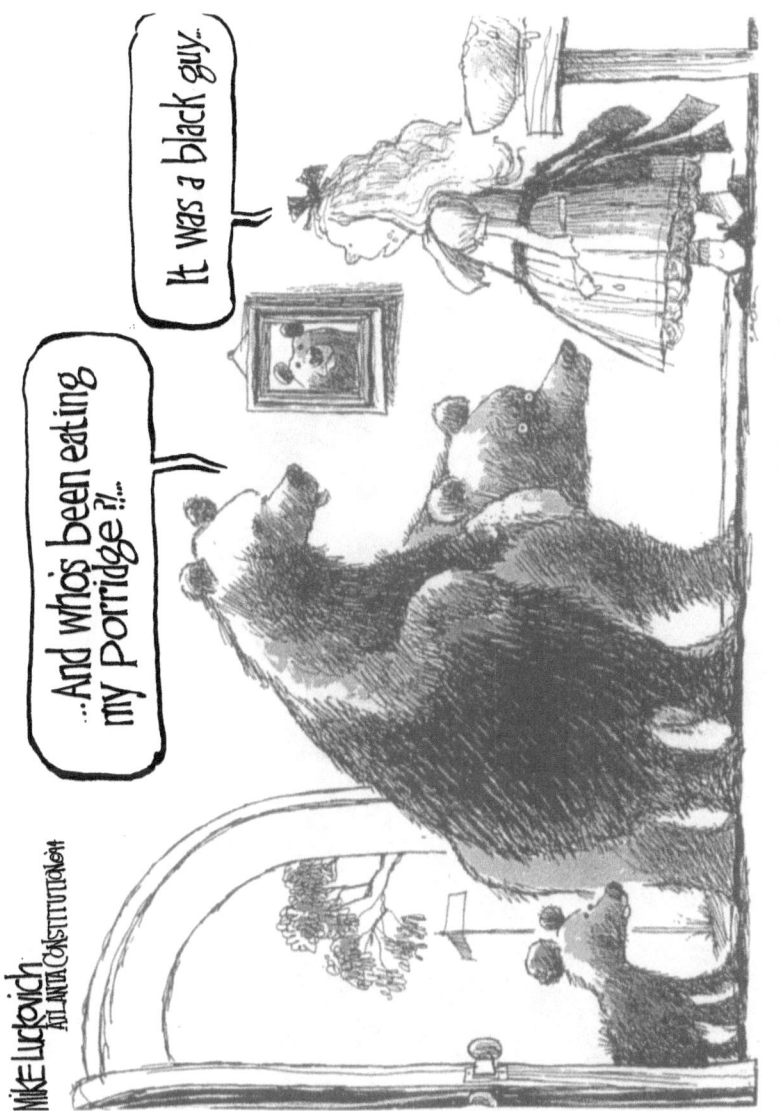

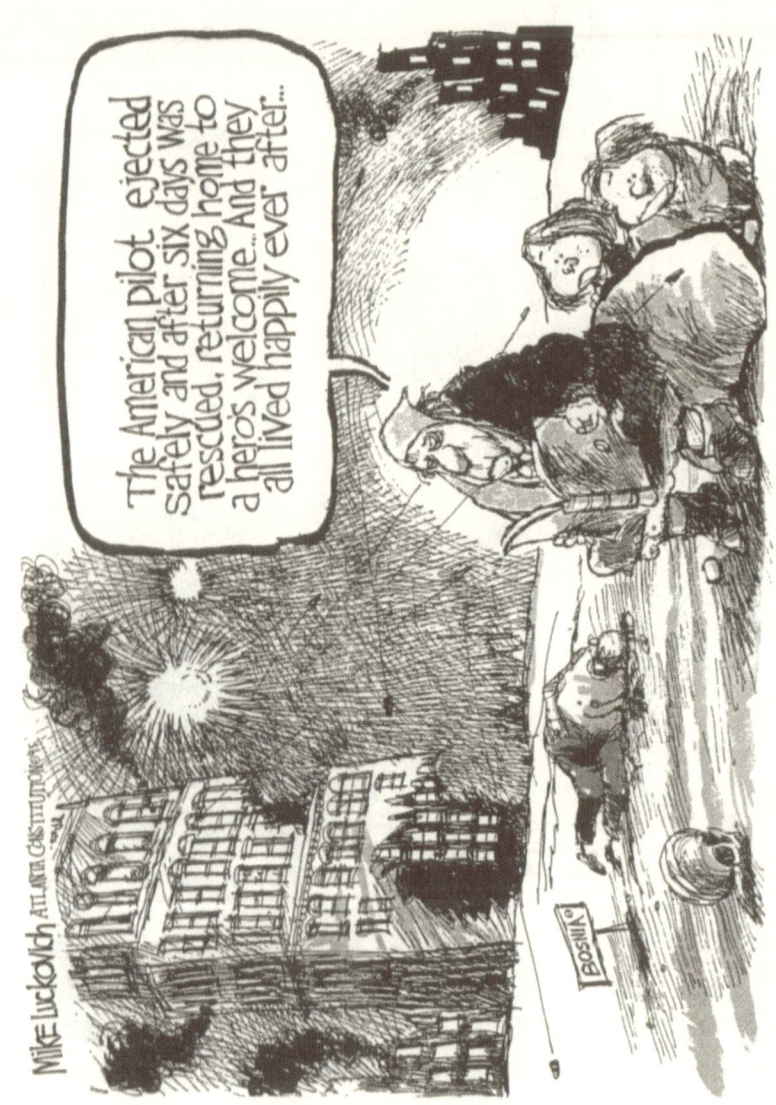

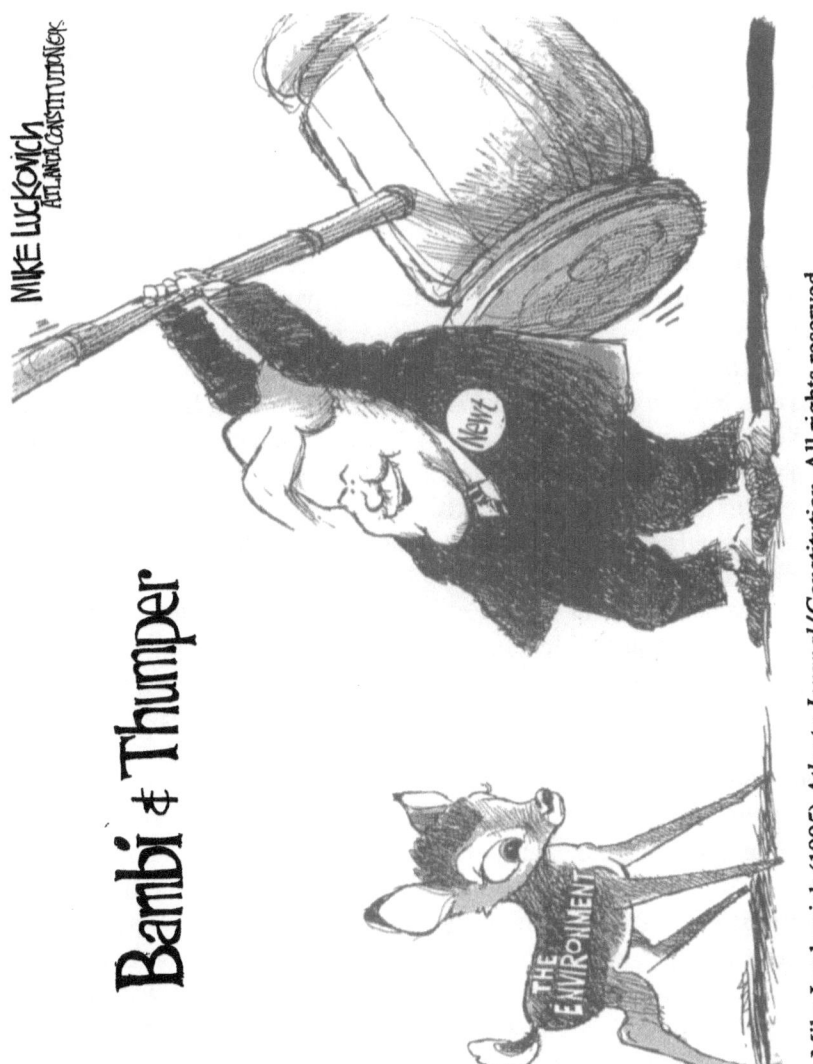

up for the same distinction in 1995. In recent years he has also won the Overseas Press Club award, 1990, 1994, and the National Headliner award, 1992. For many years his colleagues and fans also considered him the top prospect to receive the Pulitzer Prize. In 1986 he was a runner-up for the award, but in the subsequent years Luckovich began to tire of receiving condolences time after time when he was passed over, and eventually just wanted to receive the award to "get the monkey off his back." He finally received this honor in 1995, and now feels that he can actually "relax a little" (Bennet B8).

It is fitting that Luckovich should finally feel that he can breathe a little easier at the prime of his career since he worked so doggedly from an early age on to reach this goal. Born January 28, 1960, in Seattle to John and Marilyn Luckovich, Mike knew from a very early age that he wanted to be a professional cartoonist. His parents were happy to watch their son pursue a vocation he enjoyed, but did not take an especially active role in molding his goals. Luckovich acknowledges, however, the passive influence of an artistic mother and humorous father on the early development of his skills. Growing up, Mike attended schools in Boise Idaho, Eugene Oregon, and Seattle since his father was often transferred throughout the Northeast by ARCO, his employer. In each new school Mike made friends easily and entertained classmates with his cartooning ability. It wasn't until Mike attended the University of Washington, however, that he began to get his work published and started to work seriously toward a professional career. The school paper provided an excellent training ground since it imposed deadlines and demanded that his work be suitably polished for a large audience. Because Luckovich's political vision had not thoroughly developed at this point, his satire tended to have a middle-of-the-road quality that rarely upset readers.

Luckovich also exercised his drawing skills (and funded his education) by rendering caricatures of tourists beneath the Seattle space needle as a part-time job. He complemented this informal, artistic training with the pursuit of a degree in political science. College was an enjoyable experience for him, but Luckovich relates that he had a sort of epiphany/ rude awakening his junior year when he realized that he wasn't capable of being anything other than a cartoonist in life, and so somehow he had to make his professional goals work out. This insight was pivotal—from then on he devoted himself with a passion to his work (Luckovich, Interview).

Despite Luckovich's resolve and hard work during these years in training, he met with two years of rejection after graduating from college. He sent hundreds of résumés and portfolios to newspapers, but found that there were simply no openings. By this time Luckovich had married and started a family and was forced to sell life insurance from door to door in order to make ends meet. During this difficult period he would spend three days on the road doing insurance sales, and then devote the rest of the week to his cartooning. A break finally arrived when, while driving around to his insurance appointments in his old Pinto, Luckovich noticed an ad in the classified section of *Editor & Publisher* that indicated a newspaper in Greenville, South Carolina, was looking for a cartoonist. He got the job and was soon heading across country with his family, ecstatic that he had finally landed a job in his chosen profession (Luckovich, Interview).

Greenville was not a particularly easy experience for Luckovich and his wife. They were accustomed to the city life of Seattle and found their new area to be a bit slow and provincial for their taste. The people were friendly, but Mike and his wife did not feel that they fit into the social environment. At the paper Luckovich continued to pursue a gentle, middle-of-road-brand of satire, but still had difficulty dealing with an extremely demanding and hard-to-please editor. This situation ended, nine months later, when Luckovich landed a job at a paper in New Orleans. The new location and job were enjoyable, and he cites his four years there as the period when his political vision matured and he gained the confidence to be more confrontational and hard-hitting. From New Orleans Luckovich went to the *Atlanta Journal/Constitution* where he has been for the last four years (Luckovich, Interview).

With the arrival of the Olympics in Atlanta, Newt Gingrich's rise to power, and a spate of national and local controversies in the last year, Luckovich has not had difficulty finding worthy targets. He seems to thrive in the thick of controversy, and his most brilliant recent work does not shy from difficult or delicate topics. *Newsweek* ran a readers' poll at the end of last year and Luckovich's treatment of the Susan Smith case, and resulting media attention, came out as the favorite cartoon of the year. Another cartoon that created a stir was his depiction of Newt asking for a divorce from his wife (in this metaphorical reworking of real life events his wife represents his Georgia constituents), while wrapping his arms around two "D.C. Highroller" floozies. Since most politicians tend to ignore a cartoon that attacks them, or if they do notice it, call and ask for the original, Luckovich was delighted when Newt displayed his anger at the cartoon to a national audience, and vowed from that point forward to ignore all reporters from the Atlanta paper. A political cartoonist, according to Luckovich, could not ask for better publicity and reward than threats like this (Luckovich, Interview). He has received plenty of less welcome threats too, however. In 1992, hundreds of people wrote or called to the paper to protest a cartoon that juxtaposed a drawing of a stadium flying a Nazi flag labeled "Berlin Olympics 1936," and another flying the Georgia state (Dixie) flag with the caption "Atlanta Olympics 1996." Several of the angry callers who got through to Lukovich even promised "to take necessary measures," or gave other similar, thinly veiled death threats (Walburn 86.)

Although he considers himself somewhat of a moderate, and does not want to pigeonhole himself by aligning with either dominant political party, Luckovich is obviously in sync with the left-of-center orientation of his paper's editorial staff, and is not afraid to express his distaste for the political principles touted by Gingrich and many conservative members of Congress. He says he can respect people from any point of the political spectrum if they have a strong conviction and back it up, but he finds the extreme conservatism, characterized by xenophobia, an insouciance for the plight of the poor, and a self-righteous hypocrisy, to be especially "stupid" and narrow-minded. He understands the appeal this brand of politics has to many people since it reduces difficult social problems to pat answers, but feels that he should play a small role in rebutting these simplistic social remedies. He attempts to do this by representing those people who would suffer most in Gingrich's vision of America—the poor who are blamed for their poverty, but in reality do not have the tools and opportunities necessary to simply "go for" the mythical, American dream. Luckovich does not claim to have all the answers to these issues, and acknowledges that there are problems with the present welfare state, but believes that ignoring the poor will only exacerbate the nation's problems. Job training, at least, could be a better approach to reforming the welfare system than simply cutting people off (Luckovich, Interview).

Like many political cartoonists, Luckovich is essentially self-taught. He admired and tried to emulate the work of Mort Drucker (*Mad* magazine), Jeff MacNelly and Pat Oliphant in his college years, but cannot point to any significant mentors. While working as an insurance agent, and doing cartoons in his free time, he sent letters asking for advice to Jim Borgman, Mike Peters, and Don Wright. Although he did not get to know any of them personally at that time, he was thrilled to receive their encouraging responses. That they would take the time to write back convinced him that he had some promise and should keep looking for work.

His lack of formal art training could explain his unusual style and working habits. After conceptualizing and "seeing" the cartoon in his mind he transfers the image directly to the drawing board without any pencil sketching or layouts. He occasionally has to restart the cartoon when an initial line or shape doesn't look right, but says that generally the images flow with little difficulty from his mind to the page. This accelerated, spontaneous mode of working allows him to devote more time to refining his concepts and even getting a head start on the next day's piece. He generally does not even begin his cartoon until after he has had lunch. A mechanical, drafting pen is his principal drawing tool, but he also occasionally employs "brush-pens" for thicker lines and large areas of black. Gray tones are created with the help of duo-tone paper that reveals a medium, screened shade, or dark cross-hatching depending on which of two chemicals are brushed on the surface of the drawing.

Luckovich laments that he is swamped with too many extra projects since he won the Pulitzer and so has little time for recreation, but relates that in the past his accelerated working style allowed him to have a relative amount of free time to pursue hobbies and be with his family. He continues to work out three mornings a week at the gym, with an intensity and "surly attitude" that might scare the people with whom he shares his exercise space. He admits that he does not really enjoy this workout in the normal sense of having fun, but attests that he gains a sense of accomplishment and physical rush *after* he's done. At work he is more jovial—joking with the writers on the editorial staff and given to leaving odd messages on his answering machine. Two recent installments: "I've been temporarily sent home for poor hygiene, but I'll return your call as soon as they allow me to return," and "I'm asleep under my desk right now, but I'll be sure to call you when I wake up." When time permits, he browses through vintage clothing stores, trying to add to his collection of unique suits, ties and shoes. His semi-vintage car—a 1970 Mercedes convertible—also gives him a release from his pressures at work. Luckovich states that his greatest, pleasure, nevertheless, is spending time with his wife, Margo, and three children, John, Mickey, and Micaela.

Luckovich may not be the cleanest, most talented draftsman among his peers—indeed, the figures in his cartoons occasionally exhibit a sketchy, lumpy, half-baked quality; but what he lacks in visual virtuosity is made up for in the sharp and consistently accurate use of satire in his concepts and writing. In all of his work it is obvious that he has attempted to refine his concept until it effectively addresses the core incongruities, foolishness, or absurdity of an individual or issue. His seeming carelessness with the visual elements of his cartoons may even *enhance* the impact of his work since the reader's eye is attracted to the central metaphor, or "point" of the cartoon and is not distracted by careful—but peripheral—aesthetic flourishes that are often employed by other prominent cartoonists. In other words, there is nothing precious or self-congratulatory about his style—it is the equivalent of a working-class aesthetic that pulls no punches and does not get sidetracked by formal concerns in the pursuit of making a strong point. Luckovich's greatest strength—validated by his professional awards—is his ability to harness a consistent, compassionate political vision to a powerful mix of indignation and humor. Much like the disparate facets of Luckovich's personal character, these seemingly contradictory sides of his work—the serious integrity of his vision, and the playful, mischievous use of humor in his cartoons—combine synergistically to create excellent satire.

Sources

Bennet, Tom. "Luckovich Wit Always Sharp, Say Admirers." *Atlanta Journal/Constitution* 19 Apr. 1995.

Bookman, Jay. "Friendliness, Rambunctious Style of Work Suit Him Fine." *Atlanta Journal/Constitution* 19 Apr. 1995.

Luckovich, Michael E. Interview. By Kerry Soper. 28 July 1995.

Walburn, Steve. "Drawing Blood." *Atlanta Magazine* Oct. 1992.

14

Jimmy Margulies, *(Bergen County) Record*

Jack Colldeweih

"Wild and crazy" are not the words that come to mind upon meeting *Bergen Record* editorial cartoonist Jimmy Margulies. Neat and conservative in appearance, soft-spoken and careful in manner, he hardly looks the part of the one-time antiwar demonstrator and activist he was in his youth. Yet the habit of protesting the abuses and folly he sees has not changed, only the means; he now uses brush and paper in place of placards and marches. In addition, this Brooklyn, New York, native (born Oct. 8, 1951) has developed a much more incisive style of commentary than the proverbial Brooklyn raspberry. Despite his own reservations about his art, Margulies drawings use strong, bold strokes to create images honed by the text to cut precisely and deeply. He is morally and intellectually honest in refusing to avoid any issue, no matter how touchy, a stance that has caused him some trouble from time to time. His targets may complain, but there are rarely charges of unfairness, even when dealing with his primary bete noirs: intolerance and racism. Barbed though they may be, his points are tipped with humor, not venom.

A flair for the arts was common in the Margulies family: his father, Henry, was a graphic designer; his mother, Miriam, and an uncle were both fashion artists; his father's cousin was a founding partner of an industrial design firm. Margulies seemed destined therefore to study for a career in some area of graphic arts. While Carnegie Mellon was "a hotbed of rest," atypical of the volatility of campus life in the late 1960s and early 1970s, Margulies was fully involved with protesting the Vietnam War, among other causes, often driving fellow protestors to Washington, D.C., in his VW van. He also drew editorial cartoons for the campus newspaper, switching his major from architecture to graphic design. Cartooning thus encapsulated a combination of all the things that really interested him: politics, humor, and art. His parents were very accepting and supportive of his career choice, although the university was rather less so; consequently, Margulies is generally unresponsive to appeals for alumni donations.

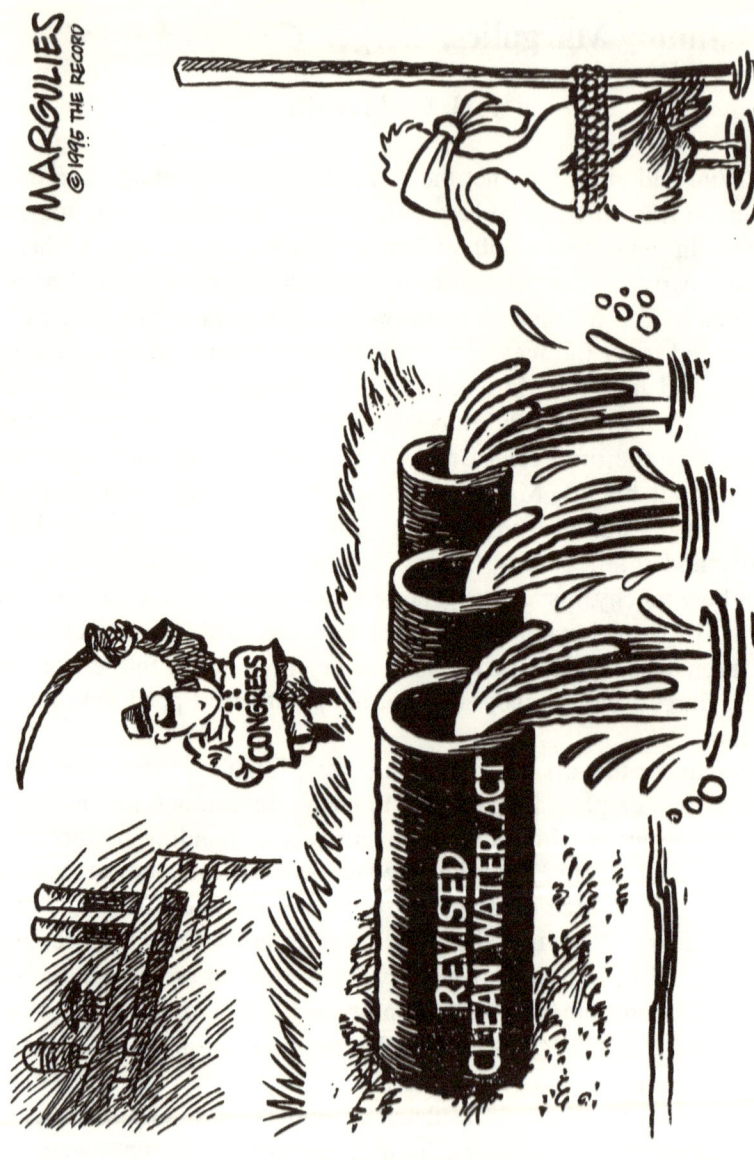

Jimmy Margulies (1995) *(Bergen County) Record.* Reprinted with special permission of North American Syndicate.

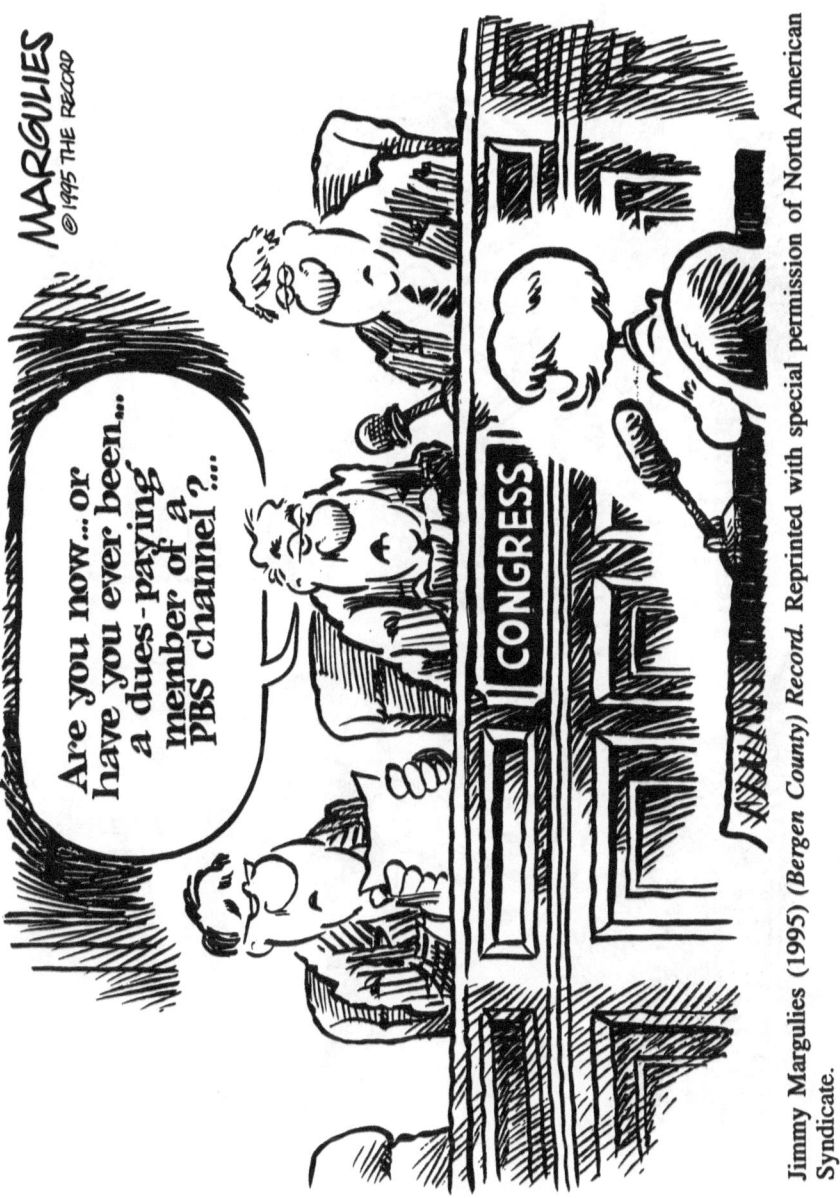

Jimmy Margulies (1995) *(Bergen County) Record.* Reprinted with special permission of North American Syndicate.

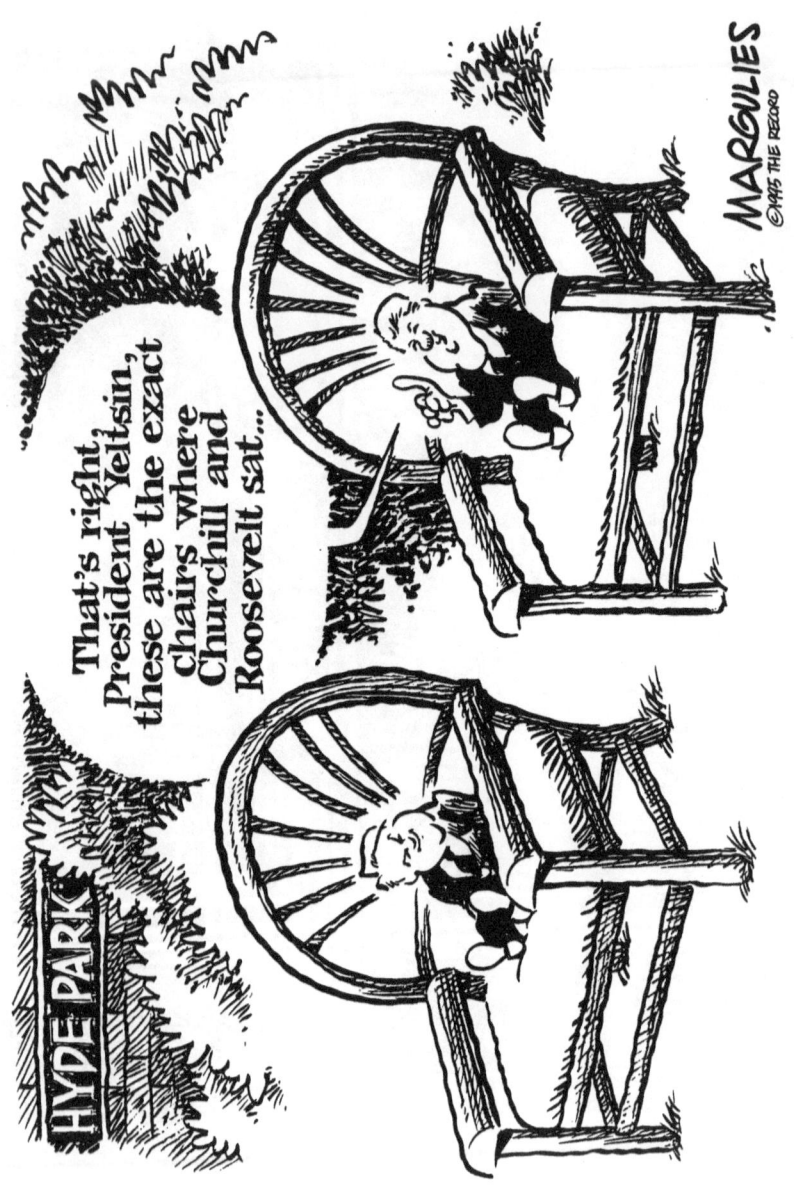

Jimmy Margulies (1995) *(Bergen County) Record.* Reprinted with special permission of North American Syndicate.

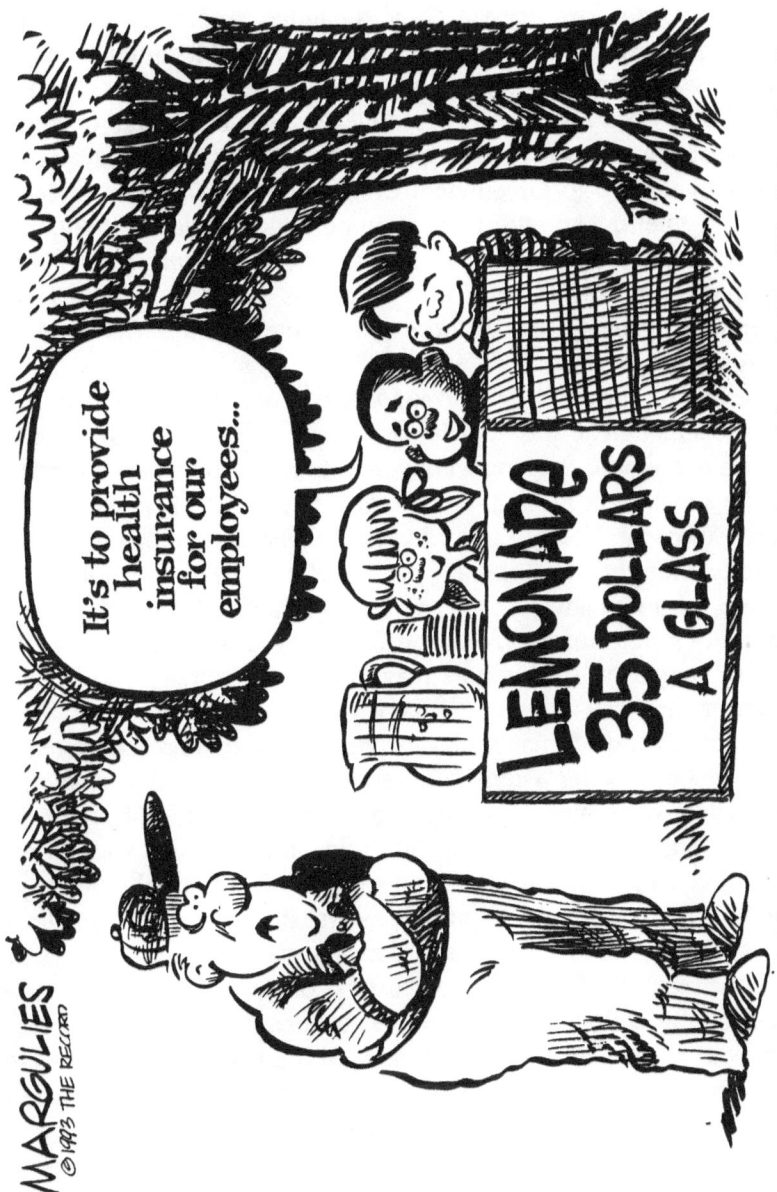

Jimmy Margulies (1995) *(Bergen County) Record.* Reprinted with special permission of North American Syndicate.

After graduation he began drawing for Rothco Cartoons, a small distribution company, for the exposure. He also got a job with CETA, a federal program that paid artists to be cultural resources for the urban underprivileged. As a free-lancer, he submitted cartoons to a New Jersey suburban newspaper, the *(Bergen County) Record,* a fortunate step that later proved fateful in helping him gain his current position there. The portfolio of work he assembled in college was good enough to convince cartoonist Ranan Lurie to take Margulies under his wing and apprentice him at his studio in Greenwich, Connecticut, giving him advice and encouragement. The additional training and experience there, and at Rothco and the *Record,* led to the ironic job at *Army Times Journal Newspapers* in Washington, D.C.; he claims that it "felt weird to work for military papers after all those years protesting the Viet Nam War" (Margulies, Interview).

Drawing for the *Journal Newspapers* a year later, he felt frustrated because although he was at the nation's capital, he was restricted to local politics and issues. Seeking an opportunity to do some national cartooning, he sought a position at the *Houston Post,* which had just been purchased from the Hobby family by the *Toronto Sun* company. Although initially thought too "liberal" for the *Post* by *Sun* cartoonist Andy Donato, who was advising the paper to seek a "moderate conservative," Margulies sent a "toned down" portfolio and got the job.

Although the *Post* editors may have been apprehensive about the reception their new cartoonist's work would receive, they never tried to influence his subject matter or viewpoint, and only once interfered with his efforts after submission—one cartoon that dealt with a local citizen was censored because it was seen as unfair. Margulies's urban, East-Coast liberal viewpoint did stir things up, at a paper that had not previously had a staff cartoonist and consequently had run only bland syndicated cartoons, but it also captured readers' attention. A 1985 *Post* reader survey found that 61.6% of the respondents said that they "always read" him (Bennett 12). He never had to fend off lawsuits, but threats were occasionally called in to his editors. Ironically, his "most unpleasant experience" there as a cartoonist dealt with a panel depicting an Israeli tank aiming at a CBS video truck. The *Houston Herald Voice,* a Jewish paper, called the *Post* anti-Semitic for printing it, but the editors backed up Margulies, who argued that "my feeling is that certain things Israel has done have embarrassed me, and I'm not alone in that" (Bennett 13).

Margulies has dealt with a wide range of topics, local, national and international, but his primary focus has always been on racism and intolerance, broadly conceived. He believes strongly in " the concept of a pluralistic society where people with different religious beliefs and moral views are able to coexist"; therefore he actively opposes the religious right and any other groups who "want to ram their point of view down [people's] throats and force them to live by their beliefs and values." He believes that antiabortion is one "prime example" of that, adding, "there are also other things such as prayer in school, teaching creationism, and book-banning; those are the things I cheer on groups like the ACLU and other groups about. I'm Jewish and I feel as though my ability to exist in society is threatened by people who want to impose their views on the law of the land, rather than just on their home and their church" (Margulies, Interview).

Influenced in normally rebellious teen years by the social and political turmoil of the 1960s, its reexamination—and frequent condemnation—of America's values, Margulies cocks a skeptical eye at much of what he sees in society today. Admittedly a politically liberal on current affairs, he is generally considered fair and evenhanded, if not universally loved. Lynn Ashby, his *Houston Post* editor wrote, "It is now a badge of honor to be humiliated by a Jimmy Margulies cartoon. His works stand proudly in waiting rooms and offices of mayors and senators and governors. His targets have become his fans—well, some of them. . . . But to be fair to him, he is fair to his readers. He takes on all comers, neatly turning lifelong friends into sworn foes while endearing himself to the strangest collection of followers since Noah" (Margulies, *My Husband* Foreword).

Although he voted for Bill Clinton in 1992, even before the election Margulies took him to task for his evasiveness about avoiding the draft during the Vietnam War. Since the election he has hammered at Clinton's indecisiveness in a number of policy areas. He also has prodded the news media about its recent campaign coverage in cartoons such as one in which two bystanders are discussing the sight of men digging through the garbage in a dumpster. One character says, "How sad, in our affluent society, people rummaging for scraps . . ." The other responds, "If it makes you feel any better, they're reporters covering the presidential campaign . . ."

Like a number of more prominent activists of the 1960s, such as Abbie Hoffman, Jerry Rubin and Tom Hayden, Margulies subsequently found a way to express his values while working within the social system rather than against it. "Rather than look at issues from a fixed, ideological position, I try to look at whatever it is that is inherently ridiculous in each situation and react accordingly" (*Editorial* 3). He prefers to use humor as his primary device for making his point, rather than stark messages of political philosophy: "Something too ideological simply turns me off" (Weeks 52).

It is not surprising, therefore, that Margulies cites fellow cartoonist Mike Peters (*Dayton Daily News*) as the leading influence on his work. "His irreverent, off-the-wall humor really turns me on, and I feel as though the reader will remember more what's funny than what he thinks is politically correct. In this way, humor reaches out to those people who may not agree with you—which is why, I think, I got the *Post* job. Humor can appeal to a broader spectrum of readers." He adds, "I may not agree with Jeff MacNelly's [*Chicago Tribune*] views but he generally presents them so humorously that I'd rather see a MacNelly I disagree with than, say, a Herblock I agree with. That doesn't mean I believe that a cartoonist is a Carson who draws. Peters, for instance, occasionally gets so gag-oriented he has almost no political message. I like sometimes to strike deeper than just a joke, but for me it mostly boils down to how you say something, not what you say" (Weeks 52, 57).

One example of "striking deeper" is a 1994 panel depicting a black man and a white woman standing arm in arm, he in a tux, she with a cast on her arm, a black eye and a battered face, both smiling: "O. J. and Nicole Brown Simpson in happier times." More common, however, are cartoons like the 1991 panel with a department store Santa seated in front of a line of children, exclaiming to the girl on his lap, "Peace on Earth? Good will to all? How do you expect to revive the economy with a wish list like that?" Another typical example from 1993 shows two pilgrims standing on the stern of the Mayflower just offshore, with one avowing, "It's a low wage country, environmental laws are practically nonexistent, and they're eager for development . . . we can't go wrong . . ."

According to Margulies, "Humor reaches out to those people who may not agree with you. Humor can appeal to a broader spectrum of readers. I don't like cartoons that seem stridently ideological or dogmatic. I like to see subject matter dealt with on its own rather than have to conform to how a liberal or conservative is supposed to think. I think the reader will remember more what's funny than what he thinks is politically correct" (Bennett 13).

Margulies's style of drawing is in fact close to that of Peters, but he is not alone in that: so are a number of others. Despite the demand for it for a variety of illustrative purposes, Margulies feels a bit self-conscious about his art, that it is not as good as it ought to be. In fact, while not as finely drawn as some, his cartoons are fairly rich in detail for the eye to appreciate; the detail enhances, rather than overwhelms the ideas being supported.

Because his drawing style is not that distinctive, he takes more pride in the titles and dialogue of his cartoons; he feels that his creativity lies more in the ideas of his cartoons rather than the art. For example, in a two-panel 1994 cartoon, the first panel shows a rather battered and disheveled boy with an overhead statement: "This child is unvaccinated, unsupervised, abused, ill-fed, and never read to." Below the child is the question, "What can he hope to become?" The second panel depicts a pair of adult hands extending out from behind prison bars, accompanied by the printed answer, "Eligible for parole." The lettering of his titles and dialogue is also a source of some pride; it is done Times-Roman style, since 1987, by hand and is in fact distinctive. He considers it a way of "showing off." A few, like Temp, may roughly approximate it, but one has little difficulty picking out a Margulies cartoon from a pageful. The lettering adds a certain weight and grace to the art it accompanies.

To stay current and to get ideas for his cartoons, Margulies reads several newspapers every day, the news magazines weekly, and watches television news shows every evening. "I think a lot of people get their news from TV, and a lot of visual images are helpful" (Bennett 13). He is irritated by people who call in to give him suggestions or ideas, "thinking that I need prompting from someone to tell me what to put in the newspaper." Although he participates in the newspaper's editorial board meetings, Margulies makes his own decisions on the content of his cartoons, which he sees as his own "graphic editorial." As a creative artist, he decried that "many people were using their creativity to sell other people's messages, and I [don't] want to do that; as a cartoonist, I use my creativity to sell my own message."

Beyond attaining a certain level of skill, he feels the most difficult part of the profession is in fact coming up with the ideas every day. But once he has the idea, supporting images come fairly quickly. Very occasionally, the process works in reverse. The image of a nude and very pregnant Demi Moore which appeared on the cover of *Vanity Fair* magazine was one that struck him immediately: "As soon as I saw that I knew I had to use it in a cartoon . . . but that is the direct opposite of what you are supposed to do in a cartoon; you are supposed to identify an issue that you have feelings about, and then figure out a way of expressing it. [In this case] I had to find some issue that could be applied to that image, and I sort of thought backwards in doing that" (Margulies, Interview). What he came up with in 1991 was an image of a similarly posed Saddam Hussein with an atom nucleus and the words "Under Construction" printed on the bare distended stomach. Other cartoonists were similarly influenced: Mike Peters used virtually the identical concept that same week, and shortly thereafter Bill Day (*Detroit Free Press*) used the idea for a comment on Mikhail Gorbachov and "The Mother of All Economic Problems."

He has published one collection of his work, and won many prizes, including the Fischetti Award, 1996; second prize from the National Press Foundation, and the Berryman Award for Editorial Cartooning, 1993; the John Peter Zenger Award from the New York State Bar Association; Global Media Award from the Population Institute, and the International Salon of Cartoons in Montreal, 1985. His cartoons are currently distributed by King Features.

Margulies does the majority of his reading in the office every morning, and then thinks. "Once I'm satisfied that I've got the best thing I can come up with that day—once I actually sit down with the pencil—I can do the drawing in about two and a half hours" (Bennett 13). He does six of these per week, skipping only Saturday. Of these, two are usually local or state cartoons, and the others national or international. He feels that local issues are important to the readers and often gets some of his strongest responses to them. He tries to maintain variety in both content and tone in his work because he feels that you lose readers if you pound on them every day. "I try to be more funny than mean—but funny with a message," adding, "but sometimes being funny is enough."

Sources

Bennett, Elizabeth. "Margulies—the Art of Hard-Hitting Humor." *The Magazine of the Houston Post* 27 Oct. 1985: 6-7, 12-13.

"Editorial Cartoonist Joining *The Record*." *The Record* (of Bergen County, Hackensack, NJ) 2 Sept. 1990: 3.

Margulies, Jimmy. "Book Publishing." *Cartoonist Profiles* Mar. 1990: 26-31.

——. Interview. By Jack Colldeweih. May 1994.

——. *My Husband Is Not a Wimp.* Austin, TX: Eakin P, 1988.

North, Steve. "Drawing Laughter—and Wrath—with Cartoons." *The Two River Times* 2 Oct. 1991: 1, 23.

"Special Bonus Issue: Jimmy Margulies." *Political Pix* 15 Aug. 1988. Bonus Issue 2: 1-4.

Weeks, Jerome. "Margulies—The Houston Post." *Cartoonist Profiles* June 1985: 52-57.

15

Jim Morin, *Miami Herald*

S. L. Harrison

Pat Oliphant has noted that Jim Morin possesses "all the attributes of a first-rate cartoonist, including a signature that is suitably illegible." Readers do not need a Morin signature to recognize a Morin creation, however. His Pulitzer Prize–winning editorial cartoons are immediately recognizable with their population of troll-like, bug-eyed, sawed-off characters who observe and comment on the fashions and foibles of political, social and economic events.

Jim Morin, editorial cartoonist for the *Miami Herald* since 1978, with a decidedly liberal bent levels his attacks on politicians of all stripe without favor. His work has been collected in *Line of Fire*. Even a casual examination shows that Morin does little "holding back" and that almost every public figure has been skewered. Some are more fun to ridicule than others. Of H. Ross Perot, for example, Morin says, "He is such fun to scorn because he's so obviously over the edge. Anybody that's pure evil is going to be fun to draw" (Morin, Interview). Pat Oliphant says of Morin: "He has a clear idea of how he feels about the issues and wants you to know about it. He then expresses himself clearly and concisely in a manner that is both exciting and explorative" (Morin, *Line of Fire* Introduction). He consistently takes dead aim on the subject of the day and delivers a devastating bulls-eye on target with venomous satirical humor and draftsmanship. And this has been recognized through many prizes, such as the 1993 National Cartoonists Society Editorial Cartooning Award; Overseas Press Club Award (twice); Sigma Delta Chi Green Eyeshade,1986; Inter-America Press Award, 1988; National Press Foundation's Berryman Award, 1996. He won a Pulitzer Prize in 1996.

Morin's interest in politics and art began early. He was born in 1953 in Washington, D.C., a town whose entire business is politics, and grew up in Boston, a hotbed of activism during the 1960s. By the age of seven he was already drawing. His earliest political recollections were of the 1968 Democratic presidential convention in Chicago. He was outraged over the treatment of the antiwar protesters. But his interest in political cartooning did not begin to jell until he attended Syracuse University,

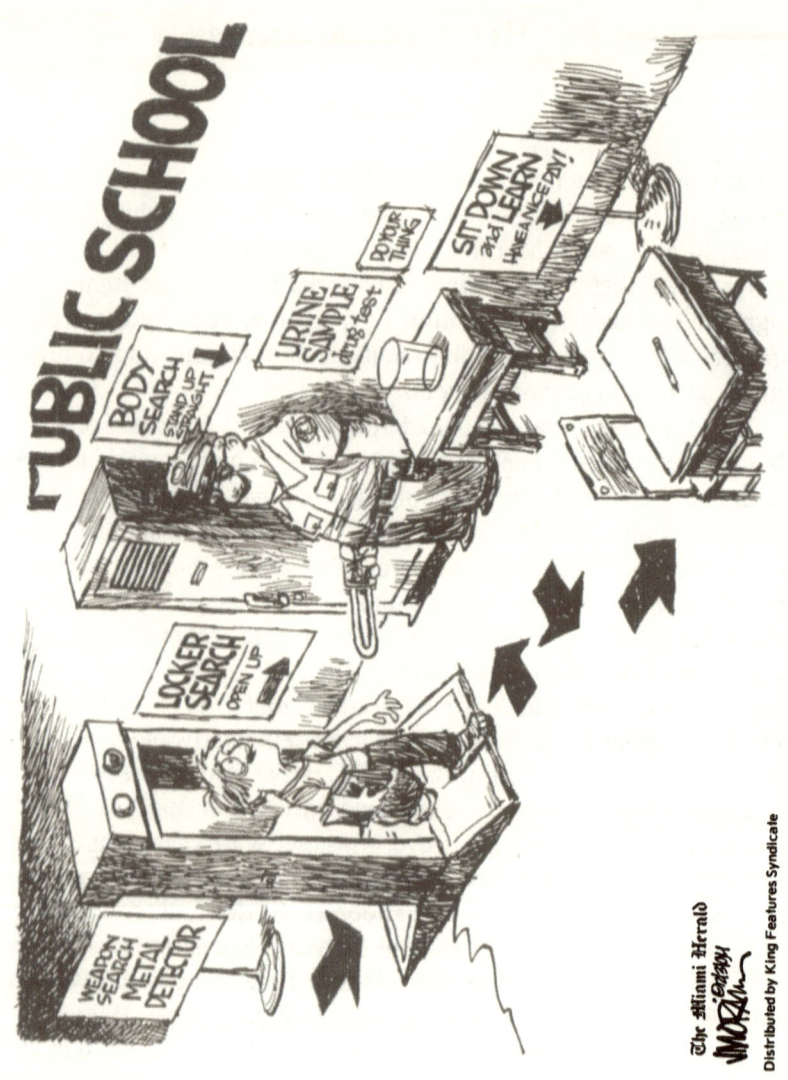

Jim Morin (1994) *Miami Herald* and *King Features Syndicate*. Reprinted with permission.

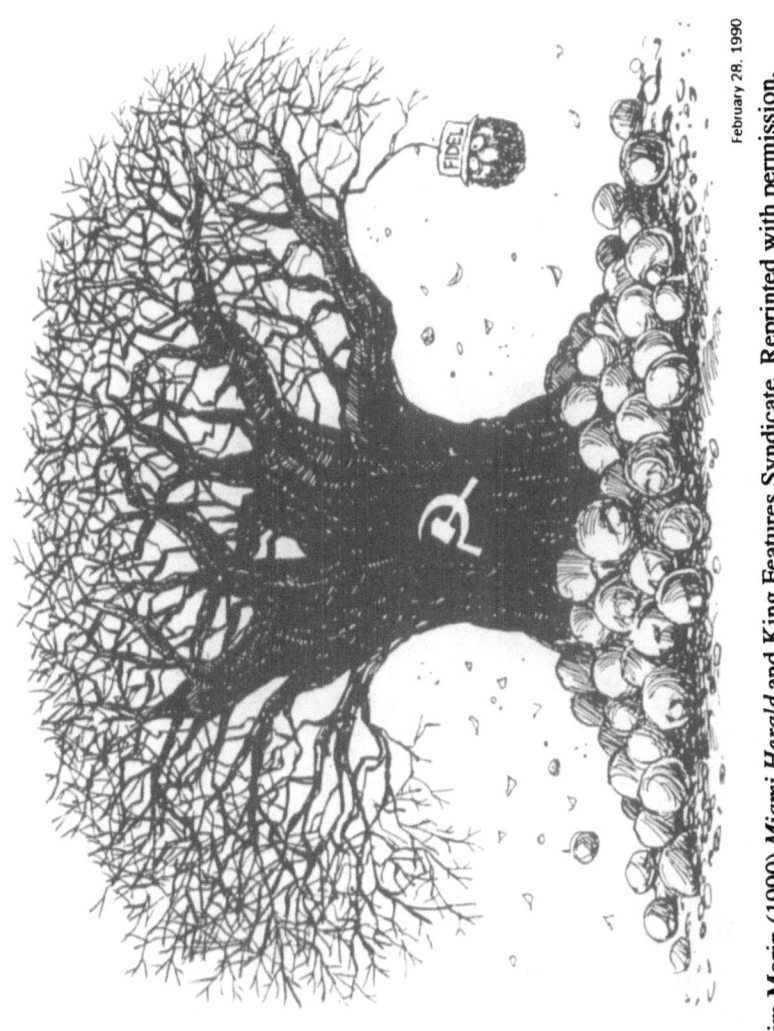

Jim Morin (1990) *Miami Herald* and King Features Syndicate. Reprinted with permission.

Febuary 28. 1990

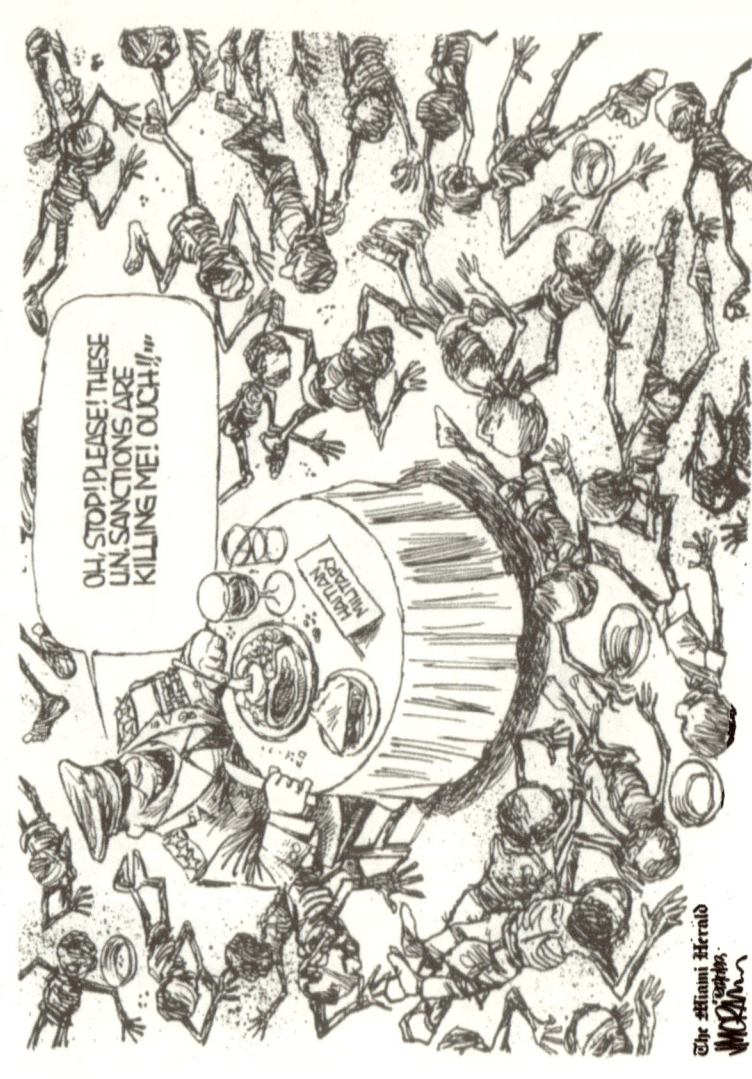

Jim Morin (1993) *Miami Herald* and King Features Syndicate. Reprinted with permission.

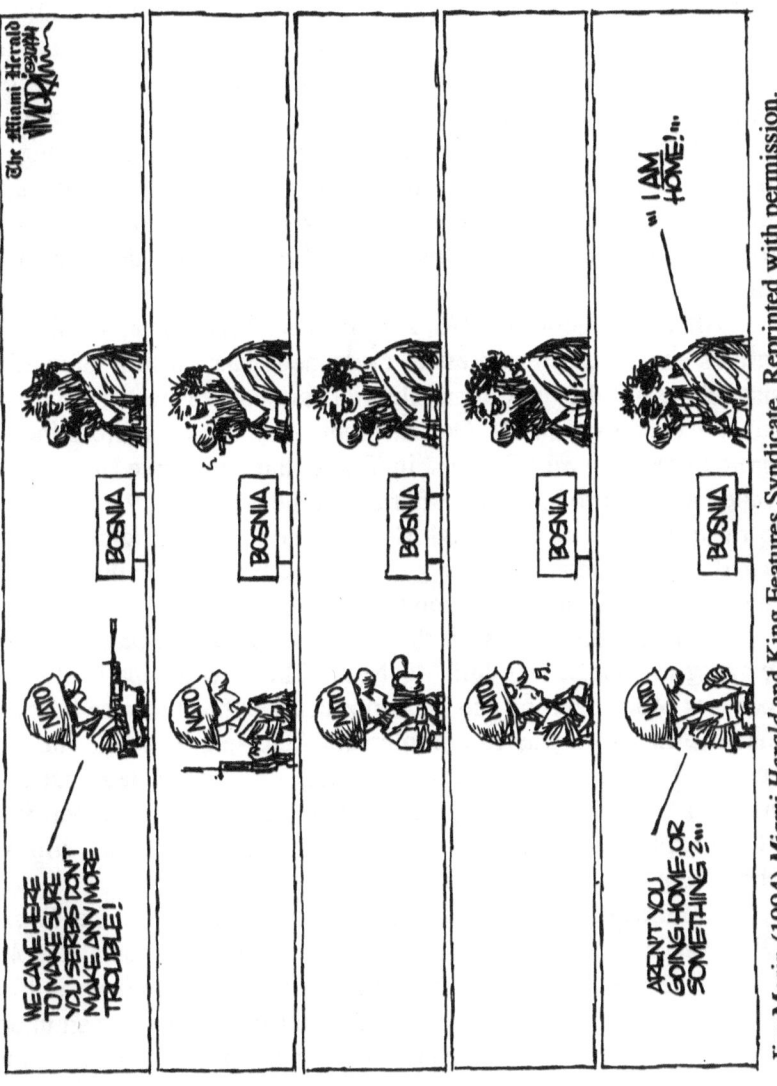

Jim Morin (1994) *Miami Herald* and King Features Syndicate. Reprinted with permission.

where he was studying "serious art." In 1974 he began to do caricatures for the *Daily Orange*, inspired by the work of Ed Sorel and David Levine, who combined art and politics. Morin has always had an affinity for cartoonists and illustrators who combine moral integrity and honesty, in particular Low, Daumier, Steadman, and Grosz. As an undergraduate, Morin submitted at first two cartoons a week, then eventually five; during his senior year he returned to Washington, D.C., to take in the Watergate hearings. His original intent was to do some sketching, but he recalls he did more listening than artwork. It was an educational process and convinced him that he was hooked on politics. His mother suggested that Jim combine his two great interests, politics and art, although he recalls that "she was scared to death I wasn't going to get a paycheck after I graduated" (Morin, Interview). He did, eventually, but it took some doing.

After graduation in 1976, Jim freelanced for a year, sending applications and letters of interest to every newspaper with a circulation of sixty-thousand that lacked an editorial cartoonist. It was a long process but it eventually paid off. One favorable response came from the *Beaumont Enterprise and Journal* in Texas; the paper liked his work but lacked a budget to hire him. After a year, however, the *Journal* managed to raise the money and hired Morin as editorial cartoonist. That post lasted for nine months. "The guy that had brought me down there got fired and I knew that I was soon to go," Morin recalls.

He next caught on with the *Richmond Times-Dispatch*, where the reigning cartoonist was Jeff MacNelly. This was a beneficial environment for Morin until he and his editor clashed; the editor had concluded that Morin's role was to complement MacNelly's work, and consequently drew up "arbitrary, ever-changing, and unpredictable rules," creating an "intolerable atmosphere in which to work" (Commer 58). So, Morin explains, "I told them to stick it" (Morin, Interview). Jim was at liberty to pursue other outlets.

A colleague, Doug Marlette, who was then with the *Charlotte Observer*, suggested that Jim look into the possibilities at the *Miami Herald*. The *Herald*, then as now the largest-circulation daily in Florida, lacked an editorial cartoonist. Morin travelled to Miami for an interview and was hired on the spot. The relationship has been a productive one for all concerned.

Morin's cartoons run atop the editorial page five days a week and the *Herald* generally allows Morin a great deal of latitude. But there have been times when a cartoon has been pulled. In one such incident, though it did not run locally, King Features Syndicate distributed Morin's controversial work. But by and large, the relationship has been a good one. And Morin recently began a Sunday strip cartoon, with a purely local focus, called "Magic City," that appears in the *Herald's* magazine. His subjects are local issues: the terrible traffic problems, dangers to tourism in downtown Miami, development run amok in the Everglades and the Keys, and the struggles of the University of Miami's Hurricanes. "I have been very fortunate to have worked in Miami through the most turbulent period in its history," he deadpans (Morin 53). His acid commentary on such topics clearly fails to reflect the views of the local Chamber of Commerce, and unsurprisingly a number of these cartoons have raised readers' ire. But management likes the work and Jim enjoys doing it, for "drawing cartoons about tragic circumstances you witness yourself is an indescribable experience" (Morin 53).

For his "Magic City" panel, Morin usually develops a subject over some weeks and then proceeds to blast the smug and self-satisfied. But for his editorial cartoons, which must be timely and meet a daily deadline, Morin begins early each day after gathering his ideas by "reading like crazy" all the newspapers and magazines available and C-Span and CNN. By mid-morning he has sketched out a half dozen or more ideas for his editors to approve.

Drawing takes time and the work reflects that. His medium is preferably pen-and-ink, with heavy crosshatching. Little brush work is evident. He works on an 13" x 9 1/2" Bristol board with a Coquille No. 6 pen laid on a well-defined blue-pencil drawing. Usually, his cartoons carry a caption of his own creation. Like most cartoonists, Morin gets many ideas from friends and admirers, and like most he usually ignores them. Unlike many editorial cartoonists, Morin does not suffer from a lack of ideas, so he often has dilemmas about which one to use. Above all, he is always conscious that after fifteen years of drawing cartoons it is easy to slip into a rut in which the only aspect that changes is the daily face and target (Morin, Interview).

The several samples reprinted here are representative of Morin's work. For example, his view of Haiti preceded the interest of most Americans and runs contrary to our government's policy. Haiti is not now and never has been a democracy and Morin's views of the UN sanctions were right on target. His cartoon, clogged with dying and starving Haitians, may seem reminiscent of the work of "Ding" Darling, with its array of figures and well-populated panel. But despite the seeming chaos of the encircling bodies, the vision point is perfect and the draftsmanship accurate; and Darling never took such a dark tone in his cartoons. Morin deplores gag humor editorials; no funny messages here.

Education problems reflect a recurrent theme in Morin's view of modern learning and his vision of the modern school, replete with its ironic messages of "do your own thing" and "have a nice day," slams both the mantras and current pedagogy. Morin's message is not meant to be reassuring.

Morin frequently resorts to a comic strip approach in his editorial message, as seen in NATO's confrontation with the Serbs. Not many Americans know exactly what side is which in Bosnia or exactly what the Croats or Muslims want. We do know that we became involved, but not why. So the multipanel approach, with "takes" and punch lines, is highly appropriate.

Morin's stark drawing of an apple tree with Fidel's head about to drop is an excellent example of mastery with basic pen-and-ink drawing. He makes effective use of white space to contrast with the basic subject, a tree that becomes somehow very menacing. Like many of Morin's drawings, this cartoon requires no caption to convey its meaning.

Morin's targets vary, and his work remains fresh through an iconoclastic viewpoint. When all of Miami was welcoming new Dolphins' coach Jimmy Johnson, Morin burlesqued his ascent into heaven with a chorus singing hosannahs. One onlooker reminded the throng, "It's only professional football." That kind of message keeps Morin controversial.

His caricatures so clearly indicate who is being portrayed that Morin can avoid the obvious labels that so often accompany editorial cartoons. At other times he realizes the need for dialogue balloons and narrative panels to clarify his often-acerbic commentary.

Morin's editorial cartoons elicit comment. That means that his work often riles a lot of readers. Many, in fact, do write or call to compliment him but more often he hears from defenders of special interest groups and organizations, like the National Rifle Association. A number of these, Morin notes, have called for his removal or dismissal. He is careful about the use of stereotypes, but contends that even if his cartoons are at times brutal, they are accurate. He is never guilty of "holding back" because "if you do that, you are editing. It's better that the newspaper do that it" (Morin, Interview).

Asked who his favorite cartoonists are, Jim Morin speaks highly of the work of the late Duncan McPherson of the *Toronto Star* and notes that "his draftsmanship and sense of satire were unparalleled" (Morin, Interview). Generally speaking, Morin holds the work of Canadian artists in high esteem. Though fewer in number than cartoonists in the United States, the Canadians' level of draftsmanship, artistic ability, and variety of style is much higher.

Besides McPherson, another past artist who influenced Morin was T. S. Sullivant, a pen-and-ink artist for the old *Life* magazine at the turn of the century. Sullivant was not an editorial cartoonist but was, in

Morin's opinion, "the single greatest animal caricaturist that ever lived," and responsible for "loosening up" (Morin, Interview) the otherwise restricted and rigid pen-and-ink work of that era. Morin is a collector of Sullivant's work. Sullivant has influenced him in one other way. He enjoys editorial cartooning but has followed Sullivant's example in two other books. *Famous Cats* and *Jim Morin's Field Guide to Birds* display his wicked humor through a series of paintings of birds and cats unknown to any zoological category.

Sources

Commer, Dick. "Jim Morin." *Cartoonist Profiles* 43 (July 1979): 56-61.
Harrison, S. L. *Florida's Editorial Cartoonists.* Sarasota: Pineapple, 1996.
——. Interview with Jim Morin. Feb. 1997.
"Jim Morin." *Cartoonist Profiles* 83 (Sept. 1989): 46-63.
Morin, Jim. *Line of Fire: Political Cartoons by Jim Morin*. Miami: Florida International UP, 1991.

16

Jack Ohman, *(Portland) Oregonian*

Kalman Goldstein

Back in 1987 Jack Ohman of the *(Portland) Oregonian* explained why, unlike some other political cartoonists, he was not also creating a strip: "Doing both a comic strip and a political cartoon is a little like being a commodities broker and an emergency room surgeon at the same time; the money is great, but the stress can be absolutely unmanageable" (Ohman, *Drawing* 11). However, in April 1994 he began "Mixed Media," a daily two-panel noncontinuity strip lampooning and fantasizing popular culture, not solely for the additional income. Jack Ohman's writing and drawing have always reflected his fascination with many aspects of our society, while he has held paradoxically to an older purist standard of proper editorial content. While others currently use editorial cartoons for social or cultural comment, "When I do a political cartoon, it's about a policy issue. It's not about fat content or the latest health story that runs in *USA Today*" (Ohman, Interview).

Once the youngest full-time cartoonist on a major daily paper, now in his mid-30s "the dean of the younger generation," Ohman has seldom been able to contain his creativity within six daily editorials. Between 1986 and 1993 he produced three collections of humorous illustrated essays on favorite pastimes (golfing and fishing). His 1986 book *Back to the '80s* combined satiric essays and cartoons to portray the Reagan era's cultural trends as retreads, nostalgic reflections of an exhausted society's unimaginative public policies. "Mixed Media" similarly examines the political refractions of popular culture as well as silly human foibles, allowing Ohman to have the "fun" that he claims is sometimes unsuitable to editorial cartooning (Harvey 34).

Since his editorial cartoons are witty, pun-filled and often contain high comedy, Jack Ohman's stance seems paradoxical, but this is characteristic of the complex man. For a cartoonist who never had formal art training and claims to have learned to draw only recently, his cartoons are effectively composed and visually focused. Ohman is also a skilled miniaturist. He criticizes cartoons based on personalities rather than issues, but is quite proud of his very subjective caricatures. His formats

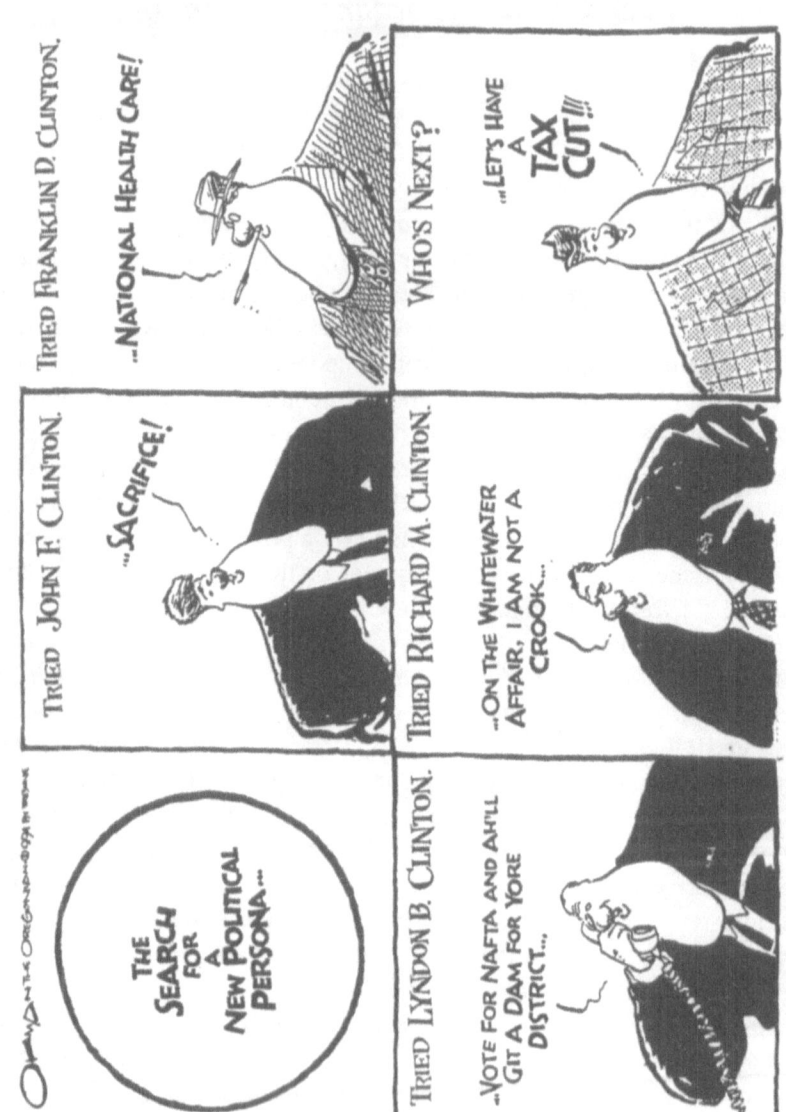

Jack Ohman (1994) *(Portland) Oregonian* and Tribune Media Services. Reprinted with permission.

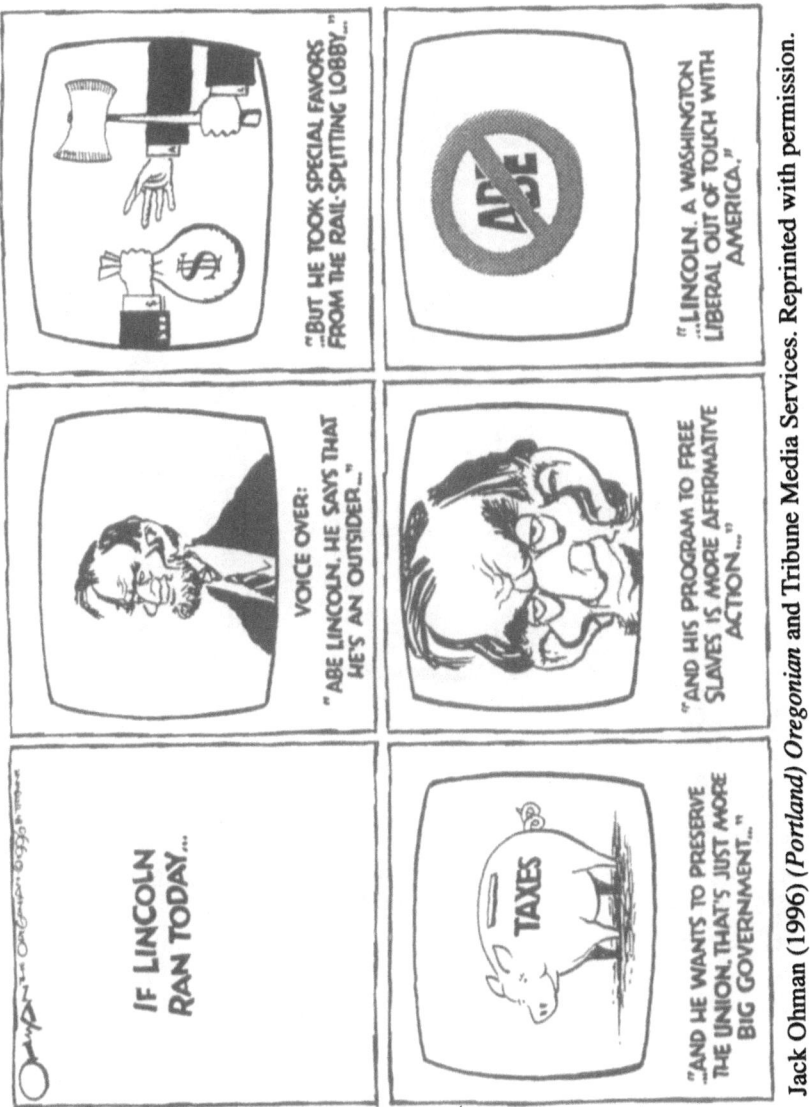

Jack Ohman (1996) *(Portland) Oregonian* and Tribune Media Services. Reprinted with permission.

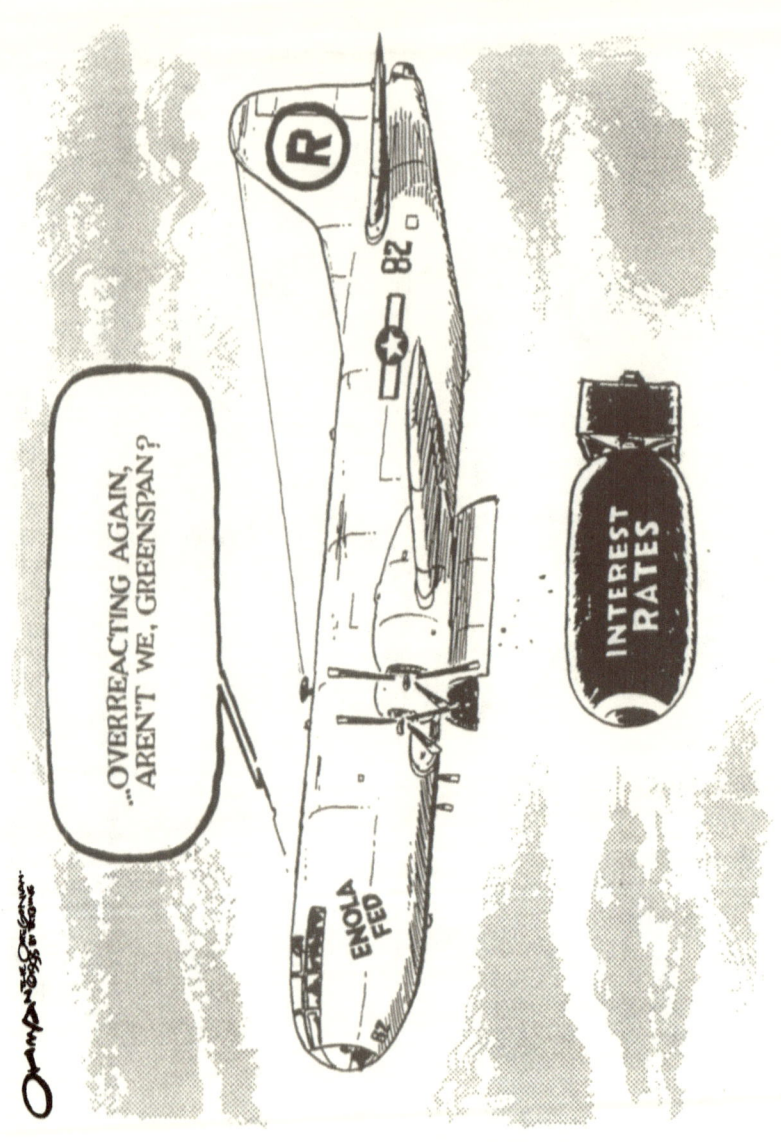

Jack Ohman (1995) (*Portland*) *Oregonian* and Tribune Media Services. Reprinted with permission.

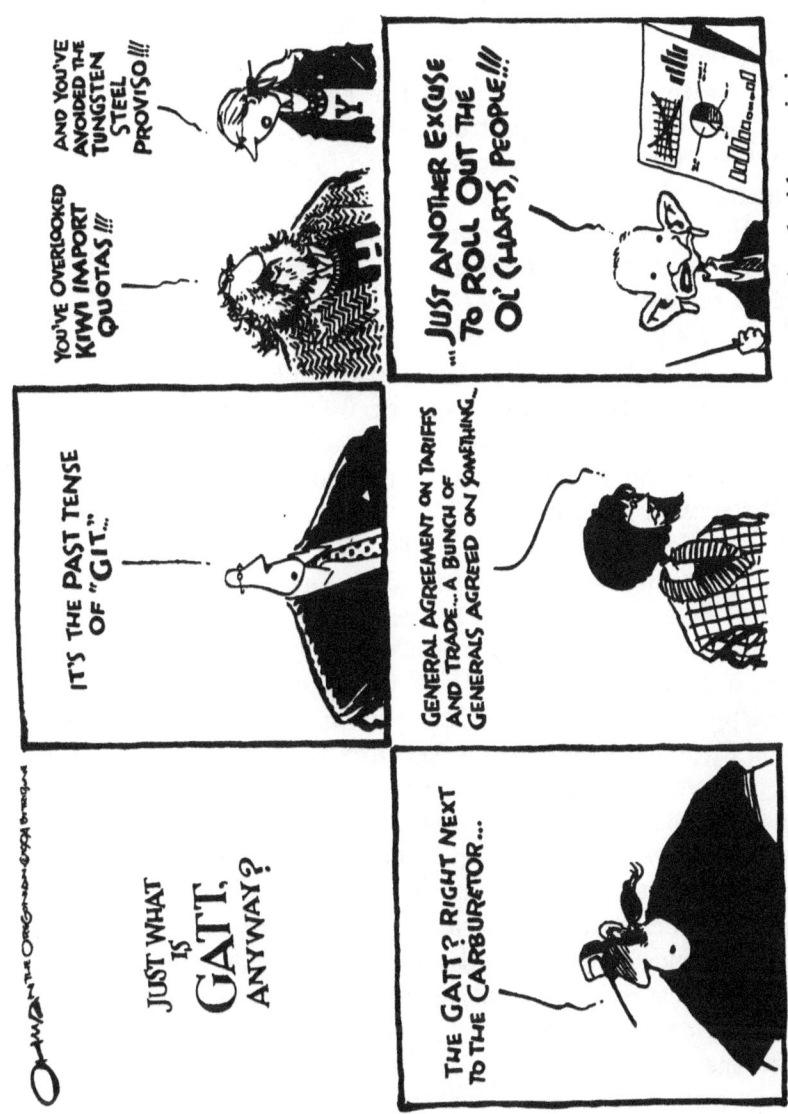

Jack Ohman (1994) *(Portland) Oregonian* and Tribune Media Services. Reprinted with permission.

are unpredictable: on any given day his cartoons may consist of from one to six panels, depending upon the topic, its complexity and the viewpoint he wishes to convey. He insists that "I probably have the worst kind of political ideology to be a political cartoonist. I am truly moderate, and. . . . there aren't a lot of angry moderates" (Ohman, Interview). Yet he consistently takes strong, sometimes even angry or sarcastic stands on a number of sensitive issues: he is pro-choice, favors gun control, satirizes "New Right" politicians and vigorously supports the First Amendment. And he repeatedly calls national leaders to direct account for their meanderings on domestic and foreign policy—though without echoing recent antigovernment rhetoric.

Born in St. Paul, Minnesota in 1960, as a youth Ohman became fascinated by Watergate; he jokes that he was the only kid on his block doing impressions of North Carolina Senator Sam Ervin. Ohman campaigned for political candidates during his teens and majored in political science at the University of Minnesota. While on the college paper, he was already self-syndicating cartoons. By age 19 his work had appeared in both *Newsweek* and the *Washington Post*. *Newsweek* had accepted the first cartoon he submitted, on the Iran hostage crisis. In 1981 he both affiliated with Tribune Media Service and won a full-time cartooning job with the *Columbus Dispatch*. He left the Ohio paper after a year and a half, quarreling over editorial freedom, and spent the next year at the *Detroit Free Press*. Marrying native Oregonian Janice Dunham in 1982, Ohman moved to Portland in 1983 to join the *Oregonian* staff. Since then, his cartoons have been both widely syndicated and anthologized; they appear regularly in *Best Editorial Cartoons of the Month, Best Editorial Cartoons of the Year,* the *New York Times* and *Foreign Affairs*.

Ohman's cartoons are distinctive in many ways, and these provide an explanation of his success. One hallmark of his work is its relative political sophistication and serious intent. Ohman hopes his cartoons will educate his readers as well as offer him an outlet for wit, though sometimes he does assume a greater amount of reader information about domestic and foreign policy issues than do many other cartoonists. He also finds that on occasion his choice of topics is at variance with that of others. "Some days you will sit down and do the same type of cartoon as everyone in the country. The next day somebody comes up with something so off the wall you wonder what planet he's on." He explains this as due in part to the cautious stance of syndicate editors who would prefer an Op-Ed piece "about the relative ease of using a fax over a 32-cent stamp" to something more controversial. But he adds, "I think most cartoonists are their own worst enemies. They'll come up with some things that are a lot more provocative than what they bring to their editors. My thinking is, why not bring in your most provocative idea and let him make the decision? Sometimes they'll surprise you" (Ohman, Interview).

Ohman will not avoid any topic and has no quarrel with cartoonists that are bold, even shocking, in order to have an impact. "There are some cartoons that I call 'Jesus Christ' cartoons. Even if you look at it and agree with it, you have to say 'Jesus Christ!' What was this guy thinking when he drew that!" Yet he expects the cartoonist to be able to defend or explain it to an angry or puzzled caller, and therefore has had some misgivings even about his own shockers, in particular a reaction to the 1994 Congressional election returns captioned "Shift happens!" Ohman judged this cartoon acceptable though tasteless. Another, one of his infrequent visual metaphors, showed a goggle-eyed Newt Gingrich smoking a huge marijuana joint labeled "Power" while alleging that 25% of the White House staff used drugs (*National Forum* Jan. 1, 1995, 5).

Many of his cartoons are wordy, or at least word-based. For Ohman, "Sometimes a picture *isn't* worth a thousand words" (Ohman, Interview). One major exception to this aphorism can be found in Ohman's cartoons about our foreign policy. Perhaps expecting reader familiarity with the general setting, Ohman here is more likely to use visual metaphors and show off his striking ability to draw military hardware (which he insists others do better). Among the images he has used to describe our policy toward the Bosnian wars have been vacuum cleaners, gravestones, werewolves, wrist-slapping pilots, autos all of whose gears are marked "reverse," a falling floor safe labeled "Bosnia Escalation—U.N. Designated Safe Zone," and President Clinton hanging upside down in an ejection seat. Some of his other foreign policy cartoons even hearken back to the allegorical style of David Low and other World War II artists: Bill Clinton embracing a hand-shaking King Hussein (labeled "Jordan") and an Israeli leader (with a star of David on his jacket) juxtaposed with "Death" embracing hand-shaking figures labeled "Hezbollah" and "Hamas," with pipe bombs in their teeth (*National Forum* Nov. 13, 1994, 15).

Generally, Ohman believes that writing, not art, should drive his cartoons; he uses neither symbols nor visual metaphors very much. He begins with a phrase or a pun, then does word associations, and only then will he decide on the images he will use. Occasionally he will settle for an easy illustrated pun; on January 2, 1995, he drew homeless people, seeking warmth, talking about this being a "grate" country (*Oregon-ian*). Or, when inspired to do a visual pun after breaches of White House security, he portrayed the Presidential residence as a shooting gallery duck with the Disney character's head—another exception to his usual avoidance of popular culture symbols in political cartoons (*National Forum* June 11, 1995, 4). On January 5, 1995, the day of my visit to his office, his cartoon for the *Oregonian* illustrated one of his tricks of the trade,"a repeated image of a woman, which underlined his great concern for the verbal message and the issue: recent shootings at abortion clinics.

But, since his forte, despite his disclaimers, is as much caricature as verbal satire, when he draws politicians, with or without identifying labels, he does so in order to express his visceral feelings economically and simply and to pass shorthand judgment for readers about the policies these leaders espouse. Just after their party's Congressional landslide in 1994, he drew hilarious caricatures of Republican leaders Jesse Helms, Strom Thurmond, and Bob Dole as wizened and dyspeptic, as a bystander enthused: "Oh Joy! Here come our dynamic new agents of change!!!" (*National Forum* Nov. 27, 1994, 4). Late in 1994, to criticize Bill Clinton's shifting imagery, he drew the president in a series of subtle facial caricatures as John Kennedy, Franklin Roosevelt, Lyndon Johnson, Richard Nixon and even Ronald Reagan, uttering characteristic phrases ("The Search for a New Political Persona," *Nat. Forum* Jan. 8, 1995, 7). Finally, "The Least Credible Campaign Statements of 1996" gathers Steve Forbes, Phil Gramm, Bill Clinton and Richard Luger, adds ludicrous tag lines, and culminates with a funereal Bob Dole glowering and intoning: "Happy to Be Here" (*New York Times* Feb. 4, 1996).

Most of his multipanel cartoons do not simply rely on this visual shorthand, however, for they go far beyond the repetitive talking-head style associated with Jules Feiffer. Many of these are either sequential narratives, as in an "exposé" of President Clinton's ineptitude in making appointments, or an attack on Speaker Newt Gingrich's proposed school prayer amendment set to a parody of "The Lord's Prayer" (*National Forum* Dec. 18, 1994, 6; Mar. 5, 1995, 8). Whether they tell a story, examine the facets of a complex issue, or reveal the ironies behind a political stance; they all necessitate a multiplicity of images. For Ohman, too often a single panel is insufficient to serve reader understanding or appreciation of what lies behind a given event or issue. For example, a six-panel cartoon on proposed budget cutting showed representatives of different interest groups (the elderly, the military, students, farmers, retirees) demurring about sacrificing for the "common good," with a repeated refrain: "Don't touch . . ." (*National Forum* Nov. 13, 1994, 6). But those cartoons that show off his ability at caricatures are most distinctive, as in the example accusing President Clinton of scrabbling about for a "new political persona" while posing as Kennedy, Roosevelt, Johnson, Nixon and even Reagan. Another equally impressive tour de force dates from late January 1995; it caricatures "declared presidential candidates" Lamar Alexander, Bob Dole, Phil Gramm, Arlen Spector and Dan Quayle—not only to show off the artist's technique, but to link them to President Clinton, *all* of whom have to study how to be presidential (*National Forum* Feb. 5, 1995, 3).

Whether doing single, double or multipanel cartoons, Ohman seems happiest when making instructive comparisons; he is a master of juxtapositions. Many cartoons compare "Then" and "Now," rhetoric and realty, the "is" and the "should be," "friend" and "foe," even facile puns ("Ich bin ein Berliner . . . Ich bin ein Beginner") distinguishing successful and unsuccessful policy-making episodes in the Kennedy and Clinton administrations.

Jack Ohman specifically credits three cartoonists for the evolution of his style. Besides Pat Oliphant and Jeff MacNelly, who revolutionized their profession, Bill Mauldin provided a model combining fine writing with dramatic political art and criticized the power structure subtly but effectively during the 1950s and early 1960s, a time of editorial caution. But Ohman's inspirations are not limited solely to other political cartoonists. He has learned much from such comic strippers as Charles Schulz ("Peanuts"), Bill Griffith ("Zippy the Pinhead"), Bill Watterson ("Calvin and Hobbes"), and Robert Crumb. Their work helps him keep his antennas out beyond the Washington Beltway views and pronouncements. While we ate lunch, he noted a young woman wearing barrettes, wondered whether this was a trend, and meditated that anything in daily life might carry clues to understanding politics in a democracy. "That's the hard part. It's like being on guard duty 24 hours a day, watching the shadows on the perimeter and trying to decide if it's friend or foe. I feel like I'm constantly working" (Ohman, Interview).

Sources

Black, Ed. "Youth on the Editorial Page." *Cartoonist Profiles* June 1983: 50-57.

Harvey, Robert C. "Jack Ohman, Mixed Media and Editorial Cartoons." *Cartoonist Profiles* 1 Dec. 1994: 32-41.

National Forum Gallery of Cartoons. Washington, D.C., weekly.

Ohman, Jack. *Back to the '80s.* New York: Simon & Schuster, 1986.

——. *Drawing Conclusions.* New York: Simon & Schuster, 1987.

——. Interview. By Kalman Goldstein. 4. Jan 1995.

17

Joel Pett, *Lexington (Ky.) Herald-Leader*

Jack Colldeweih

Although a staunch and consistent liberal on issues of social policy, Joel Pett is among the most conservative of contemporary political cartoonists in his views about his profession. His seriousness of approach places him back among the "grand old men" of crusading newspaper cartoonists, in the tradition of Nast, Keppler and Fitzpatrick, of Herblock and Conrad. He even considers that artists who rely solely upon the "gag" cartoon make the profession irrelevant to both readers and the publisher, and ultimately to society. He is also adamant about the necessity of political cartoonists remaining in touch with the problems of their local communities and dealing with those on a regular basis, another stance that puts him in the minority of his peers. In fact, Pett sees himself more as a journalist using graphics as well as text rather than as a graphic artist, once again placing himself in the minority. While all this might make him seem to be a rather quarrelsome and cranky sort, Pett is known among his colleagues as a man of quick wit and ready sense of humor, well suited to both his profession and community.

Pett spent many of his formative years growing up in Nigeria, arriving there at age six and returning five years later to the Midwest heartland of Indiana where he was born (Bloomington, Sept. 1, 1953). His father was a professor of education at Indiana University who had gone to Nigeria to set up an educational television network at a university there. When Pett returned to the United States, he felt that he did not fit in with his classmates, and consequently became "super-square" in an attempt to do so. He became a golfer on the high school varsity team, did not drink or smoke, and, looking for groups to feel superior to, disapproved of hippies and their culture. However, he did not maintain this stance for long, and in contrast to the Midwestern conservative norm, Pett is socially and politically very liberal.

Pett began drawing cartoons in high school as an amusement and continued the practice at Indiana University, which he attended for two years as a French major. Although interested in cartoons, Pett feared that he didn't have the talent for them as a career, especially when he looked

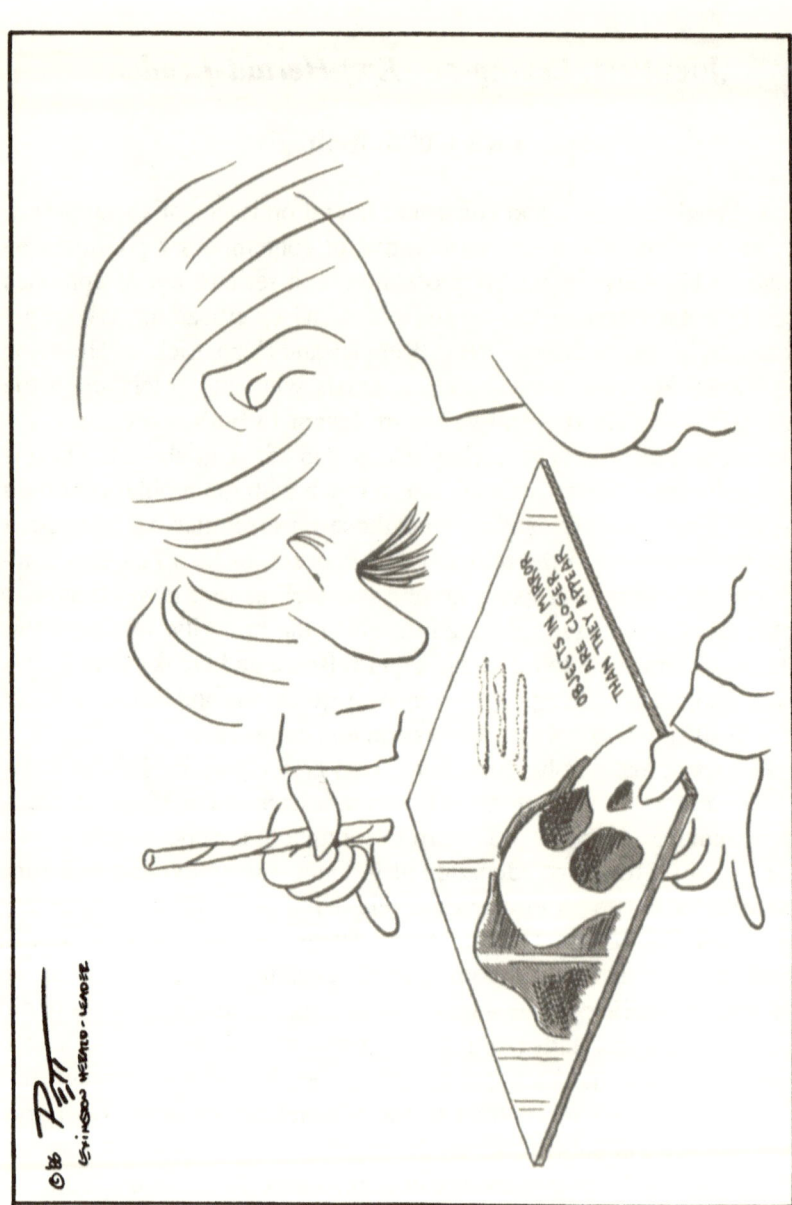

Joel Pett (1986) *Lexington (Ky.) Herald-Leader.*

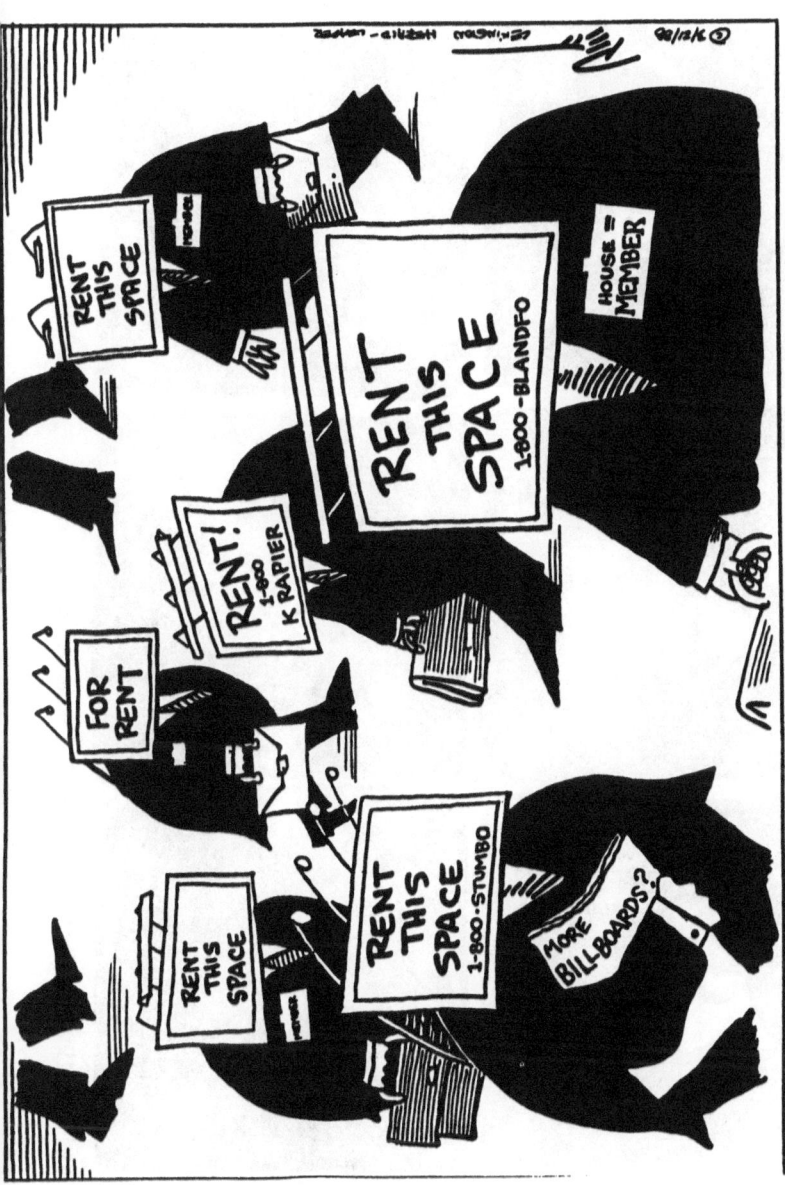

March 21, 1988
Joel Pett (1988) *Lexington (Ky.) Herald-Leader.* All rights reserved.

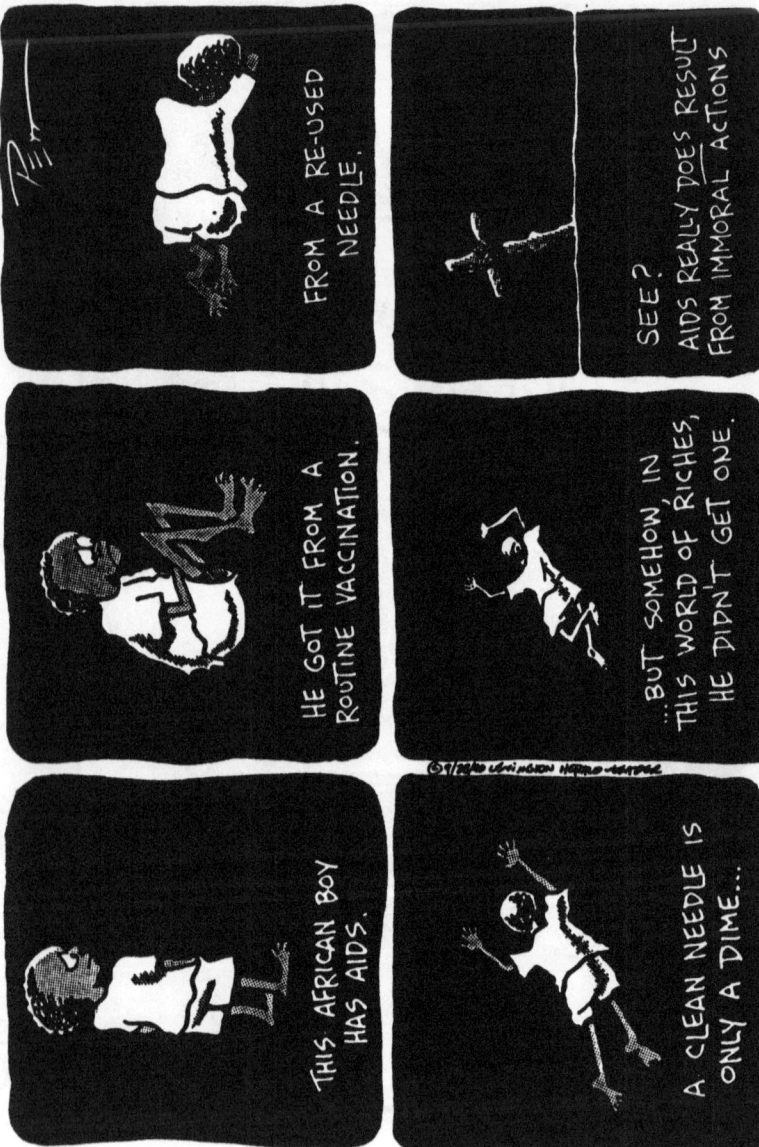

Joel Pett (1990) *Lexington (Ky.) Herald-Leader.* All rights reserved.

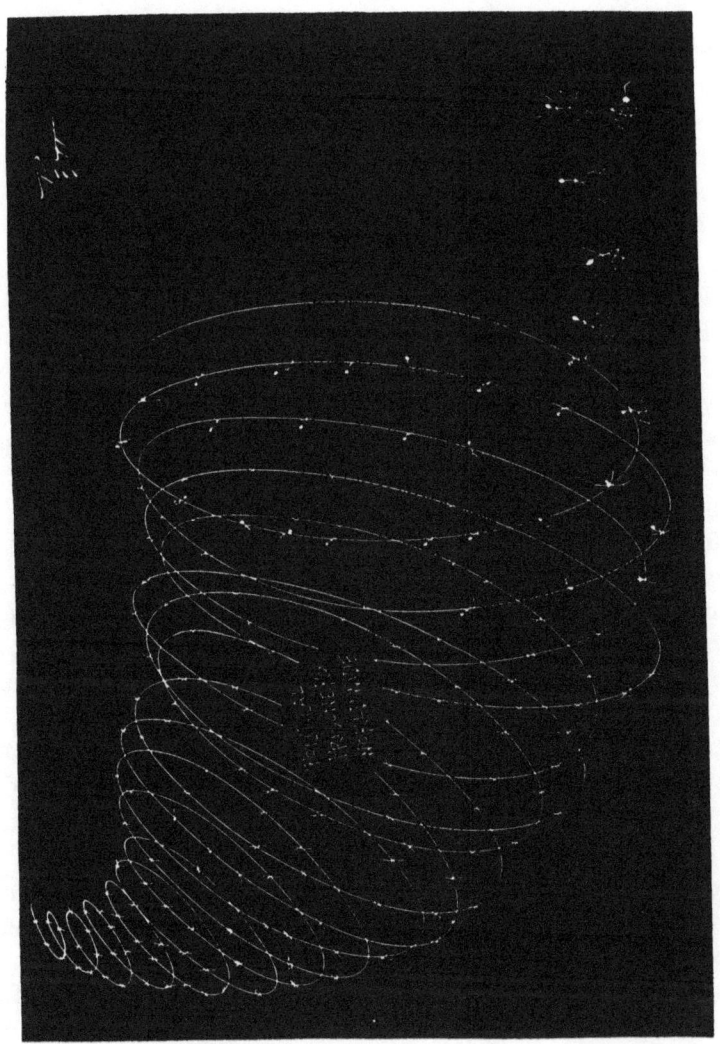

December 5th, 1991

at the work of Oliphant and MacNelly, or of Hugh Haynie, whose work he saw every day in the *Louisville Courier-Journal*. His moment of awakening came from the most unlikely of "mentors," the gag cartoonists whose work appeared weekly in the *New Yorker* magazine. Like the cartoonists' lightbulb that turns on over a character's head, Pett realized that "it's the *thought* behind all this . . . those *New Yorker* cartoons are just a few sketched-out lines and you realize they got a thousand bucks for that. It was what was in their head that made it valuable, not the rudimentary art style" (Pett, Interview).

Pett found it very liberating to realize that he could teach himself some kind of very simple drawing style with which to illustrate his opinions. He subsequently discovered other political cartoonists, such as Signe Wilkinson and Wayne Stayskal, who also successfully draw with simplicity of line. He credits Tony Auth as an influence for his looseness of style, and Tom Toles for the setup, the cadence of the multipanel cartoon. Herblock he acknowledges for an overall approach, for his concept of the political cartoon rather than for artwork. He continued to develop his style through ten years of free-lance work, doing illustrations, working as a newsroom artist and drawing editorial cartoons for the *Herald-Times* of Bloomington, Indiana, from 1978 to 1984, when he joined the *Lexington (Ky.) Herald-Leader*, where he has remained.

From day to day, Pett's cartoons vary quite a bit, which he feels makes them more interesting for the regular reader. "One day it's dark, and the next it's very, very sparse and liney, and the next day it's got a bunch of panels, and the next it's vertical, that kind of thing" (Pett, Interview). The consequent absence of a standardized presentation does not mean that there is no way other than his signature to recognize his work; it becomes quite easy to identify a Pett cartoon. His cartoons often have an "empty, vacant, or not-dressed" look to them, even when he fills in more background in them than some other cartoonists do. His characters usually have a "sketchy" appearance; for example, his "everyman," the cartoonists' representation of the ordinary man, is now usually drawn as nearly a "finger-figure," without shoulders, chin, or even ears to hold up his glasses. The top of his head is represented by three wavy lines serving as hair. On the other hand, literally, one finds a full set of five fingers even on a very tiny hand, in contrast to the more typical four, because, "I never thought of doing it any other way." Pett admits that, "If you look at it too long and analyze it, you realize that I have no idea of how the human form fits together whatsoever" (Pett, Interview).

This is in fact false humility, a humorous reference to his evolved minimalist style. His early work, during his free-lance days, was much less idiosyncratic than it is now. A quick look at his first book of cartoons, *Pett Peeves,* shows standard, properly proportioned cartoon people with full, undistorted faces and bodies. Objects and buildings were well drawn and in spatial perspective. He made a lot of use of Grafix paper, and no hatching, for shadows and background balance. Some elements remain in his present style: the flatness of his characters' bodies, a general sparseness of background, simplicity of line and, in terms of content, seriousness of approach to issues. And one can compare the development of certain of his standard characters, such as the above-mentioned "everyman," who originally looked like a normal person but evolved into the "finger-figure." His original Uncle Sam looked the standard part, dressed in striped pants, starred coat and top hat, with the neat Van Dyke white beard on his chin; the character now appears as a rather scruffy old man with unkempt whiskers all over his face, his top hat battered and bent and his suit rumpled: in short, a 1960s hippie.

Although he denigrates his own artistic ability, only a man supremely confident of what he was doing would take some of the risks Pett does within his cartoons. A 1989 cartoon, for example, consisted of only the word "lies" in large script, with a photo of President Bush pasted into the loop of the "l." In 1987 he drew an Internal Revenue Service W-4 form consisting entirely of the hand-drawn document. And in 1989 he used as a cartoon a photo of a portion of a news story from the front page of the *New York Times* depicting Vice President Dan Quayle holding a rocket launcher in South America, with an overlay of a note identifying Quayle as a "Babyboomer at Play." While these examples may in fact connote a certain sense of artistic inferiority, a reluctance to commit one's own art to paper, more important is that they indicate his belief that the *idea* is what is significant in an editorial cartoon. "The message was in the image and I couldn't improve on them in my own silly style. The impact was better this way" (Pett, Interview). Pett is confident about his *ideas.* He doesn't believe that his own work is always artistically impressive,

but at least I feel I know what I ought to be doing, even if I'm not able to summon the drawing talent [that others have]. . . . The ones who have nothing to say and are wasting the space I think are doing a lot of damage to our particular niche in the field and to journalism at large. . . . I just don't think there's any doubt in the world that those of us who regard it a serious occupation are right about it and those who don't—I just don't understand their motivation. I truly don't. (Pett, Interview)

One of Pett's strongest and most passionate beliefs has to do with the role of political cartoonists in the press and in society.

Journalism is supposed to be important. We have constitutional protections, for the specific reason that it's supposed to be serious. That means that we're supposed to be keeping our eyes open so that we're helping people, who get busier and busier and more flooded with information, make some sense out of the world that they live in and give them some explanation of why they feel bad and less empowered over their own lives. (Pett, Interview)

His big quarrel with many of his peers is that he doesn't feel they believe this, that they are merely talented gagsters. He cannot understand why anyone would get into his line of work who had no anger in them about public issues. He feels that if one wants to be an entertainer he should write for television. "It's not a joke. It's not supposed to be."

Pett takes on the standard controversies of the day such as abortion, civil rights, the plight of the homeless, sex discrimination, environmentalism, age discrimination, strip mining, privacy. These comprise issues of public policy that he believes should be publicly discussed, even though he fears that "we are a culture that has no interest in public policy. We get the kind of leadership we deserve because of it, and it's disturbing to me" (Pett, Interview). To all these questions he applies a politically liberal imagination that challenges the reader to think, not laugh, about possible solutions. One two-panel cartoon concerning the NAFTA Treaty and its effects, for example, shows an academic speaking at a lectern in the first panel, stating, "What education needs is a dose of marketplace magic." The second panel depicts a classroom blackboard upon which is written, "Notice—today's class has been moved to Mexico. The Management" (*National Gallery,* June 14, 1992, 22). Another shows a contractor examining construction plans in front of a large billboard that states, "On This Site: another tacky commercial enterprise you'll never need, but will end up paying for" (*National Gallery,* Sept. 25, 1994, 22).

Pett also takes up issues that are not fodder for many other cartoonists, although he thinks they should be. He may be, for example, the only cartoonist to comment on the decision of airlines to end the practice of special low-price fares for bereaved families (*National Gallery,* Aug. 30, 1992, 22). He has pointed out that the promised "environmentally safe electric car" would in reality be powered by the nonenvironmentally safe nuclear and coal-power-generating plants (*National Gallery,* Apr. 17, 1994, 22). He is also one of the very, very few cartoonists, in these ethnically sensitive days, to casually and habitually include nonwhite characters within cartoons unrelated to racial issues. No doubt due to his childhood experiences in Nigeria, he sees African Americans simply as parts of the social scene. This is so, despite the fact that Lexington itself does not have a large nonwhite minority, so African Americans could be as safely ignored as they are in many other newspapers.

Pett's cartoons on international subjects focus often on the African continent and the often terrible plight of its peoples, due to war, famine, disease, commercial exploitation and political oppression. He draws with great sympathy here, often relating causes and effects back to the United States. A 1988 cartoon, for example, shows a starving African child holding up a large ashtray as a food bowl, while a text note relates the news item that the United States is increasing tobacco exports to the third world (*Rough Sketches,* June 14, 1988). Another presents a bleeding and dying black African lying on the ground wearing a T-shirt inscribed "South African Miners On Strike," while in the background a television set shows a woman's neck surrounded with a necklace and says, "Vanna's wearing this *fabulous* gold and diamond necklace . . . tell 'em the cost, Jack!" (*Rough Sketches,* Sept. 7, 1987).

Pett also relates international problems to local issues, as in the 1988 cartoon labeled "Machinery of Apartheid," which had South African Prime Minister Botha bulldozing and burying a native village in the first panel, and then showed South African stone being used for a new library in Lexington, Kentucky (*Rough Sketches,* May 1, 1988). Pett takes great pride in the emphasis he places on dealing with community and state issues, comprising about 40% of all his cartoons. One of the reasons his cartoons are not more widely seen is that local cartoons are rarely syndicated. Yet he was one of three finalists for the Pulitzer Prize in 1989, on the basis of a portfolio of solely local cartoons.

In fact, some of Pett's most inventive work has been done on local issues. During the 1987 governor's race, one candidate had labeled the other "weasel." Pett was delighted to adopt this metaphor, showing Wallace Wilkinson as a weasel (and his opponent as Mr. Toad) throughout the campaign. When Wilkinson was ultimately elected, Pett issued a "correction" cartoon clarifying the differences between a true "common dwarf weasel" and the "Governor of Kentucky," explaining that "Due to a conceptual error, the images below have been used interchangeably in this space. We regret any confusion" (*Rough Sketches,* Apr. 13, 1988). Pett hectored the governor's administration for the next four years in a series he called "Wally's World," which continued Wilkinson's depiction as a weasel. Kentucky Speaker of the Assembly Blandford was depicted as a skunk cozying up to the swine of "Polluting Industry" in a 1992 cartoon (*Read My Clips*). This attempt to prop up Kentucky's ailing economy by offering to serve as a dump for other states' trash served as a focus for another Pett campaign. Other local issues have included the plight of the poor and homeless, the worsening unemployment problem, mining accidents and lack of support for the state educational system.

Despite his seriousness of purpose, Pett's sense of humor still emerges in various ways in his work. He loves wordplay, and this emerges in unexpected places, such as a 1991 multipanel cartoon on the "smart bomb," which has the bomb "thinking" in its "Palindrome function option": "Drat! Saddam . . . A Mad Dastard!" (*Read My Clips*). As part of his trash receptacle series, he relabeled "Future Kentucky Counties" as: Bulldozitt, Oozeley, Graves, Phlegming, McCoffin, Brackish, Leachate, and the like. "Eco-Weasel" (Gov. Wilkinson), as part of his "Save the Stoat" campaign to preserve his administration, confronted the "envarmint," a conceptualization of environmental concerns.

With or without humor, Pett believes strongly that he, like all other political cartoonists, has a journalistic function that must be met to serve the readers.

Our attitude is that we're not telling you *what* to think; we're telling you what *we* think, and I think that to provoke your readers by a certain set of thoughts that they don't hold is a lot closer to what you should be doing than just to reassure them that what they already think is fine. If you are going to do cartoons that bash the U.S. mail or something that everyone agrees with already, what's the point of just reassuring everybody's anger? It's more fun to challenge them. It's tremendous good fortune to have this job, tremendous good fortune. Nobody, but nobody, gets to complain in public to such a great number of people all the time, as we do. Cartoons not only attract the eye, because any cartoon can do that, but once they've attracted the eye, they must have some payoff because they take up so much space. As far as I'm concerned, if something is going to take up two thirds as much space as a column, it had better be good. (Pett, Interview)

What more can one add to that?

Sources

Pett, Joel. Interview. By Jack Colldeweih. Jan. 1995.
——. *Pett Peeves.* Bloomington: *Herald-Times,* 1982.
——. *Read My Clips!* Lexington: *Herald-Leader,* 1992.
——. *Rough Sketches.* Lexington: *Herald-Leader,* 1989.

18

Bruce Plante, *Chattanooga Times*

Kerry Soper

While working as a caricature artist at Six Flags over Texas, several years before beginning his editorial cartooning career, Bruce Plante received an introduction to the visceral, angry reactions hard-hitting cartoons or caricatures can elicit from their targets. One particularly hot summer night, a middle-aged matron of conservative bearing, displeased with the liberties Plante took in rendering her face and figure, knocked him on the back of the head with a wooden purse. As a result of the blow, Plante fell unconscious to the ground and chipped his teeth on the pavement. No less passionate, but fortunately less physical, are some of the reactions Plante's subsequent editorial cartoons have provoked in the readers of several of the newspapers for which he has worked. During his first stint as a political cartoonist—a three-cartoon-a-week job at the *Arkansas Democrat* from December 1978 to October 1981—an advertiser dropped a $10,000-a-week account in protest to one of Plante's cartoons (*Chattanooga Life & Leisure* Oct. 1986: 39). At his next job with the *Fayetteville Times* in North Carolina (Oct. 1981-Feb. 1985), he managed to offend an entire military base by skewering Green Berets who had worked for Khadafy as mercenaries. This cartoon even elicited a number of death threats (*Just for Laughs: The Comedy News* Oct. 1989: 12).

Perhaps because of these extreme reactions, and in the hope of finding a more permanent home, Plante has taken a less confrontational tack in his latest position at the *Chattanooga Times*. As a relatively liberal cartoonist in a "*very conservative* town" (Plante's emphasis), he has been careful to court his new readership with a more palatable mix of friendly humor and gentle prodding (Plante, Interview). Plante feels that unlike the larger markets where cartoonists can be consistently hard-hitting, this smaller city requires a cartoonist who can satirize with tact and restraint. After a decade of building respect and trust, Plante feels that he can now address with more frequency such controversial topics as religious extremism and radical antigovernment movements without having his hard-core conservative readers take up arms against him. His restraint in the past, he hopes, will encourage the folks on the other side

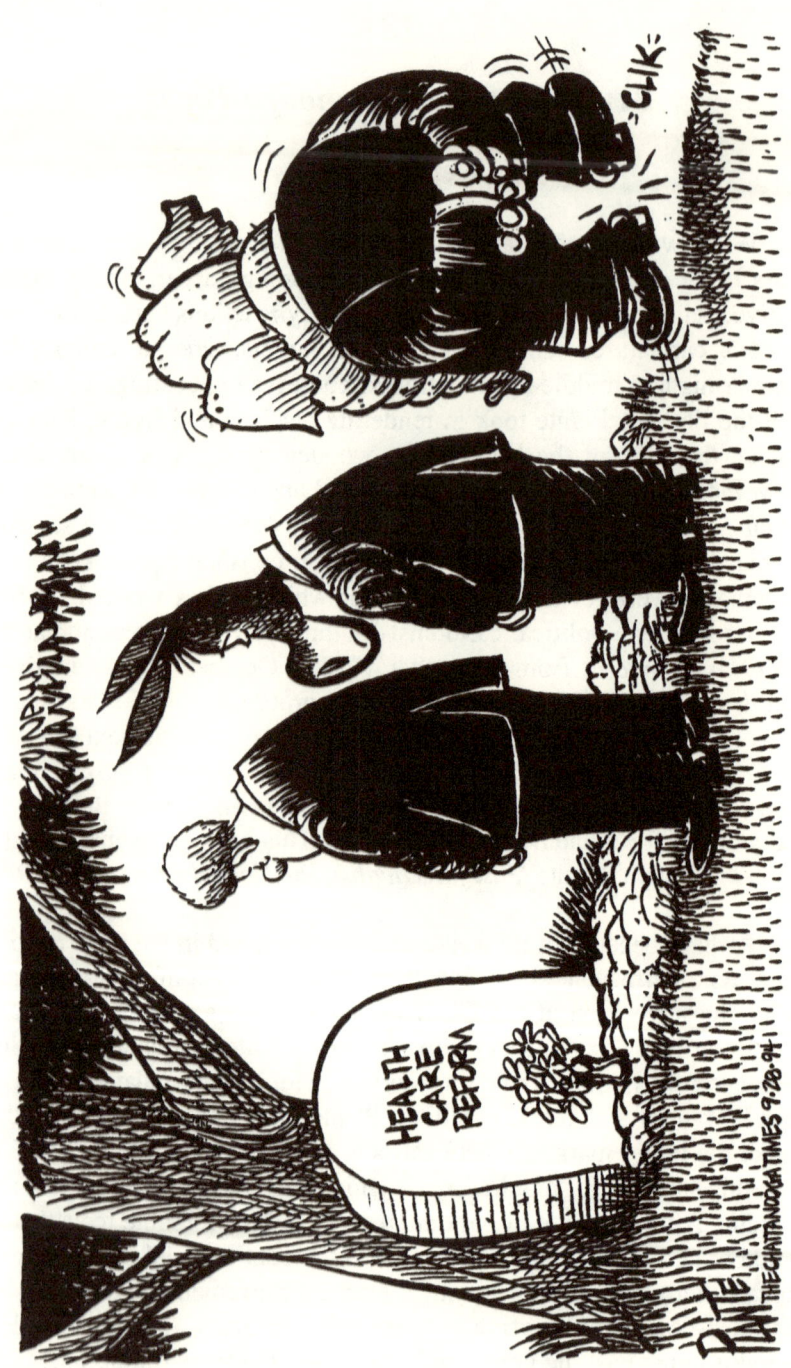

Bruce Plante (1994) *Chattanooga Times*.

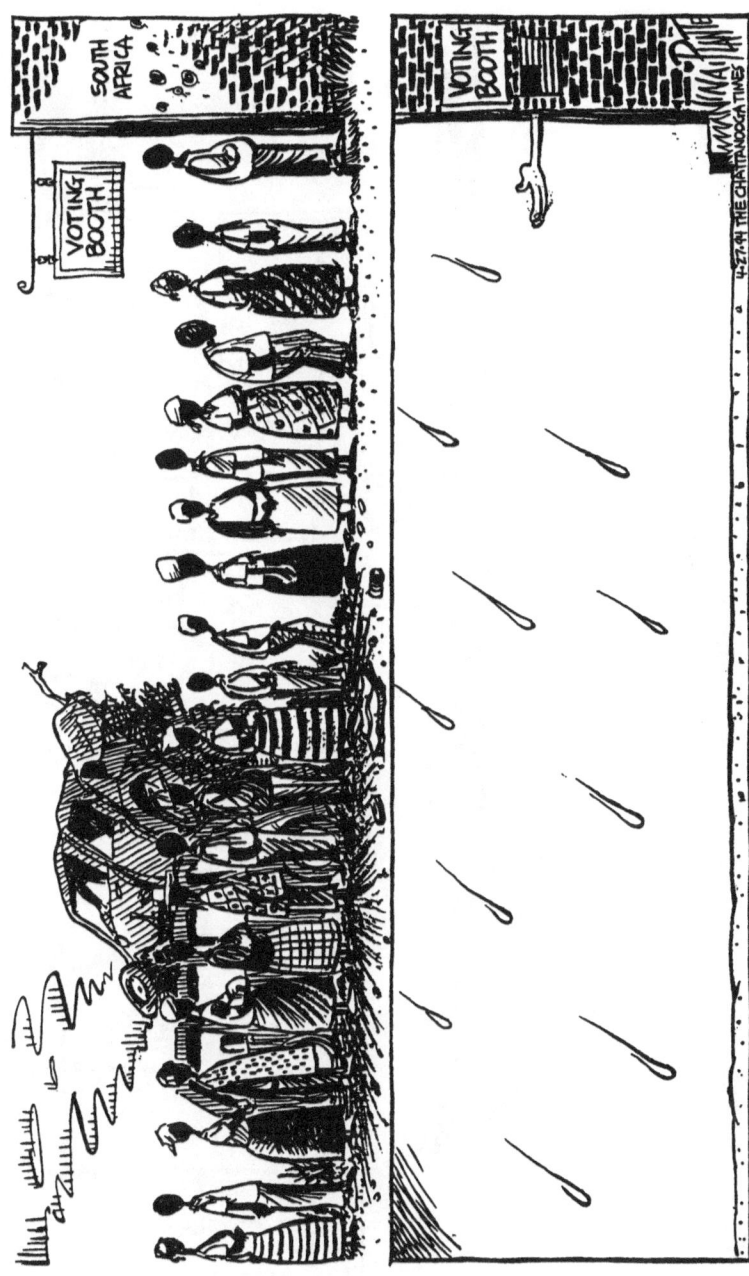

Bruce Plante (1994) *Chattanooga Times*. All rights reserved.

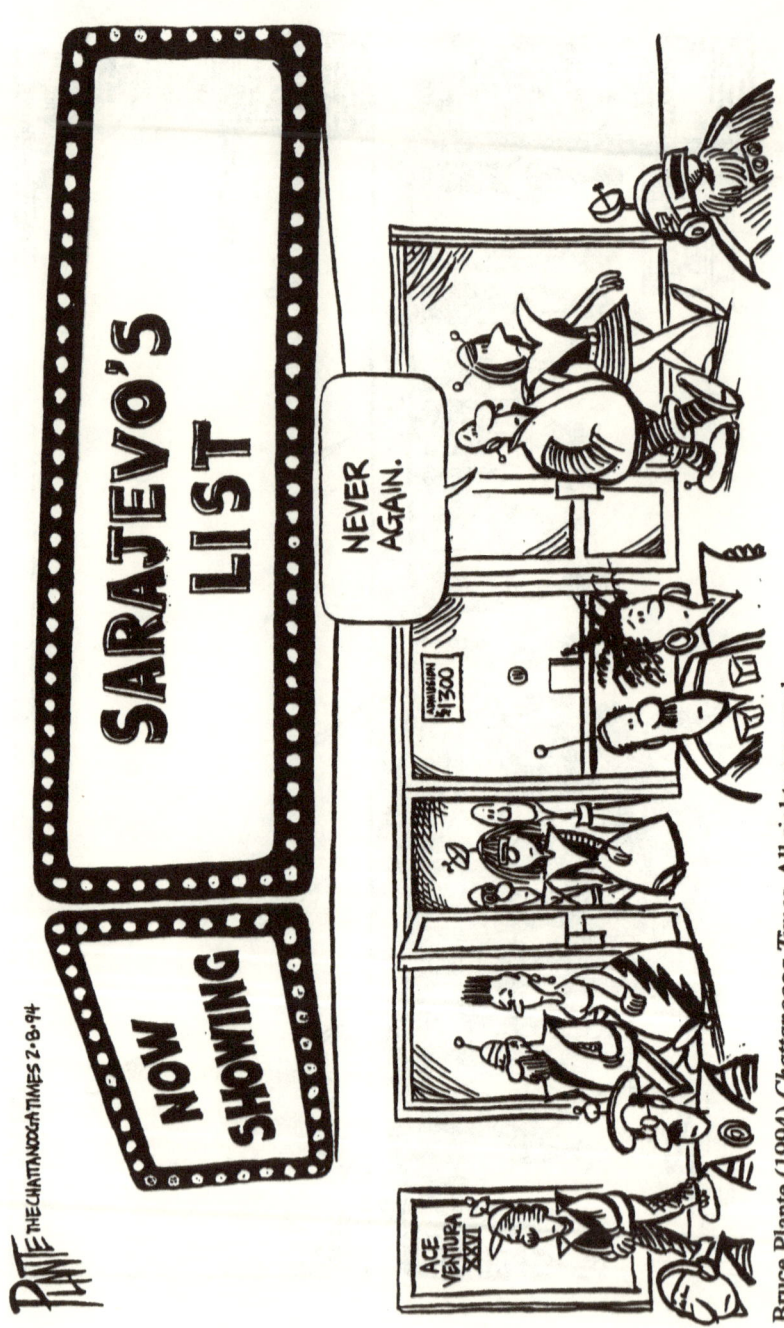

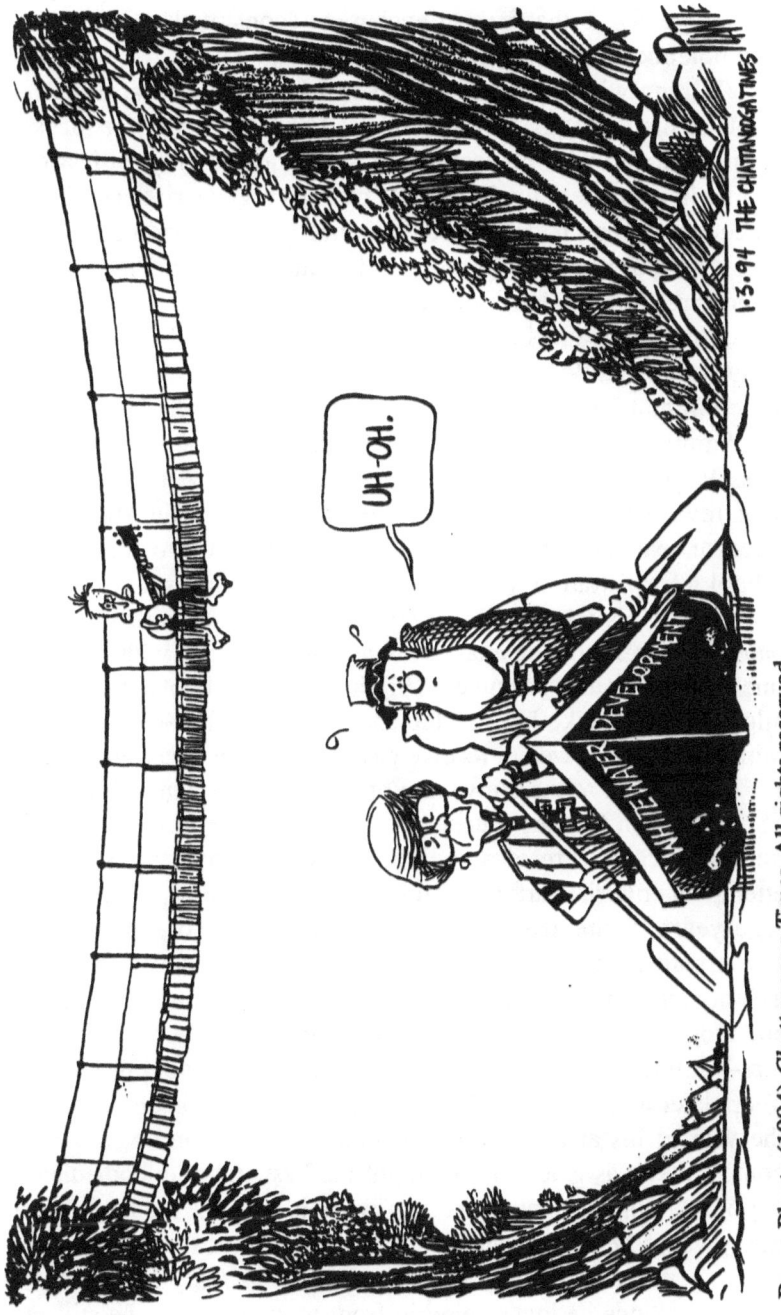

of the political fence to seriously consider his opinions. Although he can't resist the occasional, merciless jab at the provincialism or reactionary tendencies of the people in his adopted hometown, he prefers to satirize gently so that he can encourage "constructive dialogue" rather than polemical name-calling (Plante, Interview).

Talking with Plante, it is clear that he cares a great deal about the reaction his cartoons elicit in his readers. He craves feedback and is often frustrated with his isolated existence as the only professional cartoonist in a smaller city. Plante has perhaps a greater interest in immediate feedback than many cartoonists since the path leading to his present career has put him in front of many live audiences that have given spontaneous reactions to his comedy.

Born in Grand Island Nebraska September 9, 1954, to Delbert Plante and Nina Wilson Plante, he spent most of his childhood as a "construction brat" traveling from town to town, following his father's work. His family settled in Texarcana, Arkansas, (the other side of town from Ross Perot's birthplace and 30 miles from Hope, Arkansas), and Bruce soon revealed his comic abilities and desire to entertain. His early caricatures of teachers and classmates often got him into trouble with the school administration, but his parents were enthusiastic in their encouragement of his talents. They were, to him, the "quintessential, perfect parents." After winning a talent contest in fifth grade with a comedy routine that included a costume of hip-high wading boots, his parents even allowed him to take his standup shtick to a nearby adult cabaret. (As a minor, he was allowed to receive payment only in meals and T-shirts.)

In college, at the University of Arkansas, he continued to entertain at parties with his caricatures. A challenge at one of these gatherings to publish a caricature of a student officer led to Plante's first serious attempt at editorial cartooning for the local college paper. During his college years Plante seemed to be torn between two equally promising career paths: the stand-up comedian and the political cartoonist. Perhaps as a compromise, he spent his summers as a caricature artist at Six Flags and Dogpatch U.S.A.—a theme park based on Al Capp's cartoon characters—entertaining with a unique mix of his cartooning and comedy. Years later he still successfully combines the two careers. In fact, during the year of his arrival in Chattanooga he entered and won a Showtime contest that was geared to highlight the best stand-up comedians in the nation. Although Plante's standup work is now on the back burner, for many years he made regular appearances at local comedy clubs, and even opened concerts for entertainers such as Gary Morris and Lewis Grizzard. Since he loves being in front of an audience, he still manages to fit in performances for local civic groups and schools. Over the past decade Plante has been so eager to receive, for his newspaper work, the same type of immediate feedback that he's enjoyed as a standup comedian, that he'll often visit local breakfast places with the express purpose of observing morning readers' reactions. On one occasion he anonymously tipped a fellow who gave an especially enthusiastic response to a cartoon.

Plante's experience as a standup comedian has made him sensitive to the potential satire has to entertain, but he takes his work very seriously, subscribing to Pat Oliphant's ethic of indignation and pointed commentary taking precedence over gag-driven humor. Plante admits that there are always subjects that lend themselves to silliness, but he attempts to research all of his cartoons as if were an investigative journalist. He wants to avoid the knee-jerk reactions that many cartoonists adopt out of laziness or narrow-mindedness. Although Plante never had a natural interest in politics while growing up, he has, since becoming a political cartoonist, taken to assiduously following current events on CNN and Headline News and making efforts to research local, political issues (particularly environmental issues—one of his passions). Because of his interest in current events, one of his greatest frustrations is dealing with the fact that few of his readers are as well informed as he. He feels limited in the references he can make or the complexity with which he can construct his visual metaphors. For example, he was disappointed that many of his readers failed to spot his allusion to the film *Deliverance* in his cartoon of Clinton heading, literally, into whitewater troubles.

Plante cites Don Wright and Pat Oliphant as the working cartoonists that he admires the most; Wright for his original drawing style, and Oliphant "for completely changing the course of modern cartooning" (*Chattanooga Life & Leisure* Oct. 1986, 45). He also admires Steve Benson and Jim Borgman for their ability to create work that is both serious and funny. He lists as his mentors two Arkansas cartoonists who have received little national attention—George Fisher of the *Arkansas Gazette* (now defunct) and Jon Kennedy of the *Arkansas Democrat*—and Sam Rawls ("Scrawls") of *Creative Loafing* in Atlanta. George Fisher, Bill Clinton's "favorite" cartoonist, taught Plante when he was a novice the importance of making a point quickly and clearly, and the need to consistently address local issues. He also passed on the custom of including a loved one's name hidden in each cartoon—Fisher hid "Snooky" in honor of his wife in each drawing, and Plante includes "Nina" in honor of his deceased mother. (Many readers have assumed that this is an homage to Al Hirschfeld who included "Nina," his daughter's name, in his famous caricatures.) Plante occasionally regrets beginning this practice since many readers seem more interested in solving this visual puzzle than reading the cartoon, but he muses that perhaps there are people that wouldn't normally read editorial cartoons who might begin to pay attention when initially attracted to the drawings for this bit of fun.

Jon Kennedy, an artist who kept turning out excellent cartoons even when he was blind in one eye, and suffered from cerebral palsy, helped Plante get his first real newspaper job. Sam Rawls, who worked for many years at the *Atlanta Journal/Constitution,* before being unceremoniously dropped in favor of a younger cartoonist, encouraged Plante to keep struggling when jobs looked scarce, and helped him secure his current position at the *Chattanooga Times.*

Plante feels that he was perhaps too impressed with some of his mentors' work since he spent his early years trying to copy other cartoonists' styles. By his own admission, Plante's style can occasionally be generic; he attributes this to failing to let his own style develop naturally. Despite the praise he has received from other cartoonists for his "clean," bold approach to composition and inking, and his effective use of powerfully contrasting fields of white and black, he is often dissatisfied with the results of his work, and is still striving to find his own distinctive style (Plante, Interview). He inks his work with Windsor Newton series seven no. 1 or 00 brush and does some cross-hatching and lettering with a "le pen" felt tip marker. Recently he has been experimenting with computer-generated fields of shading (similar to the old Zippetone cut and paste shadings).

The simplicity of Plante's composition and brush work actually lends itself well to his unique form of self-syndication: scanning his cartoons into a computer and then faxing them directly to subscribing newspapers. Since Plante keeps his work clean and simple and faxes from a computer, rather than from a fax machine, the quality of the work that comes out in the receiving newspaper office is high enough to be transferred directly to the layout page. Plante saves himself a great deal of time and money using this method of distribution, and his twenty or so subscribers are impressed with the immediacy and convenience of the arrangement. But despite the success he's found with this novel form of distribution, self-syndication has been a daunting task. He won't go back to working with a syndicate (he was displeased with their lackluster promotion of his work), but he's considering forming a co-op of cartoonists that will help independents promote their work. He hopes that the information superhighway will eventually allow him to offer his cartoons directly to individual subscribers.

Like many political cartoonists, Plante is hoping to supplement his income by successfully syndicating a cartoon strip. "Noogie Elementary," the title of his strip creation, appears now only in the *Chattanooga Times*, but he has been working on it for four years and feels that it is refined to the point of being ready for a national audience. Plante's simple, cartoony style seems to be well suited for this genre—the characters are iconic but well developed, and the contrasting blacks and whites and dynamic, brush-created, line variation makes for a visually exciting graphic style. The humor shies away from anything political and is most successful when poking fun at pre-adolescent social life. Plante is aware that few cartoonists have successfully self-syndicated a strip (Nicole Hollander being one exception), but he's determined to make it work and has developed a complex promotional campaign that includes contests, T-shirts and lending his characters for public service announcements.

Producing both an editorial cartoon and comic strip six days a week allows Plante little free time. He spends his mornings absorbing news; conceptualizes, draws, and sends off his completed editorial cartoon by mid-afternoon; and then stays at the office into the evening until the next day's comic strip installment is complete. Unlike syndicated cartoonists who must remain up to a month ahead of their daily strip story line, Plante thrives working against a daily deadline, often coming up with ideas only because he has that intense pressure inspiring his thoughts. Despite this grinding schedule, he finds time to coach a little league team and participate in a men's baseball (*not* softball he's careful to point out) league. Other hobbies that he enjoys, but finds little time to pursue, are fishing and following the Razorbacks. He also makes an effort to spend as much time as possible with his wife, Betsy, and two sons, Jonathan and Benjamin. He and his wife see perhaps more of each other than couples in similar life situations since she also acts as his business manager.

Plante has won numerous public service and smaller-market newspaper awards including the Society of Professional Journalists Mark of Excellence, and the Associated Press First Place Managing Editors Public Service Award, but admits that he hasn't had the time to enter many national competitions. He plans on remedying this situation and has set the lofty goal of winning the Pulitzer while at the *Chattanooga Times*. In some of Plante's best work, such as "Sarajevo's List," and his treatments of local environmental issues, he appears to have the potential of attaining this prize. The fruition of Plante's career objective seems contingent on the maturation of his drawing methods into a more distinctive visual style, and a more consistent use of his sharp, satiric—and often confrontational—voice. Considering that the residual effects of Plante's early brushes with cartoon-related violence and abuse are beginning to fade, and he feels capable of taking a harder line in his local market, he may be primed and ready for this ascent to a Pulitzer-quality level of work.

Sources

Brescia, Andrew. "The Times' Resident Funnyman." *Chattanooga Life and Leisure* Oct. 86.

Plante, Bruce. Interview. By Kerry Soper. 17 May 1995.

Zimmerman, Joy. "Punchlines and Editorial Cartoons." *Just for Laughs: The Comedy News* Oct. 1989.

19

Michael Ramirez, *Memphis Commercial Appeal*

Thomas S. Langston

Kids are rushing to their deaths by joining gangs and doing drugs; Justice herself is in handcuffs; a burly man dressed in woman's clothing checks into the Las Vegas Hilton, hoping to cash in with a sexual harassment suit after the next Tailhook convention; and the President's Legal Defense Fund has put the White House up for sale. As these images from Michael Patrick Ramirez's editorial cartoons suggest, Ramirez is a conservative cynic. "Part of this job is to point out human error, and when you do that day after day, you become somewhat cynical," Ramirez explains. And besides, cartoons are on the editorial page so that issues can be presented sharply. "You've got to push the issue to the extreme," Ramirez believes. Ramirez does so, and admits to feeling neither regret nor guilt about his work, even when some people find it offensive.

When Ramirez won the Pulitzer Prize, gay militants in ACT-UP demonstrated both in Memphis, and at Columbia University during the awards ceremony, claiming that his cartoons were homophobic. They cited two in particular: a six-panel cartoon about a gay soldier "coming out" during formation roll-call (soldiers on either side of him move away); another showed a gay man, sitting on a tombstone, complaining that AIDS testing was cramping his lifestyle. Ramirez's response: "I believe in the right of extreme groups to express their opinion and I had hoped that they understood I have a constitutional right to ignore them" (*Editor & Publisher* June 25, 1994, 55).

As Ramirez sees things, while editorial textualists may wield scalpels of criticism, the cartoonist chooses from a more deadly array of implements. A cartoonist's integrity as a researcher ensures that his issues are "legitimate," and his or her editor, Ramirez says, "should set the parameters of good taste." Within these bounds, a cartoonist should use his or her autonomy to the fullest extent possible. There are three ways that cartoonists look at their work, according to Ramirez. Some cartoonists are humorists who draw: standup caricaturists. A second type, Ramirez continues, "illustrates current events." In a third school, in which Ramirez claims membership, cartoonists make "poignant state-

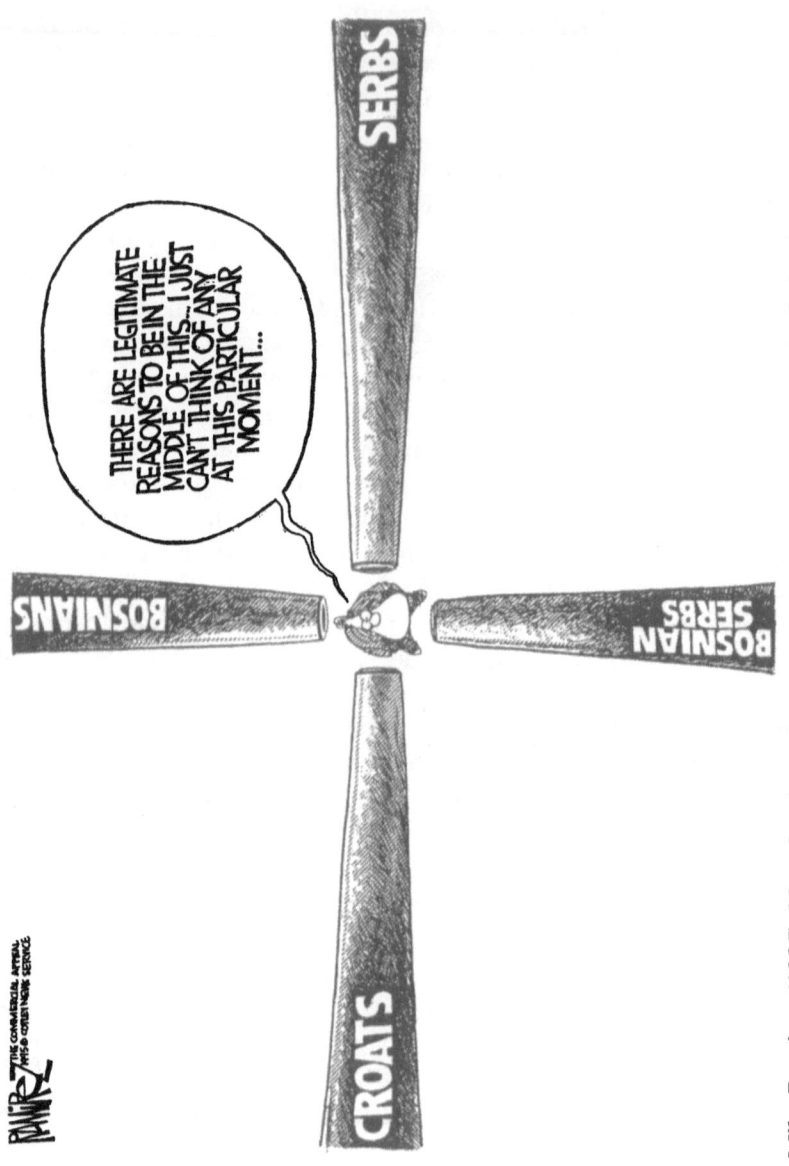

Mike Ramirez (1995) *Memphis Commercial Appeal*. Reprinted with special permission of Copley News Service.

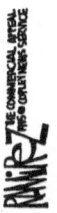

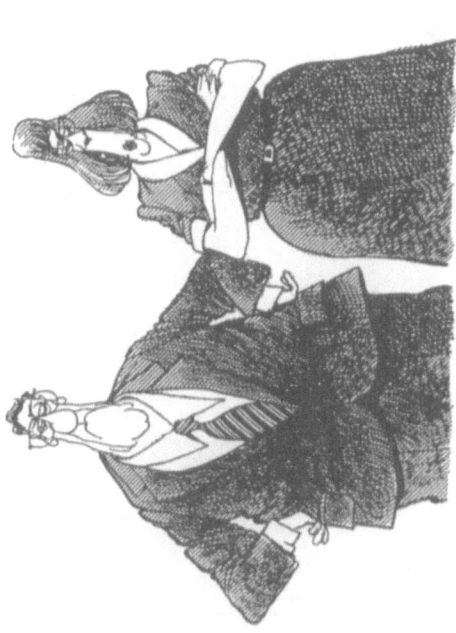

Two things that can immediately reduce teen smoking:

Parents.

Mike Ramirez (1995) *Memphis Commercial Appeal*. Reprinted with special permission of Copley News Service.

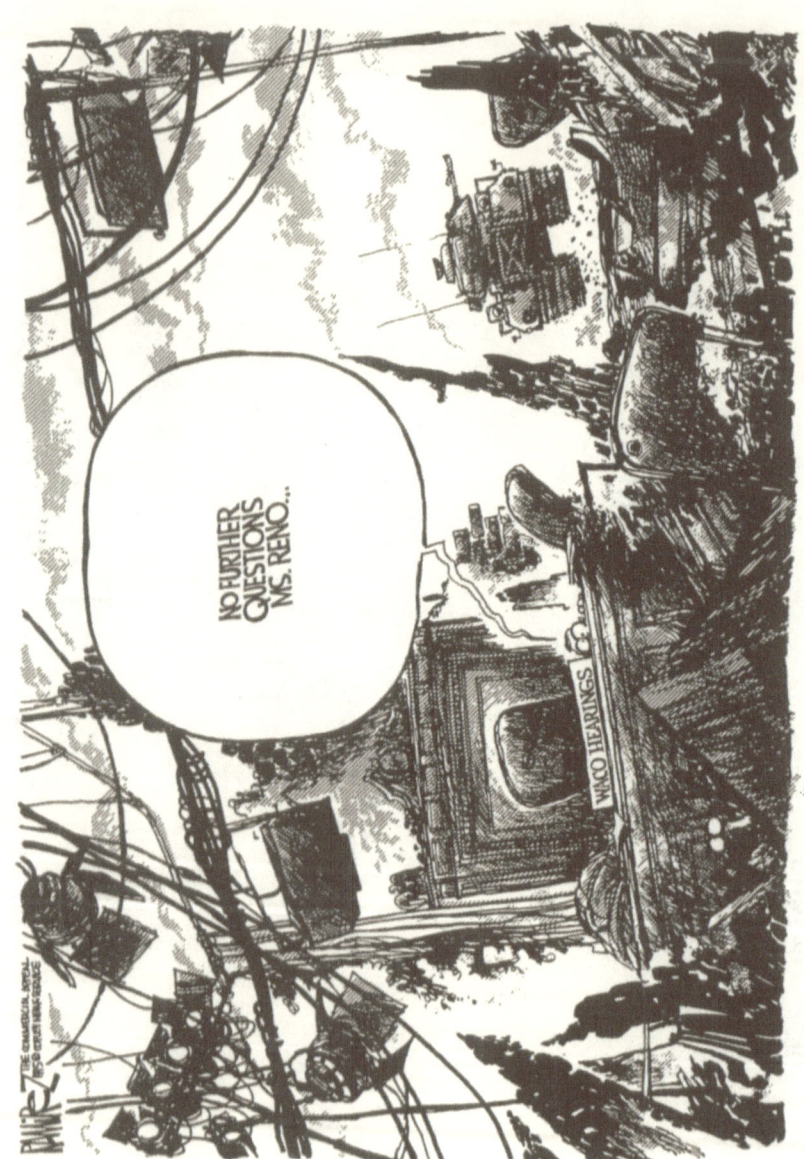

Mike Ramirez (1995) *Memphis Commercial Appeal.* **Reprinted with special permission of Copley News Service.**

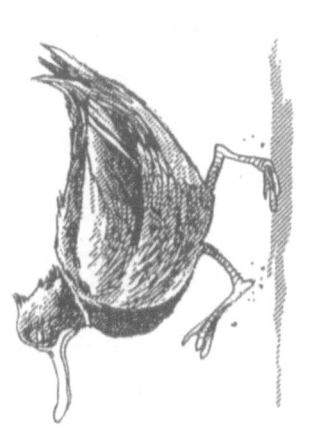
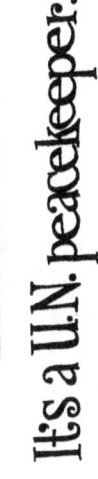

Mike Ramirez (1995) *USA Today*. Reprinted with special permission of Copley News Service.

ments . . . not just to provide levity, but to point out injustices." And if this requires, as it often does, that someone's ox gets gored, so be it. This is a tough view of cartooning. Its sources go back to Ramirez's childhood.

Ramirez was born to Fumiko and Irenio Ramirez at a United States army base in Tokyo. His father is a devout Catholic, and the younger Ramirez credits his father with instilling in him the conservative philosophy embodied in his cartoons. Later influences included George Will, William F. Buckley, Jr., and Whittaker Chambers, star witness for the notorious (or heroic, depending on who is telling the story) House Un-American Activities Committee's investigation of Alger Hiss, and author of the influential conservative memoir, *Witness*.

A dominant theme in the works of these conservative luminaries is the inestimable value of individual liberty. It was thus fitting that, once he began drawing, Ramirez would be moved by these authors. For Ramirez took the first step toward a career as a liberty-defending editorialist while in the pursuit of liberty as a teenager. As a high school student in southern California, Ramirez loved a single sport: surfing. Getting out of school to pursue his passion was, however, a problem. The solution became apparent when Ramirez noticed that staffers for the school newspaper could virtually write their own passes out of class.

In college, Ramirez again worked for the campus paper, but devoted most of his energies to other endeavors. His four siblings are today either medical doctors or on their way to becoming medical doctors, and Michael too graduated with a bachelors in biological sciences, from the University of California at Irvine. He also graduated with a major in fine arts. And while the latter degree serves him well as a cartoonist, at the time he thought of it as fodder for his medical school applications. Medical schools, he knew, would be impressed with a student who had demonstrated such catholic talents. Cartooning, and business, however, suggested other paths, and the elder Ramirezes would have to content themselves with an eighty percent progeny medical-school success rate. Michael, as he jokingly says, became "the black sheep" of the family.

In his junior year at Irvine, Ramirez co-founded what became a highly profitable corporate enterprise, Global Express Travel. He is no longer associated with the company, but its demands and rewards consumed Ramirez's ambitions until another seed planted during his college career began to grow.

The college paper at Irvine, *The New University,* was small enough that when the editor needed a cartoon and the cartoonist was not present, he knew that Michael could at the very least draw some sort of picture to go in the cartoonist's usual space. Michael drew a cartoon about an obscure campus conundrum. The response was more than he could have asked for, as he was hauled before the student body and publicly chastised. Far from a humiliation, this experience was an epiphany. With a well-chosen image, Michael realized, a cartoon can get a more immediate and visceral response than any number of well-reasoned editorials and expertly researched articles.

After drawing, and doing some writing as well, for two Irvine area newspapers, the *Newport Ensign* and *San Clemente Daily Sun and Post,* Ramirez headed to Memphis just as the 1980s were heading to a close. He had done well in California, having won several California Newspaper Publishers' Awards and becoming syndicated with Copley News Service in 1986. At the *Memphis Commercial Appeal* since 1990, he has done even better, winning the 1994 Pulitzer Prize for editorial cartooning.

The response to the Pulitzer afforded Ramirez an ironic opportunity to sharpen his definition of himself as a cartoonist with a conservative, but independent vision. When it was announced that Ramirez had won the prize, a representative from a Spanish-language television station called to request an interview. The interview never took place. It was bad enough, from the station representative's point of view, that Ramirez would have to do the interview in English. But when Ramirez said that "only if we stick to food" could he do the "Hispanic angle" for the entire time he would be on the air, it became clear that the cartoonist's story was not going to fit within the box that the television producers had already crafted for it.

It was thus fitting that the 1994 Pulitzer for best commentary was won by William Raspberry and Ramirez's cartoon in the *Commercial Appeal*. Raspberry and Ramirez are both opinionated men who defy stereotypes. Raspberry has black skin; Ramirez has a Hispanic surname. Just as the columnist would likely object to being thought of as a black columnist, Ramirez considers it the "essence of racism" to categorize persons, himself included, by ethnicity. In fact, the only way in which his Hispanic background is integrated into his work is that, as Ramirez acknowledges, his last name does "allow [him] to go further than other cartoonists" on such issues as American restrictions on illegal immigration from Mexico (Ramirez, Interview).

Ramirez takes his ideas seriously. That seriousness is not always thought becoming in a cartoonist is a fact of which Ramirez is painfully aware. The cartoonist recounts with humor what one exasperated colleague told him after yet one more editorial board meeting turned into an exchange of philosophical perspectives between Ramirez and another editorial-page contributor: "You know, Mike, you don't have to come to these meetings." It was all in fun, Ramirez insists, and he continues to attend meetings and to enjoy the debate that goes into setting the tone of his paper.

Ramirez draws his ideas largely from the day's events. For his *Commercial Appeal* drawings, he works at his office at the paper. For his cartoons that appear in *USA Today*, he uses an identically-equipped studio at his home.

Some of his favorite cartoons are those that suggest a principled response to social issues. A teenager climbs a diving-pool ladder in one panel. The board leads back to the ground, and to a grave marked Drug Deaths. The caption reads: "What goes up must come down." A similarly hard edge is evident in many of Ramirez's more explicitly political drawings. In response to President Clinton's early meanderings on Haiti, for instance, Ramirez depicted a ship, the "U.S. Haitian Policy," floating at sea. Attached to the anchor chain is a Haitian, face-down in the water. On the ship's deck, an officer announces: "Grab another anchor . . . We seem to be drifting again." And in the cartoon that the *New York Times* used to illustrate their announcement of Ramirez's Pulitzer Prize award, Yitzhak Rabin, and Yasser Arafat recognize each other through the burning rubble of what was moments before their common homeland: "Yitzhak?" "Yasser?"

Few of Ramirez's cartoons depend upon caricature. He draws a dependable, big-foreheaded and unerringly dumb Bill Clinton, and a savagely jug-eared, crazy-eyed, sour-grapes Ross Perot. His "ordinary" people are drawn cartoony in shape and proportion, with elongated faces and broad beams. But Ramirez's artistic talents and editorial interest seem put to better use in more abstract and symbolic representations. Artistically, Ramirez draws inspiration from his fine arts background, and his cartoons always show a strong concern for composition—a focal center, with either blank or sweepingly inked backgrounds for balance. Dialogue balloons are oversize, with words printed small in order to isolate and highlight the text. In addition to Oliphant, he cites Caravaggio, Rembrandt, and Mondrian as inspirations, and reports that he completed his first bronze statue just last year. In addition to pursuing art outside of the office, Ramirez is a musician. One of his great ambitions in life, he asserts, is to write "one really good song."

In looking through scores of cartoons in preparation for interviewing Michael Ramirez, one cartoon did not seem to fit with all the rest. On one side of the panel were sports cards of Pete Rose, O. J. Simpson, Darryl Strawberry, and other fallen greats. These were labeled "Perceived Heroes." On the other side of the panel were organ donor cards.

This pile was labeled "Real Heroes." The cartoonist seemed to be making a very personal statement. He was. Ramirez's father received an organ transplant several years ago. The transplanted organ is now dying, and because the demand for organs so greatly outstrips the supply, Michael's father will die along with the transplanted tissue inside of his body. Michael Ramirez will, of course, continue to cartoon, and to keep the focus of his work on the principles that his father taught him.

Sources

Editor & Publisher 25 June 1994: 55.
Ramirez, Michael. Interview. By Thomas Langston. 14 Dec. 1994.

20

Steve Sack, *Minneapolis Star-Tribune*

Roy E. Blackwood

Steve Sack is shy. Not the "painfully shy" of purple prose, but shy, nonetheless. Whether because of, or in spite of, that shyness, he's always gotten attention second-hand: through his art. His older brother, Mike, was captain of sports teams; he set records. "I had zero ability in sports, so I looked at art as a way to set my own little niche" (Sack, Interview). Other than "a few odd jobs" during college, he's never made his living any other way.

Stephen Richard Sack was born December 10, 1953, in West St. Paul, Minnesota. Even as a child he thought he might become a commercial artist. He says he thinks all young children like to draw, and he was no exception, but by second or third grade, his drawing stood out. His three brothers and two sisters didn't pay much attention to his efforts. His father Dick, a plumber, and his homemaker mother, Betty, were supportive, but it was from his peers at school that he drew most of his encouragement. "I always liked to draw funny things, and always got attention for my drawing ability," he says. "I wasn't any good in sports, and I was an average student, so I got attention for my art" (Sack, Interview).

After graduating from high school in West St. Paul, he enrolled at St. Cloud State University, about an hour's drive northwest of his home. He opted for an experimental program called "self-selection," taking a mix of classes in many areas rather than a traditional major. "I went at it with gusto, taking fencing, anthropology, and the like" (Sack, Interview). He even took a drawing and a design class. However, put off by his teacher's sneering attitude toward commercial art, he avoided taking more; little in his art comes from formal training. One of his earliest influences was *Mad* magazine, followed by animation, and various humorous cartoonists—especially those in the *New Yorker*.

Sack transferred to the University of Hawaii, for a semester of marketing and film classes, until he ran out of money. Returning home, then at the University of Minnesota, he took a part-time job as an illustrator for the university's *Daily*. After he'd been there a year, the paper's editorial

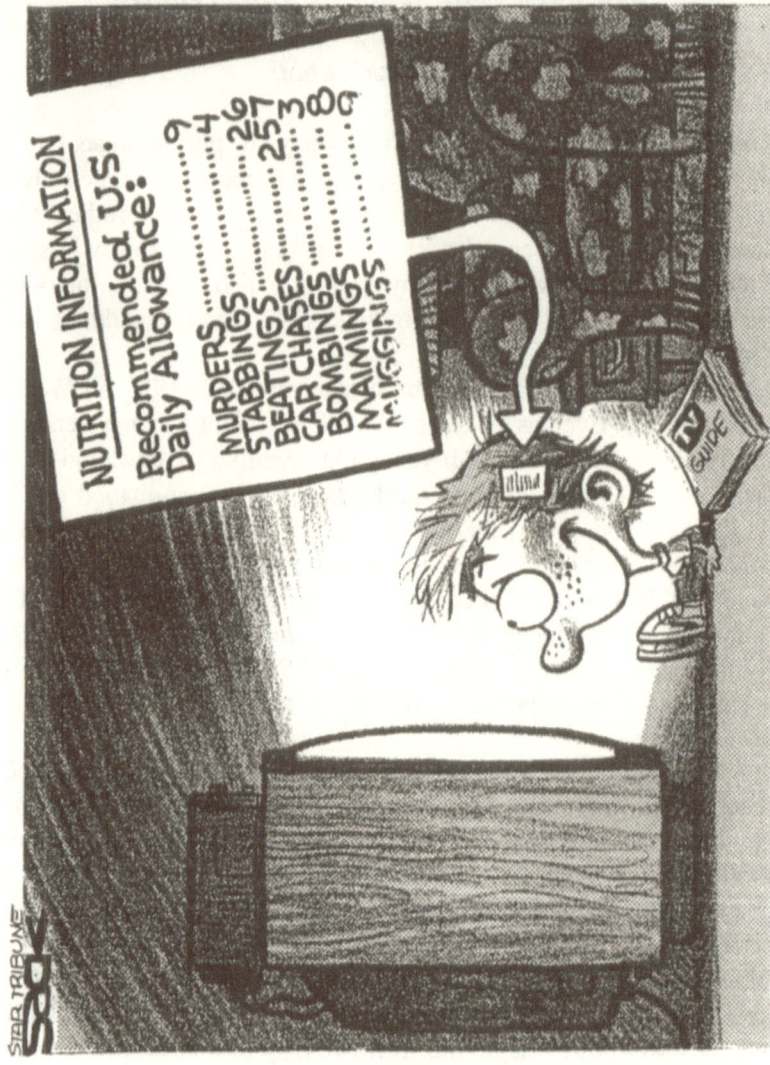

Steve Sack. *Minneapolis Star-Tribune.*

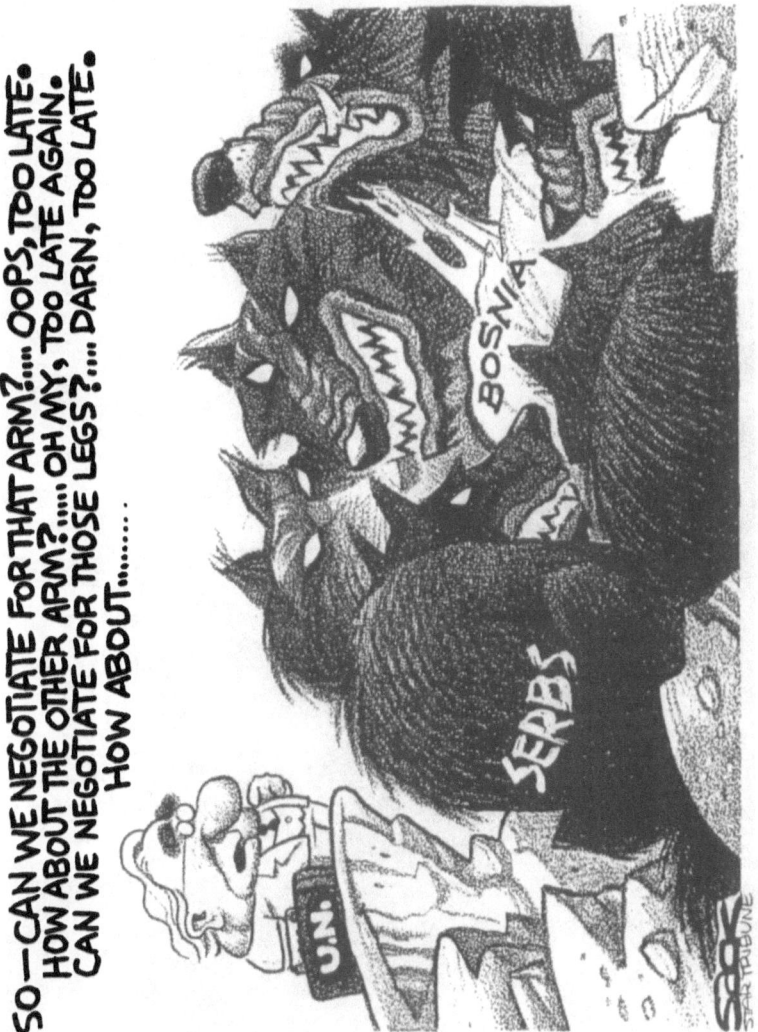

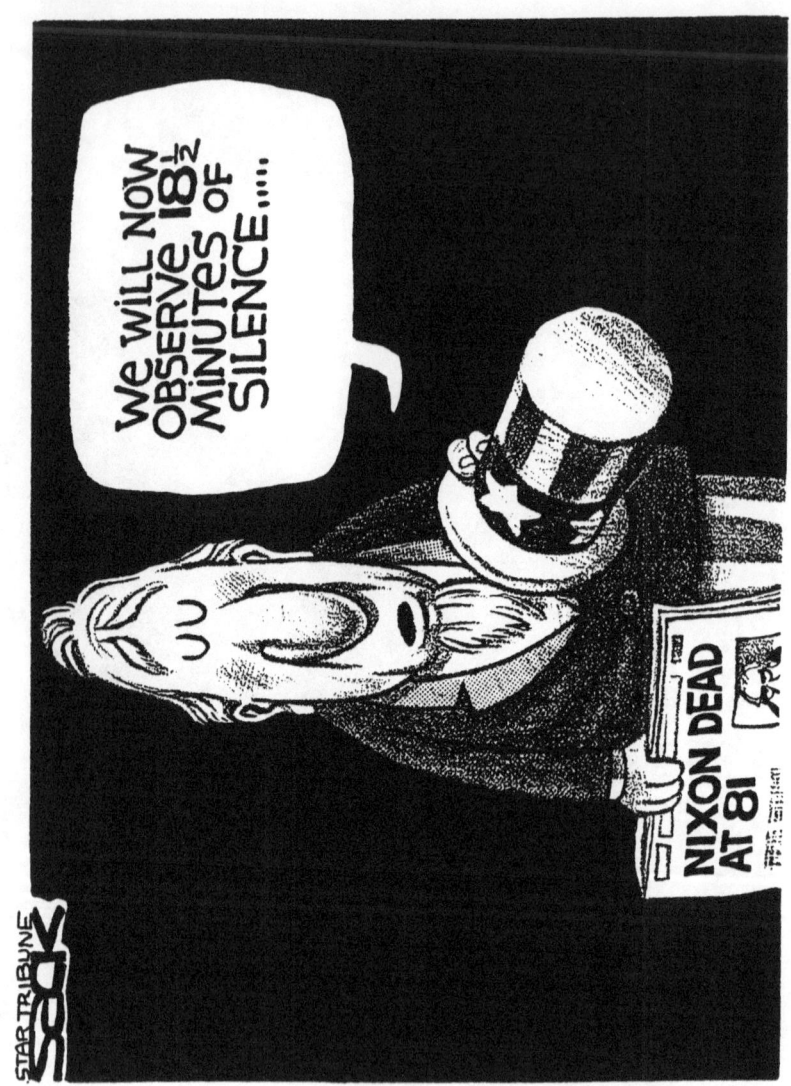

Steve Sack. *Minneapolis Star-Tribune.* All rights reserved.

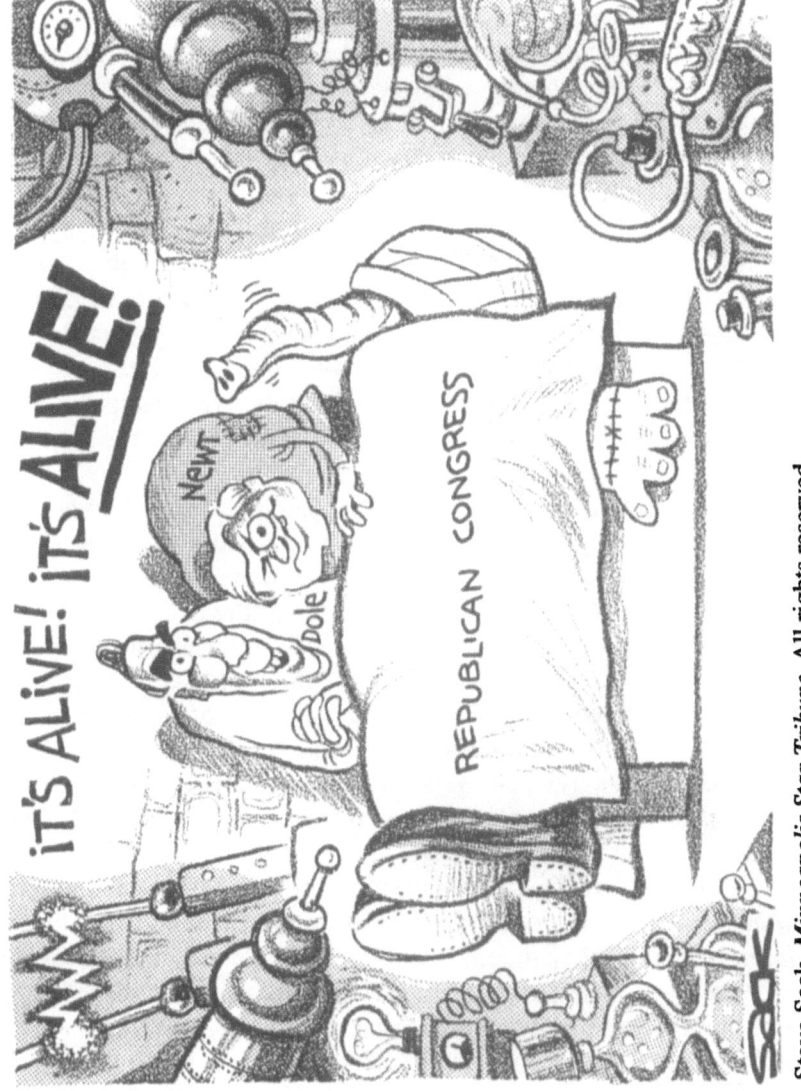

cartoonist ran for student president, promising that if elected he would quit as cartoonist. He lost, but quit anyway, so Sack took over as cartoonist. He says the *Daily* paid quite well, and had he wanted to work harder, he could have made "pretty good money" drawing a daily cartoon for them. "It was the first time that I realized you could do [cartooning] for a living" (Sack, Interview). Nonetheless, he chose to live modestly, by drawing about four cartoons a week, as well as occasional illustrations for feature stories. Having to be at least a part-time student to work for the paper, he registered for a few drawing classes, "but never came close to getting a degree." After two years, he decided to start looking for a "real" cartooning position.

From other student cartoonists, he had heard of an opening at the *Los Angeles Herald-Examiner*. He applied, but Bill Schorr from the *Kansas City Star* got the position. As it seemed logical to Sack that the *Star* then would need a cartoonist, he applied there. He was right; but they hired Dan Lynch from the *Ft. Wayne Journal-Gazette*. Not easily discouraged, Sack applied at the *Journal-Gazette*. He was spared further back-tracking: he got the job, and there he stayed for the next three years.

During this first "real" cartooning job, Sack says he was much influenced by MacNelly, Peters, and Oliphant, both in style and humor. Since then, he has made a dedicated effort to move away from them and develop his own style. "It's surprisingly difficult to do; you almost have to force yourself to draw in a different way." Sack has little patience for cartoonists who don't grow past their original influences: "I have nothing against influences; I just wish we'd look for more areas to be influenced from. The work of the real masters has all changed—grown—over the years. Some cartoonists get stuck on one period of some master's work, instead of reaching into themselves after their own work" (Sack, Interview).

While at the *Daily,* he had occasionally sent cartoons to the *Minneapolis Tribune,* a practice he continued while at the *Journal-Gazette.* Scott Long, cartoonist for the *Tribune,* retired in 1980, and the next year Sack was selected to replace him from among nearly 50 applicants. In 1982 the *Tribune* merged with the *Minneapolis Star,* and the resulting *Star-Tribune* found itself with two editorial cartoonists. Sack drew five cartoons a week, and Craig McIntosh drew three, as well as illustrating the Op-Ed pages. Sack and McIntosh also began collaborating on "Professor Doodles," a children's puzzle and comics page for the Sunday edition. Through syndication with Tribune Media Services, "Doodles" has since been picked up by about 80 other papers. Sack's editorial cartoons appear in about 40 newspapers, through the same syndicate. In 1993, McIntosh resigned from the *Star-Tribune* to concentrate on drawing the popular "Sally Forth" cartoon strip written by Greg Howard.

To ensure growth, he wages continuous combat against complacency in his own style. He periodically changes the type of paper, pencils, and other tools he uses, but chief among his weapons for change is his subconscious. "I have looked at sketches in the margins of my own work, doodles I make while on the phone, drawings I've done for fun, rough sketches that I have enjoyed shading and blending." He has tried combining newer styles with older materials. Rather than the ink many cartoonists use, he has tried using pencils, crayon, chalk, and colored pencils. "I'm not comfortable with it yet," he says. "Every few months, you think you've found just the right thing, and you'll use it the rest of your life; then after a couple of weeks, you begin to find things not quite right with it" (Sack, Interview). He says the actual aesthetics are less important than that the artist exhibits a personal style.

The artwork in Sack's editorial cartoons and that in "Professor Doodles" is, not surprisingly, quite different. His real departure as an artist, however, is squirreled away in the basement of his suburban Bloomington home, where he lives with his wife, Linda, and their son, Adam. There are stored numerous "Rube Goldberg"-style mixed-media, mechanical sculptures. "We need to do outside art," he insists, "to give us fresh views of what we do in cartooning." He says he has given some of his creations away, and sold a few "almost by accident," but has no desire to mount shows or to put them on display. He says simply: "They're for me" (Sack, Interview).

Sack says he is philosophically opposed to contests, and enters them only under editors' orders. Consequently, he has won only "a couple" statewide awards, which he refuses to remember specifically. Nor has he accepted offers to publish collections of his cartoons. "It's a lot of work; it doesn't interest me. I've already seen these cartoons. There's just no real reason I want to [publish], rather than any reason I don't" (Sack, Interview).

His working hours are flexible, but he generally starts by reading the *Star-Tribune* at home, after Adam has gone to school. An hour with the paper usually garners four or five topics that he sketches and works with all morning. He is still mulling over those topics when he gets to his office after lunch. There, he often spends some time with the *New York Times*, and may skim *USA Today*, but he says that "almost always" one of the original topics from the *Star-Tribune* will become his cartoon for the day. He eliminates a couple of topics, but keeps three or four with which to try several presentation ideas. He says he likes to draw a wide range of topics, but draws on sports or business only if they have become front page news. He does not consciously choose among local, state, national, or international topics, but goes with "what people are talking about." "By people, I mean my mother, wife, friends, co-workers. I mostly do what's in the news, what interests me at the time. [The subjects] don't all have to have heavy meaning" (Sack, Interview).

Although Sack says there are no topics he does not like to draw, there are a few, including gun control, that he prefers to comment on because he thinks they are important. "On some topics, such as race or women's issues," he says, "I wish I could think of good ideas that would add to the conversation. Sometimes a topic almost demands coverage: a new president, a big death, a disaster." In such cases, his time is spent not choosing a topic but determining its best presentation. Ideas for presenation don't always flow the way he'd like. "Sometimes I can't focus, so I go on errands, walk around, make some calls, wait for it to come to me" (Sack, Interview). After he has several roughs—some from home, some from the office—he shows them to fellow workers (but not his editor) for their reactions. He stresses that the decision is always his own, but he likes to avoid making up his mind until he hears what others have to say.

Once the idea is set, it takes him only about an hour and a half of "really focused art work" to complete the cartoon. "That's the fun part," he says, "where it sort of flows from me." The reason the ratio of time spent on the idea, compared to the execution, is so great is that Sack considers the concept more important: "A good idea with bad art is still a good cartoon; good art with a lame idea will produce a lame cartoon" (Sack, Interview).

Sack is very critical of his own work. "I draw about two cartoons a week that I'm satisfied with, and three a week that I'd just as soon not have my name on. I keep looking for the perfect one, and it never comes" (Sack, Interview). He has no favorite cartoons that he has drawn, but the ones he best remembers are those that people have reacted strongly to. The paper got about 100 angry calls about one Sack cartoon that pictured Uncle Sam, hat over his heart, holding a newspaper with a headline announcing Richard Nixon's death. The caption: "We will now observe eighteen and a half minutes of silence."

Sack says angry reactions don't much bother him; he realizes that there are just as many cartoons he does that people like but he does not hear about. "If they like it, they clip it; show it to a friend. If they don't, they call or write to the paper. No matter what you do, somebody will always have a different opinion." More than 50 people called to express outrage the day he reacted to headlines about toxic substances in a regionally distributed ice cream by drawing a group of people holding cones and shouting: "I scream, you scream, we all scream. . . ." After all, according to Sack, "Editorial cartoons are not necessarily funny. A cartoon about Bosnia should't be. If you use humor with such topics, it's in bad taste. I prefer to draw good cartoons, whether angry or hilarious. The temptation is to go for the joke; often that's what's rewarded. But I prefer cartoons with a little more bite, some message to them." He recognizes the need for words in most cartoons; in some, he says, "copy is crucial." In such cartoons, however, "The art and copy must have the same tone, be intertwined. You can't really separate them. It's important that they match" (Sack, Interview).

Sack would have people keep the importance of editorial cartoons in perspective. "They are simply one feature in the newspaper;" he says, "one person's opinion; their value is based on how readers see it. Cartoons, I don't think, change many minds, and I don't know if they should. Anybody whose mind is changed by what they see in a cartoon would have it changed by what they see in the next commercial, as well.

"They are a tiny part of what people pay for a newspaper for, but they are one part we offer people. The cartoon is our message; we speak to our readers through our work. It's a personal thing, like a column. I don't think of myself as a journalist; I'm a citizen who's offering one view of a topic. But it's fun; I love to draw. It's a good way to express myself, but especially, I love to draw" (Sack, Interview).

Source

Sack, Steve. Interview. By Roy Blackwood. 22 Nov. 1994.

21

Mike Shelton, *Orange County Register*

Kalman Goldstein

Mike Shelton of the *Orange County Register* is nothing if not pungent. Introducing himself as a conservative with libertarian bones—whose bones are increasingly prominent—during our conversation he repeatedly castigated big government and expressed contempt toward those editorial cartoonists who tread the "middle of the road," referring to "dead skunks" or to "a yellow stripe." He seems puzzled by others' surprise at his ideological stance; just because he was born in Houston in 1951 and raised by poverty-stricken grandparents in the traditionally Democratic stronghold of hardscrabble East Texas, people apparently expected him to become a Fair Deal moderate. Rather, the older he got the less use he had for liberal, "big government" policies that he was convinced were depriving citizens of initiative and self-reliance. In a November 24, 1991, cartoon, he joked that the Democrat he liked "better than Bush" was Thomas Jefferson (with laissez-faire champion Grover Cleveland a close second?).

The older he got, the more outspoken as well. Returning from a tour of duty in Vietnam as a Marine, he began cartooning for self-expression and enrolled in Sam Houston State College as an art major. When he realized he probably could make a living at cartooning, he dropped out of school during his junior year and was taken on by Copley News Service in 1981. In 1982 he got his first full-time newspaper job, with the *Fort Worth Star Telegram*, but left there after a year of confrontations over cartoons that House Speaker Tip O'Neill thought were insulting to Congressman Jim Wright. In 1983 he affiliated with King Features Syndicate and accepted his present position in Orange County, California. The *Register* is a right-wing libertarian paper, so Shelton feels at home, lambasting Democrats like Ted Kennedy (the "epitome of the other side's philosophy") and President Clinton on any number of issues, and supporting conservative Republicans.

But he cannot fully trust any politicians; in his estimation most are either trimmers or opportunists due to the very nature of their profession. This cynicism forms the basis for one of the strongest recurring themes

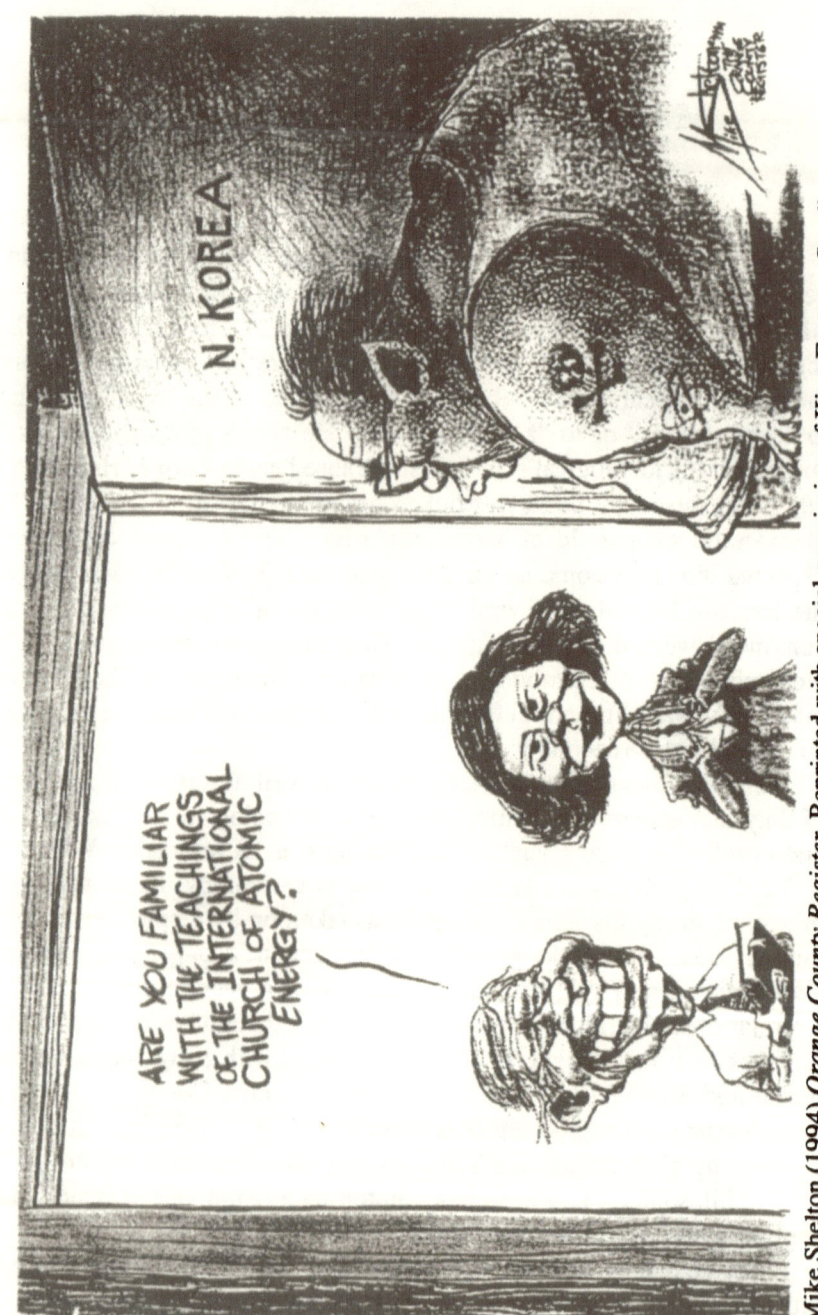

Mike Shelton (1994) *Orange County Register*. Reprinted with special permission of King Features Syndicate.

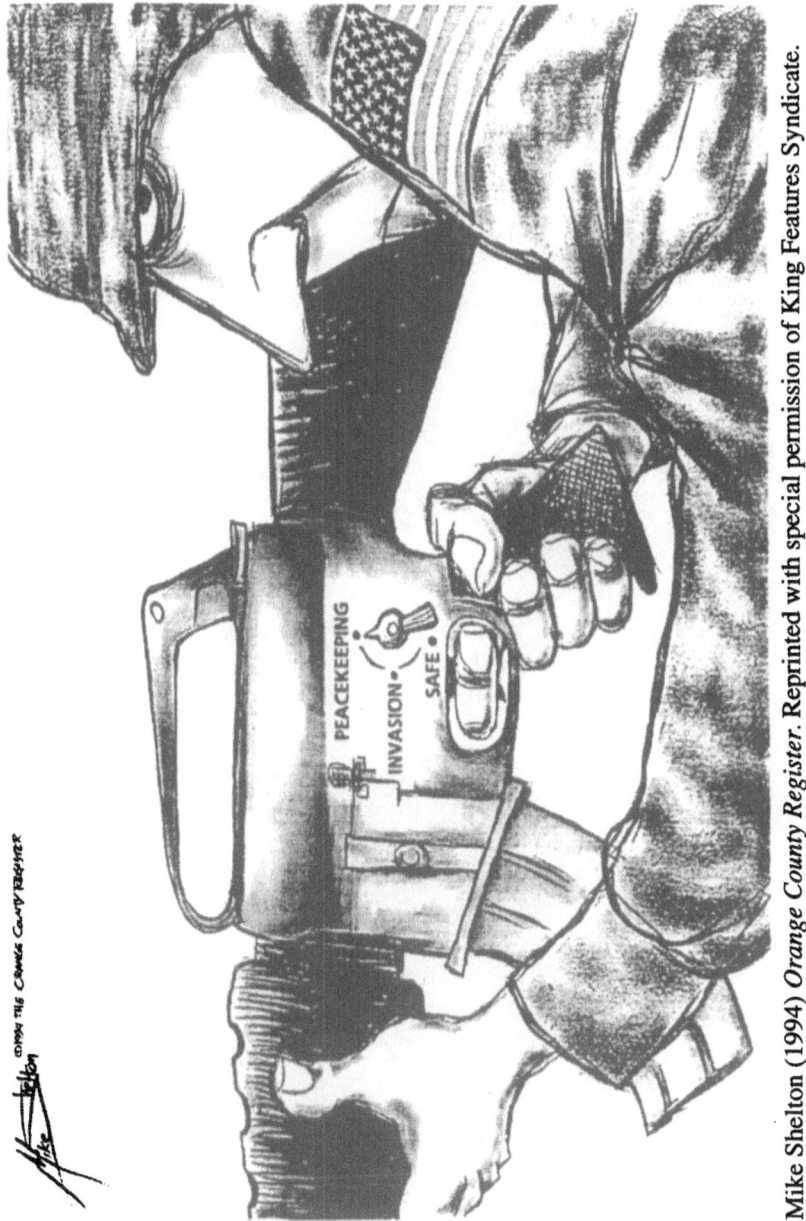

Mike Shelton (1994) *Orange County Register.* Reprinted with special permission of King Features Syndicate.

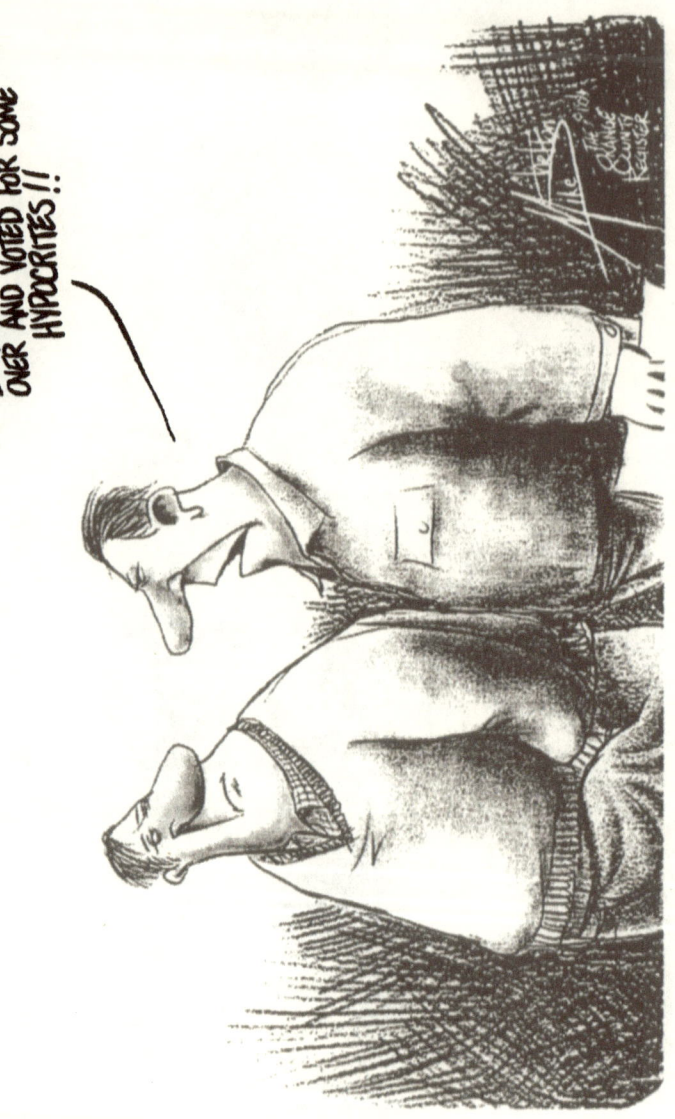

Mike Shelton (1994) *Orange County Register.* Reprinted with special permission of King Features Syndicate.

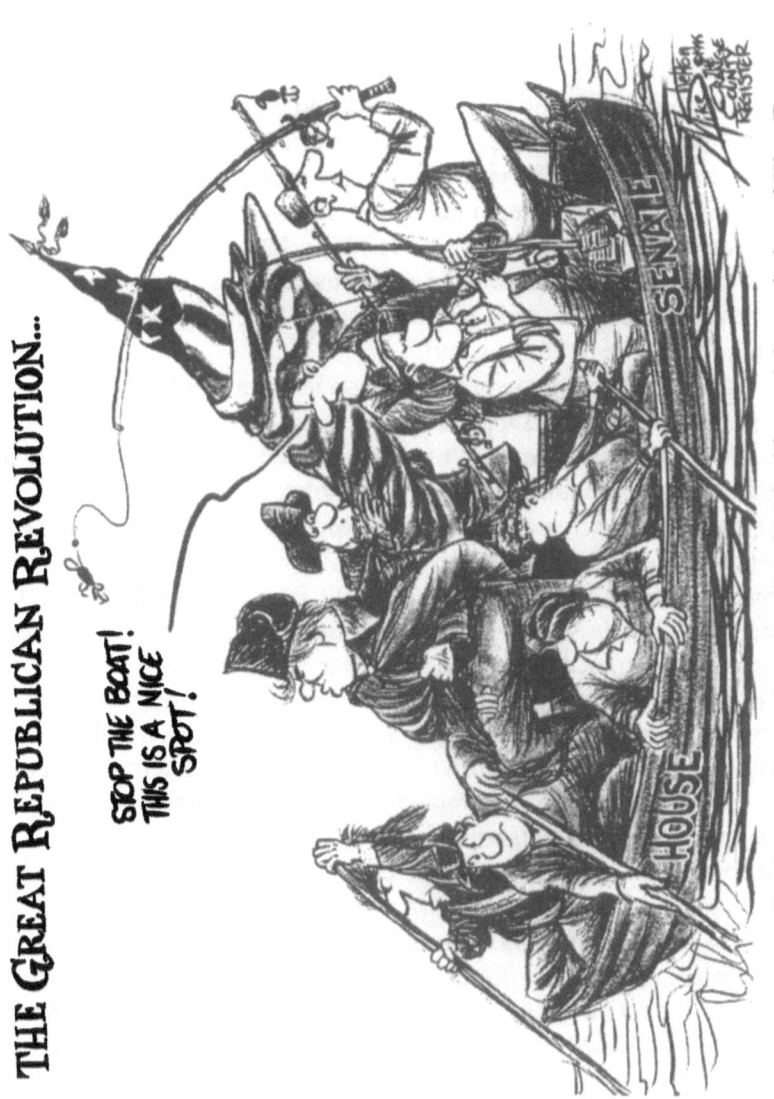

Mike Shelton (1994) *Orange County Register*. Reprinted with special permission of King Features Syndicate.

in his attacks on Bill Clinton, summed up in a computer-generated triple image of the President enunciating his "vision for America" (*New York Times* Feb. 5, 1995). When the 1994 election returns were in, he drew three Marines holding crutches and a wheelchair labeled "Lame Duck One." So Shelton had to be happy that so many right-wing Republicans were elected. "But I'm going to watch them pretty closely, because I just don't trust them. They are going to need a little motivation to continue to do the right thing (Shelton, Interview). So he has also created a running series of cartoons comparing Speaker Gingrich and the House firebrands with the more genteel Republican Senators and Bob Dole, the wittiest of which is "The Great Republican Revolution," or "Newt Crossing the Delaware" (*Bergen Record* Mar. 21, 1995). More exasperated is a series of chastisements of Republican legislators for their reluctance to push for promised term limitation proposals, and "the people's" confrontation with a life tenure Supreme Court.

In the same spirit, and in opposition to other California and national conservatives, Shelton supports legalized drugs (many of the new political leaders themselves smoked marijuana at one time) and opposes anti-smoking laws (though himself an ex-smoker); he also deplores the current nativist fervor as a denial of our historic promise of the American Dream to hard-working, tax-paying immigrants. Home-grown libertarian armed militias he finds either illogical or hysterical (*New York Times* June 4, 1995). He sees his function as that of a gadfly against inconsistency or rationalized hypocrisy. "If you can't afford to be an idealist and constantly follow your philosophy, at least you need somebody who can, to remind you where you are going wrong. It is necessary that there are people like me, who can afford to be perfectionists" (Shelton, Interview).

Because he is uncompromising in calling governments or the citizenry to task, most of his cartoons have a sharp edge to them, and even a menacing look. Sometimes this is expressed in populist terms, as in his "liars and hypocrites" cartoon (*Bergen Record* Nov. 16, 1994). Or he may sneer at a smarmy Ted Kennedy, down to his shorts, inviting sexual harassment complainant Anita Hill to his hotel room for a "de-briefing" (Brooks 145). Or, in one of his infrequent takes on the O. J . Simpson case, in July 1994 he berates the citizenry for being more interested in voyeurism and souvenirs than in alleged violations of the Fourth Amendment. His humor is always rough.

But his meanest and most vitriolic cartoons concern foreign policy, and may arise from his own military experience; he is furious with any decision that might involve pointless risk to American soldiers, or result in their betrayal. On December 15, 1994, he accused President Clinton of caving in to Somalia's warlord Mohammed Farah Aidid while standing over the bodies of UN soldiers killed by Aidid's faction. At least a dozen times during 1994, he opposed American intervention in Haiti; some of his most startling images in this cause represented Haiti as a grenade whose pin was being pulled by soldiers raising the "flag" of Clinton's foreign policy, and a truly arresting closeup of a nervously wide-eyed American soldier whose weapon has settings for "peacekeeping" and "invasion." His most emotional cartoon on foreign policy, however, was done in early February 1995, when he likened Clinton's rapprochement with Vietnam to a lynching of American prisoners of war, with the President personally pulling the rope.

Yet Shelton would undoubtedly reject being called an isolationist. His cartoons about Bosnia either represent wishful thinking about our planes destroying Serbian tanks (*Bergen Record* Apr. 12, 1994), or condemnation of UN irresolution for failing the Bosnians. Here, again, Shelton not only pulls no punches, but creates a visceral image that both shocks and offends. As the UN soldier's trousers are pulled off, his blouse resembles a short skirt exposing net stockings held up by a garter belt. The distraught Bosnian mother is reminiscent of Munch's *The Scream.* Shelton believes we have a role to play in Bosnia, and should long ago have exerted pressure against Cuba; he is impatient with any diminution of the defense industry or the cancellation of overseas base leases, and distrusts Russian intentions. Rather than an isolationist he is a skeptic, epitomized by his reaction to Jimmy and Rosalyn Carter's "naive" mission to North Korea.

His attitude toward the Clinton administration's foreign policy is related to skepticism about both its anticrime initiatives and its health care proposals; he considers them transparent smokescreens for other failures. During 1994 he satirized Congressional investigations into the Whitewater affair, alleging White House coverups of financial scandals that might implicate Bill Clinton or Hillary Rodham Clinton. In one cartoon, the President autographs jockey shorts to raise money for the Defense Fund, a reference to a "revelation" about his underwear preferences; Hillary sells chocolate chip cookies, a reference to a "defense" of her feminine role during the campaign. In another, Bill Clinton tries to pass all responsibility for the imbroglio onto his wife. And two others attacked Whitewater committee chairman Henry Gonzalez, a Democrat, for trying to downplay the whole issue. In both 1993 and 1994 he drew a series of attacks on the Brady Bill for handgun control either as hypocritical in the face of American involvement in international arms sales, or as unworkable in any case. Significantly though, he also commented on those Republican candidates who repeated pieties about "law and order" while campaigning (*Bergen Record* Aug. 30, 1994).

Mike Shelton prides himself as much on an innovative graphic style and approach to technology as he does on the unsparing vitriol and ideological purity of his cartoons. Most editorial cartoonists still compose at the easel, or will finish off cartoons through computerized colorization, but Shelton is one of the first editorial cartoonists to compose directly upon his computer. He uses a computer, printer, scanner and modem, with an electronic drawing board, which he is proud to show off. With them, he can create any type, shading, tactile quality of background, and sixteen million hue combinations. The *Register* has been running his cartoons in color since the fall of 1990; they have the look of having been painted on canvas, and are almost three dimensional. His move to using the computer for composition has markedly transformed his style. He employs fewer and larger figures, leaves more white space, draws smoother but thicker lines without the ink splatters of earlier cartoons, and employs far less dialogue than previously. He now aspires to create 30-second animated political cartoons, and expects that a proliferation of special interest cable programs will outflank the Federal Communications Commission's "fairness doctrine," which has hobbled past attempts at presenting controversial political graphics on commercial television.

When we spoke, Mike Shelton was returning from a lengthy vacation during which he was contemplating the future direction of his work. He had had to engage in some disagreements with his paper over cartoons, which he insists were misrepresented as racist, and were not printed. The situation is unlike that on the Fort Worth paper, because while the editors do disappoint Shelton in some cases, "sometimes they surprise me—sometimes they print cartoons I thought never would get printed" (Shelton, Interview). However, it had forced him to do gag cartoons about sports (the baseball strike) and Elvis Presley's hypothetical reaction to his daughter's marriage to Michael Jackson. Shelton generally dislikes using puns or "easy" popular culture references, though he does not categorically reject humor cartoons. "Otherwise the job can get to you, put you in a dark mood and rob you of humor, and [then] you *always* go for the jugular." But in going for the humor, cartoonists should never lose sight of the stronger point they wish to make. Few of Shelton's cartoons are neither directly political nor pointedly ideological.

Stung, for a while he thought that his insistence on self-expression might not be worth the grief, so he avoided sensitive topics such as race, gender and abortion rights. But he has now gotten over this reaction, and vowed not to make such concessions in the future. Mike Shelton is prepared once again to shock rather than simply to entertain his readers. "I don't want to be cute; I'd rather somebody open their paper in the morning, just as they are lifting the coffee cup to their mouth, and just sputter hot coffee all over the place as they turn to the cartoon" (Shelton, Interview).

Sources

Bergen Record. Hackensack, NJ: 1993-94.

Brooks, Charles, ed. *Best Editorial Cartoons of the Year.* Gretna, LA: Pelican, 1992.

"Color Political Cartoons Being Syndicated." *Editor & Publisher* 19 Jan. 1991: 40.

Shelton, Mike. Interview. By Kalman Goldstein. 19 Jan. 1995.

22

Mike Smith, *Las Vegas Sun*

Jack Colldeweih

Like the city he lives and works in, Mike Smith has a very broad outlook on things such as politics, social customs and people's idiosyncrasies. Las Vegas offers an uninterrupted view of the distant horizon from this wide open city, which is reflected in Smith's outward gaze and liberal views of American society. His artwork, increasingly matured, is now clean and unfussy, his drawings simple and straightforward. His editorial ideas are equally direct and bold, and therefore effective in their punch. Unconcerned with the debate over humor in editorial cartoons, Smith draws what he thinks and feels about an issue or event, willing to accept either a chuckle or a wince as a reaction.

Born in San Francisco on May 20, 1960, and raised there during the turmoil of the hippie-free love scene, student activism and Vietnam—protest years—Smith opted for the relative tranquility of Loyola Marymount University in Los Angeles for his higher education, where he was a humanities major. His background had not prepared him for this relatively subdued Catholic college milieu, however. His father was a lawyer who dealt with commodity fraud and his mother was a Veterans Administration psychiatric nurse who helped Vietnam survivors struggling with post-traumatic stress disorder. They both saw some of the dark side of American society, consequently gradually shifting from being moderate Republicans to becoming Democrats. Smith brought the effects of the frequent domestic political discussions and street political action with him to college.

Smith had often drawn and doodled while growing up, and started drawing cartoons for the college newspaper. Influenced by what he saw Paul Conrad doing for the *Los Angeles Times,* Smith also tried editorial cartooning. "And once I saw how much trouble I could get into, I said this is really fun, I want to do this for real" (Smith, Interview). One cartoon he drew was critical of a campus Latino organization that had complained of bias by the campus newspaper. In the ensuing campus reaction over the cartoon, the college administration closed the newspaper. This action prompted a number of faculty and newspaper staffers to pro-

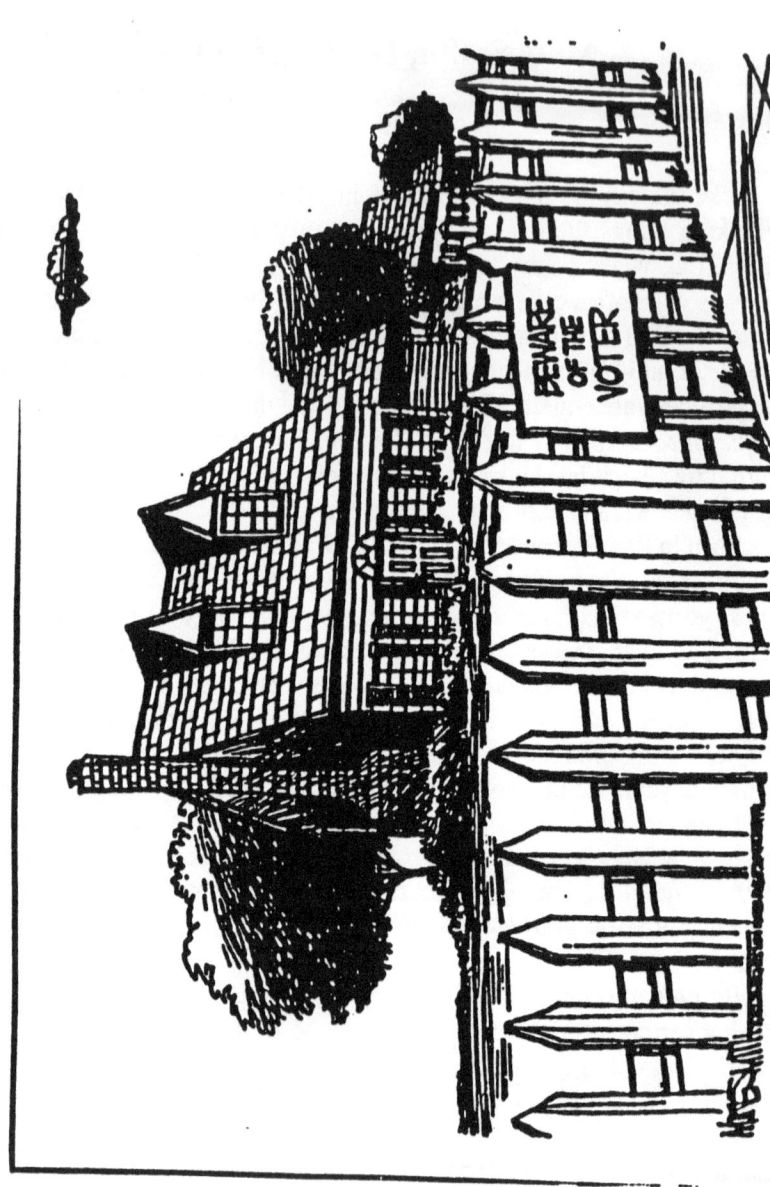

Mike Smith (1994) *Las Vegas Sun*. Reprinted with special permission of North American Syndicate.

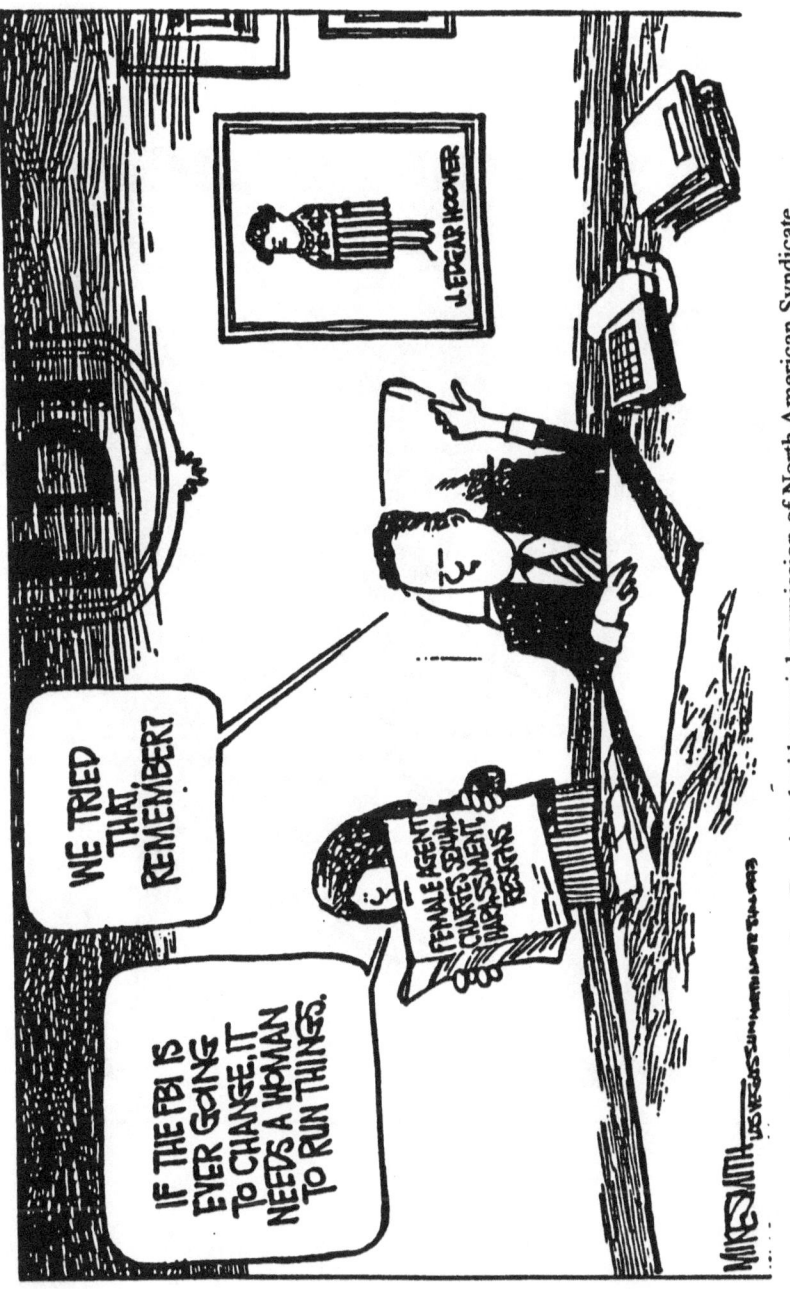

Mike Smith (1993) *Las Vegas Sun*. Reprinted with special permission of North American Syndicate.

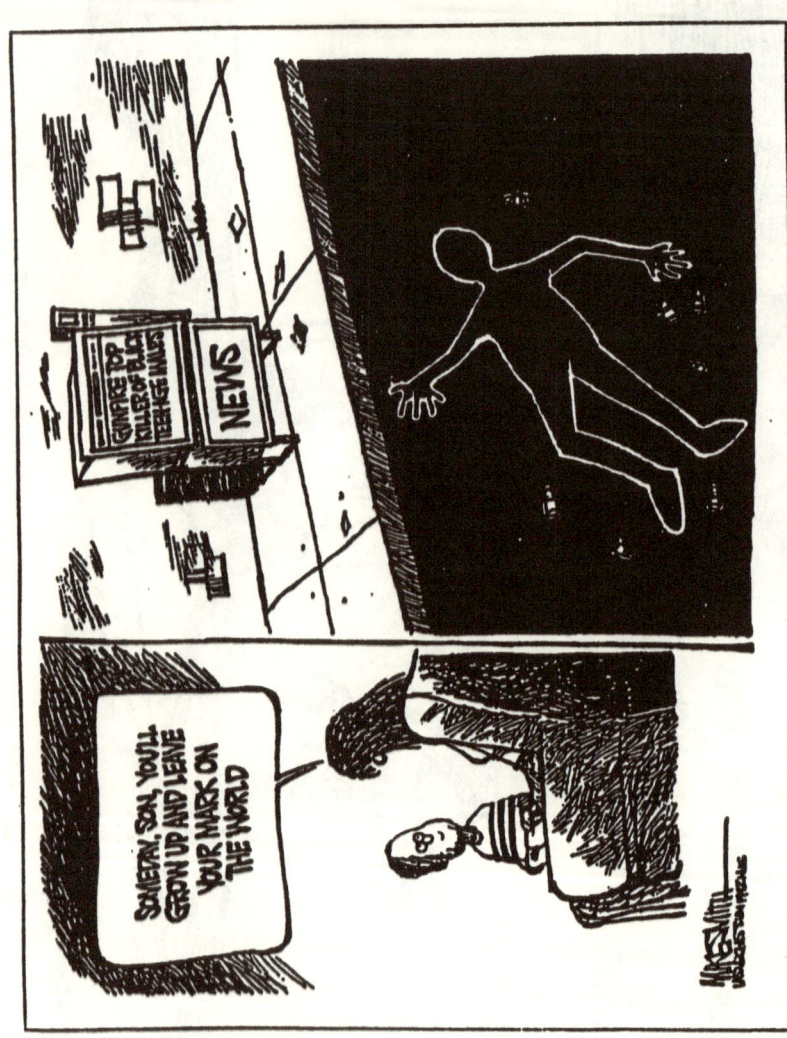

Mike Smith (1992) *Las Vegas Sun*. Reprinted with special permission of North American Syndicate.

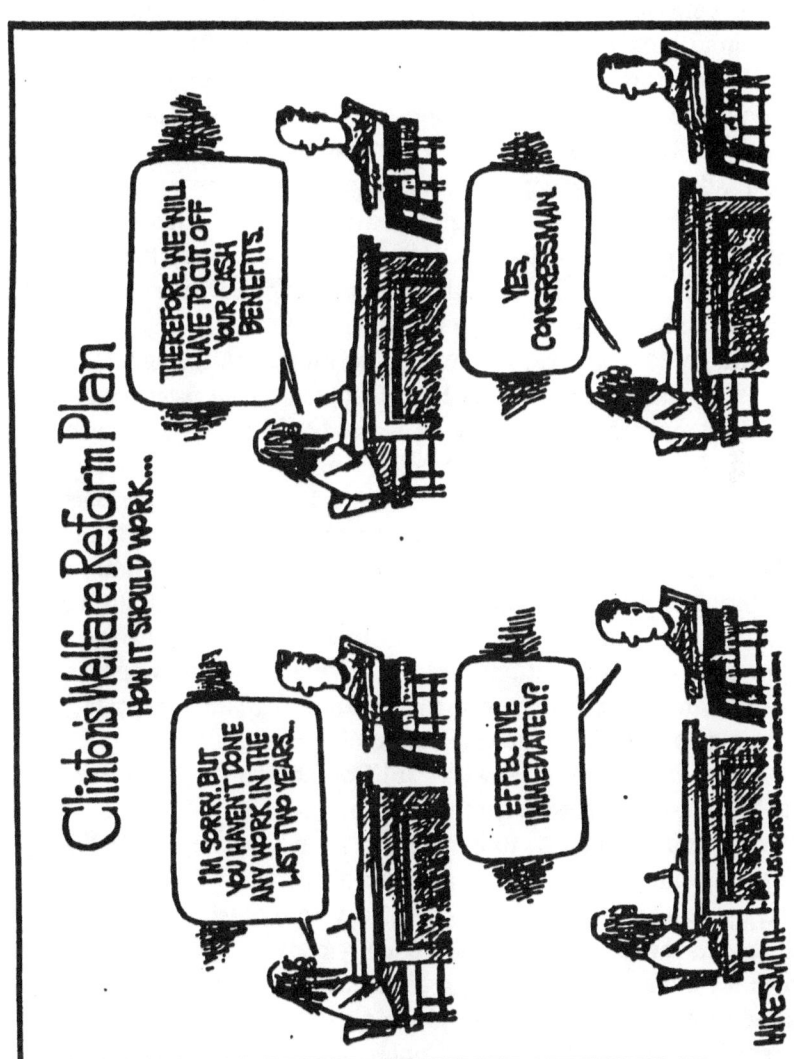

Mike Smith (1994) *Las Vegas Sun.* Reprinted with special permission of North American Syndicate.

mulgate a petition for Smith's expulsion from school. His matriculation there was saved only by the timely and influential intervention of contacts made while attending a Jesuit high school in San Jose.

Although he found the art classes at Loyola Marymount of little interest, Smith did nag cartoonist Paul Conrad into seeing him and analyzing his cartoons. After deconstructing them artistically and ideologically, Conrad suggested that Smith learn how to draw if he ever hoped to get a job as a cartoonist. This reluctant mentor also told him to draw every day, and that the key to being creative, to coming up with good cartoons, and the key to developing his own style and way of thinking was to read good newspapers every day and keep up on every little development in the news. Taking the advice to heart, Smith pretended that he had a job as a cartoonist. He would get up every morning and draw a cartoon, eventually accumulating a portfolio that he sent out to newspapers in hopes of securing a job upon graduation.

Smith got to Las Vegas in a manner befitting an Angeleno. He saw a movie set in Las Vegas (Francis Ford Coppola's *One from the Heart),* and decided that there was where he wanted to work. The editor of the *Sun* liked Smith's portfolio and bought a few at "about $8 a cartoon" (Smith, Interview). Smith continued to send him about four cartoons each week for about six months, and then asked for a job. Although the *Sun* did not have a staff cartoonist, and was interested in Smith, it did have a hiring freeze and so declined. Continuing to draw, Smith worked at National Car Rental at Los Angeles International Airport for about eight months after graduation until one of his college newspaper cartoons won an award from the then *Chicago Tribune* syndicate. That award was enough to convince the *Sun* to hire him on staff.

Because he was so taken with Paul Conrad as a model cartoonist— liberal ideology, fearlessness, tenacity, and especially drawing style— Smith consciously had tried to imitate him from his college days through his first few months at the *Sun*. He then realized that "if I wasn't careful I'd end up being a clone, and a clone of any cartoonist is never going to be as good as the original," so made equally conscious efforts to develop his own style and way of thinking (Smith, Interview). He is now satisfied that over the past decade he has achieved his goal.

Smith's style is now much simpler than that of Conrad in nearly every respect. His characters have no unnecessary features or shading, and their faces are drawn with as few brush strokes as possible. Clinton's face, for example, consists of two tiny dots for eyes, another for the mouth, and an upturned semicircle for a nose. No cheeks, no brows, no furrows or wrinkles; it's as if the face were drawn upon an egg. Only in profile does one get a sense of a three-dimensional protrusion of the nose. For other characters, the face is essentially the same, differentiated perhaps by glasses and hair, but the primary difference is in head shapes. In addition, the characters' bodies are often extraordinarily two-dimensional, especially when sitting: they are drawn as if they were paper dolls, folded at the knee and waist to fit the furniture.

Smith does not use shading but rather a form of cross-hatching that he calls "slop-hatching—it's a little messier, a little more spontaneous" (Smith, Interview). He does not like to use stippling or Zipatone graphics paper, claiming that the faxing process does not handle shading very well, thus interfering with the distribution of his cartoons. Bodies are usually not slop-hatched, but when they are the hatching often continues uninterrupted into the background of the cartoon, suggesting external shadow cast over that part of the scene. This occasionally merges the character into the background, but it also encourages a greater involvement with the cartoon. This hatching technique, for which he uses a pen instead of a brush, also often obscures the background features of the cartoons, so that vertical and horizontal breaks virtually disappear. In essence, the cross-hatching serves more for visual balance and effect in the overall cartoon than for reflecting shadows or multidimensionality. Consequently, it frequently appears at the top and/or bottom of the drawing and behind part of the dialogue balloons.

Although it is not his primary interest, Smith can be a fine draftsman, carefully detailing buildings and other structures. Sometimes, however, his perspectives are askew even though the distortion has nothing to do with the cartoon's point. One drawing, for example, shows a finely crafted White House behind the wrought-iron fence. The perspective is straight and clean (*National Gallery* June 16, 1991, 6). Similarly, a cartoon with the Capitol in the background shows careful attention to detail and both the lower and upper columns straight and parallel (*National Gallery* June 2, 1991, 6). However, a later image of the Capitol from virtually the same perspective shows the upper portion far larger than it should be in comparison with the base, and the horizontal lines canting at varying degrees; the impression is that of a leaning tower of Pisa in development (*National Gallery* Dec. 13, 1992, 20). His distortion of perspective also occurs in portraiture. In one cartoon, Clinton is seated at his desk in the Oval Office, mulling over a problem. To his side are two people commenting on his actions. In relation to their size, however, they are either seven years old or some forty yards away (*National Gallery* Aug. 1995, 30).

Like many others, Smith frequently uses the multipanel format for his cartoons, but his are rarely bordered to separate the panels. If anything, some background "slop-hatching" serves to corral the eye within each panel. In addition, it is often only the text balloons that distinguish one panel from another, the graphics changing only in the last panel as a reaction to the text.

Smith's most personal, or signature, device in his cartoons is the way he draws clouds in the background of many cartoons. Most cartoonists don't bother to include clouds at all, and when they do the clouds are nearly invariably the big white puffy variety that look like dumplings clumped together. To a desert-dweller, clouds are important and Smith's clouds are those that a westerner might see far off over the desert or distant mountains, a few little puffs with little tails stretching off to either side, the top light and the bottom dark.

While sharing that common western concern over water, Smith parts company with many over a number of other high-profile issues in the Rocky Mountain states. A special interest of his is the use of federal lands, not unexpected in a state in which the federal government owns most of the land. Policies for mining, livestock grazing, timbering and water allocation from the various rivers and aquifers are frequent targets of his brush. He is a strong believer in environmental protection and the fair use and preservation of our limited natural resources. Consequently he has often opposed proposals and actions of many powerful economic interests in his own state and throughout the West. Smith does admit, however, to enjoying "four-wheeling" in the desert, a practice opposed by some others in the environmental movement.

What really sets Smith off are "lying, cheating and stealing," especially in the public business. This, he finds, gives him no end of villains to take after, including not only public officeholders, but also businesses and organizations that deal with government. His daily contemplation of news events has led him to be less partisan now than when he started. He claims to have been mad only at the Republicans at the start of his career, and now he's angry with both parties. He believes that Clinton "is the only politician that I've seen who's got this tremendous ability to tell the truth and say it in such a way that it sounds like a lie" (Smith, Interview).

Other special targets for Smith are the National Rifle Association, "hate radio," the "far right," abortion violence and gun control. A frequently used device is the image of a character representing the NRA or the "far right" manipulating a generic congressman or specifically Republican Senator Bob Dole of Kansas. Another device is that of an armed and threatening public or group, as with school children, dressed in camouflage and armed to the nines after the Supreme Court rejected a law banning guns in school zones, holding a trussed teacher hostage while they discuss grades (*National Gallery* May 14, 1995, 5).

Even when taking on issues that have local relevance, Smith rarely deals with them on the local level. His cartoons are, by his own reckoning, nearly 100% nationally or internationally oriented. And he is as likely to comment on an issue involving the mayor of New York City as he is about the mayor of Las Vegas. This characteristic, of course, makes his cartoons more easily syndicated and they are widely seen in a variety of publications.

Another practice, which also makes the cartoons' symbolism and referents easily recognizable, is his frequent use of icons of popular culture, especially the movies. *The Wizard of Oz* is a particular favorite, and it often shows up in terms of character or dialogue. For example, during the 1992 presidential campaign, he has the three candidates on stage for debate; Clinton, as the Scarecrow, wishes, "If I only had your trust"; Bush, as the Tinman, wishes, "If I only had a plan"; and Perot, as the Lion, wishes, "If I only hadn't quit" (*National Gallery* Nov. 8, 1992, 3. In an earlier one, he has Bush hiding behind a curtain as the Wizard, while his representative is telling the Ayatollah to "Pay no attention to that man behind the curtain" (*National Gallery* May 26, 1991, 16).

Smith also uses comic book characters, such as Spiderman, and television shows in his cartoons, but not always with success, he confesses ruefully. He once used the goofy cavalrymen from *F-Troop* as symbols of ineffective staff, only to discover that many people had no idea of what he was talking about because, except for occasional syndication, the series had been off the air for three decades. Other characters from current events or movies and television shows are used much more successfully, but perhaps with short comprehension life. A cartoon showing Tonya Harding performing her community service sentence for the attack on a rival skater's knee, for example, has her telling child skaters exactly where to strike with a baton (*National Gallery* Apr. 3, 1994, 21). Other examples include Lorena Bobbitt, FBI Director J. Edgar Hoover as a transvestite, Attorney General Janet Reno, and movies such as *Home Alone*.

Smith believes that there is less use of themes and iconography from the classics than there used to be, and notes that even his mentor Paul Conrad now employs fewer. This is in part because public education has changed its curricula and emphases, and in part because the nature of the medium has changed. He claims that "cartoons are much more dialogue-oriented now. You don't have as many single panel cartoons with no words or with maximum of seven words in them like you used to. Cartoons have a lot more words and the contemporary approach is much different" (Smith, Interview).

A 1989 experiment that Smith tried, both as a means of involving his readers and as a promotional device for the *Sun*, is an example of one of the ways in which contemporary cartoons have changed from the old format. Asked to create a cartoon caption-writing contest for the Sunday edition, he drew the graphic and then readers submitted appropriate captions, the winners getting public notice and a $25 prize. From the large response to the feature, called *Smithereens,* Smith decided that it had potential on a national basis. It was distributed for about four years by Lew Little Enterprises, under the title *Brainstormers,* but eventually canceled because too few newspapers subscribed.

Smith's regular work is syndicated by North American Syndicate (King Features) and he also draws for *USA Today* every Thursday. He occasionally draws color illustrations for *Sun* feature stories and used to draw caricatures for Bally's when it had celebrity roasts in Las Vegas.

Smith is unconcerned with the debate over humorous cartoons versus pointed and controversial ones, believing that cartoons can be both or either and still be valuable. He feels that the real debate should be over "the level of guts the editor has" to run what the artist creates. Smith just asks himself what the news subject is, and how he feels about it, and then goes to work. He plans to work for a long time, finding and picking off his targets like a western sharpshooter.

Sources

Brooks, Charles, W. *Best Cartoons of the Year.* Gretna, LA: Pelican, 1992.
Smith, Mike. Interview. By Jack Colldeweih. Aug. 1994.
National Forum Gallery of Cartoons. Washington, D.C., 1991-1995.

23

Jeff Stahler, *Cincinnati Post*

Jack Colldeweih

One of the first books Jeff Stahler can remember having as his own was a copy of Walter Lantz's *Learn to Draw Woody Woodpecker,* a film cartoon character whose sunny attitude and indefatigable spirit seem to have rubbed off on him. Both personally and in his work Stahler leaves the impression of a man at peace with himself and his society. There are no demons being exorcised in his cartoons. This is not to say that there is no critical comment presented, however; Stahler just prefers to make his points with a lighter, less bitter form of humor than some other cartoonists do. He also prefers to focus more on social and cultural issues than on Washington, D.C. Beltway political issues, which perhaps accounts for his more pleasant disposition. Although he feels uncomfortable with the purely political issues of Congress and the White House, when Stahler does take on what he feels are the more important national issues he deals with them within his own middle-American context. Consequently, his cartoons usually have a "local" feel about them no matter what the issue is.

A native Ohioan (born May 3, 1955, in Bellefontaine), Stahler was raised in an environment right out of Norman Rockwell, whose illustrations influenced his own views. His father was a pharmacist who was active in local politics, despite being "probably the only Democrat in the county" (Stahler, Interview). His mother was an art teacher and his primary teacher from elementary school through high school, with someone else occasionally stepping in. She exerted a strong reinforcement to his interest in the field of art, which he pursued to a fine arts degree at the Columbus College of Art and Design. Along the way he was an inveterate doodler and sketcher, and one of the few his age "who would turn on television to watch Jon Gnagy draw a covered bridge" (Stahler, Interview).

Stahler's career path was typically indirect, but in retrospect seems an orienteering achievement. While at a print shop to get a résumé done, he was recruited by a local advertising agency to do illustrations and, when possible, advertising cartoons. He also did free-lance work for the

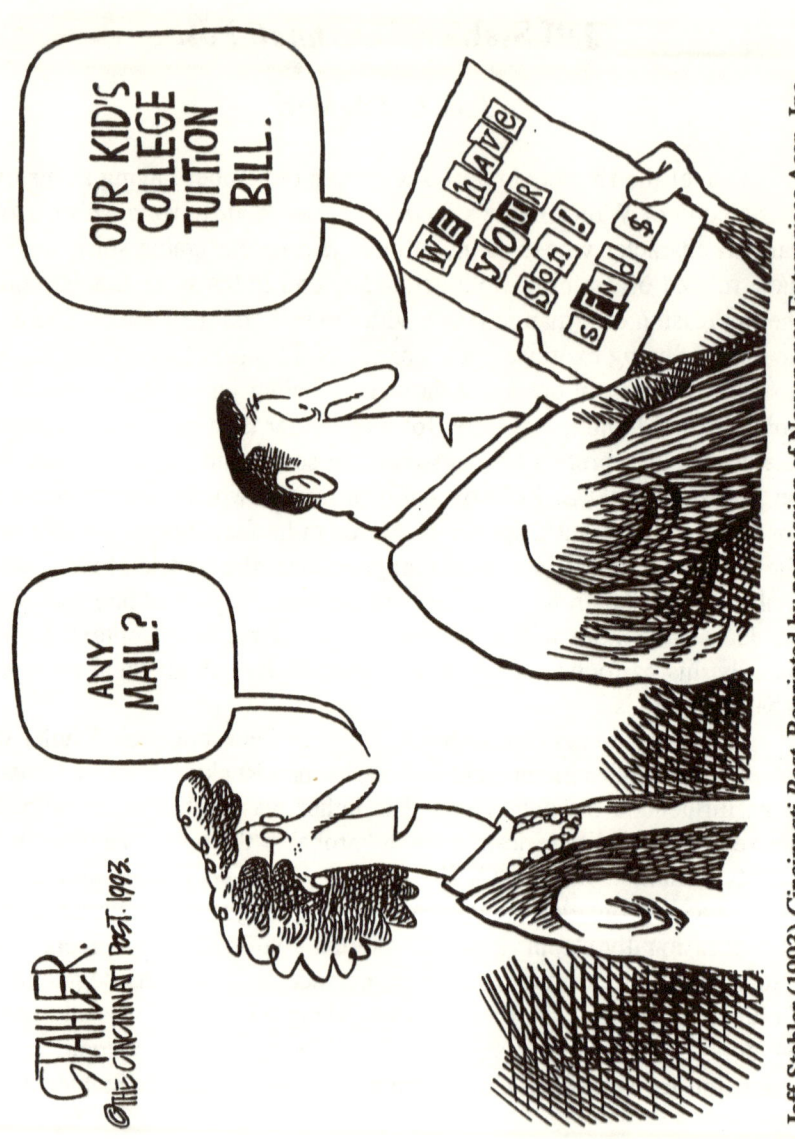

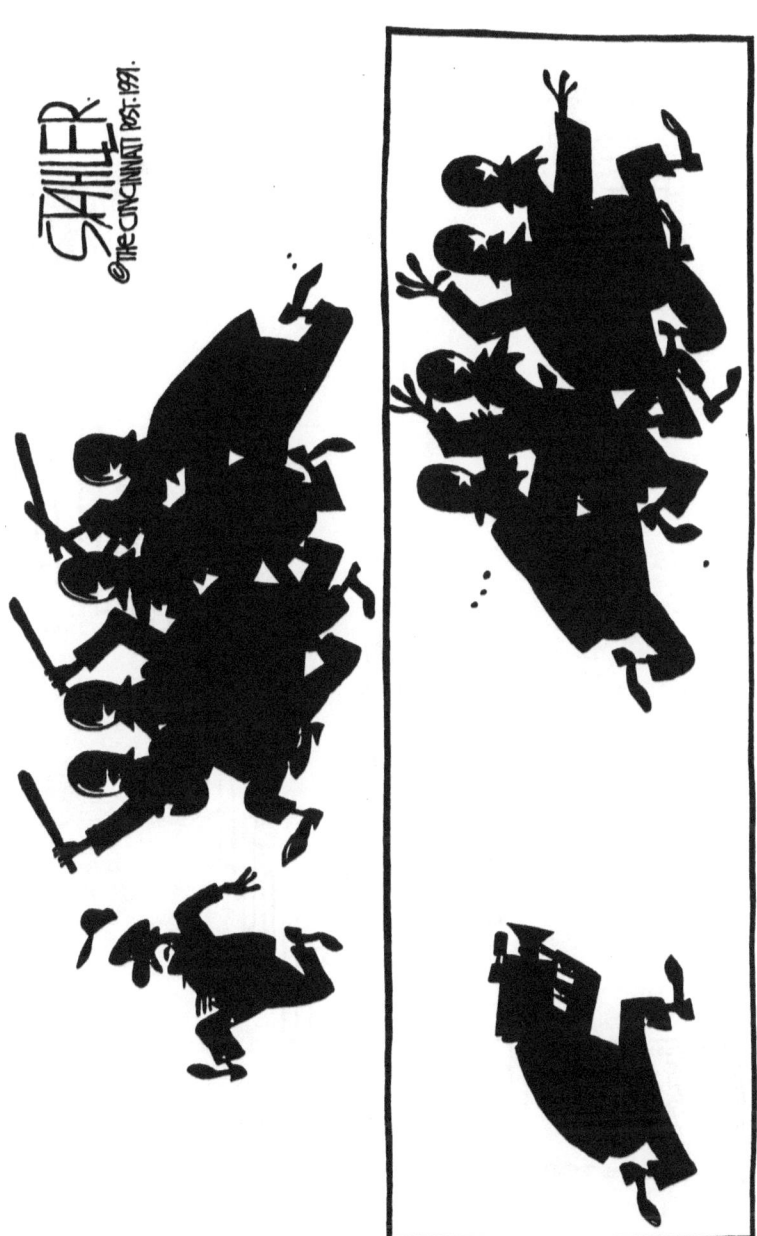

Jeff Stahler (1991) *Cincinnati Post.* Reprinted by permission of Newspaper Enterprises Assn. Inc.

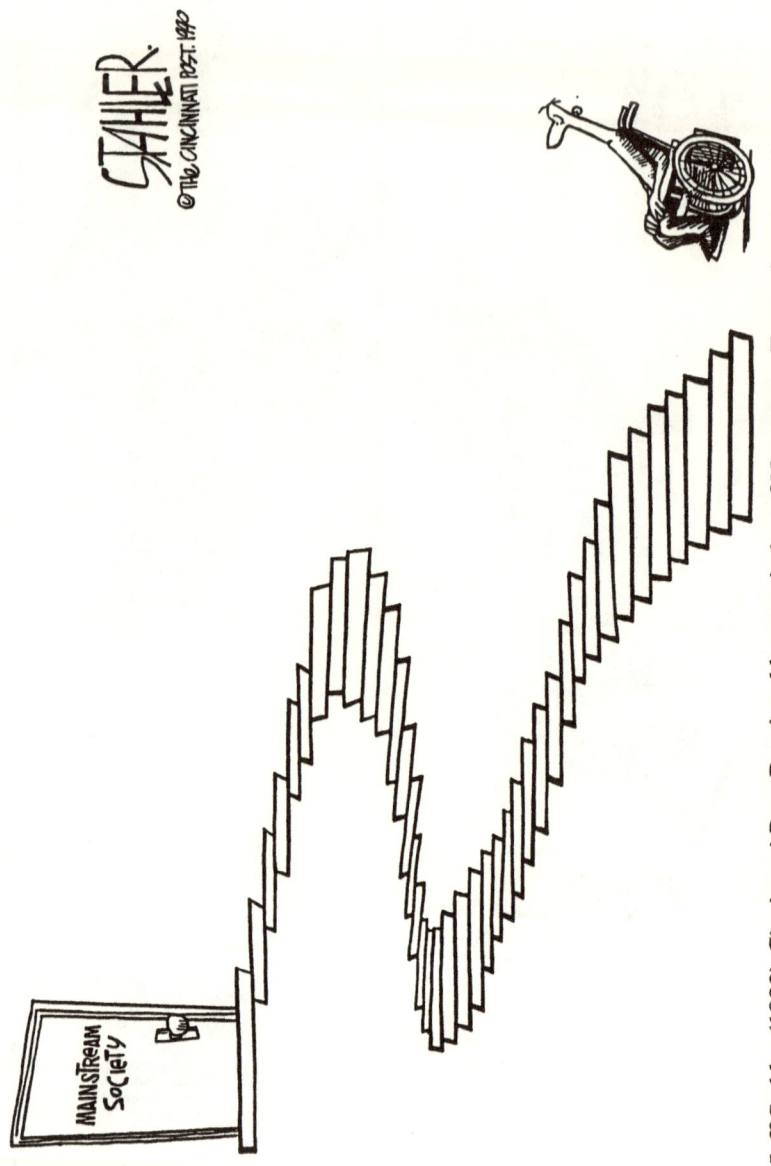

Jeff Stahler (1990) *Cincinnati Post*. Reprinted by permission of Newspaper Enterprises Assn. Inc.

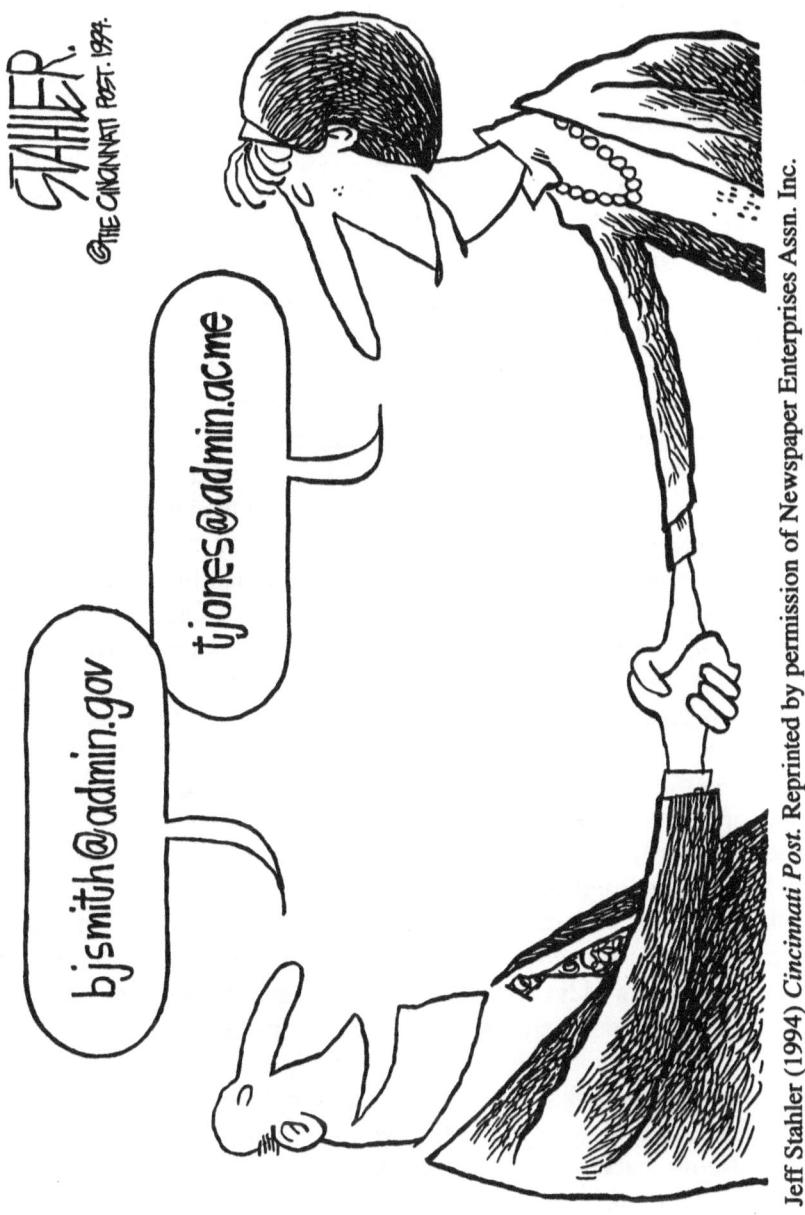

Columbus Monthly, a local magazine, and after a few years left the agency to work for the magazine full time as graphic artist, art director and illustrator. While there he began producing political cartoons for *The Booster*, a small weekly newspaper that had recently added an editorial page. The editor of the *Columbus Citizen Journal* lived in the neighborhood and noticed his work. When that paper's editorial cartoonist retired, Stahler was offered his position. This Scripps-Howard paper folded after a year, but the *Cincinnati Post* editor had been watching his progress and told him that whenever he wanted to move, a job would be waiting for him there. The *Post* had been running syndicated cartoons since Bill Watterson had left in 1980 and now wanted its own cartoonist again. A week after the *Citizen Journal* closed at the end of 1985, Stahler began drawing for the *Post*, where he has remained.

He makes sure that he draws at least one essentially local cartoon each week, although there may be more. Even after a decade in Cincinnati he feels a bit uncomfortable handling local issues, "But there are a lot of times when you can bend and twist a cartoon in a number of ways so that a local issue is also a national issue, even though it's not out right now in the national news" (Stahler, Interview). For example, Stahler has been bothered by the sizeable homeless population in Cincinnati, many of whom he sees not too far from the *Post* building. One of his responses to that was a 1992 cartoon depicting a woman with three small children sitting on a heating grate next to a building, their possessions in a large shopping bag; the title was "The Grate Society." Most of his cartoons are on issues that affect the nation at large, but they are done with such a midwestern flavor that they have local salience throughout much of the nation. The effect is similar to that conveyed by the midwestern style of speech used by most television newscasters, generally accepted as standard American English.

Like most cartoonists, Stahler is a "news junkie," reading several local and national newspapers each day, news magazines each week, and keeping up with radio and television news and the AP wire throughout the day. As his ideas jell, he makes sketches, picks his favorite, and then seeks reactions from the editors, a working habit he picked up in his days at the advertising agency. This lets him know if his approach to a problem is likely to be successful. He is sometimes offered suggestions for cartoons, but the topic and approach are always his.

Using a brush for his cartoons, Stahler's work is very stark. A proponent of the dictum "less is more," he puts all his efforts into his characters and leaves the background of the panel as empty as possible. Unless it is absolutely required for the art, for example, he will omit a picture hanging from a wall in the background; in fact, he will omit the wall if he can. Lamps, tables, windows—gone, if not required. He likes the bare look that forces the eye to focus on exactly what he wants you to see. No complications, no extra gags, he gets directly to the point. His characters have a rounded three-dimensionality, with shading where appropriate. Neither they nor any other objects in the frame often cast shadows, however, in part because he has omitted any background on which shadows might appear, and in part because they aren't really necessary anyway.

This bare look extends to text in the cartoon. He puts in as little as is necessary, none at all if possible. He hates labels and he labors to remove every word that he can from dialog and still get his point across. A dialogless cartoon with only a title is better, and one with only a newspaper headline or a title on a door is better still. If the text is in a newspaper headline, he may omit even the tiny lines other cartoonists use to indicate smaller text on the page; Stahler's newspaper is essentially all headline and no stories. He loved the "silent" comic strip "Henry," and admires Dana's "Bound and Gagged" strip for a similarly minimalist approach. His disinterest in text seems to extend to his lettering, which is inconsistent in style and size. Generally in sans serif capitals, he mixes in lower case vowels and script occasionally. While usually erect, his letters sometimes lean to the side and the size variation can extend to several points. It sometimes begins to approach the look of a ransom note pasted together from various publications. The appearance is carefully calculated, however, because in fact he meticulously edges each letter for crisp legibility.

Stahler's primary interest is children, and anything that may revolve around or affect them. As issues arise into the public arena, he will first relate them to his own family and how he thinks they will affect his two children, and then extend the analysis outward. Issues such as education, nutrition and television programming have obvious relationships; other topics in the news, such as the exponential growth and effects of the computer and its related industries, are more arbitrary in their familial connection. For example, Stahler's own experience, trying to do his taxes via computer instead of the old fashioned pencil and calculator method, was handled in a two-panel comparison cartoon. The only difference between the two panels was that a computer was included in one; the piles of books, forms, scratch paper and the like were the same and, presumably, the time to complete the forms was also.

Other examples of localizing and "personalizing" national topics include such things as violence in professional baseball, which was presented in the form of two boys discussing the merits of various players on trading cards, one boy exclaiming over a player who led the league in bench-clearing brawls. The availability of handguns was dealt with by a textless drawing of a gigantic revolver installed on a playground as a recreational structure, with parents pushing their kids on swings suspended from it and other children playing around the trigger, hammer and handle. This approach has its obvious advantages in terms of reader identification; there is no sense of remoteness or uninvolvement.

Stahler also enjoys turning his hand to mainstream cultural issues such as fads, fashions and other items of popular culture. One of his favorite devices is often used here, showing one character speaking in one context and the listener ironically hearing it in another. For example, a 1990 cartoon shows an art history teacher telling her class that they will be studying four great Italian masters tomorrow: Raphael, Michelangelo, Donatello, and Leonardo; the thought balloon over the students' heads shows the four Ninja Turtles. In a clever reverse play using that device, a 1994 cartoon has a father telling his wife that the Beatles are reuniting; the thought balloon over his young daughter's head shows a gathering of insects.

Stahler is partial to using fairy tales as a foundation for his commentary. The *Three Little Pigs* is a particular favorite, used for a variety of issues such as low-interest home loans and recycled plastic as a home-building material, for stock and commodity markets, and as parents reading to their own piglets. He also had Sleeping Beauty challenging the proffered apple because of its protective chemical coating, and a mother reading to her child the Russian version of Cinderella wherein at the stroke of midnight "everything turned back into rubles."

He does not employ many references to classic myths, art or symbols, preferring to stay with more contemporary references. He does enjoy using the irony of a past-present comparative to comment on society's progress, however. A 1992 cartoon shows an Elizabethan couple gazing at a sign listing the Globe Theatre's fall season of *Othello, Macbeth*, and *Hamlet*, and remarking, "Whatever happened to traditional family values?" In a 1994 cartoon, he took a finely detailed etching of the Battle of Manassas and modified it to include Mickey Mouse strolling through the scene of death and destruction saying, "What a great place for a theme park!" Although he tries to avoid the clichéd image, such as Grant Wood's *American Gothic* or the Marines atop Mt. Suribachi on Iwo Jima, he will use such images when he feels it is the best solution. For example, for the cover of his book he drew himself as *The Thinker*, sitting nude atop a rock and staring intently at a television screen while wearing earphones plugged into a portable radio and with a newspaper open on his lap.

Stahler does get upset at people and events from time to time, but tries to moderate such feelings before commenting on the subject. "I'm not an angry person," he claims.

I go for the joke. I like humor—it's a humorous spot on the page. I can appreciate the cartoonists who do go after the straight and hard—and I've done it too, where you just don't have a laugh in the cartoon, but I prefer to have it. I think you can find humor in just about anything; if not immediately, then if you sit back for a day or two something will develop. I'll bet you'll find the humorous edge. (Stahler, Interview)

Congress, and its frequent inability to get beyond politically motivated stalemate, is one subject that frequently disturbs him. Although he has become somewhat more conservative over the years, he hasn't found that control by either political party makes much difference. He sees most congressmen as "liars and low-down dirty culprits." Even here, however, his viewpoint is more joshing than slashing. This style does not necessarily keep him out of trouble, however. A 1990 Earth Day cartoon in which cut trees fell in a manner as to spell out Earth Day with their trunks and branches also showed the last felled tree lying atop the logger. When it was reprinted in the *Coos Bay (Oreg.) World*, local loggers protested by completely encircling the newspaper building with logging trucks and parading a picket line at the front entrance. A concerned editor called Stahler to demand to know what he meant by the cartoon. When Cincinnati Reds owner Marge Schott revealed that she had a collection of swastikas, Stahler drew her in a Nazi uniform in a field lineup with her players. This stirred a lot of comment, but on this occasion no protest, even from Schott.

Other topics that preoccupy him include defending the First Amendment, confronting a high crime rate, and wrestling with the problem of gun control in a society that seems to enjoy violence in both its fictive media and sports. A 1990 cartoon shows Blind Justice with a clothespin on her nose and "First Amendment" printed on her gown entering the Mapplethorpe museum exhibit while saying: "Honestly, the things I must protect some days." And a 1993 drawing has both the Roadrunner and Wiley Coyote cringing together in front of a television screen while holding a newspaper with the headline "Television Violence."

He's not too concerned about having an impact on society, about influencing the course of events, or even of changing anyone's mind. Some cartoonists may have done that, he believes, but he knows of no instance when he has. He feels that it would be an honor if it did, but he doesn't know if "people realistically think that way." This approach to his work allows him to be more relaxed and to express himself more freely.

Stahler has not branched out as much as some cartoonists. Although he would like to try a comic strip, he has not yet hit on a formula that he felt was right for him. He still does do illustrations for the *Columbus Monthly* magazine, where he draws for the closing article. He also loves to do caricatures, although that talent is rarely exhibited in his editorial cartoons. He concentrates on "generic" people, rather than real ones. Cincinnati Reds owner Marge Schott, a local target, is a frequent exception. Few Clintons, Doles, Gingriches, or other newsmakers appear. He likes color cartoons and would like to work in color himself, although he is unclear exactly how he would approach it, given his minimal style. What he would not like is to have his black and white cartoons "colorized" the way some old films are. He sees his crosstown colleague Jim Borgman doing Sunday color cartoons and marvels at his ability to do them on a computer. At this point, Stahler is limited to doing some of his illustration work in color.

He was syndicated with Newspaper Enterprise Association and United Features within six months of starting at the *Post*, and now also draws once a week for *USA Today* and for the *Kentucky Post*. Working in the same town as Jim Borgman at the *Inquirer* will either sharpen or ruin you as a cartoonist. Stahler has responded by winning the 1990 John Fischetti Editorial Cartoon Competition and receiving Honorable Mention in the following year. He believes that "you have your parameters so you know what you have to work in and it's up to you to use that space to the best you can" (Colldeweih).

Sources

Lamb, Chris. "Cincinnati Creator Is Nationally Known." *Editor & Publisher* 7 June 1997: 39.

Stahler, Jeff. *Cartoonist Profiles* Mar. 1992: 38-43.

——. Interview. By Jack Colldeweih. Jan. 1995.

——. *Tooned In*. Cincinnati: *Cincinnati Post*, 1994.

Wolsey, Jane. "Cincinnati Post Editorial Cartoonist." *Cartoonist Profiles* Mar. 1992: 38-43.

24

Dana Summers, *Orlando Sentinel*

S. L. Harrison

Dana Summers, editorial cartoonist for the *Orlando Sentinel*, is another of that increasing number of serious newspaper artists who also create a strip for the comic page. In fact, he manages to produce two— "Bound and Gagged," which he does solo and "The Middletons," a Sunday strip that he produces in partnership with Ralph Dunagin, a colleague also with the *Sentinel*. Summers has been in residence there since 1982 and loves Florida and his work.

"It's fun," Summers says. "What other job pays you to criticize people?" But he reminds anyone who cares to ask that editorial cartooning is a tough field to break into. Before landing his first job, Summers sent out more than 150 resumés.

Summers, a native of Massachusetts, attended the Art Institute in Boston, and free-lanced after graduation. His first newspaper job came in 1975, in North Carolina, when he joined the *Fayetteville Times* as a staff artist.

He spent four and a half years performing a variety of illustration work there before his career as an editorial cartoonist began in February 1981, for the *Dayton Journal*. This was a great position, he says, except that his cross-town competition was the *Dayton Daily News,* which had Pulitzer Prize–winning Mike Peters as its editorial artist.

The two artists got along fine. Peters was friendly, kind, generous, helpful and sympathetic. Peters had, in fact, almost all of the requisite nice-guy, Boy Scout qualities. "He was also," recalls Summers ruefully, "the bane of my existence. I felt like Avis or the Goodrich Rubber Company in a town that's used to seeing the Goodyear blimp" (Summers, Interview). Summers left Dayton after eighteen months and joined the *Sentinel* in 1982.

Summers is serious about his work and considers editorial cartooning to be on a professional plane. It bothers Summers that editorial cartooning "seems to be gravitating to the 'Jay Leno' level," as more and more cartoonists opt for the gag humor approach. This is partly, Summers thinks, because the "unfunny" topics, like the abortion issue,

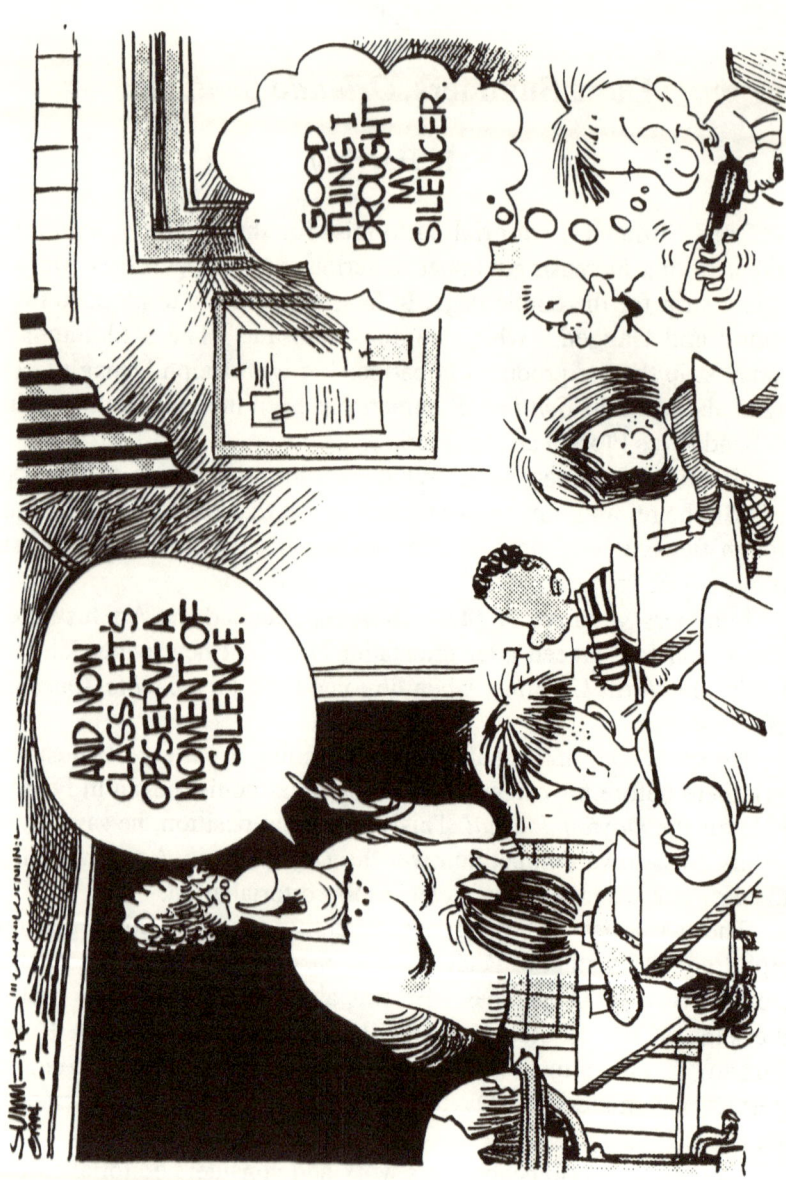

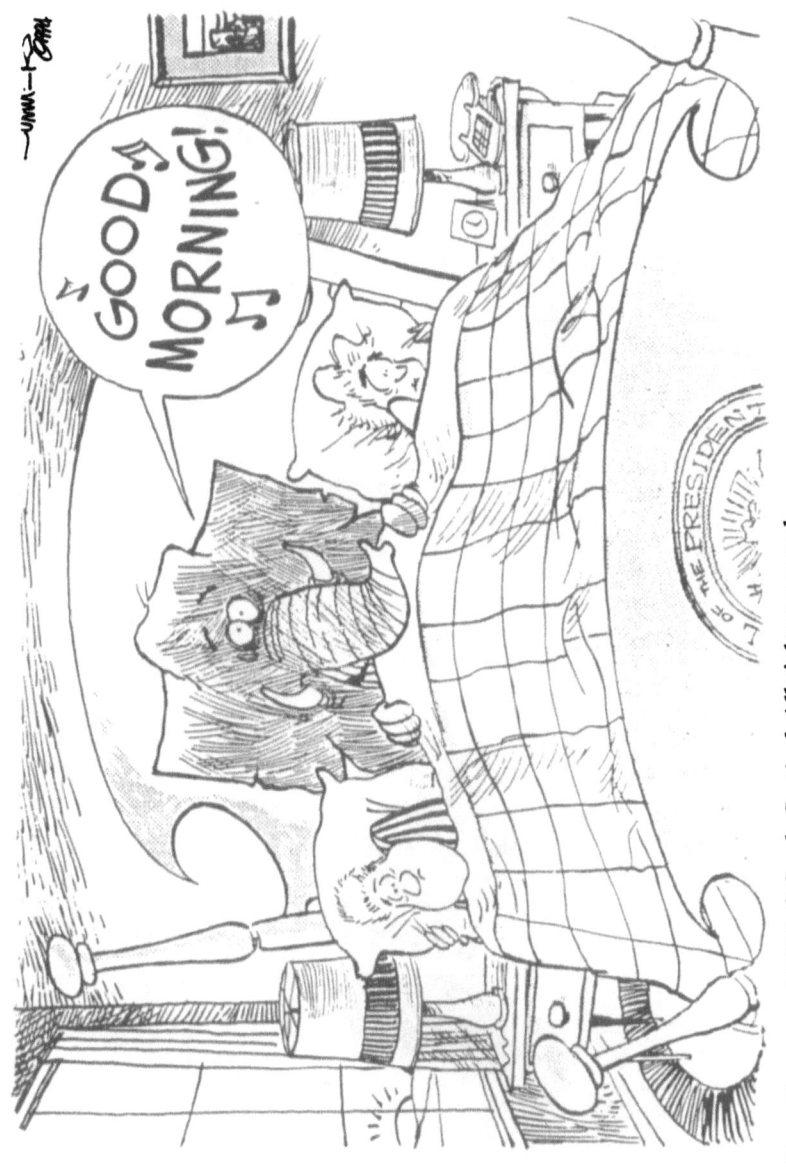

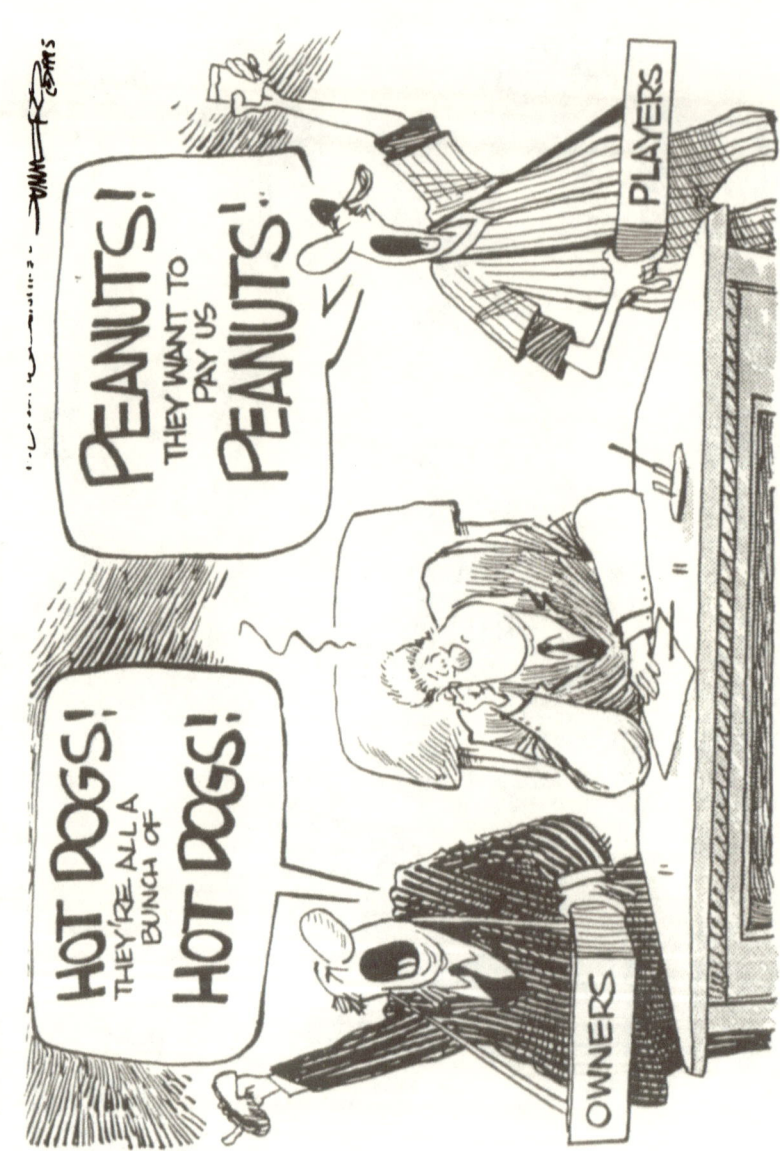

Dana Summers (1995) *Orlando Sentinel.* All rights reserved.

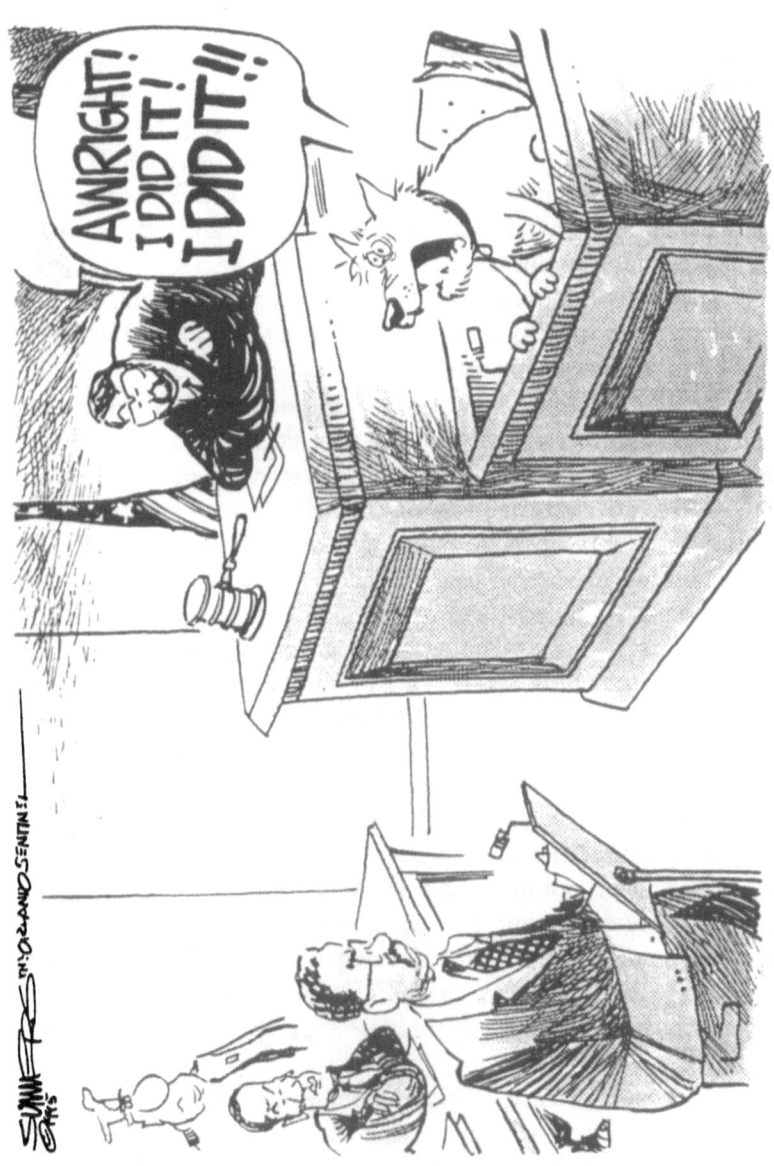

for example, tend to draw readers' ire. Editors, by and large, tend to avoid offending readers.

Summers sees his work as genuinely professional. A couple of generations ago, of course, newspaper artists and editorial cartoonists enjoyed a reputation as a raffish bunch. But Summers is typical of the new breed. He puts in a hard day of work, usually beginning at 7 a.m., and the most difficult part of his routine is coming up with a good idea for a cartoon. He usually produces three different cartoon sketches. By mid-morning, he presents his ideas to the editorial staff and once an idea is approved, he goes to work. Summers sees his editorial role as part of a team but he does not follow the party line.

"Usually, I will not run a cartoon that takes a line opposite an editorial on the day it runs, but later I will not hesitate to take an opposing view," he said. And his paper backs him on that stance.

"I usually sell the idea that I like the best and they usually choose it," he said. Summers works on a Grafix board with a uni-shade 321 using a #4 Winsor & Newton brush and a variety of pen sizes. His work is usually slightly oversize—approximately 8" x 6" and takes a slight reduction for reproduction. Summers works from his rough drafts, which are done on a yellow legal pad. Often, he notes, the finished art differs radically from his roughs. He saves the shading until the very last and uses it sparingly, "only when I think it absolutely needs it" (Summers, Interview). Summers is not affected by the modern technological innovations; the computer gets his product to his syndicate faster, but he leaves the problem of scanning to others to contend with.

Summers' editorial cartoons are invariably without a printed or type-set caption; the content and balloons carry the message. He deals with the issues of the day, national and international, usually in a humorous manner, not in a traditional gag style, and often the humor is ironic. The several examples here illustrate the eclectic quality of his range and work and his editorial viewpoint. Asked about aesthetic or technical theories, Summers responds: "I just do it. I know what to draw and how; very few cartoonists worry about theory" (Summers, Interview).

Like those of many of his contemporaries, Summers's cartoons sometimes contain panels, but he usually confines himself to a single panel to convey the meaning. President Clinton and wife Hillary find their connubial bed occupied by a GOP elephant. The early Thomas Nast symbols are still employed but Summers's depiction owes more to a Bill Hanna creation. Only a nit-picker would object that the morning sun peeping in the window is on the wrong side. Daniel Fitzpatrick, two-time Pulitzer Prize–winning editorial cartoonist for the *St. Louis Post-*

Dispatch, was fussy about such details. But the message is clear—the Republicans moved into Washington in a big way.

Summers looks at domestic issues and manages to take a swipe at baseball's establishment, the owners and players alike, and the costly strike that denied a World Series to fans in the 1994 season. Indirectly, of course, Summers manages to show that President Clinton, if exasperated, failed to do anything to resolve the issue. And more voters are likely to remember that than whatever the President does in Bosnia.

The drawn-out O. J. Simpson murder trial in Los Angeles captured the nation's attention through the long summer months in 1995 and Summers made a number of comments. One, not shown here, depicted the media as a maddened pack of wild dogs assaulting the judge. But here Summers clearly shows his impatience with the antics of Judge Ito, who, playing to the media himself, clearly let the trial get beyond his control.

Summers, like many of his contemporaries, addresses one of the primary issues of citizen discontent, the out-of-control conduct in the classroom. And he relates this troubling social issue with the equally vexing problem of easy access to guns.

His comic strips, "Bound and Gagged" and "The Middletons," deal in a lighter vein with humor and these are fun to draw. The "Bound and Gagged" strip, running weekdays and Sunday, Summers does solo. "The Middletons," worked in collaboration with Ralph Dunagin, is a traditional strip, thankfully humorous and not freighted with the heavy social messages that burden too many of today's "comic" strips and make the Sunday funnies an arena for social commentary.

Summers is aware that no issues clutter his comics; the contrast makes a welcome respite in his work day. His "Bound and Gagged" strip is clearly comic, sometimes several panels, sometimes one. "The Middletons" portrays a middle-class put-upon family's travails with the vicissitudes of daily life and is full of quiet chuckles. His usual routine is to turn to these outlets after his editorial cartoon is put to bed. The regimen makes for a long day.

Summers's editorial cartoons are syndicated through the Tribune Media Services and his work has appeared in a number of national publications. He makes regular appearances, for example, in the *Washington Post* weekly publication that is distributed nationally and the *New York Times* "Week in Review" that collects cartoons from the nation's press. Summers has won recognition for his work with awards from the Overseas Press Club and Sigma Delta Chi, the Society of Professional Journalists.

Summers considers himself a newspaperman and journalist first and foremost and an artist second. But he has feet planted firmly in both camps.

Sources

Harrison, S. L. *Florida's Editorial Cartoonists*. Sarasota: Pineapple, 1996.
Summers, Dana. Interview. By S. L. Harrison. May 1997.

25

John Trever, *Albuquerque Sentinel*

Jack Colldeweih

He is probably the only editorial cartoonist whose career was spawned by a cartoon character, in this case Walt Kelly's "Pogo." Fascinated by the strip as a child, Trever began drawing the character every day and entered a contest requiring a drawing of one's favorite comic character. Winning national first prize, at age 13 Trever was taken to New York for lunch with Walt Kelly and received a three-year scholarship for a correspondence course in cartooning from the Famous Artists School. Such an odd beginning is but one of the different ingredients constituting this most interesting man. Most readers find it hard to get a fix on his point of view, since he pokes at the programs and personalities of Democrats and Republicans alike without restraint. Once they perceive that his political philosophy is libertarian, however, his approach to political problems and solutions falls into place. A gentle man in both manner and appearance, he has an agile brush and an even more agile wit, but his targets nevertheless have to laugh even as they tend to their wounds. His drawing style is bold and confident, and the cartoons exhibit a pleasurable sense of balance in both concept and content.

Born in Santa Monica, California, on June 13, 1943, Trever was not there long. His father, an ordained Methodist minister, spent most of his career as a college teacher in various small colleges around the Midwest and California, although as a postgraduate fellow in Jerusalem in 1948 he was the first American to see, photograph and date the Dead Sea Scrolls. Young Trever, of course, followed along, gaining educationally from the exposure but suffering from a sense of rootlessness that still affects him today. While on the one hand encouraging him to stay in one place for the sake of his family, it also frees him from inhibiting ties to place and culture that sometimes restrain other cartoonists.

His mother and father gave him a rather strict rearing that affected his career as a cartoonist in at least two ways. First, he responded to parental constraints by accenting humor as a relief valve, directly leading into an interest in comedy in general and comics and cartoons in particular. Second, he developed a perfectionist attitude toward his work,

247

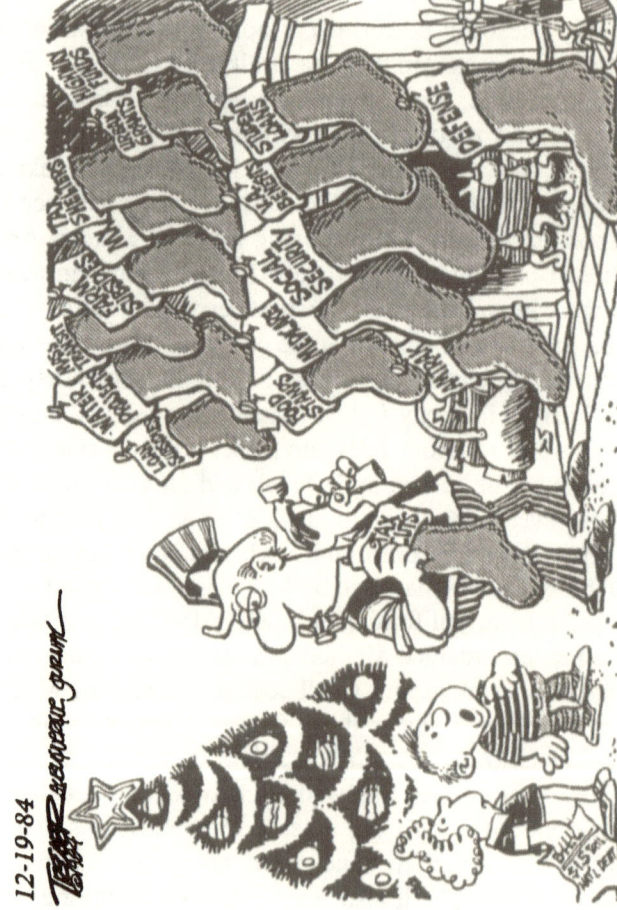

"UNC, WE THINK YOU'RE OLD ENOUGH TO KNOW... SANTA CLAUS IS REALLY ME AND SIS...."

The skyrocketing national debt was creating a huge burden for future generations.

John Trever (1984) *Albuquerque Sentinel.*

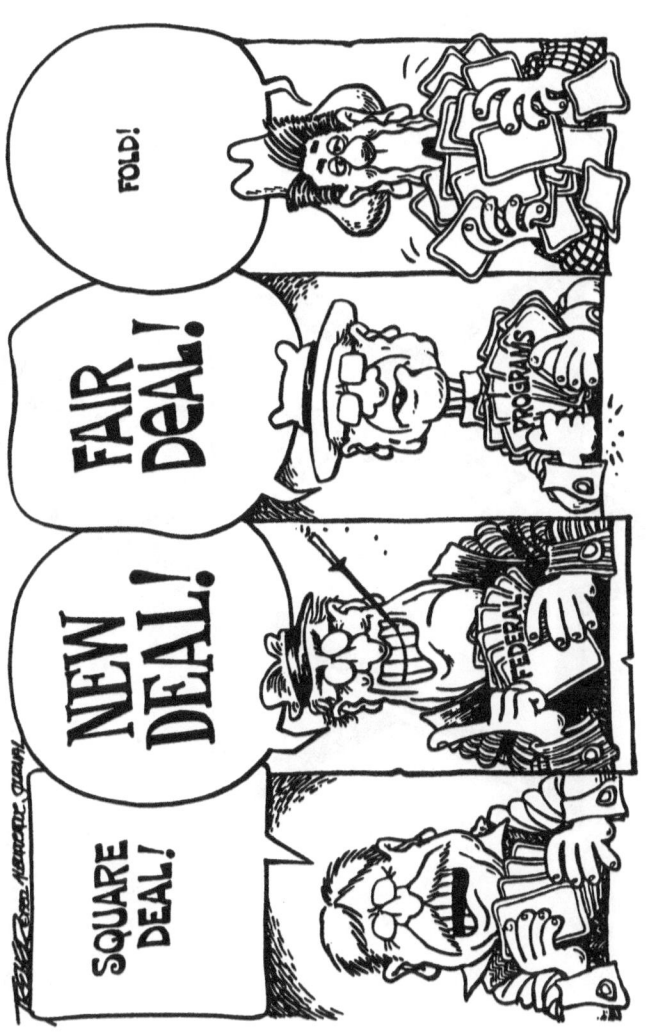

Declaring that "government is not the solution to our problem, it is the problem," Ronald Reagan vowed to reduce the size of government.

John Trever (1982) Albuquerque Sentinel. All rights reserved.

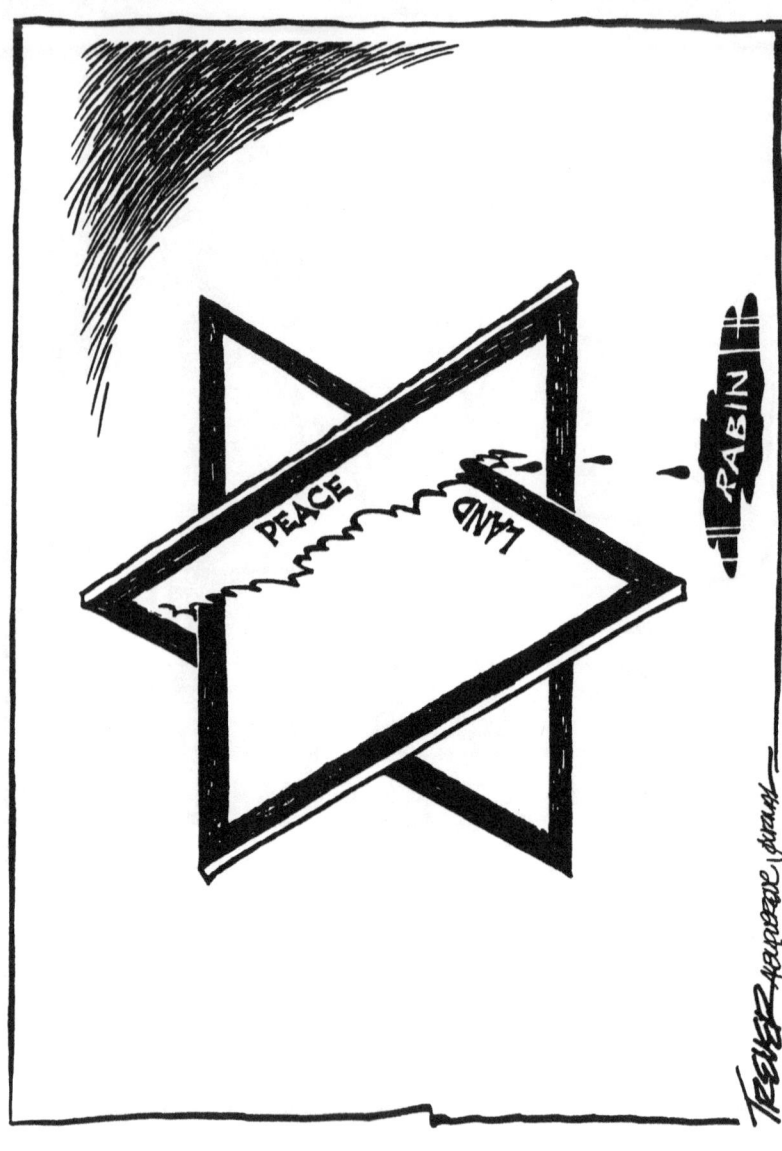

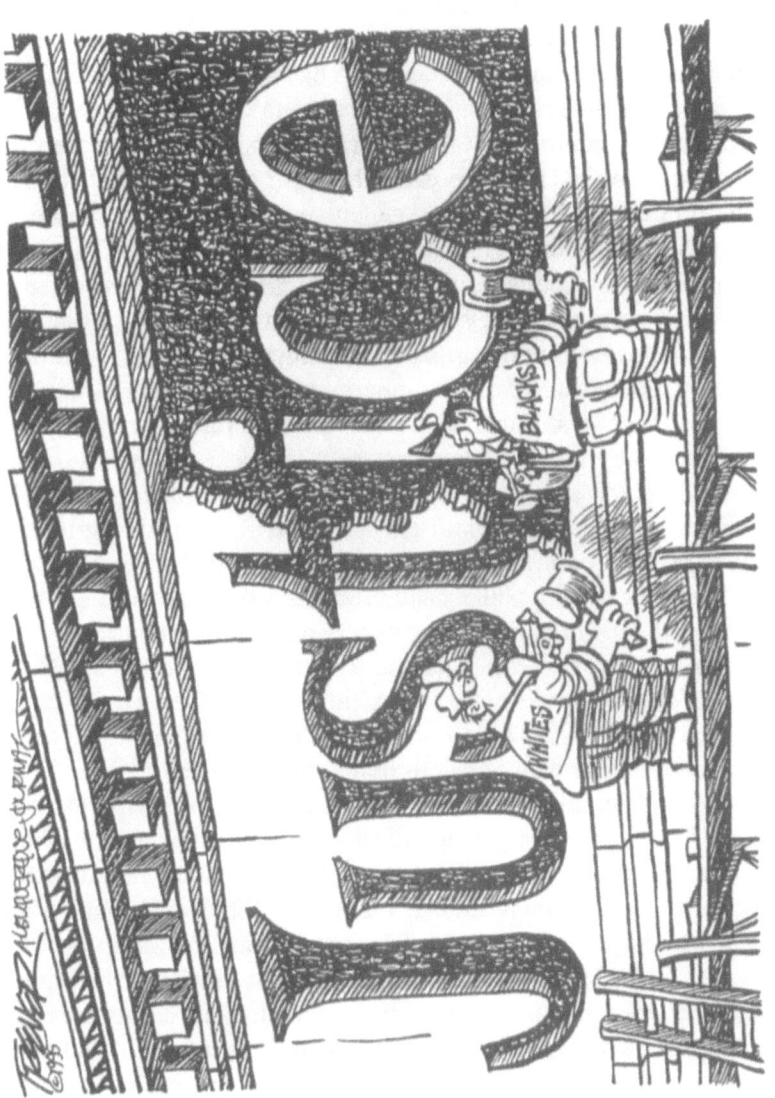

eschewing casual adequacy, and striving for the peak every day. This is clearly seen in his work, where seemingly nothing necessary is omitted but not one superfluous line included; he does not embroider.

Because one had to be at least 16 to start the cartoon scholarship, Trever had to wait until his junior year in high school, finishing the third scholarship year while attending Syracuse University. Although initially a mathematics student, his interests eventually moved toward literature, politics and cartooning for the school newspaper, the *Daily Orange*. Graduating Phi Beta Kappa in 1965, just as the Vietnam War was building up, with his antimilitary family background, Trever did what many other young men did in those years: he went to graduate school. A fellowship in political science from the University of Chicago exposed him to that school's academic rigor and its activist student spirit. The contrast with his previous experience was enormous. He finished his courses and comprehensive exams that year, but given an opportunity at the *Cleveland Plain Dealer* to intern in its art department, he never went back to complete graduate studies. After nine months at the *Plain Dealer*, since he was no longer a student, Trever was drafted. Taken into Officer Candidate School by the Air Force, he spent the next four years in underground silos in Wyoming as a Minuteman missile launch officer, insulated from much of the social and political ferment that gripped the country. His long and, fortunately, very quiet shifts gave him time to extend his education in politics and economics—and practice his art.

An ordinary-looking young man, Trever found that his Syracuse newspaper cartoons on campus hijinks gave him a social recognition and power he felt he could not have achieved any other way, a fact that impressed him deeply. These were gag cartoons only. "Political cartoons didn't really interest me. They weren't really interesting" (Gullet 45). But although initially thinking of a career drawing strip comics, the emergence of a new wave of political cartoonists such as Pat Oliphant, and of his own interest in politics, had gradually turned him toward editorial cartooning. Leaving the Air Force in 1972, Trever found a job as staff artist and editorial cartoonist for the Sentinel Newspapers, a chain of weeklies in the Denver, Colorado, area. Four years later he joined the *Albuquerque Journal* as editorial cartoonist, where he has remained.

Trever's working methods include going through local and national papers first, to get some overview of that day's news, and coming up with a topic. If that fails, he has a "metaphor box, a file packed with slogans and sayings he's compiled for inspiration. He shuffles through news clippings filed away by subject—business, economics, politics, foreign policy" (Gullett 45). After pondering possible approaches, he then sketches out some ideas in pencil, finally selecting the one he will use.

In about two hours he completes his brush and ink drawing, which he likes to have gallery presentable. For lettering he uses a Sharpie Ultra-Fine pen, outlining the letters first and then filling them in. His lettering has been called "greeting card style," but it is one that he gradually adopted after dropping the practice of having mistake-prone typesetters lay out his captions for him. He has the odd habit of using a lower case "e" in all dialogue balloons, but an upper case "e" in all signs, although he doesn't know why.

Trever uses Grafix paper about half the time and plain Strathmore bristolboard the remainder. Like many cartoonists, his choice and use of Grafix paper was influenced by Oliphant; Trever finds that it works especially well for the wide sky in New Mexico landscapes. Less successful with duotone, he uses the single grey and then crosshatches it when he needs a different shading. When not using the Grafix paper, he merely hatches in the shading with his brush.

Although he took a few art courses in college and completed the three-year correspondence cartooning course, Trever credits many years of practice and persistent perfectionist attention to detail for the quality of his work. Never sketchy, his cartoons demonstrate a sure hand in the art and a confident approach to the subject. His perspective and shadow are very good, as is his depiction of machinery. Where he excels is in the background details surrounding the cartoon focal point, as in a cartoon depicting Beirut, Lebanon, after the departure of the Israeli army, which shows the rubble, sandbags, and trash littering the streets and battle-scarred buildings in very realistic detail (*Albuquerque Journal* May 28, 1985). Similarly, another cartoon shows several boys looking at a book on a street corner; behind them is a board fence with the wood grain and knotholes exquisitely rendered, tufts of grass growing at the base, and pebbles and a puddle of water in the street at curbside (*Albuquerque Journal* Sept. 16, 1987).

Trever's libertarian philosophy means that he stands outside any formal party organization, and is registered as an independent. He pointedly opposes most of what passes for modern government today, on local as well as national levels. Government is generally seen as a tool of coercion and to be reduced to its fundamental purposes wherever and whenever possible. He is not an anarchist, however, only a minimalist. There is a role for government in providing for the public defense and for ensuring the social order and liberties. He favors privatization of such items as Amtrak and air-traffic control, and abolition of a whole range of activities such as business, farm and ethanol subsidies, tariffs, and minimum wage laws. He remains deeply skeptical of public education, the welfare system, and "drug wars."

In contemporary America, this approach allows for the broadest range of targets, and Trever takes full advantage of that fact. He frequently attacks school bureaucracy and funding, but does not omit pointing out public responsibility for placing so many non-academic demands upon the schools that their primary function is jeopardized. At the same time he also hits the public's contrary attitudes about their schools. For example, in a three-panel cartoon he has President Clinton speaking to the public with Hillary at his side, saying, "Hillary and I are fully committed to public education! The public schools must be strengthened so that *every* child can grow up and get a good job . . . so that he can afford to send his kid to private school!" (*National Gallery* Jan. 24, 1993, 11).

Trever has had a reputation for being astute on the subject of economics, in part because he frequently draws on economic topics, but also because he is in fact well-read on the subject, stemming from his days in Chicago under the influence of such lights as Milton Friedman. Taxes, free trade and foreign and domestic markets are all targets to be highlighted with his brush. The other side of the coin, the disbursement of public funds and their recipients, get their share of attention as well. School lunch programs do not fare any better than social security or social welfare in his panels. And, of course, he is as irascible toward Republicans as Democrats when they promote governmental involvement in these issues. He feels that even though their approaches differ, each party has its favorite groups to subsidize and is thereby equally culpable.

Environmentalists are a particular irritant to Trever because they always seem to be blocking development, and solutions to problems, without any creative input of their own. He sees their opposition as delaying solutions to the nuclear waste disposal problem, perhaps eventually closing down the nuclear power program. Although he is not pronuclear, such a disposal site has been proposed for New Mexico and it is a local issue for him. Other environmental concerns that he targets include endangered species, logging, and livestock grazing on public land. "I've gotten upset with 'bad science' . . . and I'm skeptical of global warming and . . . acid rain" (Trever, Interview). One cartoon shows a baggy-eyed Uncle Sam glaring at a Victorian-style house with a sign in front reading "Society of Professional Worriers" and an external alarm system blaring out "Asbestos, Alar, Logging, Popcorn, Acid Rain, Margarine, Genetic Engineering, Red Meat, (etc.)"; alongside is a uniformed policeman with wirecutters saying, "Sorry—I don't know how to cut that one off" (*National Gallery* June 19, 1994, 23).

Lobbyists and the whole culture of special pleading agitate his brush. He doesn't draw as many cartoons on "single issues," such as gun control and abortion, as other cartoonists. When he does, it is often because of what they illustrate about the modern tendency to try to "get something" from Washington, D.C. In one cartoon, for example, Trever has a couple standing in a corridor looking at two doors—one labled "Whites Only" and the other "Minorities Only." One character is commenting, "Gee, I dunno—if that's the restrooms, then it's blatant segregation. If it's the Governmental Contracts office, it's affirmative action" (*National Gallery* Mar. 19, 1995, 8). He was also very upset over the way the Robert Bork and Clarence Thomas Supreme Court nominations were handled. He believes that these were further examples of interest group excesses, and that whatever sympathy he had for liberal positions on a number of other issues was dissolved by these.

Trever's range of interests extends to international issues as well, although usually not keyed to specific events. For example, in one cartoon he shows a Serbian tank with smoking cannon moving past a body of water, surrounded by destroyed and smoking buildings and a sign reading, "Bosnia." The reflection in the water looks similar, but the name "Serbia" on the tank turret now appears as a swastika and the sign's reflection reads (upside down), "Warsaw" (*National Gallery* May 9, 1993, 3). Similarly, a later cartoon shows Clinton driving a car labeled "Peace," and carrying Arafat and Peres, on a very narrow road carved from a mountain labeled "West Bank." As they pass a sign pointing to "Settlement" ahead, they are faced with a huge truck labeled as "Greater Israel" and carrying half a prefabricated house labeled "Settlements" (*National Gallery* Mar. 20, 1994, 7). Trever even had the Canadian Conservatives hockey goalie drowning in a hole at goal in a game against the Liberals (*National Gallery* Nov. 14, 1993, 14).

He draws twice as many national/international cartoons than local ones, but unlike many cartoonists today Trever does deal with true local issues. An example is one he did on a controversial proposed bridge across the Rio Grande. The bridge halves extending from either bank do not meet in the middle, reflecting the opposing views of the authorities on each side (*Albuquerque Journal* Aug. 8, 1995). Another shows two armed guards wheeling two bags of chilies from an armored car into a supermarket, reflecting the bad harvest of chilies in New Mexico this year (*Albuquerque Journal* Aug. 4, 1995). These cartoons are unlikely to be understood by nonlocal readers. On the other hand, Trever sometimes combines local and international issues into a single cartoon; one depicts two men walking past a graffiti-covered wall speaking of support for ". . . that Singapore paint treatment . . . public flogging" (*National Gallery* Apr. 17, 1994, 20).

Only occasional use is made of classical or mythological imagery in his art. Perhaps the most common symbol is that of Uncle Sam, but he is a rather casual, disheveled figure; his top hat is bent askew and his vest is unbuttoned and loose; he wears no coat and his shirt is loose and baggy. He is not an imposing figure of power but rather an ordinary guy. Sam shares the characteristic common to most of Trever's people, a prominent nose, somewhat reminiscent of the way Virgil Partch used to draw them. He does use popular culture from time to time as a frame for his comments, but it's not a frequent occurrence. Included here are items such as *The Old Man and the Sea, Dr. Strangelove, The Little Shop of Horrors,* and *Dances with Wolves.* Great delight is taken with the contrivance of "Rube Goldberg"-type devices to illustrate the conceptual idiocy of one government policy or another. These provide a chance to exercise and play with his detailed perfectionism, knowing that it is leading nowhere—perhaps a bit of revenge upon the constant demand of his parents that he always work very hard.

Although he occasionally runs a sketch past his editors for an opinion, Trever makes his own decisions about what and how he draws. He claims to have been overruled by the newspaper only a half-dozen times in his career. Once, he had drawn Jesus lugging a cross made of a TV antenna as a comment on TV evangelists who were getting into financial and sexual difficulties. When the *Journal* did not want to run it, he sent it to his syndicate instead (Trever, *First Strike* 179). There are the occasional complaints from the wounded, but nothing serious enough to end in a lawsuit.

An engaging conversationalist, Trever loves to discuss his hobbies: collecting wines and Lionel toy trains, playing bluegrass banjo (currently inactive, he claims), and fly-fishing. At one time he tied all the lures that he used himself, but it got to be too time-consuming and expensive after he started his family. He is also not as active in professional organizations as he once was; he was awarded the Sigma Delta Chi Distinguished Service Award in 1980 and the Free Press Association Mencken Award in 1983, among others.

Sources

Graham, Tim. "Drawing Dissent." *Reason* Jan. 1988: 37-45.

Gullett, Scott. "The World According to John Trever." *Albuquerque Living* Apr. 1988: 40-45.

Trever, John. *A Cartoon History of the Reagan Years.* Washington, D.C.: Regnery Gateway, 1988.

——. Interview. By Jack Colldeweih. Aug. 1994.

——. *The Trever Gallery.* Albuquerque: Albuquerque Publishing, 1992.

——. *Trever's First Strike.* Andover, MA: Brick House, 1983.

26

Signe Wilkinson, *Philadelphia Daily News*

Kalman Goldstein

Signe Wilkinson was ambivalent about winning a Pulitzer Prize. On the one hand, she feared it might tempt her to vanity. On the other, she was moved by the ceremony as a "call to maintain high standards," feeling uplifted and rededicated in her mission (Astor 46). Because she considers editorial cartooning a calling rather than solely a profession, and is one of the very few women successful in what is generally considered a "man's field," Wilkinson is concerned more with the social and human dimension of politics than with the "horserace" of electoral campaigning and legislative maneuver. Her feminist self-consciousness and dedication to ideological consistency shape both her choice of issues to illustrate and her spare but spry artwork. For Wilkinson the message far outweighs the medium in her "daily sermonette" ("Interview: Signe Wilkinson" 17).

Wilkinson is not interested in a florid autobiography. She was born in 1950 in Wichita Falls, Texas, but her family moved to Philadelphia when she was young. Earning a B.A. in English from the University of Denver, she was politically energized during the late 1960s and 1970s, and personally motivated during a year in Cyprus (1974) observing relief work. Subsequently she spent a decade periodically taking courses at the Pennsylvania Academy of Fine Arts and other schools. During that time, Wilkinson was layout artist and occasional cartoonist for the *Philadelphia Inquirer,* publications director for the Academy of Natural Sciences, stringer and artist for a suburban journal in West Chester, Pennsylvania, and free-lancer with a number of magazines. For four years (1982-1986) she was editorial cartoonist at the *San Jose Mercury News,* then returned East to assume her current position with the *Philadelphia Daily News.* Signe Wilkinson won the Pulitzer Prize for political cartooning in 1992; that same year she affiliated with the Cartoonists and Writers Syndicate. In 1994 she became president of the Association of American Editorial Cartoonists.

For a number of reasons, her years in San Jose were strenuous ones professionally. The leap from occasional freelancer to daily editorial car-

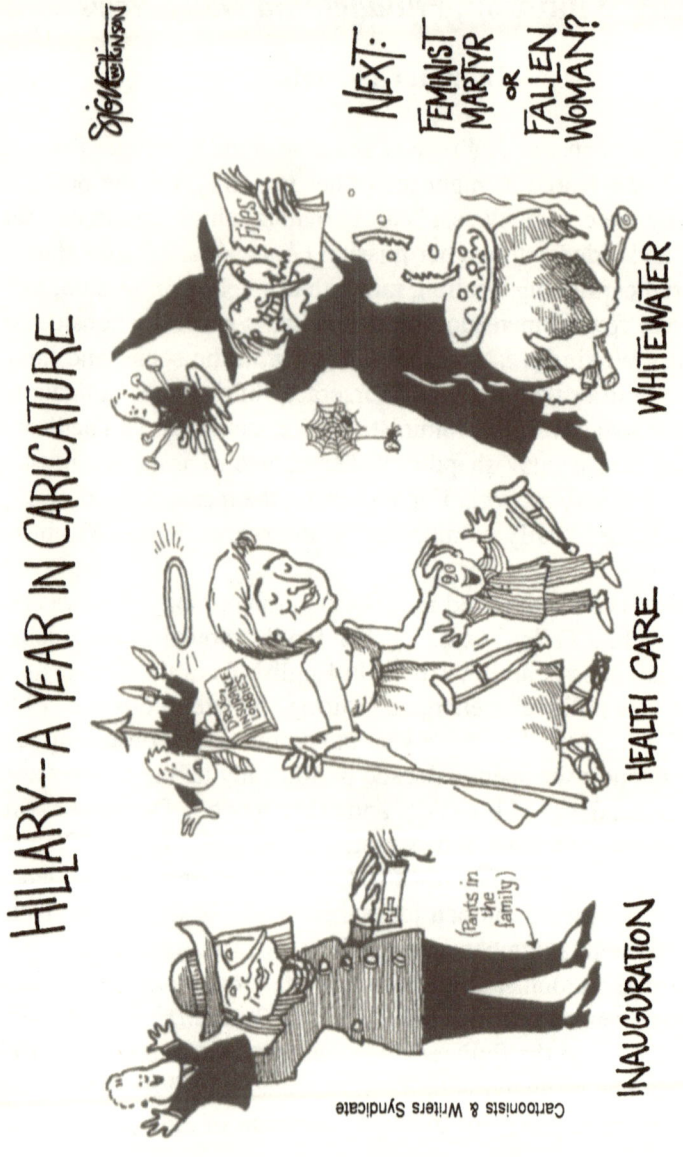

SIGNE
PHILADELPHIA DAILY NEWS
Philadelphia
USA

Signe Wilkinson (1994) *Philadelphia Daily News.* Reprinted by permission of Cartoonists & Writers Syndicate.

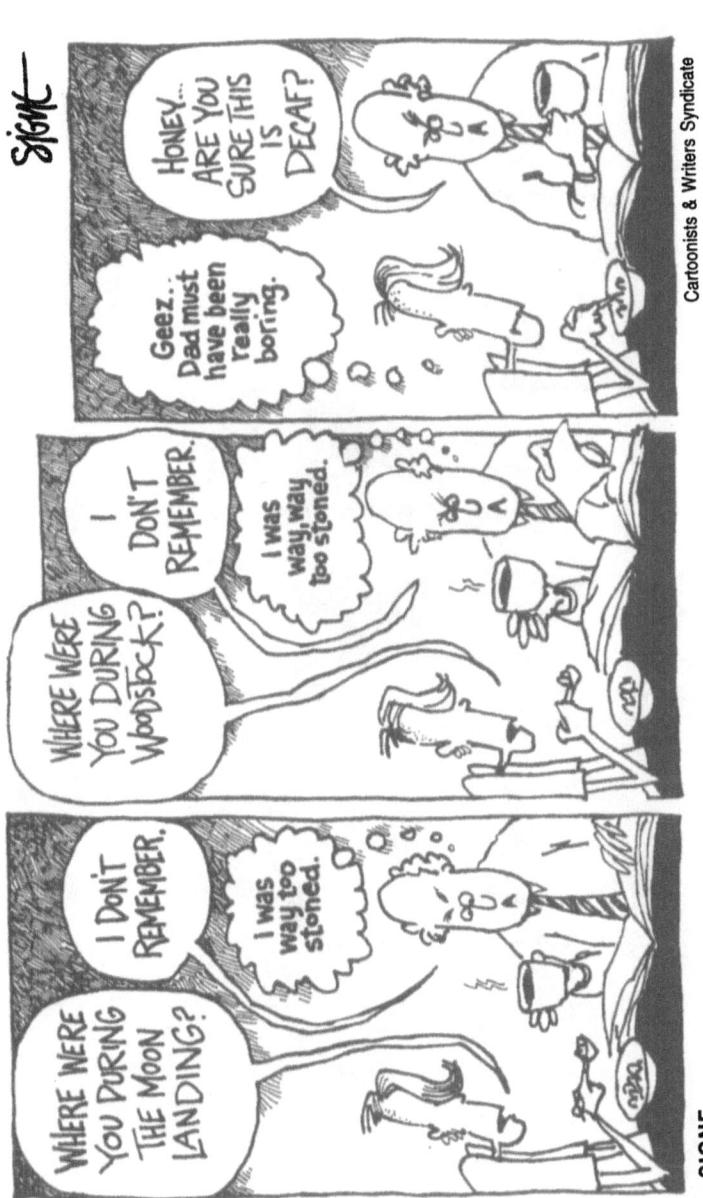

SIGNE
PHILADELPHIA DAILY NEWS
Philadelphia
USA

Signe Wilkinson (1994) *Philadelphia Daily News*. Reprinted by permission of Cartoonists & Writers Syndicate.

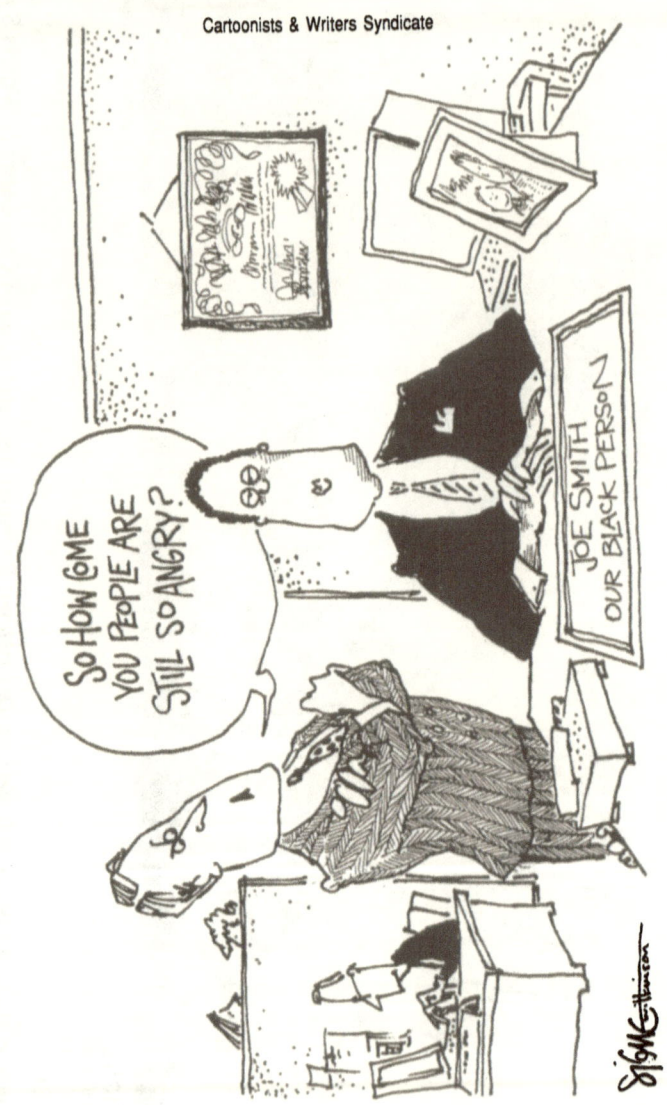

SIGNE
PHILADELPHIA DAILY NEWS
Philadelphia
USA

Signe Wilkinson (1994) *Philadelphia Daily News.* **Reprinted by permission of Cartoonists & Writers Syndicate.**

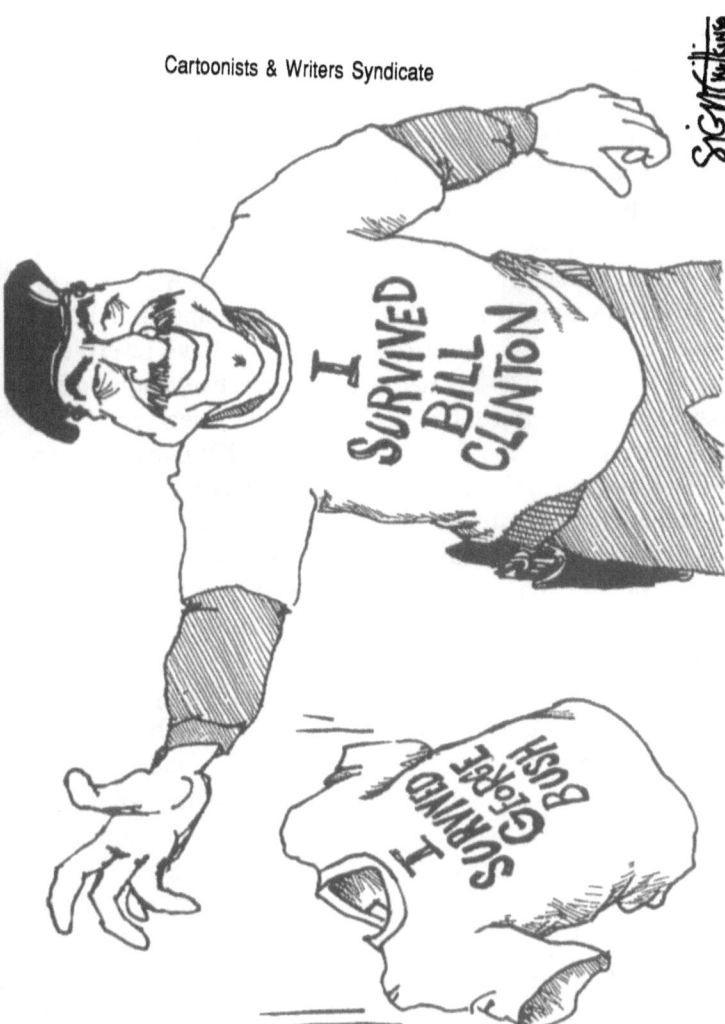

Cartoonists & Writers Syndicate

SIGNE
PHILADELPHIA DAILY NEWS
Philadelphia
USA

Signe Wilkinson (1993) *Philadelphia Daily News*. Reprinted by permission of Cartoonists & Writers Syndicate.

toonist was rocky, as it took a while for her to become familiar with state and local politics. This was also the case with California lifestyles. Local issues resonate strongly in her work, giving it freshness and distinctiveness, and providing her great enjoyment. But from habit she kept drawing overweight, overdressed East Coast people and brick rowhouses in a land where people wore running shorts to work and lived in their cars on the freeways.

Above all, in San Jose Wilkinson was the only cartoonist in town. Working in Philadelphia in the same building with Tony Auth of the *Inquirer* provided creative competition, incentive to improvement, and helped attract ample reader and professional response. Her work habits reinforced a preference for such contacts; she will talk on the phone "with all sorts of people and procrastinate and generally draw at 4:00 in the afternoon" (Wilkinson, Interview).

While her major influences include Johnny Hart, Edward Sorel, Gary Larson, Nicole Hollander and Modigliani, as well as Auth, Wilkinson aspires to a style "which is probably the most unpopular in the United States," that of M. G. Lord of *Newsday*. "I have rarely met anyone who likes M. G.'s style. It's flat, not in perspective, not rounded, not Renaissance, not chiaroscuro. It's black and white, linear, and I love it. I think that's a trait of many female cartoonists" (Wilkinson, Interview). Wilkinson's figures are more elongated and awkwardly posed than Lord's; sometimes almost desiccated, many have angular, jutting features and stick-spindly legs, although increasingly she has begun to fill out their figures. And, on occasion she can be inspired to do a fully articulated and realistic caricature, as in her 1993 portrayal of Iraq's Saddam Hussein (see illustration).

For many years Wilkinson was not affiliated with a syndicate, in part because she preferred to do a large number of local-reference cartoons, and because she did not trust syndicate editors to decide which of her drawings to package. She also resents it that many syndicates squeeze out new cartoonists, encouraging newspapers to let go of their own editorial cartoonists and subscribe to a cheaper package. This not only injures the profession, but forecloses local commentary and true reader loyalty. Nonetheless, she affiliated with Cartoonists and Writers Syndicate to get her work out to a wider audience. CWS includes a large number of international members, who provide intriguingly different stylistic and political viewpoints.

Wilkinson prefers not to cite popular culture references or parodies, nor to draw gag cartoons to make her points. She is one of a growing number of younger artists who believe that gags may trivialize their comments. But she also deplores kneejerk oversolemnity toward sensitive issues; cartoon commentary should be insightful as well as visceral. She is concerned that glib popular culture parodies quickly date one's work or deprive it of distinctiveness. Yet she also concedes that "there are only so many images to go around" (Barron C6).

In the end, what makes a cartoon distinctive, and thus potentially influential, is its integrity of viewpoint. While Wilkinson can do devastatingly grotesque caricatures of political leaders, her work is much more effective if a broader purview is involved. On November 8, 1992, she portrayed Bill Clinton being carried over the threshold of the White House by a woman, who kicks open the door with a loud THWACK! shaking a little table and knocking a patriarchal portrait askew. A year earlier, after the Anita Hill-Clarence Thomas hearings (Oct. 29, 1991), she envisioned a "Congressional Men's Group," in Stone Age loincloths, hunkered in a circle. Senator Alan Simpson, standing, piously testified: "And after totally humiliating her I felt, yes, I felt a little (sniff) hurt!" To which a drum-beating Ted Kennedy grunts: "Ho!" (Wilkinson n.p.).

There is no question that Signe Wilkinson is a feminist; her published collection *Abortion Cartoons on Demand!* testifies to that. She is outspokenly concerned about the paucity of women as well as African Americans in her profession and their poor career opportunities. Her caricatures of Hillary Rodham Clinton support the First Lady against her eager detractors. And since so much of her work reveals how political decisions impinge upon women and children, she is unsparing of insensitive or hostile policymakers.

But while she has found a number of occasions to vent her anger at officeholders, she caricatures standard political targets sparingly. Her concerns embrace much more mundane problems than government; she finds as many faults in self-delusive or hypocritical social mores. "Participatory Democracy" highlights how facile it is for people to denounce loudly the symptoms of social disorder, find a scapegoat, and then ignore or blame the victims. Another, captioned "Mind Lending Me a Hand?" shows a teacher, overburdened with assigned responsibilities for curing society's ills (boxes are labeled "Nutrition," "Sex Ed," "Discipline," "Anti-Drug Program," etc.) vainly asking assistance of an irresponsible, gum-chewing young mother whose son is smoking marijuana, toting a gun, and totally absorbed in a Walkman and a computer game.

While a committed reformer—her editor calls her an "Attack Quaker" (Davis 23)—Wilkinson is annoyed at "political correctness" ideologues. Too many groups, she is convinced, foster or maintain "incredible paranoia" about how they are portrayed in the media; frequently antipornography crusaders behave no differently from the Moral Majority ("Interview" 18). She sees them all largely as resentful whiners—but so are those who retreat under their criticism into "centrist mono-chromo-somatic cartooning," drawing only situations about white males (Wilkinson, Interview). She refuses to do so, citing her "high tolerance for stereotypes" in portrayals ("Interview" 19). By the same token, she is careful to use mixed groups of "reaction characters" in her work.

She has survived at least one controversy over her irreverent attitude toward political correctness. While in San Jose, she drew cartoons that so angered the governor that he tried to have her fired. However, Claire Booth Luce, a friend of the publisher, requested a copy of her lampoon of contemporary alternative lifestyles in a wedding photo which included the groom's daughter from first marriage, the bride's mother's lesbian lover, and the bride's sperm-donor father ("Interview" 19). Now she is simply amused when someone complains that one of her African American characters looks "kind of gay" ("Mightier" 46).

There is ample place for humor in her work, but rather than use slapstick, she prefers the arch comment in order to illustrate the ludicrousness of a situation or public position. On its November 12, 1992, Op-Ed page, the *New York Times* featured her take on Madonna's book *Sex;* Wilkinson offered some "Shocking Excerpts from the Suppressed Mid-Life Edition" which celebrated some of those banal little triumphs which grace "real" people's undramatic lives. Or, in a "Sic Transit Gloria" vein, she presents a "baby boomer" family at breakfast commenting on Richard Nixon's death as "the end of an era." Replies their teenaged son: "What band was he in?" Another teenaged son and father grope unsuccessfully across the generation gap in the 1994 "decaf" cartoon accompanying this essay. In a more pointedly ironic 8-panel cartoon for *Working Woman* magazine, Wilkinson surveys 30 years in the life of a feminist, from youthful firebrand to middle-aged C.E.O., now accused by her own daughter of "patriarchal" power (*Editor & Publisher* Jan. 7, 1995, 68). And on January 20, 1994, she used one of her infrequent "gag" approaches to solve the Serbian situation: penis-slasher Lorena Bobbitt with knife, set loose in the Balkans.

The cartoon about Nixon's death underlines another reason that Wilkinson avoids popular culture or topical references; she capitulates to what she's convinced is a lamentable lack of common historical knowledge among readers. One of her cartoon punchlines, about the Golden Rule, completely escaped community college students who did not understand the reference; in Italy she once encountered Americans who wanted directions to get to the Renaissance! So Wilkinson is a traditionalist on school curriculum issues, fearing that unless a common body of knowledge is taught, only historians or Bible scholars will understand her work—and she is not so sure about historians! "I feel that there is plenty that pulls us apart and very little that is being done to bring us together as a country and as a culture" (Wilkinson, Interview). Several of her cartoons on this theme have been picked up by conservative journals.

Falling back on popular culture or contemporary sensationalism also may trap cartoonists into dealing with a hot issue long after they have anything new or good to say about it. Regarding the O. J. Simpson murder trial, Wilkinson has commented on the media's relative indifference about the victims, and our national obsession with trivia to the neglect of truly important issues. For her to go further with O. J. cartoons might now make her seem a pedantic scold. She would also hate to feel that she has become obliged to do a certain cartoon. However, the one time that she was pressured to do a "command performance," about Operation Desert Shield, she produced a bravura anti-intervention piece that went against the national pro-invasion mood. But it was run, despite editorial doubts, since her local readers don't generally respond threateningly to her national or international cartoons, except on abortion and gun control. (Significantly, the only cartoon she remembers her editor refusing used a "limp bat" to symbolize the current impotence of the local baseball team.)

Readers *do* respond viscerally to issues that reflect social fears. Recently she did a cartoon of a black child looking at a rubble-strewn inner city field and a suburban child looking at a beautiful green field. "Somebody drew over the cartoon and sent it back, with the black kid pregnant and holding a child. That's where the social issues are being fought now. If that's where people are pissed and angry, that's where cartoonists ought to go" (Wilkinson, Interview).

Sources

Astor, David. "Signe Wilkinson's Significant '92." *Editor & Publisher* 25 Sept. 1992: 125.

Barron, James. "Cartoonist Feasts on a President." *New York Times* 31 Aug. 1994: C1, 6.

Davis, Nancy M. "Signe Wilkinson." *Presstime* Feb. 1995: 23.

"Interview: Signe Wilkinson." *Bull's Eye* Dec. 1988: 16-21.

"Mightier Than the Sorehead." *The Nation* 17 Jan. 1994: 45-54.

"Sex!—What Madonna Didn't Reveal." *New York Times* 12 Nov. 1992: A: 25.

Wilkinson, Signe. *Abortion Cartoons on Demand*. Philadelphia: Broad Street, 1992.

——. Interview. By Kalman Goldstein. 13 July 1994.

Conclusion

Kalman Goldstein and Jack Colldeweih

During mid-summer 1996, while the movie *Independence Day* was attracting huge crowds, Don Lee of the *Sandusky (Ohio) Register* drew an audience reacting oddly to the scene where alien invaders "zap" the White House. One viewer projected George Bush into the flying saucer; another thought that the destructive laser beam represented a nagging Clinton Administration scandal. A third simply wished to be at his drawing board. An usher explained: "Editorial Cartoonists" (*Best Cartoons* July 1996, 32).

Cartoonists' japes about their own profession seem plentiful today, and not always as good-humored as Don Lee's. As we have noted, the most recent AAEC conventions have vented soul-searchings about cartoonists' tunnel vision, tendencies toward pack journalism, indulgence in repetitive clichés or banal use of popular culture, and editors' preferences for relatively innocuous gags over confrontational satire. Newspaper editorial cartoonists have also revealed trade association pessimism about evolving challenges within and to their profession in the face of newspaper downsizing and technological imperatives. By focusing on two dozen prominent editorial cartoonists currently in their late 30s and 40s, *Graphic Opinions* samples the range and intensity of these concerns by probing each cartoonist's approach to political commentary. Despite their bickering, we also discovered their dedication to further honing their craft even while their profession is in flux.

As the reader has already surmised, the two dozen cartoonists in this collection have relatively little in common save for their general similarity in age, and their entry into their profession about 1980. Most, but not all, were first introduced to political commentary during the Johnson-Nixon era, and were as inspired by comics, animation, and *Mad* magazine as by earlier editorial cartoonists. Ideologically they run a gamut from liberal to libertarian. The largest number consider themselves political liberals: Boileau, Keefe, Luckovich, Margulies, Morin, Pett, Plante, Sack, Smith, and Wilkinson. Duffy, Horsey, Ohman, Stahler, Summers, and Lowe are moderates. Cullum, Godfrey, Hitch, Kelley, and Ramirez are conservatives. Shelton leans toward libertarianism, and Trever so proclaims himself. In comparison with cartoonists of earlier generations, few are political partisans, though Hitch and Shelton are Republican stalwarts, and Margulies generally supports Democrats. As a libertarian, Trever philosophically distrusts both established parties. The remainder feel free to lambaste stupidity in all quarters.

What they did have in common, and were very eager to comment about during the interviews, were shared professional concerns. *Graphic Opinions* highlights their opinions about the appropriateness of gag humor versus visual satire; how best to format and communicate ideas; and the possible impacts of electronic production and dissemination of cartoons: how prepared, willing, or "encouraged" they are to enter cyberspace.

Actually, cartoonists' in-house sniping over questions of purpose and direction is nothing new; those familiar with the literature might get a sense of *déja vu*. During the late 1970s and early 1980s a number of journals hosted acrimonious exchanges about the growing use of gag humor and popular culture references in editorial cartoons (see Sources). A deep chasm existed between an "old guard" insisting that editorial cartoons be "relentless" (Henry 22), driven by high-minded conscience and political outrage, and a "new wave" more interested in social commentary through jokes and humorous dialogue. Traditionalists derided the gag cartoon as "empty," the gag cartoonist as an opportunistic "courtier" intent on syndication in mass-circulation weekly magazines (Sanders 13; Bok 13). In rebuttal, gag cartoonists used the "honey-vinegar" analogy, but also insisted that in a "society immersed in visual media beyond the two-dimensional, or static, graphic," humor was one way to compete with television for attention (Harvey 117). Only the rare cartoonist like Jim Morin then took a middle position, that "while nothing is more boring than hitting the reader on the head day after day, nothing is more tedious and boring than trying to give them a belly-laugh day after day either" (Commer 61).

Almost all of the artists profiled here were becoming newspaper cartoonists while the debate hit its previous peak, and it is significant that although the profession is divided still (or anew) over humor, their stances on the issues are more complex than formerly. Rather than simple polarization, the cartoonists in this sample may be located within a spectrum of attitudes toward humor.

There are those who consider themselves serious journalists, eschewing humor in favor of startling or dramatic images in order to gain and hold reader attention for their ideas. Rex Babin, David Hitch, and Mike Shelton belong in this category. Other dedicated graphic satirists stress wit or sarcasm over humor, whether commenting on personalities or political events. Linda Boileau, Mark Cullum, Jack Ohman,

Joel Pett, and Signe Wilkinson belong here. It is significant, however, that among these opponents of gag editorials, Ohman will pun and Pett invoke slapstick; in their interviews both Babin and Shelton wished that they could cartoon with more humor and less mordantly. A third category includes those who are moderately antigag, but who as caricaturists use grotesquerie to diminish persons or policies through exaggeration or slapstick. In this category we include Brian Duffy, Linda Godfrey, David Horsey, and Dana Summers. A fourth category embraces those who accept the premise that readers' attention may sometimes be gained through jokes but sometimes through more serious commentary. Jim Morin, quoted above, has the most mixed palette, but Mike Keefe, Bruce Plante, Mike Ramirez, and Chan Lowe also qualify for this group. A final group are champions of broad humor, consistently using gags and jokes—and arguing that such a light approach is more effective in presenting serious issues than solemnity or satire. These cartoonists are as likely to joke about cultural and social issues as on traditionally political ones, and include Mike Luckovich, Jimmy Margulies, Jeff Stahler, John Trever, and above all Steve Kelley. Only one of the 24 cartoonists, Mike Smith, professed indifference about the question.

Despite continued criticism by some cartoonists of "gag" editorial cartoons, it would not be surprising if more of them continue to appear. In our introductory chapter, and certainly in the trade journals, are cited cases of recent contretemps between editors and cartoonists about specific cartoons or over controversial stands on sensitive issues. Some cartoonists have lost their jobs for these reasons. There is also ample evidence that, personalities or specific topics aside, there are intrinsic conflicts of interest between cartoonists and editors (see Lamb 48). Doug Marlette put it intriguingly: "Because editors are word people, they are more comfortable with words and the civilization that language brings. . . . The restriction and restraint that civilization entails feels better to them than the wild untamed passion, energy and humor of art. Of course, the best editors recognize that good cartoons shade more towards art than journalism [but] the fundamentals of cartooning are distortion, hyperbole, and subjectivity" (157-58). Realizing this can cause self-censorship, or recourse either to a "safer" humorous stance or to a less visceral topic. A number of cartoonists have testified to this in trade and scholarly journals, and among the cartoonists we interviewed, Jack Ohman was particularly open about this dilemma.

None of those surveyed admitted to having current tensions with *their* editors, but were aware of incentives as well as subtle pressures to be "funny." In 1991 *New York Times* Week in Review section editor Dan Lewis noted that "Most cartoons coming across my desk tend to be funny. . . . Sometimes I choose editorial cartoons that just make me laugh" as an anodyne to life's seriousness (Astor May 18, 1991, 45). Retired editor George Lockwood argued in 1996 that "newspaper readers just don't understand or appreciate parody and satire in comics or cartoons" (qtd. in Lockwood 39). An increasing number of editorial cartoonists have recently branched out into comic strips, and more strips have introduced serious political and social commentary. Most cartoonists understand that editorials and strips differ in tone. As Berke Breathed once put it, "Many editors won't put up with much editorial comment on the comics page. So you have to slip it under the door, through metaphor and subtlety and my particular fashion, which is silliness" (qtd. in Prendergast 22). And S. L. Harrison is concerned that when either cartoons or comic strips "attempt to carry a meaningful message of moral uplift or a social sermon" they may bore younger newspaper readers and lose their future audience (Harrison 48). On the other hand, Breathed's approach won him a Pulitzer Prize in 1987 for political comment, which could tempt cartoonists in both genres toward "silliness." Conditions do not seem to have changed too much from 1979, when Don Wright complained that "Magazines like *Newsweek* want cartoons that don't take too strong a position, that are funny" ("Hitting Between the Eyes" 80).

In a brief article about recent Supreme Court decisions tangentially affecting cartooning and libel (*Hustler Magazine vs. Jerry Falwell* [1988], *Milkovich vs. Lorrain Journal Co.* [1990]), J. P. Toomey patronizingly concluded that "if the work could be taken seriously enough to be regarded as a statement of fact, then it probably wouldn't be considered a cartoon" (Toomey 35). This is litigiously reassuring but does little for the "serious" graphic journalists' sense of confidence in their calling.

*   *   *

Shortly following his award, 1997 Pulitzer Prize–winner Walt Handelsman of the *New Orleans Times-Picayune* was quoted briefly on many of the issues explored throughout this book: commentary on both social and political topics (his split is 60/40 social), avoidance of partisanship and a dogmatic ideology ("more liberal than conservative, but I'm more issue oriented"), and striking a balance between humor and satire ("I like to be funny and have an edge, too"). Like most of his colleagues, he not only reads widely and watches television but has his antenna out for his readers' daily concerns: "I always try to draw what people are talking about over the dinner table" (qtd. in Astor, "Back to Work" 94-95).

Handelsman also took a decided position about another issue: the relationship between an editorial cartoonist's artwork and his or her writing ability. We had expected that those we interviewed would want to talk about their individual approaches to communicating editorial opinions most effectively, and were gratified by the vigor and thoughtfulness with which they responded. Sometimes the cartoonists and their interviewers delved knowledgeably into matters of technique: compositional procedures, types of pens or brushes used, preferred inks and paints, paper stock—and specific ways in which their drawing or lettering skills were evolving. At other times they were more interested in the cartoonist's identification of early influences and sources of inspiration. But in either case, the cartoonists either were outspoken about how they employed and balanced words and pictures, or their approach was consistent enough for the editors to discern patterns that, as with the "humor" issue, fell into general categories.

Handelsman believes that writing is more vital than drawing to an effective political cartoon, that the idea outweighs its execution. "If I drew stick figures and said something funny or made a point, that's better than a beautiful illustration with bad writing" ("Back to Work" 95). American political cartoonists are reputed to rely upon words as well as pictures, aspiring to create clever captions or biting dialogue as well as producing evocative images. Therefore relatively few in this book should be pigeonholed exclusively into one kind of approach, just as many of them feel as comfortable doing multipanel as drawing single panel cartoons.

Nevertheless, an unusual number generally follow the European style, combining stark economic of image with a minimum of labels or captions in order to crystallize issues visually. Rex Babin, Linda Boileau, Linda Godfrey, Chan Lowe, Joel Pett, Bruce Plante, Mike Shelton, and Jeff Stahler are most interested in "miming" the news—though never completely to the exclusion of the bon mot. At the other extreme are those who echo Handelsman, stressing dialogue or captions to produce statements that illumine graphic images. Their cartoons highlight editorial soliloquies or pointed conversations without which the pictures might remain incomplete. Brian Duffy, Steve Kelley, Mike Luckovich, Jimmy Margulies, Jack Ohman, Steve Sack, and Signe Wilkinson adhere most frequently to this approach. Then there are those cartoonists who enjoy exhibiting their artistic skills; their captions and labels underline the images, but the tableau, not the words, most weightily delivers the massage. We would include David Hitch, David Horsey, Mike Keefe, and Jim Morin Here. Finally, some cartoonists try consistently to lavish attention equally on words and images: Mark Cullum, Mike Ramirez, Mike Smith, Dana Summers, and John Trever.

Such thumbnail characterizations are merely suggestive of the varying ways in which cartoonists are expressing themselves during the mid-
1990s. Certainly none seem set in their ways, and all with whom we
spoke had refined their styles within the past few years or had experimented with presentation, lettering, or format. Some, including Mike
Shelton and David Horsey, were among those who had moved from
black and white to color. And not even the recent Pulitzer Prize winners
we included were resting on their laurels.

None felt that they could afford to. We've seen that the cartooning
community periodically fears that it's going stale. Even during the
Oliphant Revolution, as cartooning was re-energized by a "fresh, exciting way of saying something," Jim Morin scoffed that "a glut of lazy
artists" could imitate and plagiarize the profession back into a renewed
crisis of creativity (qtd. in Commer 61). As early as 1981, Don Wright
was speculating about changes that the computer, newsprint shortages,
and the rising price of paper might eventually force on newspaper cartoonists, including a possible "wedding between television and journalism" ("Don Wright" 11).

As sensitive as they are to their political and social environment, and
to a lesser extent the business of their profession, most of the artists
included here were relatively uninformed about technological and legal
issues related to editorial cartooning. They were asked in the interviews
about use of drawing, colorizing and lettering by computer in their work;
few had even experimented, much less made any regular use of such
electronic techniques. Jeff Stahler tried drawing by computer, but was
unsatisfied with the results: it was comparatively clumsy artistically; nor
does he like lettering by computer even though idiosyncratic fonts can be
created. Some, like Mike Smith, are computer literate but don't use the
computer at all for their art. Mike Keefe is an enthusiastic embracer of
the power of the computer as an artistic and ideational aid, but he uses it
only for database and colorization purposes for his cartoons, and animation functions for his dePixion website. Mike Shelton is the only cartoonist in this group who is not only comfortable, but even enthusiastic about
fully using the computer as a creative tool in his work. He draws, col-
orizes and letters directly on the computer, and feels that he does a better
job more efficiently than before. Most cartoonists professed either indifference or studied ignorance of the potential of the computer as an artistic
tool. And there is Mike Luckovich, who is somewhat of a Luddite with
respect to the computer in cartooning; he doesn't have one in his office
and is hostile to the Internet as a shallow and user-unfriendly device.

Nevertheless, many cartoonists now include a Web address with
their signature in their cartoons. And even if they didn't, their news-

papers and/or distribution syndicates include their work in other sites. Mike Shelton's cartoons have been offered in color by King Features through both the mail and AP GraphicsNet since 1991 (Lamb 40). Earlier attempts by syndicates to utilize computer-to-computer transmission of cartoons were only partially successful, but the businesses had confidence that this was the wave of the future and most persisted through the slow start (Astor, "Slow Growth" 34). By 1995, some 60 daily papers had already started online services and an additional 35 were planning to do so (Garneau 72). While this was only a small percentage of the Newspaper Association of America, it is an indication of a future direction of distribution, a fact noted among attendees at the 1995 Festival of Cartoon Art (Astor, "Oklahoma" 34).

The potential monetary and legal ramifications of this trend were almost universally unremarked by our cartoonists. None had thought about the fact that appearance on a web site constitutes an additional publication, for which they are uncompensated. Most felt that because their paper already pays them under contract, what the paper subsequently does with the art in terms of display is not their concern. As far as syndicate web site presentation is concerned, they considered that as a promotional device, even though any casual browser could download the cartoon free. At this time the downloaded images are not of very good quality but that could change.

Although the new rules related to decency on the Internet had not yet been formulated at the time of our interviews, all the cartoonists felt very safe from legal problems of libel, privacy, copyright, and indecency or pornography, and properly so. None had thought about international problems related to any of the above issues, however. Because the Internet makes material available everywhere, what may be permissible in one nation may not be in another, as many reporters and some cartoonists have discovered. In addition, copyright protection is rather uncertain internationally, relying as much on exposure and shame as upon the law. In general, however, political cartoons tend to travel less well from one national culture to another at this time than do comics and are consequently less vulnerable. The trend of national cultures homogenizing into a global culture seems relentless, however, despite the best efforts of the French Academy, so the degree of this protection may diminish in step.

Despite their reluctance to change the way they work, or even to experiment with it, cartoonists are finding the profession changing around them; willingly or not, they will adapt and come to terms with it. There are no good political cartoonists with closed minds.

*   *   *

When cartoon scholar Roger Fischer addressed the Association of American Editorial Cartoonists' 1996 convention, he was unintentionally ironic. He began by congratulating them: "I am convinced that a larger number of gifted cartoonists are doing better work today, and doing it more consistently, than ever before." But later, he concluded that 1969 through 1985 had been a "golden age" (Astor, "Cartooning" 24); had their gravy days passed? Lucy Rollin, another cartoon scholar, profiled Kate Salley Palmer of South Carolina for *Inks* early in 1997, characterizing her "quirky" humor, visual imagery, and outrage at injustices, as epitomizing "all successful editorial cartoonists" (Rollin 30-31). But she prefaced this assessment by noting that Palmer was unemployed. Amid all the reports in *Editor & Publisher* of newspapers downsizing, cost slashing, being absorbed by chains, or even going out of business, the litany of pessimism in David Greenberg's cartoons stands out. Besides being that trade journal's cartoonist, Greenberg is David Horsey's colleague on the *Seattle Post-Intelligencer*—but not even a cartoonist with two positions can feel comfortable about the "fourth estate" today. Early in 1997, veteran Bill Schorr of the *Kansas City Star* remarked that his was a "constantly evolving profession" (qtd. in Harvey 118). Doubtless many newspaper editorial cartoonists grit their teeth at that.

Editorial cartoonists have always been expected to meet daily deadlines, and have something interesting to say and arresting to look at. They have had to reconcile their individualistic and distinctive viewpoints with their editors' more cautious definitions of appropriate content. Now they are also pressured to be funny rather than satiric, and expected to comment wittily on social and cultural trends as well as political developments. The recent trend toward topical comic strips challenges editorial cartoonists' ingenuity both in format and content. An essay in *The Economist* (Nov. 2, 1996) reviewed a contemporary exhibit of political art, found it boring and flat, and warned current cartoonists that the future of their profession might lie with "alternative" or otherwise unaffiliated illustrators. And increasingly they have to huff along beside the speeding chariots of technological change. They are running, but running scared.

Sources

Astor, David. "Back to Work after Post-Pulitzer Frenzy." *Editor & Publisher* 26 Apr. 1997: 94-95.

——. "Cartooning Views from Non-Artists." *Editor & Publisher* 13 July 1996: 24-25.

——. "Do Too Many Funny Editorial Cartoons Get Reprinted?" *Editor & Publisher* 18 May 1991: 45-48.

——. "Downbeat Look at a Profession's Future." *Editor & Publisher* 25 June 1994: 110-11.

——. "Editorial Cartoonist Having a Big Year." *Editor & Publisher* 28 Sept. 1996: 32-33.

——. "Oklahoma City Bombing Cartoon Angers Many Readers in Tacoma." *Editor & Publisher* 10 June 1995: 33.

——. "Slow Growth for a New Delivery Method." *Editor & Publisher* 11 Aug. 1990: 34-35.

——. "Tacoma Cartoonist Tackles the Issues." *Editor & Publisher* 27 Apr. 1996: 90-92.

Bender, Jack. "The Outlook for Editorial Cartooning." *Journalism Quarterly* 30 (Spring 1963): 175-80.

"Bile Needed." *The Economist* 2 Nov. 1996: 83-84.

Bok, Chip. "The Courtier Cartoonists." *Target* 4 (Summer 1982): 13.

Bragg, Rick. "Some Cartoons Are Original; Alas, the Also-Rans Also Run." *New York Times* 3 Apr. 1994, IV: 12.

Case, Tony. "Cartoon World Has Its Ups and Downs." *Editor & Publisher* 29 Apr. 1995: 50.

Commer, Dick. "A Baker's Dozen of Questions for One of America's Brightest Young Cartoonists." *Cartoonist Profiles* 43 (Sept. 1979): 56-61.

"Confronting People with What They Don't Want to See: A Tony Auth Album." *Civil Liberties Review* July-Aug. 1977: 60-67.

"Don Wright. Crusading Journalist." *Target* 1 (Autumn 1981): 4-11.

Garneau, George. "Campus Press Races Online." *Editor & Publisher* 22 Apr. 1995: 72-75.

"Getting Angry Six Times a Week: A Hugh Haynie Album." *Civil Liberties Review* May-June 1977: 62-69.

Gorrell, Bob. "A Responsibility to Fairness." *Target* 1 (Autumn 1981): 12-13.

Harrison, S. L. "What's the Trouble with Newspapers?" *Editor & Publisher* 15 Mar. 1997: 48.

Harvey, Robert C. "The Bill Schorr Interviews." *Comics Journal* 193 (Feb. 1997): 115-19.

Henry, William A., III. "The Sit-Down Comics." *Washington Journalism Review* Oct. 1981: 22-28.

"Hitting between the Eyes Every Day: A Don Wright Album." *Civil Liberties Review* Jan.-Feb. 1979: 80-91.

"I Have a Bent for Satire: A Paul Szep Album." *Civil Liberties Review* Nov.-Dec. 1977: 67-73.

Jones, Stacy. "Too Harsh for Comfort." *Editor & Publisher* 25 Jan. 1997: 9-10.

Kirste, Ken. "Crossbreeding Comic Strip and Editorial Cartoonists: New Type of Humor Born?" *Cartoon Art Museum Newsletter* 1 (Spring 1986): 4.

Lamb, Chris. "Editorial Cartoonists Pessimistic about Their Profession." *Editor & Publisher* 14 Oct. 1995: 36, 48.

Lockwood, George. "Stay Away from Talking Frogs." *Cartoonist Profiles* 109 (Mar. 1996): 34-40.

Marlette, Doug. *Shred This Book!* Atlanta: Peachtree, 1988.

Paul, Angus. "Colleges Are Rich with Artists." *Chronicle of Higher Education* 17 Nov. 1982: 6-8.

Prendergast, Alan. "Of Penguins and Pulitzers." *Washington Journalism Review* Oct. 1987: 19-28.

"The Pressure of Pulitzer." *Editor & Publisher* 6 July 1996: 16.

Rollin, Lucy. "Kate Salley Palmer: A Profile." *Inks* 4 (Feb. 1997): 29-34.

Sanders, Bill. "Using the Knife." *Target* 3 (Spring 1982): 13.

Sorel, Edward. "The Limits on Drawing Power." *Washington Journalism Review* Oct. 1981: 30-32.

Toomey, J. P. "How Far Is Too Far in Political Cartooning?" *Editor & Publisher* 11 Mar. 1997: 35, 48.

Wines, Michael. "Cartoonists See a Future That's No Joking Matter." *New York Times* 3 July 1995: 41.

Contributors

Diana Beeson has been director of University of Iowa Television since 1983. Previously she was a television reporter and public information director both in Missouri and Iowa, as well as an instructor in journalistic writing/reporting and broadcast reporting both at the University of Iowa and at Kirkwood Community College. Beeson has an M.A. in journalism and mass communication and has completed her doctoral course work at the University of Iowa. She has published essays on Nancy Drew and currently is writing her dissertation on American women who worked as war correspondents during the Chinese Civil War.

Roy E. Blackwood, a professor of journalism since 1992 and chair of the Department of Mass Communication at Bemidji State University, Minnesota, since 1997, is a much-published specialist on Canadian editorial cartooning. Born in Pennsylvania, he was a U.S. Marine for four years, then traveled in Asia, and was a reporter in Anchorage. He earned his Ph.D. (continuing education and communication) from Cornell University. He has taught journalism, literature, and communication in China and Thailand.

Jack Colldeweih is emeritus professor of communications and coordinator of the communications and speech area in the School of Communication Arts at Fairleigh Dickinson University. He received his Ph.D. in Mass Communications from the University of Illinois. Although he writes most frequently on film and press history, his interest in political cartoons was sharpened considerably during the heyday of the underground press of the 1960s and 1970s and he has written on the most prominent of their cartoonists, Ron Cobb.

Kalman Goldstein has been at Fairleigh Dickinson University since 1967, and professor of history since 1983. His Ph.D. is from Columbia University. An NEH summer seminar conducted by Lawrence Levine turned him from traditional political history toward political humor and graphics. Since 1980 he has published articles on Al Capp and Walt Kelly, as well as print humorists George Ade, Finley Peter Dunne, Harry Golden, and Marion Hargrove. A survey essay on American political cartooning, and several on GI era cartoons, are in press. He is also interested in Civil War satire.

S. L. Harrison, an associate professor of communication at the University of Miami, holds a Ph.D. from American University and has taught both there and at the University of Maryland. He has worked for newspapers, industry, and government research agencies, and has held staff positions in both houses of Congress. With a particular interest in political cartoons, he has written about Gib Crockett and John Stampone, as well as Florida's current artists. His publications include *Florida's Editorial Cartoonists* (1996) and *The Editorial Art of Edmund Duffy* (1998) forthcoming.

Thomas Langston, an associate professor of political science at Tulane University, received his Ph.D. in political science from MIT. He has published two books: *Ideologues and Presidents: From the New Deal to the Reagan Revolution* (1992) and *With Reverence and Contempt: How Americans Think About Their Presidents* (1995). His essay on Mike Ramirez is his first published writing on editorial cartooning.

Kerry Soper is a Ph.D. in American studies at Emory University, interested in print, television, and film media, but his primary focus is on the history of satire in comic strips. In 1996 he pioneered a course in Cartoons and Comics at Emory. He holds a B.F.A. in commercial art from Utah State University, and is a freelance cartoonist and caricature artist whose work has appeared in such regional and national publications as *Southern Changes, The Spoke, U. The National College Newspaper, Cracked,* and *Campus Life.* In 1990 he won the 1990 Scripps/Howard Charles M. Schulz Award for college cartooning. In 1997 he illustrated *Chelsea Clinton's Freshman Notebook,* a book parody of the First Daughter's doodlings at Stanford.

Robin G. Weitzen is currently completing her Ph.D. in English at Tulane University, where she is a senior teaching fellow and an instructor in the freshman writing progam. Her researches focus on cultural expression as reflected in literary and social texts; as a former Westerner, she is fascinated by the Deep South. As with her university colleague Thomas Langston, this is her first published examination of political cartooning.